D1518569

CULTURE
AND
CHILDREN'S
INTELLIGENCE

David Wechsler

CULTURE

AND

CHILDREN'S

INTELLIGENCE

CROSS-CULTURAL ANALYSIS OF THE WISC-III

EDITED BY

JAMES GEORGAS

Department of Psychology
University of Athens
Athens, Greece

LAWRENCE G. WEISS

The Psychological Corporation
San Antonio, Texas

FONS J. R. VAN DE VIJVER

Department of Psychology
Tilburg University
Tilburg, The Netherlands

DONALD H. SAKLOFSKE

Department of Educational Psychology
University of Saskatchewan
Saskatoon, Saskatchewan, Canada

ACADEMIC PRESS

An imprint of Elsevier Science

Amsterdam   Boston   Heidelberg   London   New York   Oxford
Paris   San Diego   San Francisco   Singapore   Sydney   Tokyo

The sponsoring editor for this book was Nikki Levy, the senior developmental editor was Barbara Makinster, and the senior project manager was Paul Gottehrer. The cover was designed by Cathy Reynolds. Composition was done by Cepha Imaging Pvt. Ltd., Bangalore, India and the book was printed and bound by Maple-Vail, York, PA.

Cover photo credit: Banana Stock © 2003.

This book is printed on acid-free paper. ∞

Academic Press
An imprint of Elsevier Science
525 B Street, Suite 1900, San Diego, California 92101-4495, USA
http://www.academicpress.com

Academic Press
84 Theobald's Road, London WC1X 8RR, UK
http://www.academicpress.com

Library of Congress Catalog Card Number: 2003104541

International Standard Book Number: 0-12-280055-9

PRINTED IN THE UNITED STATES OF AMERICA
03 04 05 06 07   7 6 5 4 3 2 1

This book is dedicated to:
Στην Κατερίνα και τον
Αλέξανδρο, με όλη την αγάπη μου.—J.G.

To my wife, Judy, whose love of
travel opened my eyes to the world.—L.G.W.

Voor L., mijn levensgezellin.—F.J.R.vdV.

Lukas, my precious grandson, his parents Jennifer and
Jon, and his great grandparents, Frances and
Harold, Shirley and Mel.—D.H.S.

Contents

PART I

INTELLIGENCE AND THE WECHSLER SCALES FOR CHILDREN

1

THE WECHSLER SCALES FOR ASSESSING CHILDREN'S INTELLIGENCE: PAST TO PRESENT

DONALD H. SAKLOFSKE, LAWRENCE G. WEISS, A. LYNNE BEAL, AND DIANE COALSON

2

CROSS-CULTURAL PSYCHOLOGY, INTELLIGENCE, AND COGNITIVE PROCESSES

JAMES GEORGAS

PART II

STANDARDIZATION STUDIES OF THE WISC-III IN DIFFERENT CULTURES

3

THE WISC-III IN THE UNITED STATES

LAWRENCE G. WEISS

4

CANADA

DONALD H. SAKLOFSKE

5

UNITED KINGDOM

PAUL MCKEOWN

6

FRANCE AND FRENCH-SPEAKING BELGIUM

JACQUES GRÉGOIRE

7

THE NETHERLANDS AND FLEMISH-SPEAKING BELGIUM

MARK SCHITTEKATTE, WILLEM KORT, WILMA RESING, GRIET VERMEIR, PAUL VERHAEGHE

8

GERMANY

UWE TEWES

9

AUSTRIA AND SWITZERLAND

PETER ROSSMANN, URS SCHALLBERGER

10

SWEDEN

KARIN SONNANDER, BENGT RAMUND

11

LITHUANIA

GRAŽINA GINTILIENĖ, SIGITA GIRDZIJAUSKIENĖ

12

SLOVENIA

DUŠICA BOBEN, VALENTIN BUCIK

13

GREECE

JAMES GEORGAS, IOANNIS N. PARASKEVOPOULOS, ELIAS BESEVEGIS,
NIKOLAOS GIANNITSAS, KOSTAS MYLONAS

14

JAPAN

KAZUHIKO UENO, ICHIRO NAKATANI

15

SOUTH KOREA

KEUMJOO KWAK

16

TAIWAN

HSIN-YI CHEN, YUNG-HWA CHEN, JIANJUN ZHU

PART III

CROSS-CULTURAL ANALYSIS OF THE WISC-III

17

PRINCIPLES OF ADAPTATION OF INTELLIGENCE TESTS TO OTHER CULTURES

FONS J. R. VAN DE VIJVER

18

METHODOLOGY OF COMBINING THE WISC-III DATA SETS

FONS J. R. VAN DE VIJVER, KOSTAS MYLONAS, VASSILIS PAVLOPOULOS, JAMES GEORGAS

19

A CROSS-CULTURAL ANALYSIS OF THE WISC-III

JAMES GEORGAS, FONS J. R. VAN DE VIJVER, LAWRENCE G. WEISS,
DONALD H. SAKLOFSKE

CONTRIBUTORS

Numbers in parentheses indicate the pages on which the authors' contributions begin.

A. Lynne Beal (3), Toronto District School Board, Toronto, Ontario, M5T 1P6 Canada

Elias Besevegis (199), Department of Psychology, The University of Athens, Athens, 15784 Illissia, Greece

Dušica Boben (181), Center for Psychodiagnostic Resources, Ljublijana, SI-1000, Slovenia

Valentin Bucik (181), Department of Psychology, University of Ljublijana, Ljublijana, SI-1000, Slovenia

Hsin-Yi Chen (241), Department of Special Education, National Taiwan Normal University, Taipei, 106, Taiwan, ROC

Yung-Hwa Chen (241), The Chinese Behavior Science Corporation, Taipei, Taiwan, ROC

Diane Coalson (3), The Psychological Corporation, San Antonio, Texas 78259

James Georgas (23, 199, 265, 277), Department of Psychology, University of Athens, 15784 Athens, Greece

Nikolaos Giannitsas (199), Department of Psychology, University of Athens, 15784 Athens, Greece

Gražina Gintilienė (165), Department of General Psychology, Vilnius University, Vilnius 20057, Lithuania

Sigita Girdzijauskienė (165), Department of Social Work, Vilnius University, Vilnius 20057, Lithuania

Jacques Grégoire (89), Faculty of Psychology and Education, The Catholic University of Louvain, Louvain-la-Neuve, 1348, Belgium

Willem Kort (109), Department of Research and Development, Dutch Psychological Association Service Center, Amsterdam 1007 AP, The Netherlands

Keumjoo Kwak (227), Department of Psychology, Seoul National University, Seoul, 151-742, Korea

Paul McKeown (77), The Psychological Corporation, Europe, London NW17BY, United Kingdom

Kostas Mylonas (199, 265), Department of Psychology, University of Athens, 15784 Athens, Greece

Ichiro Nakatani (215), Individual Tests Division, Japan Institute of Psychological Aptitude, Tokyo 113-0021, Japan

Ioannis N. Paraskevopoulos (199), Department of Psychology, University of Athens, 15784 Athens, Greece

Vassilis Pavlopoulos (265), Department of Psychology, University of Athens, 15784 Athens, Greece

Bengt Ramund (149), Department of Education, Uppsala University, Uppsala SE-75002, Sweden

Wilma Resing (109), Department of Development and Educational Psychology, Leyden University, Leyden 2333 AK, The Netherlands

Peter Rossmann (137), Institute of Education, Karl-Franzens University of Graz, Graz A-8010, Austria

Donald H. Saklofske (3, 61, 277), Department of Educational Psychology and Special Education, University of Saskatchewan, Saskatoon, Saskatchewan S7NOX1 Canada

Urs Schallberger (137), Department of Applied Psychology, University of Zurich, Zurich CH-8006, Switzerland

Mark Schittekatte (109), Faculty of Psychology and Educational Sciences, University of Ghent, Ghent 9000, Belgium

Karin Sonnander (149), Department of Neuroscience, Uppsala University, Uppsala SE-75017, Sweden

Uwe Tewes (121), Institute of Medical Psychology, Hannover Medical School, D-30625 Hannover, Germany

Kazuhiko Ueno (215), Tokyo Gakugei University, Tokyo 184-8501, Japan

Paul Verhaeghe (109), Testing Department, H., Ghent University, Gent, B-9000 Belgium

Griet Vermeir (109), Testing Department, H., Ghent University, Gent, B-9000 Belgium

Fons J. R. van de Vijver (255, 265, 277), Department of Psychology, Tilburg University, Tilburg 5000LE, The Netherlands

Lawrence G. Weiss (3, 41, 277), The Psychological Corporation, San Antonio, Texas 78259

Jianjun Zhu (241), The Psychological Corporation, San Antonio, Texas 78259

FOREWORD

It is almost exactly 30 years since I was introduced to the concept of cross-cultural assessment. David Wechsler told me that he was on the doctoral dissertation committee of a student from Gujarat, India and asked if I would do him a favor and "review" the manuscript for him in the next day or two. I accepted his invitation a bit too quickly, totally missing the fact that both of his hands were behind his back, and failing to notice the twinkle in his eyes that was saying "Boy, did I put one over on you!" He quickly produced the dissertation from behind his back, a document of more than 1000 pages that looked like the Manhattan Yellow Pages. "Tell me your thoughts about the Gujurati WISC on Friday morning," he said, stifling a smile as he walked out, well aware that I wasn't going to sleep much during the next 36 hours.

Dr. Wechsler spent most of that Friday morning asking me questions. I wanted to talk about reliability, psychometrics, validity coefficients, linear equating, and factor analysis. I kept reciting number after number—secure in my mastery of the data and pleased with how much I had learned in so short a time. He listened patiently, paused, and asked, "Did you read the dissertation? Why have you said nothing about the Indian culture and the people? What about the role of caste and the way that the tests are actually used in Gujarat? Why did several Picture Arrangement items and many Comprehension items cause problems because of the cultural differences? Will the Gujurati WISC even be useful?" The discussion that followed opened my eyes and changed the way I thought about IQ and culture.

I had entered a new world and learned a new set of skills that I was able to put to immediate use. Dr. Wechsler told me that I would soon be meeting with a variety of psychologists from around the world to discuss the revised WISC, and that I should pay careful attention to how close people stood when they talked to me; what kinds of questions they asked (or avoided asking); and how the test was going to be used in their country. Also: Who was going to be allowed to administer the tests? What were the prevailing attitudes about IQ? What special aspects of their language, regional dialects, and culture might affect the process of revision and standardization. During the next year, I met with psychologists from Poland, Japan, England, Israel, and several other European and Asian countries. I was now alert to nuances in a burgeoning and exciting field—cross-cultural assessment— that I had scarcely known existed until Dr. Wechsler decided to "burden" me with an over-long manuscript and a Socratic lesson.

But if my mentor was responsible for opening my eyes to cross-cultural assessment, it was my students who taught me about the intricacies of cross-cultural research, adaptations, and comparisons. Toshinori Ishikuma, later to become a co-author of both the Japanese Kaufman Assessment Battery for Children (K-ABC) and the Japanese WISC-III, taught me to take nothing for granted. While doing research on IQ differences between children in the United States and Japan, we jointly discovered that Richard Lynn's initial "headline" finding that Japanese children outscored American children by 11 IQ points on the WISC-R Full Scale was largely an artifact of inadequate methodology. When the data were corrected for unequal variability, the failure of the Japanese sample to be stratified by socio-economic status, the unjustified elimination of Digit Span and Arithmetic in the computations (both tasks were essentially unchanged), generational changes (the "Flynn effect"), and other key factors, Lynn later conceded that the Japanese advantage was closer to 2.5 than 11 points. But it was my student, Toshinori Ishikuma, who made the most startling discovery of all after perusing the Manual for the Japanese WISC-R: Inexplicably, the Japanese WISC-R reduced the 120-second time limit for Coding to 90 seconds, rendering as meaningless the cross-cultural comparison on that task. Yet neither Lynn nor James Flynn (one of the main critics of the Japanese research) was aware of that basic error as they hashed and rehashed methodological issues in the literature. Indeed, a lot of time was spent by psychologists and sociologists trying to find cultural explanations for the Japanese children's "poor" Coding when the reason was simply an inadvertent 25% reduction in the time limit.

But the most fascinating cross-cultural research finding came to me courtesy of another one of my students, Soo-Back Moon (later a co-author of the Korean K-ABC), when he excitedly showed me his dissertation data. Based on American norms, the *average* South Korean school-age child (5–12.5 years) earned a scaled score of 17 (98th percentile!) on Number Recall—akin to Digits Forward. Even at the preschool level (2.5–4 years), South Korean children averaged close to the 90th percentile on this digit-repetition task relative to American preschoolers. This astonishing finding necessitated using longer number series for the Korean version of the K-ABC in order to obtain an appropriate "ceiling" for the subtest. Even more amazing was the fact that South Korean children did *not* especially excel on Word Order (memory of words in sequence), or on any other memory task in the battery, making it difficult to support possible cultural explanations for the finding that might pertain to motivation, attention, parental emphasis on achievement, and the like.

Furthermore, the literature supports a very similar finding for Taiwanese first- and fifth-grade children in Harold Stevenson and colleagues' exceptional 1985 cross-cultural investigation of Japanese, Taiwanese, and American children. The Chinese students from Taiwan excelled on a test of serial memory, as the Chinese *first* graders far outperformed both the Japanese and American *fifth* graders. These results were just as dramatic in their magnitude as the findings with the Korean K-ABC, and, once again, this incredible skill in number memory did not generalize to any other task in the 10-subtest battery that Stevenson developed, including other tests of memory. In fact, the average score on the 10 cognitive subtests was nearly equal for the three cultures studied.

As soon as I received the manuscript for this superb cross-cultural assessment book, I greedily scanned Chapters 15 and 16 for data on South Korea and Taiwan. Although the specific chapters on these countries did not provide data to address my curiosity, I quickly discovered Chapter 19 which presented a brilliant treatment of a variety of cross-cultural comparisons, including relative performance on the WISC-III subtests. And, indeed, the South Korean students excelled on Digit Span relative to all other groups studied, by a wide margin. The South Korean children also performed incredibly well on Symbol Search, suggesting a striking strength in some sort of symbolic processing or short-term symbolic memory that facilitates performance on both WISC-III subtests. I yearned to know whether the Taiwanese children and adolescents likewise had peaks on these subtests, but was thwarted to find data from Taiwan excluded from the cross-cultural subtest analysis. A quick e-mail exchange with James Georgas gave me the disappointing news that, "Regarding Taiwan, unfortunately they lost the individual level data on some tests, so we could only use the country level data."

No matter. Once again, South Korean children displayed their exceptional number-memory skill and this time excelled as well on Symbol Search, featuring medium to large effect sizes relative to other countries on these two subtests (Table 19.6). By way of comparison, all other cross-cultural "strengths" (i.e., positive effect sizes relative to the global mean of all countries) on all WISC-III subtests would be classified as "small." The four editors of this book hypothesized in Chapter 19 that the strength displayed by South Korean children on Symbol Search reflects motivation, especially for "education-related matters," and the strength on Digit Span may be related to the short time it takes to say Korean numbers, consistent with Baddeley's "phonological loop hypothesis."

I don't think so. Why would educational motivation be restricted to only one or two WISC-III subtests? Why wouldn't other countries with high motivation for educational achievement, such as Japan, not also excel on Symbol Search? Similarly, for the linguistic hypothesis, why wouldn't children from other countries with short words for numbers likewise excel on Digit Span? French numbers are spoken quickly. Numbers in English are all one-syllable, except for seven, yet American children do not perform relatively high on Digit Span. Furthermore, the analogous K-ABC Number Recall subtest avoids the digit seven, replacing it with the number ten, specifically to avoid the linguistic intrusion. Yet South Korean children greatly outperformed American children on this K-ABC subtest.

I do believe that the Baddeley hypothesis is the most likely explanation for the relatively low Digit Span scores earned by Lithuanian children, as suggested by Georgas et al. in Chapter 19, owing to the fact that numbers in the Lithuanian language not only sound alike but contain three syllables. But I believe that the high scores by South Korean children on Digit Span and Symbol Search relate to an unexplained specific cognitive strength, one that is probably akin to Guilford's Memory for Symbolic Units, as opposed to being a result of either linguistic or motivational variables.

But my disagreement with a couple of hypotheses proposed by the editors of this astoundingly good cross-cultural book actually reflects one of the book's strengths. It forces readers to think and evaluate the vast amount of information presented on diverse cultures, not to blindly accept the results or the interpretations given. The editors structured the book carefully, producing a dynamic organization for each chapter that allowed the researchers from each country to present their analyses in a systematic, easy-to-follow manner. Yet neither this structure nor the incredible and diverse array of cultures represented in the separate chapters makes this book the best text on cross-cultural assessment that I have ever seen. Rather, that exalted status comes from the role the editors themselves played in integrating the cross-cultural results with brilliance and insight, creating a marvelous gestalt out of the raw materials from each culture. The editors blended a very high level of statistical and methodological sophistication with strong foundations in research, theory, and clinical applications. The theories incorporated into the book not only included many facets of cognitive psychology, cross-cultural psychology, and developmental cognitive neuropsychology, but they extended the framework to include sociology, anthropology, and neurolinguistics.

Chapters 1 and 2 beautifully set the stage for the chapters to follow on 16 cultures, with the first chapter providing a fascinating historical account that builds the foundation for understanding how David Wechsler the man—even more so than his tests—changed the face of intellectual assessment. When the Binet was king, IQ assessment was purely a psychometric affair; the leading interpretive text was written by Quinn McNemar, a statistician. Wechsler, an astute and gifted clinician, turned intellectual assessment into a clinical process, an approach that embraces both personality and culture, and makes the cross-cultural study of intellectual ability a logical extension of his method. Chapter 2 also provides pertinent history, about cross-cultural comparisons, and offers an insightful, theory-based approach to intelligence. Further, this chapter teaches the reader the subtle distinctions among concepts that are necessary for interpreting the content of the book—e.g., culture, nation, environment—and introduces the Ecocultural Framework as a sophisticated model for understanding cross-cultural assessment.

Chapters 3 through 16, on the separate cultures with each written by assessment experts from that culture, provide extremely interesting and authoritative information. Especially illuminating are the sections on Adaptation Process, Cultural Issues, and Professional Issues, all of which pinpoint those unique aspects of history, culture, language, and test use that affect both the construction of the adapted WISC-III and its interpretation within the culture. Linguistic issues often formed the most formidable obstacles to test construction, such as the important regional differences in dialect in both the Dutch and German languages that greatly affected the development of unbiased Verbal items in the Netherlands, Belgium, Germany, Austria, and Switzerland (Chapters 7–9). The grammatical complexity of the Slovene language (Chapter 12) can affect test interpretation, depending on both the child's and examiner's language skills, and the specific definition of "similar" in the Lithuanian language ("having the same features and peculiarities") can lead children in Lithuania to give more 1-point than 2-point responses, i.e., responses that focus on outside features rather than abstractions. Typically, modification of specific test items was a function of differences between English and the specific language in question (or pertained to the metric system), but occasionally cultural differences affected item content. For example, a Picture Completion item was inappropriate in Sweden (Chapter 10) because Swedish bathtubs typically come with showers, and, in France (Chapter 6), one Comprehension and one Arithmetic item was not suitable: In French bookshops, customers cannot choose between paperback and hardcover books, and teenagers do not sell newspapers.

After one digests the culture-by-culture approach in the separate chapters that comprise Part II of the book, the editors provide an intelligent integration of the fascinating cross-cultural findings in Part III, Cross-Cultural Analyses (Chapters 17 through 19). The constructs and methodologies discussed in Chapters 17 and 18 are important, especially as they set the stage for understanding the crucial sets of comparisons that are delineated in Chapter 19, including the cross-cultural subtest comparisons referred to earlier. The topics raised in the first two chapters are brought back in this concluding chapter, as are topics discussed in the chapters on separate cultures in Part II (such as factor analysis of each version of the WISC-III), providing cohesion and unity that are rarely achieved in an edited book.

This outstanding text has so much to offer clinicians, academic psychologists, and professionals in related fields about the cross-cultural assessment of children and adolescents with the WISC-III, and its value will be felt in nations throughout the world. However, to best internalize the pertinent cross-cultural issues discussed in this book there is no substitute for direct communication with people from different cultures.

I have learned much about different cultures, and about cross-cultural assessment, from friends—and from my former doctoral students.

My personal experiences have taught me to embrace the cultural differences, to try to gain more self-insight by understanding these differences, and, most of all, to continue to grow and learn from greater cross-cultural understanding. I believe this book provides a wealth of information to facilitate such understanding and that the integration of the findings from the different cultures offers a solid foundation for making sense out of the cross-cultural analyses, both clinically and theoretically.

What is the main message of the book? The same message that I have received from my own cross-cultural experiences: That diverse cultures are more alike than different. Whether it is the universals in cognitive test performance identified in van de Vijver's cross-cultural meta-analysis (Chapter 2), the similarity of the WISC-III factor structure (Chapter 19), or the aspirations and feelings of people from different countries, I am impressed by how much more we are connected than divided.

The editors, representing four different cultures, have assembled a wealth of information from 16 cultures and have presented that information in a clear, readable format with both insight and compassion. The WISC-III, like its predecessors, the WISC-R and WISC, has had a profound influence on the world-wide assessment of children and adolescents. This book is a must for clinicians throughout the world, especially in view of the increased mobility of people in the high-tech new Millennium who readily move their families from one culture to another. The depth of the knowledge provided about each culture's unique history, language, ethnic diversity, and attitudes will enhance practitioners' abilities to interpret Wechsler profiles—indeed, profiles on any mental ability test—for children who moved to their country from a different culture.

Dr. Wechsler would be very proud.

Alan S. Kaufman
Yale University
School of Medicine
New Haven, Connecticut
April, 2003

PREFACE

This book is the first to make a comprehensive examination of the structure of the Wechsler Intelligence Scale for Children: Third Edition (WISC-III) from a cross-cultural perspective. The Wechsler tests are perhaps the most widely used intelligence tests in the world and yet, little is known about the standardization efforts in different countries or how well the WISC-III travels across country, cultural, and linguistic borders. The data for the analyses reported in this book are from the standardization programs of the WISC-III in the United States, Canada, United Kingdom, Austria, Germany and Switzerland, France and French Speaking Belgium, the Netherlands and Flemish Speaking Belgium, Greece, Sweden, Slovenia, Lithuania, Japan, South Korea, and Taiwan. While the WISC-III is used in other countries, particular criteria were established which limited the data analyses to those countries which have carried out comprehensive standardization studies that have been fully documented in technical manuals.

The initial idea of comparing the WISC-III in different nations led to the organization of a symposium at a conference of the International Association for Cross-Cultural Psychology and the International Test Commission in Graz, Austria in 1999. The participants included many of the present authors in this book. The success of the symposium stimulated the four editors of this book to study more systematically issues related to these cross-cultural comparisons and to expand the study to countries that had completed the standardization of the WISC-III.

From a cross-cultural perspective, the WISC-III studies have two characteristics that are not widely shared among comparative studies of intelligence or related constructs. The first is the care of the sampling process. It is uncommon to find studies in psychology that are based on nation-wide samples, which can claim to be representative for the larger national population. There are few examples in the literature on intelligence and cognitive processes with samples so carefully selected and representative of the social structural variables in each country. The samples represent the populations of children ages 6–16 in these countries. Second, much attention was paid to the test adaptation process in each country. Each national team has seriously dealt with the issue of appropriateness of test items for its own country. As a consequence, we can be confident that the items, which were either closely translated from the American original or created for the specific country, represent the targets of the subtests in an adequate way.

The standardization studies are discussed from two perspectives. One is cross-cultural and compares countries. The second is country-specific or indigenous; authors of each country chapter present cultural variables that may influence WISC-III test performance and interpretation, ranging from the construction, translation and adaptation in different cultures, to the analysis of its structure and function as a concept, and finally to its clinical use with different ethnic groups.

The first aim of this book is to present a comprehensive cross-cultural analysis of the WISC-III data. A second aim is to describe and analyze the adaptation and standardization of the WISC-III in each country. To achieve this, we invited key researchers from each country to write a detailed description of this process of adaptation and standardization. These country chapters outline the standardization studies including items retained and changed, norms, reliability and validity, cultural issues related to test performance and interpretation of the results, etc. An overarching theme of this book is a commentary on the clinical use of the WISC-III in each country and its potential use with ethnic groups in multicultural societies. We have also encouraged in both the country-specific chapters as well as through our own analyses an exploration of the relevance of the cross-cultural analyses with current theoretical and applied issues regarding intelligence testing, the concept of intelligence, and cognitive processes.

The book is separated into three major parts. Part I discusses intelligence and the Wechsler tests, and then extends this to include a cross-cultural perspective of intelligence and cognition. Chapter 1 by Donald H. Saklofske, Lawrence G. Weiss, A. Lynne Beal, and Diane Coalson begins by reviewing the lineage of the various Wechsler scales dating back to the original Wechsler-Bellevue, and placing these developments in context with critical events in society during the twentieth century. The chapter shows how societal needs have driven the growth of intelligence testing and even shaped the nature and purpose of the tests over time from identification of the mentally retarded to measures of cognitive processing related to academic achievement. The chapter concludes with a review of the clinical utility of recent modernizations of the Wechsler scales that are informed by developmental cognitive-neuropsychological constructs such as working memory and processing speed.

Chapter 2 by James Georgas outlines some issues related to cross-cultural psychology, intelligence, and cognitive processes. Cross-cultural psychology studies the relationship between culture and psychological variables; the degree to which there are universals in psychological processes, and the degree to which there are variations in the behavioral manifestations of psychological processes due to specific cultural influences. One issue is the similarities and differences of the concepts of environment and culture. A second issue is the concepts of nations, cultures, and ethnic groups, and the importance of these distinctions in cross-cultural methodology. Issues related to intelligence, intelligent behavior, and tested intelligence are discussed. The definition of intelligence has been a controversial issue in psychology and psychometrics, dating from the construction of the first intelligence tests. Cultures define intelligence differently according to their own ecological and social demands. There are also variations in the manifestations of cognitive processes necessary for adaptation to the ecological demands of cultures. Cross-cultural psychology and anthropology have a long history of studies of cognitive processes in different cultures. Research in cross-cultural psychology has explored universals in cognitive processes across cultures, and also variations in how cognitive processes are manifested in different cultures.

Part II presents descriptions of the standardization of the WISC-III in each country. These chapters represent the indigenous dimension of the book. Chapters written by the authors of each country chapter describe the comprehensive process of item and scale adaptation, description of the standardization samples and sampling procedures, reliability, evidence of validity, factor index scores, and a description of cultural styles or performance issues that may influence test performance and interpretation of the results. These cultural factors in performance in the WISC-III may be of particular interest to psychologists testing a child who has recently emigrated from one of the countries in this book.

The countries and authors are:

Chapter 3. United States. Lawrence G. Weiss
Chapter 4. Canada. Donald H. Saklofske
Chapter 5. United Kingdom. Paul McKeown
Chapter 6. France and French-Speaking Belgium. Jacques Grégoire
Chapter 7. The Netherlands and Flemish-Speaking Belgium. Mark Schittekatte, Willem Kort, Wilma Resing, Griet Vermeir, and Paul Verhaeghe
Chapter 8. Germany. Uwe Tewes
Chapter 9. Austria and Switzerland. Peter Rossmann and Urs Schallberger
Chapter 10. Sweden. Karin Sonnander and Bengt Ramund
Chapter 11. Lithuania. Gražina Gintilienė and Sigita Girdzijauskienė
Chapter 12. Slovenia. Dušica Boben and Valentin Bucik
Chapter 13. Greece. James Georgas, Ioannis N. Paraskevopoulos, Elias Besevegis, Nikolaos Giannitsas, and Kostas Mylonas
Chapter 14. Japan. Kazuhiko Ueno and Ichiro Nakatani
Chapter 15. South Korea. Keumjoo Kwak
Chapter 16. Taiwan. Hsin-Yi Chen, Yung-Hwa Chen, and Jianjun Zhu

The structure of each chapter is the same so that readers can easily reference the same information about each country. Each chapter begins with a brief history of why it was important to translate, adapt and norm the WISC-III, whether this was the first adaptation of the WISC or whether there were previous adaptations, the year the project began and was completed and those responsible for the adaptation, and other Wechsler tests or other intelligence tests which have been constructed or adapted in the country.

Adaptation Process. The procedures used to adapt the items from the U.S. or the UK version are described including the translation and back translation procedures for the items, the panel of experts, and their background, the procedures used for adapting the items, procedures used to verify that the new items retained the same level of difficulty, and/or that the construct being measured was the same. The pilot study or tryout data is described; the number of cases collected, if items were revised again after the pilot/tryout. Examples are presented of items in the U.S. or UK version that did not function well in the country due to culture bias, item bias, change in difficulty level, or other reasons. Some of these examples are interesting in understanding why certain items from one culture are culture biased in another.

Sample Characteristics. The important demographic characteristics of the country are described, and how closely the stratification of the standardization sample matched them: gender, age, educational level or socioeconomic level of parents, racial/ethnic composition of the sample, geographical areas of the country, etc. The sampling frame is discussed, together with the sampling procedures employed in selecting the individuals. The language of each country is described, together with issues of sampling related to language competence in countries with large ethnic groups.

Reliability. The split-half reliability coefficients and standard errors of measurement, reported in the technical manual of each country, for each subtest, IQ, and Index Score are presented in tables. The main findings are summarized and briefly discussed. Retest correlations are reported for age bands and for total sample. The age bands vary somewhat from country to country. In some countries in which the standardization is very recent, retest reliabilities may not have been gathered at the time of publication of this book.

Evidence of Validity. The table of intercorrelations among subtests for the overall sample is presented. These tables will be useful for those who scan the intercorrelations looking for interrelationships. The results of factor analysis of the data are presented in a table, which also permits comparisons between countries. The method employed for extracting factors and for the rotation of factors is described. The Index Scores are presented and discussed in terms of their meaning in each country.

Validity data based on correlations of the WISC-III with other measures of intelligence or achievement are presented. Some countries report detailed validation studies and their relationship to the literature on the WISC tests. Other countries report studies of the WISC-III with specific clinical groups.

Cultural Issues Influencing WISC-III Interpretations. This section is of particular interest to those psychologists who evaluate children from different ethnic groups, particularly those children who may have recently immigrated into the country and may not have attained language fluency in the language of the host country. The purpose of this section is to familiarize the reader about cultural issues in the home country, issues which may influence performance of a child taking the WISC-III, either in the language of the host country or in the language of the home country. Evaluation of the child's cognitive functioning on the WISC-III by a psychologist in a host country will be aided by information about some cultural and linguistic issues in the home country. Understanding these cultural issues will aid in proper interpretation of scores obtained by children in the host country. One example is that the names of numbers in Lithuania are longer than in other countries and this makes the Digit Span task much more difficult for Lithuanian children. Thus, a low Digit Span score for a Lithuanian child may not necessarily mean that he or she has a poor working memory. Japanese children show high test performances on the speed tests. In order to adjust for a ceiling effect in item response, the time limit for some subtests and some items were shortened. Because of the increase in affluence in Greece during the past 30 years, correlations between test performance on the WISC-III and measures and educational level of their parents are in the low 0.30s. Thirty years ago these correlations, on other intelligence tests, were in the 0.60s. Thus, the correlation between test performance on the WISC-III and a measure of socioeconomic status in Greece has reduced significantly in the past 30 years.

Other issues discussed here also include the WISC-III performance of different subcultures in some countries. For example, Dutch-speaking children from the Flanders area of Belgium perform differently on some subtests as compared to Dutch children from neighboring Netherlands, and these differences are thought to be due to the effects of different emphases of the educational system in the two countries.

Professional Issues in the Use of Intelligence Tests. This section describes professional issues about IQ testing that are current topics of debate in professional associations within each country. Some countries have enacted laws or legislation certifying or licensing psychologists. In some countries, only psychologists can administer psychological tests while in others, educators can also administer them. Yet in other countries, there are strict restrictions imposed by the Ministry of Education about the use of intelligence tests in evaluating educational achievement while in others there is more leeway about evaluating types of learning difficulties with intelligence tests. Clinical assessment and the use of intelligence tests from the perspective of the psychological associations of each country are briefly described.

A reading of these chapters suggests that in that past, not all efforts to standardize the Wechsler tests have been carried out in a comprehensive fashion. There have been instances of psychologists merely translating intelligence tests without copyright permission of the publisher, and thus without going through a rigorous adaptation and standardization with a representative sample.

In some countries, intelligence tests are almost entirely restricted to school psychologists with few evaluations by clinical psychologists. Also, some countries passed through a period similar to that in the United States in which intelligence tests were criticized as culturally biased and their use was either discouraged or banned in educational testing programs.

Part III presents the cross-cultural analysis of the WISC-III. Chapter 17, "Principles of Adaptation of Intelligence Tests to other Cultures" is written by Fons J. R. van de Vijver. Different options are available when test developers want to develop a test version for a new cultural and linguistic population. Test instructions can be closely (i.e., literally) translated or they can be adapted when such a translation would be culturally or linguistically inappropriate. After a description of the options in test translation, measurement issues of these translations are considered. The concept of equivalence is presented as a generic term for the comparability of item and test scores. Three types of equivalence are distinguished: structural equivalence (to what extent does a test or subtest measure the same construct in each culture?); measurement unit equivalence (identity of measurement units across cultures); scalar equivalence or full score equivalence (identity of measurement unit and scale origin).

Chapter 18, "Methodology of Combining the WISC-III Data Sets" by Fons J. R. van de Vijver, Kostas Mylonas, Vassilis Pavlopoulos, and James Georgas presents the method employed in the cross-cultural analyses. The first part of the chapter presents an overview of which items were closely translated from the American original or British version and which items were adapted in each country. This presentation provides the background for the statistical analyses reported in the next chapter; however, the overview is also interesting in its own right. It provides insight into the judgmental bias of the subtest, which refers to non-statistical procedures to identify bias, based on a content analysis of the items. All local test development teams had to address the question: which American items, or items from the UK revision, were expected to be transferable to a new cultural and linguistic context without major alterations and which items were assumed to require adaptation. As a consequence, country comparisons of the number of adapted items of the 12 subtests (Mazes was not included in the final analyses as explained in Chapter 19) provide information about the judgmental bias in these subtests. The second part of the chapter describes, in a largely nontechnical way, the statistical analyses that are reported in the next chapter.

Chapter 19 presents the cross-cultural analysis of the data sets across all the countries. The authors, James Georgas, Fons J. R. van de Vijver, Lawrence G. Weiss, and Donald H. Saklofske, are also the editors of this book. In the first part the structural equivalence is examined, using factor analysis. Cross-cultural analysis of its structural equivalence and differences or similarity in meaning across countries is of specific interest to the WISC-III. One question concerns the structural equivalence of the WISC-III across these countries. If there is structural equivalence, it would provide partial support for the universality of the kind of intelligence measured by the WISC-III in school-going populations. A second question concerns the comparative analysis of its scores on the subtests and on the Verbal, Performance and Full-Scale IQ, and the Index Scores. Are there mean differences or are there similarities in performance at the individual level and at the country-level? These analyses are, of course, conducted with the raw scores from each country and not the scaled scores, or the actual Verbal, Performance and Full-Scale IQs. Comparison of means of scaled scores across countries would result in zero differences, since each country has transformed its raw scores to scaled scores. Item Response Theory is used to estimate means of subtests with partly dissimilar items across cultural groups. The last part of the chapter presents country-level analyses. Correlations are discussed between subtest scores on the one hand and various country indicators, such as affluence and educational indices, on the other.

These countries are from different geographical and cultural zones around the world: North America, Northern and Central Europe, the Balkans, and East Asia. However, they also share similar social structural features. They are among the most affluent countries in the world. Most of these countries emerge on the same cultural cluster based on economic and educational social indices. Lithuania and Slovenia are exceptions here, although among the former socialist countries of Eastern Europe, they are among those whose economic level is increasing more rapidly than some of their neighbors. These countries all have highly developed educational systems. Their governments and people place high value on the role of education in success, in achievement of occupational success, and in a better life. These countries have all invested highly in information technology. As a consequence these countries are not representative of the wide range of cultures in the world in terms of the range of economic level and educational systems. Our sample does not include the poor countries of Africa, South America, and East and West Asia. Thus, although this is a cross-cultural analysis, the range of sampling of countries is restricted in terms of economic and educational measures.

It is our hope that the findings presented in this book will provide a contextually rich and culturally meaningful analysis of the WISC-III. We have demonstrated that the WISC-III is a remarkably robust measure of intelligence that has considerable power for assessing children's intelligence, even when cultural contexts vary as they have in this study. At the same time, the results have indicated that considerable measurement sophistication is required to adapt the WISC-III when required. Further, the chapters in this book remind of us of the professional and ethical responsibilities that go hand in hand with the use of the WISC-III when used for research or clinical purposes. We encourage further research of this kind and hope that our book has provided a template for both the cross-cultural study of intelligence but also its practical measurement.

We are very grateful to Alan S. Kaufman, Yale Child Study Center, Yale University School of Medicine, who took time from his busy schedule, for agreeing to write the Foreword for this book.

The authors of the country chapters presented a thorough and structured analysis of the process of standardization of the WISC-III and a graphic and interesting description of the cultural aspects of the WISC-III in their countries. We want to warmly thank them and the co-authors of other chapters for their level of competence and for their interest in the project.

The editors would like to thank The Psychological Corporation and its parent company, Reed-Elsevier, for their support of this project and for permission to use the data set of the American standardization for the cross-cultural analyses and tables from the WISC-III manual. We would also acknowledge with thanks permission of the publishers in the following countries to use the data sets of their standardizations and tables from the WISC-III manuals: Nihon Bunka Kagakusha Co., Ltd., Tokyo, Japan; The Chinese Behavioral Sciences Corporation, Taipei, Taiwan; The Psychological Corporation of Canada, Toronto, Ontario, Canada; Les Editions du Center de Psychologie Appliquée, Paris, France; Verlag Hans Huber, Bern, Germany, Switzerland, and Austria; The University of Athens, Athens, Greece; Special Education Publishers, Seoul, Korea; Center za psihodiagnosticna sredstva, d.o.o. and Vilnius University, Ljubijana, Slovenia; Psykologifφrlaget, AB, Stockholm, Sweden.

Warm thanks to George Zimmar who initially encouraged us to write this book. Thanks to John W. Berry for his comments on Chapter 2. The John Ranton MacIntosh Fellowship supported the work of Donald H. Saklofske on this book through a grant. The research committee of the University of Athens supported some of the work on this project. We would like to thank Rinus Verkooijen of Tilburg University for his help with checking the references.

Finally, many thanks to Nikki Levy, Publisher of Academic Press, for steering this project to port and her helpful advice along the way. Thanks also to Senior Developmental Editor Barbara Makinster and Senior Project Manager Paul Gottehrer for their work in preparing the final manuscript for publication.

James Georgas, Athens, Greece
Lawrence G. Weiss, San Antonio, Texas, U.S.A.
Fons J. R. van de Vijver, Tilburg, The Netherlands
Donald H. Saklofske, Saskatoon, Saskatchewan, Canada
April, 2003

PART

I

INTELLIGENCE AND THE WECHSLER SCALES FOR CHILDREN

1

THE WECHSLER SCALES FOR ASSESSING CHILDREN'S INTELLIGENCE: PAST TO PRESENT

DONALD H. SAKLOFSKE

*Department of Educational Psychology
and Special Education
University of Saskatchewan
Saskatoon, Saskatchewan, Canada*

LAWRENCE G. WEISS

*The Psychological Corporation
San Antonio, Texas*

A. LYNNE BEAL

*Toronto District School Board
Toronto, Ontario, Canada*

DIANE COALSON

*The Psychological Corporation
San Antonio, Texas*

The Wechsler tests have contributed substantially to the study of cognitive processes and have served as the cornerstones for the assessment of intelligence and memory for more than 60 years. To this day, the Wechsler tests remain the most often used individually administered, standardized measures for assessing intelligence in children and adults (Camara, Nathan, & Puente, 2000; Prifitera, Weiss, & Saklofske, 1998). Of particular relevance to the development of these tests is Dr. David Wechsler the person, the events and people who influenced him, and the tests that he developed. A full appreciation of the current version of the children's scale, the Wechsler Intelligence Scale for Children—Third Edition (WISC-III; Wechsler, 1991), may be gleaned from an examination of the history of the Wechsler scales. A contextual appreciation of the WISC-III comes from the current status of assessing general mental ability, and the role of the Verbal IQ (VIQ) and Performance IQ (PIQ) in comparison to the more recently developed

WISC-III index scores of Verbal Comprehension (VCI), Perceptual Organization (POI), Freedom from Distractibility (i.e., working memory; FDI) and Processing Speed (PSI). A clinical appreciation of the WISC-III comes from its current uses in school and child psychology assessment practices.

Dr. Wechsler's perspective on intelligence tests and assessment appeared to converge as a function of the influences of key individuals in his professional sphere, his experiences in the Army testing program and in his professional practice, the recognition of the strengths but also limitations of the Binet-Simon scales, and the rapid development of many new tests that appeared to address these shortcomings. After completing his master's degree at Columbia University, he joined the U.S. Army and was trained to administer individual psychological tests that included the Stanford-Binet and the Yerkes Point Scale, as well as other performance tests. Wechsler stated (1975) that it was this experience that guided his thinking that intelligence may be usefully assessed with both verbal and nonverbal tests. This would prevent much of the misdiagnosis that occurred as a result of using scales that relied heavily on the assessment of verbal abilities, which were certainly influenced by formal education. This was also recently suggested to be the thinking underlying Wechsler's decision to not include a vocabulary subtest on his first scale (Tulsky, Saklofske, & Richer, 2003).

Further influences on Wechsler most certainly resulted from his studies with Spearman and Pearson in London. It was Spearman who was a strong proponent of a two-factor theory of intelligence with g or general mental ability at the apex, reflecting the various positive correlations between more limited and specific tests. As well, Wechsler served as a part-time consultant for The Psychological Corporation, founded by James McKeen Cattell in 1921 and then took a position administering intelligence, personality, and achievement tests for the New York Bureau of Child Guidance. The director was Bernard Glueck who had also noted the shortcomings of the Binet tests, probably due to his experiences with the Ellis Island screening program for new immigrants to the United States. Wechsler's earliest views about intelligence tests were articulated in a paper published in 1926 entitled "The Influence of Education on Intelligence as Measured by the Binet-Simon Tests." Following the completion of his Ph.D., also earned at Columbia University, Wechsler later accepted the position of chief psychologist at the Bellevue Psychiatric Hospital. Apart from these specific influences, at least several other key events also helped to influence Dr. Wechsler.

CRITICAL EVENTS IN THE HISTORY OF INTELLIGENCE TESTS AND TESTING

The considerable activity directed at developing and using tests to assess intelligence in the formative years of psychology as both a discipline and profession would have a significant impact on David Wechsler and on his views of intelligence assessment and the tests he developed (Boak, 2002; Tulsky, Saklofske, & Richer,

2003; Tulsky, Saklofske, & Zhu, 2003). There is ample evidence of attempts to measure intelligence that certainly predate the formation of psychology as a scientific discipline in the mid 1800s (Boak, 2002). Early psychology was significantly influenced by the pioneering efforts of Sir Francis Galton who developed and employed a number of psychophysical or anthropometric measures to assess individual differences. These tests were introduced to the public during an 1884 health exhibition in London, England. In the U.S., James McKeen Cattell both adapted and created a battery of "mental tests" that was administered to college students. However, the publication of Binet and Simon's intelligence scale in 1905 was a significant event that has profoundly influenced our views of both intelligence and intelligence tests. The more purely psychophysical measures that dominated the measurement of intelligence to that time had not demonstrated much practical usefulness. Instead, Binet and Simon assembled a battery of brief tests that included some existing measures (e.g., digit span) as well as new tests tapping more complex cognitive skills. By grouping the subtests into age levels, this scale was then used to detect children who were deemed unlikely to benefit from the regular education programs. Thus it appeared that it was possible to both measure intelligence and then use the results for practical decisions.

The 1905 and 1908 Binet-Simon tests met with great success and were introduced into the U.S. by Goddard. Revisions by Yerkes and Bridges and by Terman further improved and demonstrated the utility of intelligence tests in the assessment of children and also adults. The Stanford-Binet Intelligence Scale published in the U.S. in 1916 by Terman clearly established the importance of intelligence testing in the schools and provided a template that has guided the format of intelligence tests to this day. The future of intelligence tests and testing was further anchored in the events of World War I. In the U.S., group tests were employed in the screening and selection process of Army recruits. Many key American psychologists including Yerkes, Boring, Thorndike, Otis, and Thurstone were instrumental in the development of the tests and the implementation of the testing program. The Alpha and Beta tests were designed to be administered to groups who were either English proficient or nonproficient in English. Individually administered intelligence tests were employed when failure occurred on one of the group tests.

Following the development of the Binet-Simon tests, and many other scales, as well as the demonstration of their utility during WWI, intelligence tests were also rapidly finding their way into the schools and clinics of post-war America. French (1990) has documented the history of school psychology and suggests that the assessment role was well-established by the 1920s. University courses in assessment methods, such as those offered by Witmer more than one hundred years ago, became more common in the early part of the 20th century so that training in intelligence testing was now being offered to teachers and medical doctors as well as psychologists. Fagan (1999) suggested that the mental testing movement in American psychology strongly influenced the training and role of psychologists. Intelligence tests and testing programs were now firmly established as part of the practice of psychology. Concurrent with the training of psychologists was the continued development of new tests such as the Kohs Block Design. Wechsler was also influenced by guiding principles from this era, resulting in the use of more cognitively complex tests, summarizing subtests to yield composite scores (i.e., IQ score), and organizing the test following the point-scale method. Clearly, these events established a solid foundation for the Wechsler tests. Beginning with the Wechsler-Bellevue Intelligence Scale published in 1939, Wechsler certainly used many subtests that were developed by others in the creation of his tests (see Boak, 2002; Tulsky, Saklofske, & Zhu, 2003).

THE FIRST WECHSLER TEST: THE
WECHSLER-BELLEVUE INTELLIGENCE SCALE

The Wechsler-Bellevue Intelligence Scale (W-B), reporting norms for 10–59 years of age, was standardized and used at the Bellevue Hospital for several years prior to it being produced by The Psychological Corporation and published in 1939. Its development has been documented in a number of publications including Boak (2002), Matarazzo (1972), Tulsky *et al.* (2003) and, of course in Wechsler's own publications of his tests. The W-B tests of 1939 and 1946 were essentially a clever integration and synthesis of tests that had already been more or less developed and were in use at that time. In fact, Wechsler (1939) stated that his aim was not so much to develop new tests as to assemble various scales that would yield a more effective measure of intelligence. Thus all of the subtests contained in the W-B-I, many of which have carried through to the WISC-III and Wechsler Adult Intelligence Scale-III (WAIS-III) can be traced to the Army Alpha and Beta tests, the Kohs Block Design, and others, although the actual item content may be quite different.

The extremely successful introduction of the W-B, and of the Wechsler Memory Scale in 1945, marked the beginning of the testing legacy that still bears the name of David Wechsler, despite his passing away in 1981. While Wechsler did not in a sense invent or create a uniquely new comprehensive test in the Binet-Simon tradition, his contributions to the theory of psychological assessment of intelligence and to intelligence testing itself are undeniable. The high regard in which he is still held is aptly described by Kaufman (1994) in the preface to his book *Intelligent Testing with the WISC-III*.

> Little did I realize then that those battles with the Master (Dr. Wechsler) would shape
> my own development as a test author and trainer of school psychologists, and would remain
> forever etched-fresh and vibrant and poignant in my memory (p. xv).

What was it that made the W-B so popular, especially since it appeared only 2 years after the 1937 revision of the Stanford-Binet? Maybe it was a need for more than one comprehensive measure of intelligence, given the demand for such tests in schools, child guidance clinics, hospitals, and the military. Certainly, the W-B did not create a major dissonance for psychologists because it included so many subtests that were already familiar to them. Maybe it was that the tests accomplished what they were intended to do. The organization of the subtests into verbal and performance scales, even if not initially based on empirical evidence, clearly reflected the experiences of WWI with the Alpha and Beta tests. The use of deviation scores and the comprehensiveness of the standardization and norming procedures were also critical factors in establishing the W-B. Boak (2002) stated that "by incorporating these technical innovations into a single scale, Wechsler accomplished a major advance in the technology of individual intelligence testing." As research on intelligence as a key individual differences variable also grew, so the Wechsler scales became very much a part of mainstream psychology.

THE WECHSLER TESTS FOR ASSESSING CHILDREN'S INTELLIGENCE

The standardization of the W-B initially included children in the 7–9 year age range, but the test manual only included norms for the 10–59 year ranges. A few years later, the W-B-II was published, but the separation into children and adult scales was marked by the 1949 publication of the Wechsler Intelligence Scale for Children (Wechsler, 1949). Essentially this was a downward extension of the W-B-II and did not introduce changes other than adding easier items to anchor the scales for children. This test was supported by a comprehensive standardization, albeit one that would be deemed biased by the demographic criteria employed in the more recent standardization projects. The WISC retained the deviation IQ and the separation of scales into VIQ, PIQ, and Full Scale IQ (FSIQ). Once again, Wechsler's test was very quickly accepted by practicing psychologists.

Over the ensuing years, further editions of the Wechsler tests were published which eventually included separate tests for adults, school-age children, and preschool children as shown in Fig. 1.1. These tests, in concert, now cover the age range of 2.5–89 years.

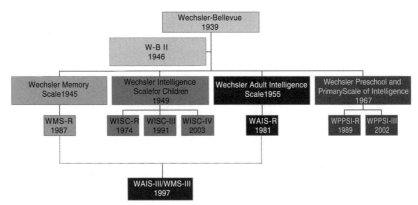

FIGURE 1.1   Revisions of the Wechsler Tests.

The revision of the WISC into the Wechsler Intelligence Scale for Children—Revised (WISC-R; Wechsler, 1974) was mainly an effort to ensure the test remained contemporary in terms of item content and norms. Kaufman (1994) has provided an insightful description of David Wechsler during the time that they collaborated on the development of the WISC-R. It appears that Wechsler was very insistent on the minimum of modifications to this test while remaining firmly committed to the VIQ and PIQ scales as well as the composite FSIQ. However, the "seeds of change" were becoming increasingly evident. The technology of test construction was rapidly advancing as were new research findings from cognitive psychology and neuropsychology that had significant implications for understanding and measuring intelligence. New models of intelligence (e.g., Das, Kirby, & Jarman, 1979) were coming to the attention of psychologists. This was complemented by other new intelligence tests of the day, some of which were quite in contrast to the g-based Wechsler tests, (e.g., Kaufman Assessment Battery for Children; Kaufman & Kaufman, 1983; Woodcock-Johnson Psychoeducational Battery; Woodcock & Johnson, 1977). Clinicians were now expecting more from their test instruments as demands increased for more in-depth and prescriptive assessments. In addition, intelligence tests were under very close scrutiny by the public and the courts (e.g., Larry P. v. Riles, 1979). There was also evidence that test norms (as well as the item content) can become dated over reasonably short periods (Flynn, 1984, 1987).

While each revision of the Wechsler tests continued to be well received, these events began the process of gradual change pursued by the caretakers of David Wechsler's legacy at The Psychological Corporation. Several research thrusts were also challenging the traditional VIQ, PIQ, FSIQ structure of the WISC and WAIS. Cohen (1959) reported that the WISC verbal scale tended to split into two factors and that the performance subtests showed differential loadings on their respective factor. The fact that three factors emerged was a critical event at a time when the search was underway for tests that could assist in differential diagnosis and had prescriptive utility.

THE WISC-III

The WISC-III (Wechsler, 1991) was developed to provide a contemporary and psychometrically sound intelligence scale with current norms. The WISC-III is shown in Fig. 1.2. However, it was not a vast departure from the WISC and WISC-R. The test certainly met all of the psychometric standards. All but one of the subtests was familiar to psychologists who had used the WISC as shown in Table 1.1. However, in an effort to strengthen the psychometric integrity and clinical usefulness of the third factor, the Symbol Search subtest was added, again changing the landscape on which this test was grounded.

The addition of the Symbol Search subtest had an unexpected effect on the factor structure of the new WISC-III. Rather than serving to strengthen the FDI factor, a fourth factor appeared that was replicated in subsequent phases of the

FIGURE 1.2   WISC-III test kit and materials.

TABLE 1.1   Verbal and Performance Subtests Included in the WISC, WISC-R, and WISC-III

	WISC	WISC-R	WISC-III
Verbal subtests			
Information	✓	✓	✓
Comprehension	✓	✓	✓
Arithmetic	✓	✓	✓
Similarities	✓	✓	✓
Vocabulary	✓	✓	✓
Digit span[a]	✓	✓	✓
Performance subtests			
Picture completion	✓	✓	✓
Picture arrangement	✓	✓	✓
Block design	✓	✓	✓
Object assembly	✓	✓	✓
Coding	✓	✓	✓
Mazes[a]	✓	✓	✓
Symbol search[a]			✓

[a]Digit Span, Mazes, and Symbol Search are considered supplementary tests, or as alternate tests in the event of a spoiled administration.

standardization program. The emergence of a fourth factor labeled Processing Speed (a more cognitive description in contrast to the behavioral term, Freedom from Distractibility) was in further contrast to the VIQ, PIQ, FSIQ description found in the previous versions of the WISC (see Fig. 1.3 for a description of the factor structure).

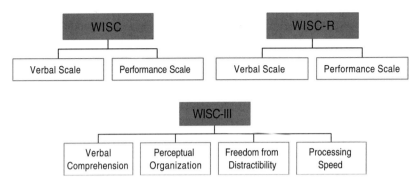

FIGURE 1.3   Factor-based scales of the WISC, WISC-R, and WISC-III.

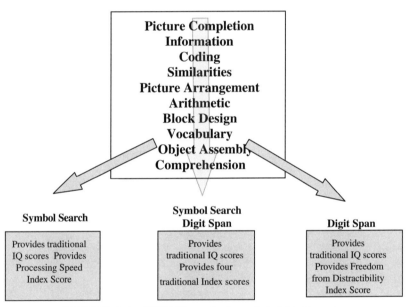

FIGURE 1.4   WISC-III organization and administration order.

Although both scoring systems (IQ and index scores) were presented in the technical manual and included on the test protocol, it was only in more recent years that greater attention has been directed at understanding the meaning of these factors and how they can be used in the clinical assessment context (Prifitera *et al.*, 1998; Weiss, Saklofske, & Prifitera, 2003). The shift can be further observed in the WAIS-III (Wechsler, 1997) where greater emphasis is placed on the four factors (Tulsky, Saklofske, & Zhu, 2003). Figure 1.4 illustrates how the WISC-III subtests combine to yield various score results.

IQ SCORES AND THE WECHSLER TESTS

Until very recently, the Wechsler scales were considered to be tests of general mental ability. Merit was seen in having a test that provided a wide sampling of intellectual skills that could be added together to provide a composite measure. This view of intelligence is in line with the theoretical views of Spearman (1904) and Vernon (1950), and was empirically supported by Carroll's (1993) analyses of more than 400 large databases. Although g has essentially been replicated in many studies of intelligence, it has also been increasingly called into question (see Garlick, 2002; McGrew, 1997). Thus, it would appear necessary to revisit the relevance of the FSIQ as a composite or summary measure of general intellectual functioning, and especially its future in clinical assessment. This follows from the more recent view that the VIQ and PIQ may also be less relevant in relation to the four-factor structure and index scores described for the WISC-III and WAIS-III.

Some writers have criticized the lack of a theoretical foundation in the Wechsler intelligence scales (e.g., Thorndike, 1990; Flanagan, Genshaft, & Harrison, 1997). A closer review of Wechsler's original conceptions and development of his scales provides important insights into his theoretical views. Wechsler argued for a unitary construct of intelligence that could best be measured by assessing an individual's performance on a wide array of tests. He considered intelligence not only as a global entity but also as an aggregate of specific abilities that are qualitatively different. Wechsler explained that intelligence is global because it characterizes the individual's behavior as a whole. It is also specific because it is comprised of elements or abilities that are qualitatively different.

The primary purpose of intelligence testing at the time Wechsler published his original scale was still focused on the classification of individuals based on their overall level of cognitive functioning. Drawing from his considerable clinical expertise, Wechsler selected those subtests that he deemed to be the most clinically useful and ecologically valid for this purpose. Although it is true that he did not select subtests based on an explicit theory of intelligence, his choice of subtests for inclusion in his scales sheds light on the cognitive aspects of intelligence that he deemed most important to assess. The subtests Wechsler selected and developed tapped many different mental abilities, such as abstract reasoning, perceptual organization, verbal comprehension, quantitative reasoning, memory, and processing speed. All of these areas have been confirmed as important aspects of cognitive ability in more contemporary theories and measures of intelligence (Carroll, 1993, 1997; Horn & Noll, 1997).

In general, Wechsler's conception of intelligence as a global construct assessed by the measurement of different abilities is consistent with current research on intelligence. The last several decades of research have included factor-analytic studies of intelligence measures to determine the specific abilities measured by intelligence tests (e.g., Jensen, 1997; Carroll, 1993). Although the terms used to describe the cognitive abilities vary with the researcher, results indicate that intelligence comprises specific narrow abilities that, in turn, cluster into higher-order ability domains. Although some have presumed that Wechsler assumed a two-factor structure of intelligence based on his split of subtests into verbal and performance tasks, Wechsler clarified the practical purpose of the split by noting:

> [The grouping of subtests into Verbal and Performance areas] . . . does not imply that these are the only abilities involved in the tests. . . The subtests are different measures of intelligence, not measures of different kinds of intelligence, and the dichotomy of Verbal and Performance areas is only one of several ways in which the tests could be grouped (Wechsler, 1958, p. 64).

NEW GROUPINGS OF SUBTESTS: BEYOND IQ SCORES

Wechsler had already noted many years earlier that ". . . the attributes and factors of intelligence, like the elementary particles in physics, have at once collective and individual properties, that is, they appear to behave differently when alone from what they do when operating in concert" (Wechsler, 1975, p. 138).

Evidence that the WISC and WISC-R subtests could be regrouped in several meaningful ways came quickly and was well accepted by practitioners as clinically useful. Bannatyne (1974) proposed a set of regroupings that have become known as the Bannatyne composites. In his influential book *Intelligent Testing with the WISC-R*, Kaufman (1979) discussed other composites that could be derived from clinically meaningful regroupings of the WISC-R subtests (e.g. ACID profile).

INDEX SCORES

As discussed above, the revision of the WISC-R provided the opportunity to not only update the test and provide new norms, but also to further define the factor structure that arose in the new WISC-III. In line with research and the increased use of intelligence tests for the evaluation of specific cognitive functions, more recent versions of the Wechsler Intelligence Scales (i.e., Wechsler Preschool and Primary Scale of Intelligence (WPPSI-III), WISC-III, WAIS-III) have included new subtests to tap more specific abilities (e.g., working memory and processing speed) and provide factor index scores to represent narrower areas of cognitive functioning than the traditional VIQ and PIQ.

Factor analyses of the WISC-III subtests resulted in four factors that have been replicated in a number of independent studies (see Sattler & Saklofske, 2001). The VCI provided a purer measure of verbal comprehension by omitting the Arithmetic subtest that now loaded on the Freedom from Distractibility factor. Further, the POI factor is a more pure measure of the kinds of cognitive abilities previously measured by the PIQ (Prifitera, Weiss, & Saklofske, 1998). Together with the new subtest Symbol Search, Coding now loaded on the PSI factor. While the VCI and POI factors were well understood by both researchers and practitioners, the two new factors expanded the measurement capabilities of the WISC-III.

FREEDOM FROM DISTRACTIBILITY:
A MEASURE OF WORKING MEMORY

Perhaps the most important of the possible regroupings was the collection of Arithmetic, Digit Span, and Coding. This composite was labeled "Freedom from Distractibility." It was first identified as a third factor by Cohen (1957, 1959) based on factor analyses of the original WISC, and confirmed by Kaufman (1979) in the WISC-R. The meaning of the third factor and its labeling have been topics of extended debate. By using the Freedom from Distractibility label, Kaufman emphasized the attention-concentration aspects of the factor. Bannatyne (1974) contended that the three subtests all require sequencing ability. Lutey (1977) noted that research on situational or "state" anxiety identifies the Freedom from Distractibility subtests as the most susceptible to test anxiety. Cohen (1957) emphasized the short-term memory and auditory memory elements of the tasks underlying the subtests. Osborne and Lindsey (1967) highlighted the numerical or quantitative ability element of the subtests because each employs numbers in some capacity.

The Freedom from Distractibility Index is mislabeled according to currently accepted interpretations, since it does not measure distractibility (Kaufman, 1994; Prifitera, Weiss, & Saklofske, 1998). While all of the views hold some validity, Wielkiewicz (1990) expressed the most prophetic view, considering subsequent research in neuropsychology, by emphasizing the role of executive processes underlying performance on the third factor subtests. This index is now understood in the context of the frontal executive functions, and would be better labeled as the Working Memory Index. Working memory is the ability to hold information in mind temporarily while performing some operation or manipulation with that information, or engaging in an interfering task, and then accurately reproducing the information or correctly acting on it. Working memory can be thought of as mental control involving reasonably higher order tasks and it presumes attention and concentration.

Baddeley's (1986, 1992) model of working memory is a generally accepted framework. He proposed an architecture for working memory consisting of two storage devices, one for verbal material and one for spatial material, and a central executive that regulates the operation of the storage devices. Neuroimaging studies of working memory have generally supported this model. Verbal working memory is known to play a strong role in normal language development (Baddeley, Gathercole, & Papagno, 1998; Gathercole & Baddeley, 1989). Many researchers have found a relationship between spoken language disorders in preschool and written language disorders later in elementary school (Aram, Eklelman, & Nation, 1984; Aram & Nation, 1980; Hall & Tomblin, 1978; King, Jones, & Lasky, 1982; Silva, Williams, & McGee, 1987). Consensus is growing that there is a language base to many reading disorders (Silva, Williams, & McGee, 1987; Bowey & Patel, 1988; Catts, Hu, Larrivée, & Swank, 1994; Kahmi & Catts, 1989; Perfetti, 1985; Scarborough, 1989; Scarborough & Dobrich, 1990; Snyder & Downey, 1991;

Stanovich, 1988; Vellutino, 1979). Two often used tests of working memory tasks are Digit Span and Arithmetic. The Arithmetic subtest is an ecologically valid measure of working memory because we are frequently called upon to mentally calculate arithmetic problems in real-life situations. However, working memory interpretations of the Arithmetic subtest are too often confounded with the examinees numerical ability. Purer measures of working memory are needed.

PROCESSING SPEED

During the 5-year development effort that preceded the release of WISC-III in 1991, researchers at The Psychological Corporation evaluated several new tasks designed to strengthen and clarify the interpretation of the elusive third factor. Ultimately the new Symbol Search subtest was included in the final battery. The unexpected result was the splitting of the third factor into two factors, creating the now widely known four-factor structure of WISC-III. Arithmetic and Digit Span loaded together and this factor retained the name Freedom from Distractibility. Coding loaded with the new subtest Symbol Search now known as the Processing Speed Index.

On the surface, the Coding and Symbol Search subtests are simple visual scanning and tracking tasks. Yet, there is consistent evidence that inspection time (hypothesized by some to be a measure of the rate that information is processed) correlates about 0.4 with intelligence test scores (Deary & Stough, 1996). The speed of nerve conduction is moderately correlated with IQ, and specific qualities of brain waves correlate strongly with IQ. There are large and obvious age-related trends in processing speed that are accompanied by age-related changes in the number of transient connections to the central nervous system and increases in myelinization. Several investigators have found that measures of infant processing speed predict later IQ scores (e.g., Dougherty & Haith, 1997). Additionally, WISC-III PSI scores have been shown to be potentially sensitive to neurological disorders such as epilepsy and traumatic brain injury. These findings have led some to posit that differences in g result from differences in the speed and efficiency of neural processing.

The processing speed and working memory constructs measured by the WISC-III are important to the individual's intellectual development. As children develop normally, more rapid processing of information results in more effective use of working memory, which enhances performance on many reasoning tasks. Processing speed is not simply one of many different independent factors that contribute to intelligence; instead processing speed is thought to be linked causally to other elements of intelligence and achievement. Perhaps most interestingly for school psychologists, FDI contributes the second largest amount of variance, after VCI, to the prediction of reading, writing, and mathematics scores on the WIAT and other measures of achievement (Konold, 1999; Hale, Fiorello, Kavanagh, Hoeppner, & Gaither, 2001).

Clinical research in developmental cognitive neuropsychology suggests a dynamic interplay between working memory, processing speed, and reasoning—one that practicing psychologists attempt to construct in their every day clinical assessment practice. As Wechsler noted:

> "What we measure with tests is not what tests measure—not information, not spatial perception, not reasoning ability. These are only a means to an end. What intelligence tests measure is something much more important: the capacity of an individual to understand the world about him and his resourcefulness to cope with its challenges" (Wechsler, 1975, p. 139).

CURRENT CLINICAL USES OF THE IQ SCORES

One operational definition of the usefulness of factors measured by the WISC-III is their use in the clinical definition of a disorder or diagnosis, such as those found in the DSM-IV (Diagnostic and Statistical Manual of Mental Disorders; American Psychiatric Association, 1994). Another operational definition would be the use of the factors in the definitions and classification systems adopted by Education and Social Services Ministries and Departments for the purposes of determining eligibility for services. For children, diagnostic categories are often linked closely to categories of educational exceptionality (called educational handicapping conditions in the U.S.). In those terms, the usefulness of general mental ability or *g* in clinical diagnosis must assume that it is measured by the Full Scale IQ, such as provided by the WISC-III. If one accepts this premise, most clinical diagnoses linked to children's learning profiles use *g* in some way.

The American Association on Mental Retardation's (1992) definition of mental retardation includes a *g* measure or Full Scale IQ measure:

> Mental retardation refers to substantial limitations in present functioning. It is characterized by: Significantly subaverage intellectual functioning, existing concurrently with related limitations in two or more of the following applicable adaptive skill areas: communication; self-care; home living; social skills; community use; self-direction; health and safety; functional academics; leisure; and work. Mental retardation manifests before age 18 (p. 1).

The DSM-IV (1994) provides essentially the same definition. The diagnostic category of Mental Retardation is then specified in four degrees, reflecting the level of intellectual impairments. Each one provides the range of FSIQ scores and related adaptive skill limitation.

Gifted children, at the other end of the learning spectrum, are most frequently identified with a *g* measure through an IQ score (Tannenbaum, 1998). Most states and American school systems usually include measured intelligence in their definition of gifted students (Renzulli & Purcell, 1996; Sparrow & Gurland, 1998), as do most Canadian provinces (Beal, Dumont, & Mark, 1999) and most school boards in Ontario Canada (Association of Chief Psychologists with Ontario School Boards, 1993).

The new definition of learning disabilities from the Learning Disabilities Association of Ontario (2001) represents the most recent thinking in defining learning disabilities. It defines learning disabilities, in part, as:

> . . . a variety of disorders that affect the acquisition, retention, understanding, organiza-
> tion or use of verbal and/or non-verbal information. These disorders result from impairments
> in one or more psychological processes related to learning . . . in combination with other-
> wise average abilities essential for thinking and reasoning. Learning disabilities are specific
> not global impairments and as such are distinct from intellectual disabilities.

While "abilities essential for thinking and reasoning" are not specifically defined here, the literature on learning disabilities makes wide use of a *g* measure such as FSIQ on the WISC-III to satisfy this criterion. The definition goes on to "invariably interfere with the acquisition and use of one or more of the following important skills: oral language, reading, written language, mathematics." The DSM-IV (p. 46) operationalizes this part of the definition: "Substantially below is usually defined as a discrepancy of more than 2 standard deviations between achievement and IQ. . ."

CLINICAL UTILITY OF THE INDEX SCORES:
THE EXAMPLE OF LEARNING DISABILITY

Carroll's (1993) landmark factor analytic study of 461 data sets clearly indicated that human cognitive abilities fell into 69 specific or narrow cognitive abilities that could be grouped into a smaller set of broad abilities, with *g* at the apex. On the Wechsler scales, the equivalent of broad ability scores are index scores. The clinical utility of the index scores can be operationalized by the extent to which the specific abilities that they measure become integral to the definitions of any human disorders or diagnoses. As an example, the Learning Disabilities Association of Ontario's (LDAO 2001) definition of learning disabilities puts deficits in certain psychological processes at the heart of the reason for reduced functioning in academic skills. The identified processes include phonological processing, memory and attention, processing speed, language processing, perceptual-motor processing, visual-spatial processing, and executive functions.

Language processing deficits may be assessed by the Verbal Comprehension Index, measuring an ability within the broad category of verbal ability. Kaufman (1994) defined verbal comprehension as a measure of "factual knowledge, word meanings, reasoning and the ability to express ideas in words." He recommended that the Verbal Comprehension (VC) Index should be interpreted when it shows a 13-point difference between a child's standard score on VC versus freedom from distractibility, or if there is scatter of 7 points of more among the five Verbal subtests used to compute the VIQ. Many theories of learning disability differentiate between subtypes of learning disability where VIQ is discrepant from PIQ (e.g., Rourke, 1989, 1998). A verbally-based learning disability shows deficits in VC, if not in VIQ.

Visual-spatial processing is assessed by the Perceptual Organization Index, measuring an ability within the broad category of nonverbal ability. Kaufman (1994) defined perceptual organization (PO) as a measure of "integration of visual stimuli, reasoning nonverbally, and applying visual-spatial and visual-motor skills to solve the kinds of problems that are not school taught." He recommended that the Perceptual Organization Index should be interpreted when it shows a 15-point difference between a child's standard score on PO versus Processing Speed; and if there is a scatter of 9 points or more among the five Performance subtests used to compute PIQ. Nonverbal learning disabilities as defined by Rourke (1998) show deficits in PO, if not in PIQ.

Working memory is an ability within the broad category of memory and attention. Working memory, as noted previously, is the ability to hold information in mind temporarily while performing some operation or manipulation with that information, or engaging in an interfering task, and then accurately reproducing the information or correctly acting on it. Working memory can be thought of as mental control involving reasonably higher-order tasks and it presumes attention and concentration. The Working Memory Index, known as the Freedom from Distractibility Index (FDI) on the WISC-III, provides a test of memory within the LDAO's list of psychological processes.

Processing speed can be measured by the Processing Speed Index (PSI) on the Wechsler Scales. This index measures the rapidity with which a student can process simple or routine information without making errors. Because learning often involves a combination of routine information processing (such as reading) and complex information processing (such as reasoning), a weakness in the speed of processing routine information may make the task of comprehending novel information more time-consuming and difficult. A weakness in simple visual scanning and tracking may leave a child less time and mental energy for the complex task of understanding new material. This is the way in which these lower-order processing abilities relate to higher-order cognitive functioning. The pattern of PSI lower than reasoning abilities is more common among students who are experiencing academic difficulties in the classroom than among those who are not (Wechsler, 1991, p. 213). Research studies have also indicated that children with attention deficit hyperactivity disorder (ADHD) earn their lowest WISC-III scores on the PSI (Prifitera & Dersh, 1993; Schwean, Saklofske, Yackulic, & Quinn, 1993; Schwean & Saklofske, 1998).

All of the index scores on the WISC-III can be used to measure the processing skills deficits that are integral to learning disabilities, giving the WISC-III broad utility as part of an assessment for learning disabilities. Since the WISC-III does not assess all of the processes that could interfere with academic learning within the definition of learning disabilities, it must be supplemented by other information processing and memory tests in a complete assessment battery.

A FINAL WORD

Revisions of Dr. Wechsler's tests continue. Each new edition involves much more than a mere update of the normative data. Each subsequent edition has included new tasks and indexes carefully designed to reflect the most current thinking in cognitive and neuropsychological assessment. These developments will be critical to maintaining a battery of tools needed to assess the identified human abilities that are integral to evolving definitions of diagnoses, disabilities, and definitions of entitlements to services.

At this writing, the research and development team at The Psychological Corporation is in the final year of a 4-year research program leading to the publication of WISC-IV. The team is studying the inclusion of a new working memory task to replace Arithmetic for the reasons stated above, and will likely rename the Freedom from Distractibility Index as the Working Memory Index. Another new task is under investigation to improve the measurement of processing speed. The Picture Arrangement subtest has been dropped from the battery because of its continuing misinterpretation as a measure of social reasoning (e.g., Beebe, Pfiffner, & McBurnett, 2000). Finally, two new measures of fluid reasoning are under consideration, one verbal and one performance.

REFERENCES

American Association on Mental Retardation (1992). *Mental Retardation: Definition, classification, and system of supports-Ninth edition.* Washington, DC: Author. (Online). Available: http://www.aamr.org/Policies/faq_mental_retardation.shtml

American Psychiatric Association (1994). *Diagnostic and Statistical Manual of Mental Disorders* (4th ed.). Washington, DC: Author.

Aram, D. M., Ekelman, B. J., & Nation, J. E. (1984). Preschoolers with language disorders: 10 years later. *Journal of Speech and Hearing Research, 27,* 232–244.

Aram, D. M., & Nation, J. E. (1980). Preschool language disorders and subsequent language and academic difficulties. *Journal of Communication Disorders, 13,* 159–179.

Association of Chief Psychologists with Ontario School Boards (1993). *Screening and Identification of Gifted Students.* (Available from the President, Association of Chief Psychologists with Ontario School Boards, Durham Catholic District School Board, 650 Rossland Road West, Owhawa, ON, Canada, L1J 7C4.

Baddeley, A. D. (1986). *Working Memory.* Oxford, England: Oxford University Press.

Baddeley, A. D. (1992). Is working memory working? The fifteenth Bartlett lecture. *The Quarterly Journal of Experimental Psychology, 441,* 3–29.

Baddeley, A. D., Gathercole, S. E., & Papagno, C. (1998). The phonological loop as a language learning device. *Psychological Review, 105,* 158–173.

Bannatyne, A. (1974). Diagnosis: A note on recatergorization of the WISC scaled scores. *Journal of Learning Disabilities, 7,* 272–249.

Beal, A. L., Dumont, R., & Mark, R. (1999). A comparison of the Canadian and American WISC-III norms for the identification of intellectually gifted students. *Exceptionality Education Canada, 9,* 29–40.

Beebe, D. W., Pfiffner, L. J., & McBurnett, K. (2000). Evaluation of the validity of the Wechsler Intelligence Scale for Children—Third Edition Comprehension and Picture Arrangement subtests as measures of social intelligence. *Psychological Assessment, 12,* 97–101.

Boak, C. (February, 2002). *From the Simon-Binet to the Wechsler-Bellevue: A century of intelligence testing.* Paper presented at the 20th Annual Meeting of the International Neuropsychological Society. Toronto.

Bowey, J. A., & Patel, R. K. (1988). Metalinguistic ability and early reading achievement. *Applied Psycholinguistics, 9,* 367–383.

Camara, W. J., Nathan, J. S., & Puente, A. E. (2000). Psychological test usage: Implications, in professional psychology. *Professsional Psychology— Research and Practice, 13,* 141–154.

Carroll, J. B. (1993). *Human Cognitive Abilities: A Survey of factor-analytic studies.* New York: Cambridge University Press.

Carroll, J. B. (1997). The three-stratum theory of cognitive abilities. In D. P. Flanagan, J. L. Genshaft, & P. L. Harrison (Eds.), *Contemporary intellectual assessment: Theories, tests, and issues* (pp. 122–130). New York: Guilford Press.

Catts, H., Hu, C.-F., Larrivée, L., & Swank, L. (1994). Early identification of reading disabilities in children with speech–language impairments. In R. Watkins & M. Rice (Eds.), *Specific language impairments in children* (pp. 145–160). Baltimore, MD: Paul H. Brookes.

Cohen, J. (1957). The factorial structure of the WAIS between early adulthood and old age. *Journal of Consulting Psychology, 21,* 283–290.

Cohen, J. (1959). The factorial structure of the WISC at ages 7–6, 10–5, and 13–6. *Journal of Consulting Psychology, 23,* 285–299.

Das, J. P., Kirby, J. R., & Jarman, R. F. (1979). *Simultaneous and successive cognitive processes.* New York: Academic Press.

Deary, I. J., & Stough, C. (1996). Intelligence and inspection time: Achievements, prospects and problems. *American Psychologist, 51,* 599–608.

Dougherty, T., & Haith, M. M. (1997). Infant expectations and reaction time as predictors of childhood speed of processing and IQ. *Developmental Psychology, 33,* 146–155.

Fagan, T. K. (1999). Training school psychologists before there were school psychologists: A history, 1890–1930. In C. R. Reynolds & T. B. Gutkin (Eds.), *The handbook of school psychology* (3rd ed.) (pp. 2–33). New York: John Wiley & Sons.

Flanagan, D. P., Genshaft, J., & Harrison, P. L. (1997). *Contemporary intellectual assessment: Theories, tests, and issues.* New York: Guilford Press.

French, J. L. (1990). History of school psychology. In T. B. Gutkin & C. R. Reynolds (Eds.), *The handbook of school psychology* (2nd ed.) (pp. 3–20). New York: John Wiley and Sons.

Flynn, J. R. (1984). The mean IQ of Americans: Massive gains 1932–1978. *Psychological Bulletin, 95,* 29–51.

Flynn, J. R. (1987). Massive gains in 14 nations: What IQ tests really measure. *Psychological Bulletin, 101,* 171–191.

Garlick, D. (2002). Understanding the nature of the general factor of intelligence: The role of individual differences in neural plasticity as an explanatory mechanism. *Psychological Review, 109,* 116–136.

Gathercole S. E., & Baddeley, A. D. (1989). Evaluation of the role of phonological STM in the development of vocabulary in children: a longitudinal study. *Journal of Memory and Language, 28,* 200–213.

Hale, J. B., Fiorello, C. A., Kavanagh, J. A., Hoeppner, J. B., & Gaither, R. A. (2001). WISC-III predictors of academic achievement for children with learning disabilities: Are global and factor scores comparable? *School Psychology Quarterly, 16,* 53–77.

Hall, P. K., & Tomblin, J. B. (1978). A follow-up of children with articulation and language disorders. *Journal of Speech and Hearing Disorders, 42,* 364–369.

Horn, J. L., & Noll, J. (1997). Human cognitive capabilities: Gf-Gc theory. In D. P. Flanagan, J. L. Genshaft, & P. L. Harrison (Eds.), *Contemporary intellectual assessment: Theories, tests, and issues* (pp. 53–91). New York: Guilford.

Jensen, A. R. (1997). The puzzle of nongenetic variance. In R. J. Sternberg & E. L. Grigorenko (Eds.), *Intelligence, heredity and environment* (pp. 42–88). Cambridge (UK): Cambridge University Press.

Kahmi, A., & Catts, H. (1989). *Reading disabilities: A developmental language perspective*. Boston: Little, Brown.

Kaufman, A. S. (1979). *Intelligence testing with the WISC-R*. New York: Wiley.

Kaufman, A. S. (1994). *Intelligent testing with the WISC-III*. New York: John Wiley & Sons.

Kaufman, A. S., & Kaufman, N. L. (1983). *Kaufman Assessment Battery for Children*. Circle Pines, MN: American Guidance Service.

King, R. R., Jones, C., & Lasky, E. (1982). In retrospect: A fifteen year follow-up of speech-language disordered children. *Language Speech and Hearing Services in Schools, 13*, 24–32.

Konold, T. R. (1999). Evaluating discrepancy analysis with the WISC–III and WIAT. *Journal of Psychoeducational Assessment, 17*, 24–35.

Larry, P. *et al. v.* Wilson Riles (1979, October). C 71 2270. U.S. District Court for the Northern District of California, RFP.

Learning Disabilities Association of Ontario (2001). *Learning Disabilities: A New Definition* (Online). Available at: http://www.ldao.on.ca/pei/defdraft.html#defn

Lutey, C. (1977). *Individual intelligence testing: A manual and sourcebook* (2nd ed. and enlarged). Greeley, CO: Carol L. Lutey.

Matarazzo, J. D. (1972). *Wechsler's measurement and appraisal of adult intelligence* (5th ed.). New York: Oxford University Press.

McGrew, K. S. (1997). Analysis of the major intelligence batteries according to a proposed comprehensive Gf-Gc framework. In D. P. Flanagan, J. L. Genshaft, & P. L. Harrison (Eds.), *Contemporary intellectual assessment: Theories, tests and issues* (pp. 151–180). New York: Guilford.

Osborne, R. T., & Lindsey, J. M. (1967). A longitudinal investigation of change in the factorial composition of intelligence with age in young school children. *Journal of Genetic Psychology, 110*, 49–58.

Perfetti, C. A. (1985). *Reading ability*. New York: Oxford Press.

Prifitera, A., & Dersh, J. (1993). Base rates of WISC-III diagnostic subtest patterns among normal, learning-disabled, and ADHD samples. *Journal of Psychoeducational Assessment, WISC-III Monograph Series,* 43–55.

Prifitera, A., Weiss, L. G., & Saklofske, D. H. (1998). The WISC-III in context. In A. Prifitera & D. H. Saklofske (Eds.). *WISC-III clinical use and interpretation: Scientist-practitioner perspectives* (pp. 1–38). San Diego: Academic Press.

Renzulli, J. S., & Purcell, J. H. (1996). Gifted Education: A look around and a look ahead. *Roeper Review, 18*, 173–178.

Rourke, B. (1989). *Nonverbal Learning Disabilities: The Syndrome and the Model*. New York: The Guilford Press.

Rourke, B. (1998). Significance of verbal-performance discrepancies for subtypes of children with learning disabilities: Opportunities for the WISC-III. In A. Prifitera & D. H. Saklofske (Eds.), *WISC-III clinical use and interpretation scientist-practitioner perspectives* (pp. 59–72). San Diego: Academic Press.

Sattler, J. M., & Saklofske, D. H. (2001). Wechsler Intelligence Scale for Children-III (WISC-III): Description (pp. 220–265); WISC-III subtests (pp. 266–297); Interpreting the WISC-III (pp. 298–334). In J. M. Sattler (Ed.), *Assessment of children: Cognitive applications* (4th ed.). San Diego, CA: author.

Scarborough, H. S. (1989). Prediction of reading disability from familial and individual differences. *Journal of Education Psychology, 81*, 101–108.

Scarborough, H. S., & Dobrich, W. (1990). Development of children with early language delay. *Journal of Speech and Hearing Disorders, 33*, 70–83.

Schwean, V. L., Saklofske, D. H., Yackulic, R. A., & Quinn, D. (1993). WISC-III performance of ADHD children. *Journal of Psychoeducational Assessment, WISC-III Monograph,* 6–21.

Schwean, V. L., & Saklofske, D. H. (1998). WISC-III assessment of children with Attention Deficit/Hyperactivity Disorder. In A. Prifitera & D. H. Saklofske (Eds.), *WISC-III clinical use and interpretation: Scientist-practitioner perspectives* (pp. 91–118). San Diego: Academic Press.

Silva, P. A., Williams, S., & McGee, R. (1987). A longitudinal study of children with developmental language delay at age three: later intelligence, reading and behavior problems. *Developmental Medicine and Child Neurology, 29*, 630–640.

Snyder, L., & Downey, D. (1991). The language-reading relationship in normal and reading-disabled children. *Journal of Speech and Hearing Research. 34*, 129–140.

Sparrow, S. S., & Gurland, S. T. (1998). Assessment of gifted children with the WISC-III. In A. Prifitera & D. H. Saklofske (Eds.), *WISC-III clinical use and interpretation: Scientist-practitioner perspectives* (pp. 59–72). San Diego: Academic Press.

Spearman, C. (1904). General intelligence, objectively determined and measured. *American Journal of Psychology, 15*, 201–293.

Stanovich, K. E. (1988). The right and wrong places to look for the cognitive locus of reading disability. *Annals of Dyslexia, 38*, 154–157.

Thorndike, R. M. (1990). Would the real factors of the Stanford-Binet: Fourth Edition please come forward? *Journal of Psychoeducational Assessment, 8*, 412–435.

Tannenbaum, A. J. (1998). Programs for the gifted: To be or not to be. *Journal for the Education of the Gifted, 22*, 3–36.

Tulsky, D. S., Saklofske, D. H., & Richer, J. H. (2003). Historical overview of intelligence and memory; Factors influencing the Wechsler scales. In D. S. Tulsky, D. H. Saklofske *et al.* (Eds.), *Clinical interpretation of the WAIS-III and WMS-III*. San Diego: Academic Press. In press.

Tulsky, D. S., Saklofske, D. H., & Zhu, J. (2003). Revising a standard: An evaluation of the origin and development of the WAIS-III. In D. S. Tulsky, D. H. Saklofske *et al.* (Eds.), *Clinical interpretation of the WAIS-III and WMS-III*. San Diego: Academic Press. In press.

Vellutino, F. R. (1979). *Dyslexia: Theory and research*. Cambridge, MA: MIT Press.

Vernon, P. E. (1950). *The structure of human abilities*. London: Methuen.

Wechsler, D. (1939). *Wechsler-Bellevue Intelligence Scale*. New York: The Psychological Corporation.

Wechsler, D. (1949). *Wechsler Intelligence Scale for Children*. New York: The Psychological Corporation.

Wechsler, D. (1958). *Measurement and appraisal of adult intelligence* (4th ed.). Baltimore: Williams & Wilkins.

Wechsler, D. (1974). *Manual for the Wechsler Intelligence Scale for Children—Revised*. San Antonio, TX: The Psychological Corporation.

Wechsler, D. (1975). Intelligence defined and undefined: A relativistic appraisal. *American Psychologist, 30*, 135–139.

Wechsler, D. (1991). *Wechsler Intelligence Scale for Children—Third Edition*. San Antonio, TX: The Psychological Corporation.

Wechsler, D. (1997). *Wechsler Adult Intelligence Scale—Third Edition*. San Antonio, TX: The Psychological Corporation.

Weiss, L. G, Saklofske, D. H., & Prifitera, A. (2003). Clinical interpretation of the WISC-III factor scores. In C. R. Reynolds & R. W. Kamphaus (Eds.), *Handbook of psychological and educational assessment of children: Intelligence and achievement* (2nd ed.). New York: Guilford Press.

Wielkiewicz, R. M. (1990). Interpreting low scores on the WISC-R third factor: It's more than distractibility. *Psychological Assessment: A Journal of Consulting and Clinical Psychology, 2*, 91–97.

Woodcock, R. W., & Johnson, M. B. (1977). *Woodcock-Johnson Psychoeducational Battery*. Allen, TX: DLM.

2

CROSS-CULTURAL PSYCHOLOGY, INTELLIGENCE, AND COGNITIVE PROCESSES

Department of Psychology
The University of Athens
Athens, Greece

Cross-cultural psychology studies the relationship between culture and psychological variables, that is, it is concerned with two questions about this relationship. The first question is to determine the degree to which there is communality of psychological processes, or universals, across cultures. The second question is the degree to which there are variations in psychological processes due to specific cultural influences. Thus, a goal of cross-cultural psychology is to understand the relationships between human behavior and the cultural contexts in which it has developed and is displayed (Berry, Poortinga, Segall, & Dasen, 2002).

This chapter will discuss issues related to the cross-cultural study of intelligence and cognitive processes. The first section will discuss the concepts of environment as employed in psychology and that of culture. Cross-cultural studies are conducted with children from different nations, cultures, and ethnic groups. The distinctions between them and measures of cultural variables are important elements in research methodology. The next section discusses issues related to intelligence, intelligent behavior, and tested intelligence. The definition of intelligence has been a controversial issue in psychology from the beginning of the construction of the first intelligence tests. Cultures define intelligence differently, according to their own ecological and social demands. There are also variations in the types of cognitive processes important for adaptation to the ecological demands of each culture. Cross-cultural psychology and anthropology have a long history of studies of cognitive processes in different cultures. A goal of cross-cultural psychology is to not only seek universals in cognitive processes across cultures, but also to explore the manifestations of cognitive processes as shaped by different types of cultures. Universals represent cognitive processes that are specific to the human species, such as encoding and decoding. These cognitive processes are shaped by the adaptation of the individual to the ecocultural demands of the specific culture.

CULTURE AND ENVIRONMENT

Psychology has traditionally employed the term "environment" rather than culture. Environment, as culture, is also an extremely broad theoretical concept, which can potentially include all features of the physical and social environment. Psychology has usually employed operational definitions of social structural elements, such as rural-urban setting, socio-economic level, educational level, etc. Some of these environmental variables have been found to be consistently related to intelligence and cognitive functioning. Socioeconomic level has been found to correlate highly with performance on intelligence tests. Another correlate of intelligence is the number of years of schooling of the person or of the parents of these children. People with more years of schooling score higher on intelligence tests than those with fewer years. Another typical finding is that parental level of education is correlated with children's performance on intelligence tests. Other measures are styles of childrearing, the family climate, teacher-child interactions, etc.

One of the criticisms of the above traditional operational definitions of environment is that they are employed as isolated units. Critics of this approach argue that environment is not merely a selection of variables which have proved to be correlated with intelligence test scores. Environment is a patterned organization of physical and social components. Schooler (1998) argues that psychology has much to learn from sociology about environmental complexity and its effects on psychological variables; that the sociological literature has considerable evidence regarding the relationship between children's exposure to a complex environment, such as current urban societies, and their effects on cognitive functioning. A number of models of ecological context and relationships with psychological variables have been proposed: Brunswik's (1955) probabilistic model of the relationships of variables within an ecological context; McClelland's (1961) achievement motivation, cultural, and ecological variables; B. Whiting's (1963) model of ecology, social systems, and the feedback effects on the normative environment; effects of history and environment on maintenance systems (LeVine, 1973); Bronfenbrenner's (1979) ecological model based on general systems theory; and the developmetal niche (Super & Harkness, 1980).

Arguments based on the relative importance of genetic factors and environmental factors on intelligence (Jensen, 1969, 1998; Herrnstein & Murray, 1994) based on the societal institutions of only one country may present a restricted picture of environmental effects. A classic principle in experimental design is to systematically vary points along the independent variable in order to measure effects on the dependent variable. That is, in order to come to conclusions based on the relative weight of genetic factors and environmental influences on intelligence, cultures should be selected to systematically vary across social dimensions, e.g., different forms and different levels of educational systems, different forms of government, different forms and different levels of economic activity, different family systems, etc. In order to generalize about the relative effect of genetics and environment on intelligence or g, this can only be done by selecting cultures which represent different points along these cultural dimensions. If not, then the conclusions regarding the dominance of the genetic basis of g, and the restriction in variation of environment may tell us only about this relationship in one country. This book cannot ask nor answer questions regarding the effect of biological factors on intelligence. Nor can it provide answers to many of the issues raised by the controversies regarding theories of intelligence and intelligence tests. But it can explore more widely the issue of environment in terms of the concept of culture. More specifically, it can provide evidence regarding cultural aspects of the Weschler Intelligence Scale for Children–Third Edition (WISC-III) and of intelligence from the viewpoint of cross-cultural psychology.

The next question is, "What is culture?" There are many definitions of culture. One, still widely accepted in cross-cultural psychology, is that of Kroeber and Kluckhohn (1952):

> Culture consists of patterns, explicit and implicit, of and for behavior acquired and transmitted by symbols, constituting the distinctive achievements of human groups, including their embodiments in artifacts: the essential core of culture consists of traditional (i.e., historically derived and selected) ideas and especially their attached values; cultural systems may on the one hand be considered as products of action, on the other as conditioning elements of further action (p. 181).

The problem with this definition of culture, is that culture is a global concept; it refers to all human activity: thinking, behavior, symbols, values, traditions, institutions, traditions, economic activity, settlements, means of transportation, means of communication, etc. Thus, it is very difficult to provide an operational definition of culture because it potentially could include everything.

THE ECOCULTURAL FRAMEWORK

A differentiated Ecocultural Framework has been elaborated by Berry (1976, 2001) in relation to cross-cultural psychology. The Ecocultural Framework studies human psychological diversity at the individual level and the group level in terms of two sources of influences, ecological and sociopolitical, and a set of variables that links these influences to psychological characteristics (cultural and biological adaptation at the population level, and various "transmission variables" to individuals such as enculturation, socialization, genetics, and acculturation). The concepts

were originally developed on the basis of the study of ecological and social influences on cognitive differentiation (Berry, 1976). The Ecocultural Framework
considers human diversity, both cultural and psychological, to be a set of collective
and individual adaptations to context. The Ecocultural Framework assumes a "uni-
versalist theoretical framework in which basic psychological processes are taken to
be species-wide features of human psychology, on which culture plays infinite variations during the course or development and daily activity" (Berry, 2001, p. 359).

NATION, CULTURE, AND ETHNIC GROUP

It is important to differentiate between *nation* and *culture*. Some cross-cultural
studies study psychological variables in three nations, some are based on more
than thirty. These studies seek differences or similarities in mean scores between
cultures. The term "nation" refers to the geopolitical delineation of a nation-state,
e.g., Germany or Switzerland. Culture, as discussed above, is a more global
concept. Germany, for example, shares similar cultural elements with Austria
and German-speaking Switzerland. One can speak, at the certain level of generalization, of German-speaking cultures. On the other hand, Switzerland has at least
three distinct cultural or ethnic groups: German, French, and Italian. The term
"ethnic" was defined by Herodotus 2000 years ago as a group of people with a
common heritage, language, religion, customs, and values. This definition has not
changed much in its usage by current cultural anthropologists and cross-cultural
psychologists. Cultural anthropologists estimate that there are thousands of ethnic
groups throughout the world.

Many societies are characterized as multicultural because of their many ethnic
groups. One can argue that the term "multicultural" may not be as accurate as
"polyethnic" or "plural." One should also take into account the overarching or
dominating "culture" of its society, with its traditional type of economic system,
system of government, judicial system, educational system, etc. Weber (1904)
argued how Protestantism shaped the capitalist system. That is, the dominant
religion of a country and its social institutions shape its laws and its culture. Thus,
ethnic groups within a host country adapt to the culture of the dominant group.
Although there may be many "cultural niches" in a nation, the question is the degree
to which a country is multicultural or polyethnic in terms of its social institutions.

The distinction between these terms is important in cross-cultural research
because of what has been described as "Galton's Problem" (Naroll, Michik, &
Naroll, 1974). This concept refers to the geographical and cultural distance
between countries. Members of nations interact, which leads to cultural diffusion. For example, despite the differences in culture among European countries,
the concept "European culture" refers to some shared aspects of culture among
these countries due to diffusion. A study that involves many European nations
and a few nations from other areas of the world can result in the overestimation
of cultural variation because of the large number of European nations. That is, at
another level of generalization, the cultural diffusion due to the relatively close

geographical and cultural distance between European countries results in their having common elements. A traditional experimental design in which a country is treated as a nominal-level variable essentially treats each nation as independent, which does not control for cultural diffusion. One way of controlling for this is to identify the position of each country on a context variable, such as country-level economic status, or other social indices.

Georgas and Berry (1995) employed ecosocial variables based on ecological and sociopolitical elements of the Ecocultural Framework to delineate some core dimensions of societies. These dimensions represent a further differentiation of the sociopolitical elements of the Ecocultural Framework (Georgas, 1993) and are based on sociological categories. These societal institutions are: (1) the subsistence or economic system, (2) the political and judicial system, (3) the educational system, (4) religion, and (5) means of mass communication. A second element, derived from social psychology, refers to bonds with groups in the immediate community. The third element refers to the structure and function of the family. In Georgas and Berry (1995), social indices on ecology, education, economy, mass communications, population, and religious sects, based on archival data from 174 nations, resulted in clusters of nations on each of these ecocultural dimensions, together with profiles of the means for each specific indicator.

In a second study (Georgas, Van de Vijver, & Berry, in review) this taxonomy of nations in terms of specific ecosocial indices, based on the Ecocultural Framework, was employed as a heuristic framework for exploring the relationships of elements of the framework to psychological variation. Religion and affluence were found to vary systematically with values and attitudes in different clusters of nations.

INTELLIGENCE, INTELLIGENT BEHAVIOR, AND TESTED INTELLIGENCE

"What is intelligence?" Sternberg (1997) refers to the distinction between intelligence, intelligent behavior, and tested intelligence, according to Hebb's (1949) discussion of these concepts.

The first six decades of the 20th century were characterized by the psychometric approach in constructing intelligence tests. Binet and Simon constructed their test at the beginning of the 20th century with a specific practical goal: to identify children with learning difficulties in school. Spearman's two-factor theory (1927) posited a general factor g, that is, an intellectual factor common to all abilities and a specific factor, specific intellectual abilities different or independent from each other. A different approach was Thurstone's Primary Abilities (Thurstone, 1938). Thurstone sought to identify specific mental abilities through factor analysis rather than general intelligence. Wechsler defined intelligence as a global intellectual capacity and specific abilities, and that ". . .intelligence is not the mere sum of these abilities" (1939, p. 3). The subsequent development of the WISC was constructed with the same concept of subtests measuring different mental abilities.

But there was no agreement on the definition of intelligence based on the psychometric approach. The issue was so controversial that in a meeting of leading psychometricians in 1921 (Resnick, 1976), a compromise was reached in which intelligence was defined for a period as, "...what an intelligence test measures." This circular definition was in fact employed in classic textbooks of psychological testing.

More recent attempts have established hierarchical models of intelligence based on the psychometric approach, for example, Vernon's model (1969) of g and specific factors at lower levels.

The study of cognitive processing as related to theories of intelligence resulted in the construction of a variety of intelligence tests based on theory in the past 20 years. For example, the Kaufman Assessment Battery for Children (Kaufman & Kaufman, 1983) is based on the neuropsychological processing theory of Luria (1973, 1980). Sternberg (1993) has developed measures of these different types of intelligence. The focus on a cognitive processing analysis of test scores has influenced changes in the Wechsler tests. The WISC-III (Wechsler, 1991) has four index scores based on factor analysis of the tests: Verbal Comprehension, Perceptual Organization, Processing Speed, and Freedom from Distractibility.

INTELLIGENCE

The question of what intelligence is was given impetus in American psychology recently by Sternberg's Triarchic Theory (1985). Sternberg proposes three types of intelligence—analytical, creative, and practical—and that most intelligence tests measure primarily analytical intelligence, the type of thinking emphasized in school learning. The constructs of "emotional intelligence" (Goleman, 1995) and "social intelligence" (Cantor & Kihlstrom, 1987) suggest that intelligence is a much broader concept than previously believed in psychology. The point is that intelligence is not only the type of cognitive activity manifested in educational settings. It also includes the types of cognitive activities involved in everyday settings, such as comparing different prices for products in a supermarket, or bargaining tactics in a bazaar, or planning for the future security of one's family, or finding one's way in a foreign country.

Cross-cultural psychology and cultural anthropology have had a strong interest in the study of intelligence and cognition. A comprehensive account of key concepts, issues, and research in this area is described in recent publications (Berry *et al.*, 2002; Mishra, 1997).

Although there are many differences in opinion regarding what intelligence is, most cross-cultural psychologists would agree that the manifestations of cognitive processes are embedded in culture. That is, although cognitive processes are universal across cultures, the different manifestations of these cognitive processes, according to Berry *et al.* (2002), represent different types of cognitive adaptations to the specific ecological demands and ecocultural patterns of cultures. Berry and

Irvine (1986) refer to Ferguson's (1954) "Law of Cultural Differentiation," that is, cultural factors prescribe what is learned and at what age, with the consequence that different patterns of ability are learned in different cultural environments. Universals can be described as aptitudes, not shaped by culture, while manifestations can be described as abilities or skill levels influenced by culture.

Thus, studies by cross-cultural psychologists and cultural anthropologists have shown that "intelligence" is defined differently in different cultures, according to the specific ecocultural demands. There are many studies of how indigenous people define intelligence in the cross-cultural, anthropological, and cultural psychological literature. Irvine (1966, 1970) asked this question, and suggested that socio-affective aspects of intelligence are found in many African cultures. In a later study Irvine (1988) describes the "dispositional intelligence" of the Shona of Zimbabwe. Some of the dimensions of intelligence among the Shona are: foresight versus not predicting outcomes, reckoning logically versus false inferences, alertness versus inattention, and skepticism versus credulity. "Social intelligence" included asking favors indirectly versus blunt approach, knowledge of limits versus fanciful ambition, and respect for elders versus poking fun at elders.

Berry (1984) cites many studies of indigenous definitions of social and affective intelligence. Wober (1974) found that the Baganda of Uganda tend to define intelligence as an "extroverted" characteristic, related to public or social issues, rather than as an introverted or individualist process. The ideas of what is intelligent behavior have also been influenced by Islam. For example, loss of faith is associated with improper functioning of intelligence. Real intelligence is not cleverness or playing with ideas on a superficial level.

Putnam and Kilbride (1980) found that among the Songhay of Mali and the Samia of Kenya, social and communal qualities and social skills were part of the definition of intelligence. Super (1983) reports that among the Kipsigis of Kenya, intelligence is a verbal quickness necessary to politicians, teachers, market traders and others who must comprehend complex matters and employ this knowledge in the management of interpersonal relations.

Thus, studies in cultures throughout the world indicate that the concept of intelligence and intelligent behavior varies considerably, with some cultures emphasizing social facets of intelligence and with different perspectives on what intelligent behavior is. Does this mean the existence of a state of cognitive anarchy, one concept of intelligence for each culture? In order to attempt to seek answers to this question, we have to examine how intelligence is measured, that is, with intelligence tests.

MEASUREMENT OF INTELLIGENCE IN DIFFERENT CULTURES

The assessment of intelligence in cultures by anthropologists and psychologists can be traced to the end of the 19th century. The issue of cognitive processes in exotic cultures was studied by Rivers (1901, 1905), Boas (1911), Wundt (1912 through 1921), and Lévy-Bruhl (1910, 1923), as cited in Berry and Dasen (1974). Two different conclusions were reached regarding the mental abilities of Europeans and peoples from these cultures. Rivers studied memory and perceptual processes in the Torres Straits Islands. He concluded that although visual acuity of these "savage and half-civilized people" was somewhat superior to that of Europeans, their overall mental operations were at the concrete level as compared to the abstract level of Europeans. Lévy-Bruhl's position was similar. He concluded that the mental processes of "primitives" were prelogical and not rational as found in Europeans. The positions of Boas and Wundt were different. Boas concluded that although there were differences between thinking processes between "primitive man" and "civilized man," these differences were more in terms of content than process and attributed to their cultural context. He denied that there were racial differences in intelligence. Wundt also argued that the intelligence of primitive man is not inferior to that of civilized man, and that the observed differences in mental processes are due to his more restricted environmental field.

The promise of intelligence testing as a means of determining the level of intellectual ability at the beginning of the 20th century led to the tests being used for a variety of purposes, such as with Army recruits in World War I. One of the results was that the mean IQs of immigrants from different countries differed, and the inference made was that the mental abilities of these ethnic groups also differed. In the years that followed, American IQ tests were employed in testing the mental ability of peoples in different cultures. Although some psychologists concluded that the mental abilities of some cultures were lower than those of Americans because of lower IQs, others such as Goodenough (1936), Porteus (1937), and Raven (1938) realized the cultural bias of these tests and attempted to construct "culture-free" intelligence tests. The issue here is that intelligence tests constructed in a culture, European or North American, were assumed to "objectively" measure intelligence in ethnic groups in their countries and also to validly measure intelligence in other countries, many of them very different ecologically and culturally. In such comparative studies mean differences on these intelligence tests were interpreted as country-level differences in intelligence, sometimes leading to generalizations about racial differences. This methodological error is often made in cross-cultural research. Intelligence tests, and other psychological tests, constructed in one culture can be simply translated and applied in another culture. The following section explains two important concepts in cross-cultural methodology related to this issue.

EMIC AND ETIC

The terms *emic* and *etic* originally referred to the difference between *phonemics* and *phonetics*. Pike (1966) employed emics to refer to study of behavior in one culture from within by the indigenous researcher and etics to refer to the comparative study of behavior in a number of cultures from a position outside the society. These are important methodological concepts in cross-cultural psychology (Berry, 1969). The emic approach is the construction of an intelligence test by an indigenous psychologist in a culture. The etic approach is the search for universals in intelligence across cultures with a specific intelligence test. A methodological error, an *imposed etic*, would be to take an intelligence test constructed in one culture, to assume that it measures intelligence in all cultures, and to interpret the differences in scores across the cultures as real differences. The approaches can be combined. For example, one can construct an intelligence test in one culture, an imposed etic, then ask the indigenous researchers in the other cultures to construct a similar intelligence test, an emic. Comparison of the etic and emic tests, a *derived emic*, will determine if the tests measure the same construct. If so, one can conclude that the test measures a universal construct of intelligence. This is the methodology employed in this book and described in detail in Chapters 17 and 18.

The traditional anthropological methodology consisted of a European or North American researcher acting as a participant-observer in a culture, relying on the aid of an indigenous informant to study cognitive processes and attempting to associate these processes with ecological and social elements and values and customs of the society. This was also the methodology among cross-cultural psychologists. In recent years, the term *indigenous psychology* (Kim & Berry, 1993) refers to an emic methodology in which indigenous psychologists take the initiative of studying psychological variables within their cultures. This emic approach essentially means that the indigenous psychologist is more cognizant of the language and the cultural variables in his/her culture than an outside observer. However, this does not imply that observations of nonindigenous researchers are less valid than those of indigenous researchers. The outside researcher may make errors in observation, attribution, and interpretation of behaviors in another culture. The indigenous researcher can also make errors within his/her culture with overemphasis on certain phenomena, with claiming uniqueness of psychological or cultural variables, etc. Thus, the combination of the etic and emic approaches which create a derived emic is a more objective methodology in cross-cultural psychology. This is the approach employed in this book, in which the country chapters represent the emic approach and the cross-cultural analyses represent the etic approach.

The next section will describe the study of cognitive processes in different cultures employing the emic approach and the etic approach.

COGNITIVE PROCESSES WITHIN
AND ACROSS CULTURES

As discussed above, the study of cognitive processes in cultures has had a long history in anthropology and psychology. Types of cognitive processes that have been studied are, e.g., sorting, learning and memory, literacy, spatial cognition, problemsolving and reasoning. The following are a few examples from the many studies in the literature.

Okonji (1971) studied the effects of familiarity of animals and objects on classification in Nigeria and Scotland. The task was to sort objects familiar to Nigerian children such as, a gourd flute, a red wooden rod, and also animals familiar to both groups, such as a dog or a goat. The criteria were different levels of abstraction. In the first stage the child was asked to name the item. In the second stage the child was asked to sort a number of items according to categories. No differences were found between the two groups in terms of their ability to shift their basis of classification of animals. Only moderate support was found regarding the effect of familiarity with objects on classificatory behavior of Nigerian children in comparison with Scottish children.

Deregowski and Bentley (1988) studied the size-distance constancy of two groups of Bushmen, the !Xu and the Kxoe in the Northern Kalahari. The ecological features, the means of subsistence, homes, and other aspects are described in detail. The procedure consisted of the subject telling the experimenter where to place red fire buckets in a line so that in the judgment of the subject, the distances would be the same. The testing was conducted under two conditions: at an airstrip (a nontraditional condition) and in the bush (a familiar traditional condition). The results indicated that both groups had perfect constancy in the bush but the !Xu also had perfect constancy in the airstrip while the Kxoe did not. The results of the remarkable perceptual constancy of the Bushmen are discussed in terms of adaptation to their habitat and in terms of the literature.

An example of a cross-cultural study based on a specific theory is Berry's studies of cognitive styles. The initial study (Berry, 1966) of hunting- and agriculture-based peoples established links between ecological demands and cultural practices shaping the required cognitive performances, that is, visual disembedding and analytic and spatial abilities. Further studies were based on the cognitive style of field dependence–field independence (Witkin & Berry, 1975). More recent advances in these studies by Berry (2001, Berry et al., 2002) analyze in terms of the Ecocultural Framework, the relationships between ecological, cultural, and acculturation variables and the expected cognitive style. These variables include the subsistence patterns, settlement patterns, population density, family type, social/political stratification, socialization practices, education, and wage employment. Some of the findings were that nomadic hunters and gatherers, with a loose social structure and with an emphasis on assertion in socialization, were relatively field independent, while sedentary agriculturalists, with tight social structures and with an emphasis on compliance in socialization, were relatively field dependent. In addition, people in societies undergoing acculturation and developing Western types of education became more field independent.

CROSS-CULTURAL PSYCHOLOGY AND
COGNITIVE PROCESSES

Studies in cultures throughout the world, such as the above examples, have documented that cognitive skills are expressed according to the ecocultural context of each culture. Can order or taxonomy be introduced into this chaos of findings from different cultures leading to general constructs about cognitive processes across cultures? Or is the relationship between specific cultures and their ecocultural context so unique that comparisons are not valid? As indicated above, one goal of cross-cultural psychology is the search for universal constructs in cognitive processes across cultures. A second related goal is the search for variations in the expression of cognitive skills attributable to the ecocultural context of specific cultures.

Some of the basic questions regarding cross-cultural studies of cognitive processes were formulated by Berry and Dasen (1974). One question is whether there are qualitatively different or similar types of cognitive processes in different cultures. A second question is whether there are quantitative differences between different cultural groups. A third question is whether there are qualitative and quantitative differences in the development of cognitive processes and in their organization across groups.

Positions different from those of cross-cultural psychology are held by cultural psychology and anthropology, which adopt a cultural relativistic position (Berry, 1984). Cultural psychology as expressed by Cole (Cole, Gay, Glick, & Sharp, 1971) and others (Greenfield, 1997) holds that the cultural context of learning and thinking is specific and unique to a particular culture. Cognitive performance is tied to specific features of the ecocultural context and to the symbols and meanings within the culture. Thus, cultural psychology emphasizes the particular features of the situation in the culture and argues that generalizations across cultures are not psychologically meaningful. Anthropology, with a longer history of research, has a similar objection to seeking cross-cultural similarities in cultural phenomena, with the exceptions of some anthropologists. Murdock created an Outline of Cultural Materials (1937, as cited in Murdock *et al.*, 1982) as a taxonomic system of a "universal culture pattern." Ember (1977) has criticized the extreme relativistic and noncomparative position of many anthropologists in the area of cognitive anthropology and emphasized the relevance of cross-cultural psychology's comparative approach in studying cognition in different cultures.

Kluckhohn and Murray (1948) employed an adage, which I will paraphrase as, "humans are like all other humans, like some other humans, like no other human," to refer to the epistemological methodology of psychology; that is, universal traits, taxonomies of traits, and traits of the individual. If the word "culture" is substituted for "human" one can argue that it depends at which level one is looking at cultural phenomena. Clinical and school psychologists would tell us that personality is unique. Cultural psychology would say something similar. However, cross-cultural psychology as well as general psychology also looks at the other two levels in this hierarchy.

Evidence of universal cognitive processes across cultures has been found by examining the structure of cognitive processes with factor analysis. Irvine (1979) did a meta-analysis of 91 factor analytic studies in countries outside Europe and North America, except for studies with ethnic groups or native peoples in the latter two geographical areas. The factors found in these cultures were reasoning, visual/perceptual processes, verbal abilities and skills, numerical operations, physical/temperamental quickness, and memory functions. In addition he reported that the factors were themselves intercorrelated, evidence of an overall *g* factor. Irvine's findings were consonant with Carroll's model (1993), based on over 400 studies. Carroll integrates the findings into a theoretical framework with three hierarchical levels of cognitive processes; a first level *g*, a second level with group factors common to subsets of tests, and a third level with very specific abilities. In a meta-analysis of 197 studies with 1555 independent comparisons, Van de Vijver (1997) came to a number of conclusions regarding universals in cognitive test performance. The absence of any cross-cultural difference was the most frequent finding in these studies. Cross-national studies resulted in larger performance differences than intranational cross-ethnic studies. Cross-cultural differences in cognitive performance were correlated with the affluence level of the countries; these differences increased according to chronological and educational age; performance differences were larger on common Western tasks, with the Wechsler tests playing a leading role, than with indigenously developed cognitive tasks.

Furthermore, the question of comparison of means between cultures on cognitive skills is of secondary relevance to the more important issue; that of structural relationships of cognitive skills across culture. Cross-cultural psychology has developed methods of determining construct equivalence across cultures or universals, that is, whether an intelligence test constructed in one culture or cognitive processes across cultures are structurally equivalent in other cultures (Berry *et al.*, 2002; Poortinga, 1989; Van de Vijver & Leung, 1997). This issue will be discussed in detail in Chapter 17, Principles of Adaptation of Intelligence Tests to other Cultures. The cross-cultural analysis of the data of the WISC-III in Chapter 19 is based on this procedure.

REFERENCES

Berry, J. W. (1966). Temne and Eskimo perceptual skills. *International Journal of Psychology, 1*, 207–229.
Berry, J. W. (1969). On cross-cultural comparability. *International Journal of Psychology, 4*, 119–128.
Berry, J. W. (1976). *Human ecology and cognitive style: Comparative studies in cultural and psychogical adaptation*. New York: Sage/Halsted.

Berry, J. W. (1984). Towards a universal psychology of cognitive competence. *International Journal of Psychology, 19*, 335–361.

Berry, J. W. (2001). Contextual studies of cognitive adaptation. In J. M. Collis & S. Messick (Eds.), *Intelligence and personality: Bridging the gap in theory and measurement* (pp. 319–333). Mahwah, NJ: Lawrence Erlbaum.

Berry, J. W., & Dasen, P. (1974). *Culture and cognition*. London: Methuen.

Berry, J. W., & Irvine, S. H. (1986). Bricolage: Savages do it daily. In R. H. Sternberg & R. K. Wagner (Eds.), *Practical intelligence: Origins of competence in the everyday world*. New York: Cambridge University Press.

Berry, J. W., Poortinga, Y. H., Segall, M. H., & Dasen, P. R. (2002). *Cross-cultural psychology: Research and applications*. New York: Cambridge University Press.

Bronfenbrenner, U. (1979). *The ecology of human development*. Cambridge, MA: Harvard University Press.

Brunswik, E. (1955). Representative design and probabilistic theory. *Psychological Review, 62*, 192–217.

Cantor, N., & Kihlstrom, J. F. (1987). Social intelligence: The cognitive basis of personality. In P. Shaver (Ed.), *Review of Personality and Social Psychology* (Vol. 6, pp. 15–34). Beverly Hills, CA: Sage.

Carroll, J. B. (1993). *Human cognitive abilities: A survey of factor-analytic studies*. New York: Cambridge University Press.

Cole, M., Gay, J., Glick, J., & Sharp, D. (1971). *The cultural context of learning and thinking*. New York: Basic Books.

Deregowski, J. B., & Bentley, A. M. (1988). Distance constancy in Bushmen: An exploratory study. In J. W. Berry, S. H. Irvine, & E. B. Hunt (Eds.), *Indigenous cognition: Functioning in cultural context* (pp. 177–185). Dordrecht, The Netherlands: Martinus Nijhoff.

Ember, C. R. (1977). Cross-cultural cognitive studies. *Annual Review of Anthropology, 6*, 33–56.

Ferguson, G. A. (1954). On learning and human ability. *Canadian Journal of Psychology, 8*, 95–112.

Georgas, J. (1993). An ecological-social model for indigenous psychology: The example of Greece. In U. Kim & J. W. Berry (Eds.), *Indigenous psychologies: Theory, method & experience in cultural context* (pp. 56–78). Beverly Hills: Sage.

Georgas, J., & Berry, J. W. (1995). An ecocultural taxonomy for cross-cultural psychology. *Cross-Cultural Research, 29*, 121–157.

Georgas, J., Van de Vijver, F. J. R., & Berry, J. W. (2002). *The ecocultural framework, ecosocial indices and psychological variables in cross-cultural research*. In review.

Goleman, D. (1995). *Emotional intelligence*. New York: Bantam Books.

Goodenough, F. L. (1936). The measurement of mental functions in primitive groups. *American Anthropologist, 38*, 1–11.

Greenfield, P. M. (1997). You can't take it with you: Why ability assessments don't cross cultures. *American Psychologist, 52*, 1115–1124.

Hebb, D. O. (1949). *The organization of behavior*. New York: Wiley.

Herrnstein, R. J., & Murray, C. (1994). *The bell curve: Intelligence and class structure in American life*. New York: Free Press.

Irvine, S. H. (1966). Towards a rational for testing abilities and attainments in Africa. *British Journal of Educational Psychology, 36*, 24–32.

Irvine, S. H. (1970). Affect and construct—a cross-cultural check on theories of intelligence. *Journal of Social Psychology, 80*, 23–30.

Irvine, S. H. (1979). The place of factor analysis in cross-cultural methodology and its contribution to cognitive theory. In L. H. Eckensberger, W. J. Lonner, & Y. H. Poortinga (Eds.), *Cross-cultural contributions to psychology* (pp. 300–341). Lisse, The Netherlands: Swets and Zeitlinger.

Irvine, S. H. (1988). Constructing the intellect of the Shona: A taxonomic approach. In J. W. Berry, S. H. Irvine, & E. B. Hunt (Eds.), *Indigenous cognition: Functioning in cultural context* (pp. 157–176). Dordrecht, The Netherlands: Martinus Nijhoff.

Jensen, A. R. (1969). How much can we boost IQ and scholastic achievement? *Harvard Educational Review, 39*, 449–483.

Jensen, A. R. (1998). *The g factor: The science of mental ability*. Westport, CT: Praeger.

Kaufman, A. S., & Kaufman, N. L. (1983). *Kaufman Assessment Battery for Children*. Circle Pines, MN: American Guidance Service.

Kim, U., & Berry, J. W. (1993), *Indigenous psychologies: Theory, method and experience in cultural context*. Newbury Park, CA: Sage.

Kluckhohn, C., & Murray, H. A. (1948). *Personality in nature, culture and society*. New York: Knopf.

Kroeber, A. L., & Kluckhohn, C. (1952). *Culture: A critical review of concepts and definitions*, 47(1). Cambridge, MA: Peabody Museum.

LeVine, R. A. (1973). *Culture, behavior and personality*. London: Hutchinson.

Luria, A. R. (1973). *The working brain: An introduction to neuropsychology*. New York: Basic Books.

Luria, A. R. (1980). *Higher cortical functions in man* (2nd ed.). New York: Basic Books.

McClelland, D.C. (1961). *The achieving society*. Princeton: Van Nostrand.

Mishra, R. C. (1997). Cognition and cognitive development. In J. W. Berry, P. R. Dasen, & T. S. Saraswathi (Eds.), *Handbook of cross-cultural psychology* (2nd ed.). *Volume 2. Basic processes and human development* (pp. 41–68). Needham Heights, MA: Allyn & Bacon.

Murdock, G. P., Ford, C. S., Hudson, A. E., Kennedy, R., Simmons, L. W., & Whiting, J. W. M. (1982). *Outline of cultural materials*. New Haven: Human Relations Area Files.

Naroll, R., Michik, G. L., & Naroll, F. (1974). Hologeistic theory testing. In J. G. Jurgensen (Ed.), *Comparative studies by Harold E. Driver & essays in his honor*. New Haven: HRAF press.

Okonji, O. M. (1971). The effects of familiarity on classification. *Journal of Cross-Cultural Psychology, 2*, 39–49.

Pike, K. L. (1966). *Language in relation to a unified theory of the structure of human behavior.* The Hague: Mouton.

Poortinga, Y. H. (1989). Equivalence of cross-cultural data: An overview of basic issues. *International Journal of Psychology, 24*, 737–756.

Porteus, S. D. (1937). *Intelligence and environment*. New York: Macmillan.

Putnam, D. B., & Kilbride, P. L. (1980). *A relativistic understanding of intelligence: social intelligence among the Songhay of Mali and the Samia of Kenya*. Paper presented at the Society for Cross-Cultural Research, Philadelphia.

Raven, J. C. (1938). *Progressive matrices: A perceptual test of intelligence, 1938 individual form*. London: Lewis.

Resnick, L. B. (1976). Introduction: Changing conceptions of intelligence. In L. B. Resnick (Ed.), *The nature of intelligence* (pp. 1–10). Hillsdale, NJ: Lawrence Erlbaum.

Schooler, C. (1998). Environmental complexity and the Flynn effect. In U. Neisser (Ed.), *The rising curve: Long-term gains in IQ and related measures* (pp. 67–79). Washington, DC: American Psychological Association.

Spearman, C. (1927). *The abilities of man*. New York: Macmillan.

Sternberg, R. J. (1985). *Beyond IQ: A triarchic theory of human intelligence*. New York: Cambridge University Press.

Sternberg, R. J. (1993). *Sternberg Triarchic Abilities Test*. Unpublished test.

Sternberg, R. J. (1997). The concept of intelligence and its role in lifelong learning and success. *American Psychologist, 52*, 1030–1037.

Super, C. M. (1983). Cultural variation in the meaning and uses of children's intelligence. In J. Deregowski, S. Dziurawiec, & R. Annis (Eds.), *Expiscations in cross-cultural psychology*. Amsterdam: Swets and Zeitlinger.

Super, C., & Harkness, S. (1980). Anthropological perspectives on child development. *New Directions for Child Development, 8*, 7–13.

Thurstone, L. L. (1938). *Primary mental abilities*. Psychometric Monographs, No. 1.

Van de Vijver, F. J. R. (1997). Meta-analysis of cross-cultural comparisons of cognitive test performance. *Journal of Cross-Cultural Psychology, 28*, 678–709.

Van de Vijver, F. J. R., & Leung, K. (1997). *Methods and data analysis for cross-cultural research.* Newbury Park, CA: Sage.

Vernon, P. E. (1969). *Intelligence and cultural environment.* London: Methuen.

Weber, M. (1904/1958). *The Protestant ethic and spirit of capitalism* (T. Parsons, Trans.). New York: Charles Scribner's Sons.

Wechsler, D. (1939). *The measurement of adult intelligence.* Baltimore: Williams & Wilkins.

Wechsler, D. (1991). *Wechsler Intelligence Scale for Children—Third Edition.* San Antonio. TX: The Psychological Corporation.

Whiting, B. (Ed.). (1963) *Six cultures: Studies in child rearing.* New York: Wiley.

Witkin, H., & Berry, J. W. (1975). Psychological differentiation in cross-cultural perspective. *Journal of Cross-Cultural Psychology, 6,* 4–87.

Wober, M. (1974). Toward an understanding of the Kiganda concept of intelligence. In J. W. Berry & P. R. Dasen (Eds.), *Culture and cognition: Readings in cross-cultural psychology* (pp. 261–280). London: Methuen.

PART

II

STANDARDIZATION STUDIES OF THE WISC-III IN DIFFERENT CULTURES

3

UNITED STATES

LAWRENCE G. WEISS

The Psychological Corporation
San Antonio, Texas

The Wechsler Intelligence Scale for Children—Third Edition (WISC-III) was published in the United States in 1991, following five years of research and development by staff at The Psychological Corporation. The primary reason for this project was to update the Wechsler Intelligence Scale for Children—Revised (WISC-R) norms published in 1974. Based on longitudinal data of cognitive functioning across time, Flynn (1984, 1987) found that in several countries cognitive scores increased significantly in a single generation. Thus, it is considered important to update norms periodically so that children's intelligence is assessed relative to a contemporary cohort.

In addition to updating the norms, each revision incorporates recent advances in understanding of cognitive ability. For example, the WISC-III included enhancements made to the working memory and speed of information processing constructs with the addition of the new Symbol Search subtest and the resultant four-factor structure. As we write, the research and development team at The Psychological Corporation is well underway with work on the WISC-IV, scheduled for publication in 2003. It is likely that this revision will not only update the norms for the U.S. population, but incorporate recent advances in the assessment of working memory and fluid reasoning.

ADAPTATION PROCESS

The process of modifying the WISC-R during development of the WISC-III involved many procedures similar to those used when adapting the U.S. version for use in other countries. Each item was examined for cultural bias with respect to gender, racial/ethnic group, and region of the country. Advice from a panel of experts and several focus groups of examiners was combined with information from the research literature to target items for revision. New items, together with experimental versions of new subtests such as Symbol Search, were pilot tested on 119 children. Subsequently, a national tryout of 450 children was conducted. During standardization, an oversample of more than 400 minority children in addition to those of the standardization sample were tested and their scores analyzed for bias. At each step in the process, every item was analyzed for bias using several methods (Angoff, 1982; Reynolds, Willson, & Jensen, 1984; Wright & Stone, 1979). Basically, these analyses evaluate the extent to which children of the same overall cognitive ability level will have the same probability of a correct response regardless of their gender, racial/ethnic group, or the region of the country in which they live. When this situation is identified, the item is either dropped from the test or rewritten before proceeding to the next phase in the development process.

The evaluation of item bias is of critical importance to the development of culturally fair tests. The process described above, however, may occasionally reveal that an item believed by experts to be biased does not demonstrate bias when examined empirically. One example is a new Picture Completion item being tested for WISC-IV. This item is a picture of a basketball hoop without the net, and the child must indicate that the net is missing. Expert reviewers consistently state that this item will be biased because basketball hoops do not have nets in most poor, inner city neighborhoods. The empirical data available to date, however, suggests that children from these environments are aware that there should be a net on the hoop and give the targeted answer. Thus, the evaluation of item bias during the adaptation phase of test development is a complex matter involving both data and judgment.

SAMPLE CHARACTERISTICS

The demographics characteristics of the U.S. population are constantly changing. Most significantly, there have been large changes in educational attainment across the generations. Approximately one-third of those over 80 years of age did not attend school beyond the 8th grade, whereas more than half of those now in their 30s either attended or graduated college. Of all the important demographic features painting the landscape of the country, perhaps the most salient to intelligence is education. Education is highly correlated with intelligence. Education is considered a proxy variable for socioeconomic status. As the educational level of the parents increase, their children are more likely to enjoy improved socioeconomic conditions. This younger cohort of 30–39 year olds is likely to be the parents of children taking the WISC-III today. The parent's greater emphasis on education may provide these children with increased intellectual stimulation and improved educational opportunities which could be reflected in higher scores on tests of cognitive ability.

There are also important changes in the racial/ethnic composition of the nation. The influx of immigrants from other nations, the high birth rates among some minority populations, and the increase in biracial marriages results in a constantly changing national complexion. The percentage of whites has been steadily declining with each successive generation as the percentage of Hispanics grows and new immigrant groups join the country. Whereas the percentage of whites is more than 80% among U.S. citizens aged 55 and over, the percentage of white U.S. children aged 2–6 years is below 65%. In some regions of the country (California), the percentage of Asian children is approaching 12%.

It is noteworthy that educational opportunity and attainment tend to co-vary with racial/ethnic group. The white majority group has higher mean levels of education than all minority groups except Asians. Given the large percentage of variance in IQ scores accounted for by education, this confounding of education level and racial/ethnic group can confuse the interpretation of bias research if not adequately controlled. This will be discussed further in the section on cultural issues influencing WISC-III interpretation.

Although the U.S. has had stable national borders for more than two centuries, a fact not true of many other nations, the demographics of the country continue to change and test developers must keep abreast of these changes as new standardization samples are collected. It may soon become necessary to track and report the percentage of Asian children in the WISC-IV standardization sample as compared to the census. Further in the future, it may also become necessary to begin to sample multiracial children according to the census, as was done for the Canadian WISC-III standardization sample. Also, as the percentage of parents with less than an 8th grade education begins to fall below 5%, the impact of this group will be less significant on the norms and might be dropped from future sampling plans.

Table 3.1 shows a snapshot of U.S. demographics taken according to the 1988 census. As shown in this table, the percentage of children in the WISC-III standardization sample very closely matches the U.S. population by parent education level and racial ethnic group at each year of age. Data reported in the WISC-III Manual further shows that these percentages are equivalent for females and males in the sample.

RELIABILITY

Table 3.2 shows the average (across age) split-half reliability coefficients and standard errors of measurement for the subtests, IQ, and index scores by age and overall. As shown in the table, the average reliability for the IQ scores are all above 0.90. The average reliability for the index scores range from $r = 0.85$ for Processing Speed Index (PSI) to $r = 0.94$ for Verbal Comprehension Index (VCI).

TABLE 3.1   Demographic Characteristics of the Standardization Sample: Percentages by Age, Parent Education Level, and Ethnic Group

Age	n	≤8	9–11	12	13–15	≥16	White	Black	Hispanic	Other
			Parent education					Ethnic group		
6	200	6.5	12.5	36.5	26.5	18.0	69.5	15.0	11.0	4.5
7	200	6.5	11.5	38.0	25.0	19.0	69.5	16.0	11.5	3.0
8	200	5.5	12.0	36.0	26.5	20.0	69.5	14.5	11.5	4.5
9	200	6.5	14.0	37.0	25.5	17.0	70.5	15.5	10.5	3.5
10	200	6.5	11.5	38.0	26.0	18.0	70.5	15.0	10.5	4.0
11	200	4.0	12.5	38.0	27.5	18.0	70.5	15.5	11.0	3.0
12	200	6.5	12.5	38.0	24.0	19.0	71.0	13.0	11.0	5.0
13	200	5.0	12.0	37.0	26.0	20.0	69.5	16.0	11.5	3.0
14	200	6.0	13.0	37.5	24.5	19.0	70.0	16.0	11.5	2.5
15	200	5.5	12.0	37.0	26.0	19.5	71.0	15.5	10.0	2.5
16	200	4.5	13.0	37.0	27.5	18.0	70.0	16.0	11.0	3.0
Total	2200	5.7	12.4	37.3	25.9	18.7	70.1	15.4	11.0	3.5
U.S. population		6.5	12.4	37.3	25.9	18.7	70.1	15.4	11.0	3.5

Note: U.S. population data for children aged 6–16 are from *Current Population Survey, March 1988* [Machine-readable data file] by U.S. Bureau of the Census, 1988, Washington, DC: Bureau of the Census (Producer/Distributor).

The average subtest reliabilities range from $r = 0.69$ for Object Assembly to $r = 0.87$ Vocabulary and Block Design. The SEMs follow naturally from the reliabilities such that those subtests with the highest reliabilities have the smallest standard errors.

Table 3.3 shows the average corrected retest correlations for the subtests, IQs and index scores by age band and overall. For the overall sample, these range from $r = 0.87$ for Performance IQ (PIQ) to $r = 0.94$ for Verbal IQ (VIQ) and Full Scale IQ (FSIQ). The retest correlations for the index scores range from $r = 0.82$ for the Freedom from Distractibility Index (FDI) to $r = 0.93$ for VCI. The retest correlations for the subtests range from $r = 0.57$ for Mazes to $r = 0.89$ for Vocabulary.

EVIDENCE OF VALIDITY

The WISC-III and its predecessors are among the most researched tests in psychology. The lines of validity for the WISC-III are long and deep, and space limitations in this chapter prevent all but the most cursory review of the evidence. There is ample evidence of validity based on test content, response processes, relations to other variables, and test-criterion relations. In this section, the focus is on validity evidence based on internal structure.

TABLE 3.2 Reliability Coefficients and Standard Errors of Measurement of the Subtests Scaled Scores, IQ Scores, and Index Scores, by Age[a]

Subtest/scale	Age in years											Average[c]
	6	7	8	9	10	11	12	13	14	15	16	
Information	0.73	0.76	0.86	0.81	0.82	0.85	0.85	0.85	0.87	0.88	0.88	0.84
(SEm)	1.56	1.47	1.12	1.31	1.27	1.16	1.16	1.16	1.08	1.04	1.04	1.23
Similarities	0.81	0.77	0.84	0.80	0.82	0.82	0.84	0.74	0.84	0.81	0.84	0.81
(SEm)	1.31	1.44	1.20	1.34	1.27	1.27	1.20	1.53	1.20	1.31	1.20	1.30
Arithmetic	0.81	0.73	0.78	0.71	0.79	0.79	0.74	0.81	0.77	0.81	0.82	0.78
(SEm)	1.31	1.56	1.41	1.62	1.37	1.53	1.31	1.56	1.47	1.34	1.56	1.41
Vocabulary	0.82	0.79	0.88	0.82	0.88	0.88	0.89	0.89	0.91	0.91	0.89	0.87
(SEm)	1.27	1.37	1.04	1.27	1.04	1.04	0.99	0.99	0.90	0.91	0.99	1.08
Comprehension	0.75	0.72	0.85	0.74	0.79	0.76	0.81	0.73	0.76	0.80	0.73	0.77
(SEm)	1.50	1.59	1.16	1.53	1.37	1.47	1.31	1.56	1.47	1.34	1.56	1.45
Digit span	0.79	0.81	0.84	0.82	0.84	0.84	0.87	0.87	0.84	0.91	0.89	0.85
(SEm)	1.37	1.31	1.20	1.27	1.20	1.20	1.08	1.08	1.20	0.90	0.99	1.17
Picture completion	0.78	0.84	0.81	0.80	0.74	0.76	0.72	0.72	0.72	0.82	0.75	0.77
(SEm)	1.41	1.20	1.31	1.34	1.53	1.47	1.59	1.59	1.59	1.27	1.50	1.44
Coding	0.75	0.70	—[b]	—[b]	0.78	0.82	—[b]	—[b]	0.70	0.90	—[b]	0.79
(SEm)	1.50	1.64	—[b]	—[b]	1.41	1.27	—[b]	—[b]	1.64	0.95	—[b]	1.42
Picture arrangement	0.82	0.84	0.72	0.72	0.74	0.70	0.79	0.76	0.78	0.73	0.73	0.76
(SEm)	1.27	1.20	1.59	1.59	1.53	1.64	1.37	1.47	1.41	1.56	1.56	1.48
Block design	0.82	0.77	0.83	0.85	0.89	0.84	0.87	0.90	0.90	0.92	0.90	0.87
(SEm)	1.27	1.44	1.24	1.16	0.99	1.20	1.08	0.95	0.95	0.85	0.95	1.11
Object assembly	0.71	0.65	0.65	0.75	0.69	0.65	0.68	0.75	0.60	0.76	0.71	0.69
(SEm)	1.62	1.77	1.77	1.50	1.67	1.77	1.70	1.50	1.90	1.47	1.62	1.67
Symbol search	0.69	0.76	—[b]	—[b]	0.72	0.79	—[b]	—[b]	0.75	0.82	—[b]	0.76
(SEm)	1.67	1.47	—[b]	—[b]	1.59	1.37	—[b]	—[b]	1.50	1.27	—[b]	1.48
Mazes	0.80	0.78	0.76	0.66	0.70	0.68	0.66	0.70	0.70	0.61	0.67	0.70
(SEm)	1.34	1.41	1.47	1.75	1.64	1.70	1.75	1.64	1.64	1.87	1.72	1.64

(Continues)

TABLE 3.2 (Continued)

| Subtest/scale | Age in years | | | | | | | | | | | Average[c] |
	6	7	8	9	10	11	12	13	14	15	16	
Verbal IQ	0.93	0.92	0.96	0.93	0.95	0.95	0.95	0.94	0.95	0.96	0.95	0.95
(SEm)	3.97	4.24	3.00	3.97	3.35	3.35	3.35	3.67	3.35	3.00	3.35	3.53
Performance IQ	0.91	0.90	0.90	0.91	0.91	0.90	0.91	0.90	0.89	0.94	0.92	0.91
(SEm)	4.50	4.74	4.74	4.50	4.50	4.74	4.50	4.74	4.97	3.67	4.24	4.54
Full scale IQ	0.95	0.94	0.96	0.95	0.95	0.96	0.95	0.95	0.95	0.97	0.96	0.96
(SEm)	3.35	3.67	3.00	3.35	3.00	3.30	3.00	3.35	3.35	2.60	3.00	3.2
Verbal comp. index	0.91	0.91	0.95	0.93	0.94	0.94	0.95	0.93	0.95	0.95	0.94	0.94
(SEm)	4.50	4.50	3.35	3.97	3.67	3.67	3.35	3.97	3.35	3.35	3.67	3.78
Percept. organ. index	0.91	0.90	0.89	0.90	0.90	0.89	0.91	0.91	0.89	0.93	0.90	0.90
(SEm)	4.50	4.74	4.97	4.74	4.74	4.97	4.50	4.50	4.97	3.97	4.74	4.68
Freedom-distract. index	0.87	0.84	0.87	0.83	0.86	0.88	0.86	0.88	0.86	0.91	0.90	0.87
(SEm)	5.41	6.00	5.41	6.18	5.61	5.20	5.61	5.20	5.61	4.50	4.74	5.43
Processing speed index	0.81	0.80	0.84	0.85	0.84	0.87	0.87	0.82	0.82	0.91	0.91	0.85
(SEm)	6.54	6.71	6.00	5.81	6.00	5.41	5.41	6.36	6.36	4.50	4.50	5.83

[a] $N = 200$ for each age group. The reliability coefficients for all subtests except Coding and Symbol Search are split-half correlations corrected by the Spearman-Brown formula. For Coding and Symbol Search, raw-score test-retest correlations are presented for six age groups, these coefficients, which are based on samples of about 60 children tested twice, were corrected for the variability of the appropriate standardization group (Guilford & Fruchter, 1978). The coefficients for the IQ and factor-based scales were calculated with the formula for the reliability of the composite (Nunnally, 1978); the values for the supplementary subtests (Digit Span, Mazes, and Symbol Search) were not included in these computations. The standard errors of measurement are reported in scaled-score units for the subtests, in IQ units for the Verbal, Performance, and Full Scale scores, and in index units for the Verbal Comprehension, Perceptual Organization, Freedom from Distractibility, and Processing Speed scores.

[b] For Coding and Symbol Search, the best estimates of the reliability coefficient at an age level for which retesting was not done is the value obtained at the adjacent age level. The exceptions for age 8, for which the most reasonable estimate is the value obtained at age 10—the closest age at which Level B of these subtests is administered. (Level A is administered to children younger than age 8.) These "best estimates" for Coding and Symbol Search were used for computing the reliabilities of the composites to which these subtests contribute.

[c] The average r was computed with Fisher's z transformation. The average SEms were calculated by averaging the sum of the squared SEms for each age group and obtaining the square root of the results.

TABLE 3.3 Stability Coefficients of the Subtests, IQ Scales and Factor-Based Scales by Age

	Age in years						
	6–7 ($n = 111$)		10–11 ($n = 119$)		14–15 ($n = 123$)		All ages
Subtest/scale	r_{12}	r_c^a	r_{12}	r_c^a	r_{12}	r_c^a	Average[b]
Information	0.80	0.80	0.87	0.80	0.87	0.86	0.85
Similarities	0.77	0.78	0.80	0.81	0.84	0.84	0.81
Arithmetic	0.66	0.66	0.75	0.79	0.75	0.76	0.74
Vocabulary	0.80	0.82	0.89	0.88	0.93	0.93	0.89
Comprehension	0.68	0.66	0.76	0.75	0.78	0.78	0.73
Digit span	0.63	0.67	0.73	0.75	0.77	0.77	0.73
Picture completion	0.80	0.82	0.78	0.80	0.85	0.82	0.81
Coding	0.73	0.70	0.79	0.78	0.83	0.80	0.77
Picture arrangement	0.67	0.65	0.59	0.60	0.68	0.67	0.64
Block design	0.74	0.69	0.76	0.75	0.84	0.83	0.77
Object assembly	0.69	0.64	0.71	0.71	0.69	0.62	0.66
Symbol search	0.73	0.70	0.74	0.74	0.77	0.77	0.74
Mazes	0.61	0.60	0.62	0.56	0.54	0.54	0.57
Verbal IQ	0.87	0.90	0.93	0.94	0.95	0.96	0.94
Performance IQ	0.86	0.86	0.85	0.88	0.88	0.88	0.87
Full scale IQ	0.90	0.92	0.93	0.95	0.95	0.95	0.94
Verbal comp. index	0.86	0.89	0.92	0.93	0.94	0.95	0.93
Percept. organ. index	0.85	0.86	0.84	0.87	0.88	0.87	0.87
Freedom-distract. index	0.71	0.74	0.81	0.86	0.82	0.84	0.82
Processing speed index	0.78	0.80	0.83	0.85	0.85	0.86	0.84

[a] Correlations were corrected for the variability of WISC-III scores on the first testing (Guilford & Fruchter, 1978).

[b] Weighted average of corrected correlations for ages 6–7, ages 10–11, and ages 14–15 were obtained with Fisher's z transformation ($N = 353$).

The intercorrelations of subtest scaled scores are reported in Table 3.4 for consistency with other chapters in this book. This will allow interested researchers to compare the internal structure of the WISC-III across the national samples reported herein. Also, the four-factor structure originally reported in the WISC-III Manual is repeated here in Table 3.5 for the same reason. A maximum likelihood factor analysis was applied, with iterated communalities (SMCs inserted initially), followed by a Varimax rotation. (Oblique rotations produced highly similar four-factor solutions.) The adequacy of reporting factor scores for the two smaller factors was verified by a cross-validation procedure designed to test the consistency of factor scores across samples. In this procedure seven random samples of 352 children each were drawn with replacement from the standardization sample of 2200. Each sample was submitted to factor analysis according to the procedures described above, yielding seven sets of four-factor scores. These seven sets of scores were then calculated for each of the children in the hold out sample

TABLE 3.4 Intercorrelation of Subtest Scaled Scores

Subtest/scale	Inf	Sim	Ari	Voc	Com	DS	PCom	Cd	PA	BD	OA	SS	Mz
Information													
Similarities	0.66												
Arithmetic	0.57	0.55											
Vocabulary	0.70	0.69	0.54										
Comprehension	0.56	0.59	0.47	0.64									
Digit span	0.34	0.34	0.43	0.35	0.29								
Picture completion	0.47	0.45	0.39	0.45	0.38	0.25							
Coding	0.21	0.20	0.27	0.26	0.25	0.23	0.18						
Picture arrangement	0.40	0.39	0.35	0.40	0.35	0.20	0.37	0.28					
Block design	0.48	0.49	0.52	0.46	0.40	0.32	0.52	0.27	0.41				
Object assembly	0.41	0.42	0.39	0.41	0.34	0.26	0.49	0.24	0.37	0.61			
Symbol search	0.35	0.35	0.41	0.35	0.34	0.28	0.33	0.53	0.36	0.45	0.38		
Mazes	0.18	0.18	0.22	0.17	0.17	0.14	0.24	0.15	0.23	0.31	0.29	0.24	

($n = 440$), and the resulting sets of scores intercorrelated. The median correlations among the same factors ranged from $r = 0.93$ for PSI to $r = 0.99$ for VCI. These results demonstrated the stability of the third and fourth factors across samples. (See WISC-III Manual for further details.)

Most subsequent studies have continued to support this four-factor structure (Konold, Kush, & Canivez, 1997; Blaha & Wallbrown, 1996; Roid, Prifitera, & Weiss, 1993; Roid & Worrall, 1996; Sattler & Saklofske, 2001; Kush, Watkins, Ward, Ward, Canivez, & Worrell, 2001), although others have supported a three-factor structure (Logerquist-Hansen & Barona, 1994; Reynolds & Ford, 1994; Sattler, 1992; Sattler 2001).

In spite of this strong empirical support for the four-factor structure of the WISC-III, factor analysis should not be the sole criterion for determining how to summarize test performance. This decision should be informed by clinically meaningful patterns in the performance of diagnostic groups as well (Prifitera, Weiss, & Saklofske, 1998). For this reason, studies demonstrating differential performance of various clinical groups on these four factors are equally important, if not more important, than factor loadings in determining how to summarize WISC-III test performance. Much has been written about the validity of the WISC-III with specific clinical populations including children with attention deficit hyperactivity disorder (ADHD), emotional disturbances, learning disabilities, language impairments, and neurological insults, as well as children who are gifted, mentally retarded, or hearing impaired. For one of the more comprehensive, recent volumes see Prifitera and Saklofske (1998).

TABLE 3.5 Maximum-Likelihood Factor Loadings (Varimax Rotation) for Four Factors

Subtest/scale	Factor 1: Verbal comprehension Ages				Factor 2: Perceptual organization Ages				Factor 3: Freedom from distractibility Ages				Factor 4: Processing speed Ages			
	6–7	8–10	11–13	14–16	6–7	8–10	11–13	14–16	6–7	8–10	11–13	14–16	6–7	8–10	11–13	14–16
Information	0.66	0.70	0.74	0.76	0.23	0.29	0.31	0.26	0.32	0.30	0.21	0.23	0.00	0.17	0.05	0.07
Similarities	0.70	0.73	0.68	0.72	0.24	0.29	0.32	0.26	0.26	0.25	0.26	0.19	0.03	0.09	0.10	0.08
Vocabulary	0.71	0.84	0.80	0.84	0.27	0.24	0.24	0.17	0.16	0.11	0.22	0.17	0.07	0.18	0.13	0.20
Comprehension	0.63	0.66	0.66	0.65	0.12	0.20	0.23	0.20	0.14	0.14	0.18	0.21	0.08	0.19	0.20	0.21
Picture completion	0.29	0.41	0.34	0.44	0.51	0.49	0.58	0.55	0.18	0.10	0.10	0.09	0.15	0.11	0.04	0.01
Picture arrangement	0.32	0.33	0.29	0.40	0.28	0.33	0.40	0.41	0.43	0.06	0.02	0.07	0.20	0.30	0.21	0.19
Block design	0.26	0.26	0.23	0.37	0.65	0.75	0.73	0.63	0.36	0.21	0.36	0.27	0.03	0.14	0.17	0.21
Object assembly	0.24	0.27	0.22	0.28	0.70	0.68	0.68	0.68	0.19	0.10	0.16	0.10	0.12	0.12	0.14	0.16
Mazes	0.06	0.08	0.09	0.02	0.32	0.38	0.31	0.39	0.36	0.02	0.04	0.13	0.03	0.14	0.07	0.15
Arithmetic	0.41	0.47	0.43	0.43	0.20	0.28	0.25	0.27	0.60	0.54	0.64	0.85	0.06	0.19	0.13	0.15
Digit span	0.32	0.30	0.20	0.27	0.19	0.13	0.12	0.22	0.39	0.33	0.44	0.30	0.03	0.20	0.21	0.18
Coding	0.04	0.13	0.11	0.12	0.13	0.13	0.10	0.14	0.12	0.10	0.15	0.08	0.98	0.84	0.85	0.81
Symbol search	0.24	0.22	0.14	0.22	0.30	0.30	0.34	0.39	0.48	0.21	0.18	0.16	0.30	0.60	0.52	0.57

CULTURAL ISSUES INFLUENCING WISC-III
INTERPRETATION IN THE U.S.

In the U.S. there is considerable literature concerning the performance of minority groups on intelligence tests. The use of IQ tests with minority students has been controversial because of concerns of test bias. Despite many concerns over test bias, the vast majority of studies investigating ethnic bias in IQ tests in general and in the Wechsler series have not produced evidence of test bias (Reynolds & Kaiser, 1990). Still, studies have consistently found that African-Americans score on average 15 points lower than whites, and Hispanics score somewhere between these two groups on IQ tests (Neisser, Boodoo, Bouchard, Boykin, Brody, Ceci, Halpern, Loehlin, Perloff, Sternberg, & Urbina, 1996). It is therefore natural to ask: Does the WISC-III show evidence of test bias toward minorities?

In studies of prediction bias (Weiss, Prifitera, & Roid, 1993; Weiss & Prifitera, 1995), the WISC-III predicted achievement scores equally well for African-American, Hispanic, and white children. The results of these studies are similar to other studies using the WISC-R (Reynolds & Kaiser 1990). Such results are interpreted as evidence that the scales are not biased against minorities. In addition item selection for the WISC-III was done in conjunction with item bias analyses and content bias reviewers (Wechsler, 1991). Results of the British and Canadian studies mentioned above also demonstrated that the WISC-III was valid for these samples.

Wechsler was fully aware of the controversies regarding IQ testing with minority children. Wechsler, however, viewed the differences in mean scores not as indicators of lower intelligence among certain groups but as indicators of differences in our society and how variations in social, economic, political, and medical opportunities have an impact on intellectual abilities. In a 1971 paper Wechsler discussed the fact that individuals from lower socioeconomic levels tended to score lower on IQ tests. He viewed this fact as evidence for a call to change the social conditions that cause these differences rather than as an indictment of the IQ test. In discussing differences in IQs among socioeconomic groups, Wechsler stated "the cause is elsewhere, and the remedy not in denigrating or banishing the IQ but in attacking and removing the social causes that impair it" (Wechsler, 1971).

If differences in IQ among groups are attributable primarily to social and economic factors, then what implications do these have for the interpretation of IQ. First it is important to view the IQ score not as a fixed entity but as a reflection of an individual's current level of cognitive functioning. All too often in psychological reports one sees a phrase which states directly or strongly implies that the IQ reflects the individuals potential or inherited ability. But there are many factors including the socioeconomic, medical, temporary and transitory states of the organism, motivation, inherent test unreliability, etc., that all may impact the person's score. It is well accepted by the professional community that IQ is not a measure of genetic endowment (Neisser et al., 1996) even though there is substantial evidence for the role of genetic factors in intelligence.

There is clear evidence from the WISC-III standardization sample as well as data from other IQ tests of a substantial correlation between IQ and socioeconomic level. One of the reasons that test developers stratify their samples by socioeconomic status (SES) variables is to control for this effect. In the WISC-III, the standardization sample was stratified by parental level of education because this variable is related to SES and considered a good measure of SES. Results show that children from homes whose parents have the highest level of education (college level or above) score considerably higher than all the other four levels of education groups (i.e., <8th grade, 8–11 years of education, high school graduate, some post-secondary education or technical school). The mean FSIQ scores for the entire WISC-III standardization sample for the five education levels from highest to lowest are 110.7, 103.0, 97.9, 90.6, and 87.7, respectively. The impact of SES on IQ scores is a "truth" generally accepted among the professional community.

As mentioned above, African-American groups on average tend to score 15 points lower than white samples on IQ tests. However, just looking at groups at this level conceals many issues and often leads to the erroneous conclusion that the intelligence of minority groups is lower than that of whites. This is erroneous because these overall group differences do not take into account other relevant variables such as SES. One issue that affects this outcome is that when developing IQ tests, developers stratify SES within racial/ethnic groups in order to obtain a representative sample of the U.S. population. The effect of this is that minority groups tend to have a larger percentage of their sample as lower SES just because this reflects the population characteristics. Therefore, a simple comparison of means between minority groups and whites will yield scores that do not take into account the impact of socioeconomic and other demographic variables that might affect scores. Also, focusing on the overall IQ score alone misses other aspects of an individual's functioning. Remember what the IQ score represents: it tells us the score or standing of an individual relative to a reference group. Thus the individual's score must be interpreted in light of the reference group characteristics.

In order to investigate differences among different racial/ethnic groups, Prifitera, Weiss, and Saklofske (1998) examined the WISC-III IQ and index scores of African-Americans, Hispanics, and whites in the WISC-III standardization sample (see Table 3.6). In addition, rather than just looking at overall means, they compared samples that were matched on SES (level of education). Through matching they also controlled for sex, age (in years), region of the country (Northeast, South, Midwest, and West), and number of parents living at home. Tables 3.7 and 3.8 present data for these matched samples.

When looking at these data, several important points should be considered. First in Table 3.6, the mean difference between the white and African-American sample is one standard deviation which is consistent with previous research on IQ tests (Neisser et al., 1996) and on the WISC-R (Kaufman & Doppelt, 1976). The difference between the white and Hispanic sample is smaller (approximately 9 points). The second point, however, is that there is considerable variation in the differences among African-Americans, Hispanics, and whites among the other

TABLE 3.6   Mean IQ and Index Scores by Ethnicity for the WISC-III Standardization Sample[a]

IQ or index score[b]	African-American	Hispanic	White
FSIQ	88.6	94.1	103.5
VIQ	90.8	92.1	103.6
PIQ	88.5	97.7	102.9
VCI	90.8	92.2	103.7
POI	87.5	97.5	103.4
FDI	95.7	95.4	103.1
PSI	95.8	100.2	101.9

[a]Total $N = 2200$; African-American group, $n = 338$; Hispanic, $n = 242$. Data and table copyright © 1997 by The Psychological Corporation. All rights reserved.
[b]FSIQ, Full Intelligence Quotient; VIQ, Verbal IQ; PIQ, Performance IQ; VCI, Verbal Comprehension Index; POI, Perceptual Organization Index; FDI, Freedom from Distractibility Index; PSI, Processing Speed Index.

TABLE 3.7   WISC-III Scores of African-American and Whites Based on a Sample Matched on Age, Parental Level of Education, Region, Sex, Number of Parents Living in the Household

IQ or index score[a]	African-American ($n = 252$)	White ($n = 252$)[b]
FSIQ	89.9	100.9
VIQ	91.9	100.8
PIQ	89.8	101.2
VCI	91.9	100.7
POI	88.8	101.6
FDI	97.0	102.5
PSI	96.9	100.9

[a]FSIQ, Full Intelligence Quotient; VIQ, Verbal IQ; PIQ, Performance IQ; VCI, Verbal Comprehension Index; POI, Perceptual Organization Index; FDI, Freedom from Distractibility Index; PSI, Processing Speed Index.
[b]All differences between groups significant; $p < 0.05$.
Data and table copyright © 1997 by The Psychological Corporation. All rights reserved.

IQ and index scores. For example, African-Americans score only 6.1 and 7.4 points, respectively, below whites on PSI and FDI scores. Hispanics continue to show a relatively higher PIQ and Perceptual Organization Index (POI) score compared to their VIQ and VCI scores which is consistent with the previous literature. The difference in the PIQ between Hispanics and whites is only 5.2 points. In addition, the Hispanic group's PSI score is virtually identical to that of whites and there is only a 7.7 point difference between the groups on the FDI score. These results strongly suggest that simply looking at the FSIQ differences

TABLE 3.8   WISC-III Scores of Hispanics and Whites Based on a
Sample Matched on Age, Parental Level do Educating, Religion, Sex,
Number of Parents Live-in in the Household

IQ or index score[a]	Hispanic ($n = 151$)	White ($n = 151$)
FSIQ	96.8	99.6[b]
VIQ	95.0	98.6[b]
PIQ	99.7	100.9
VCI	95.2	98.2[b]
POI	99.5	101.8
FDI	97.2	101.5[b]
PSI	101.1	99.6

[a]FSIQ, Full Intelligence Quotient; VIQ, Verbal IQ; PIQ, Performance
IQ; VCI, Verbal Comprehension Index; POI, Perceptual Organization Index;
FDI, Freedom from Distractibility Index; PSI, Processing Speed Index.
  [b]$p < 0.05$.

ignores relative strengths in the various domains of cognitive functioning among
minority groups. It also strongly supports the practice of using the index scores
even though factor analyses do not always clearly support the four-factor structure
for minority groups (e.g., Logerquist-Hansen & Barona, 1994).

To further investigate the relationship of SES variables with IQ scores, we
looked at matched samples of African-Americans, Hispanics, and whites. Subjects
were matched on age, region, sex, parental education level, and number of parents
living in the household. Analyses of the WISC-III standardization data found that
children who live in a one-parent household have on average a FSIQ score that
is approximately 6 points lower than children living in a two-parent household.
Therefore we matched on this variable as well. Results are provided in Tables 3.7
and 3.8.

The score differences between African-Americans and whites are significantly
reduced when one takes into account these gross SES and demographic variables.
Also of interest is that contrary to what is often assumed, African-Americans do
in fact do somewhat better on the verbal compared to the nonverbal, performance
tasks. This is contrary to the usual assumption that African-Americans perform
more poorly on the verbal tasks because it is commonly assumed that verbal
items are more culturally loaded and biased than nonverbal tasks. Also, the relatively lower score on performance measures cannot be attributed to the likelihood
that African-Americans are disadvantaged on speeded tests because the smallest
discrepancy (4 points) is found on the PSI. What these data do suggest is that
socioeconomic and demographic factors do have a strong impact on scores and
again that there are considerable variations in scores among the cognitive components measured in the WISC-III. This again underscores the value of using both

the index scores and IQ scores or else these patterns of relative strengths would be overlooked.

The score differences between Hispanics and whites are also significantly reduced when samples are matched on these demographic variables (see Table 3.8). All differences are less then four points and several scores show no statistical significance. The higher score on the PSI by the Hispanic group (although not statistically significant) is of particular interest because it is sometimes assumed that Hispanics score lower than whites on the WISC-III because of the speeded nature of some of the tasks. The reasoning behind this is that speed and time is valued differently in Hispanic cultures so on tasks requiring quick performance, Hispanics are likely to score lower. However, on the PSI which is highly speeded, the Hispanic group did not differ significantly (and actually scored high) than the white sample.

Finally, we also looked for age trends in score differences between African-Americans and whites. Table 3.9 presents the difference scores between groups by age bands. This is the same matched sample as in Table 3.7 broken up into two age bands: 6–11 year olds and 12–16 year olds. Such age trends were not found for the matched Hispanic sample.

The patterns in these tables clearly illustrate that the differences between groups are even smaller for the younger age group. The reasons for this age difference are unknown. However, it does have implications for how we view scores and how and when we intervene. The impact of earlier intervention on outcomes of children when score differences are smaller should obviously be further investigated.

These data also strongly suggest that research needs to look at more refined SES, cultural, linguistic, home environment, medical, and other variables that affect opportunity to learn and the development of cognitive abilities.

TABLE 3.9   Difference Scores between Whites and African-Americans by Age Group on WISC-III IQ and Index Scores for a Matched Sample[a]

IQ or index score[b]	6- to 11-year-old group (n = 143)	12- to 16-year-old group (n = 109)
FSIQ	8.6	14.1
VIQ	6.6	11.9
PIQ	9.4	14.0
VCI	6.9	11.4
POI	10.8	15.4
FDI	3.1	8.6
PSI	2.3[c]	6.3

[a]Total $N = 2200$; African-American group, $n = 338$; Hispanic, $n = 242$.
[b]FSIQ, Full Intelligence Quotient; VIQ, Verbal IQ; PIQ, Performance IQ; VCI, Verbal Comprehension Index; POI, Perceptual Organization Index; FDI, Freedom from Distractibility Index; PSI, Processing Speed Index.
[c]$p > 0.05$; all other differences are significant, $p < 0.05$.

The fact that IQ score differences between groups are substantially reduced when samples are matched for SES is an important finding, especially considering that parent education level is only a gross proxy for SES. Further, group differences on SES matched samples are even smaller for index than IQ scores. These findings strongly suggest that the view that minorities have lower abilities is clearly wrong. One has to ask what would the difference have been if even more refined variables such as household income, home environment variable such as parental time spent with children, per-pupil school spending, medical and nutritional history, exposure to environmental toxins, etc., had been controlled. It also strongly supports not interpreting IQ scores as indicators of some inherent or genetic endowment.

SES also interacts with racial/ethnic groups in the interpretation of intraindividual differences or profile analysis. Practitioners often examine the discrepancy between a child's verbal and performance scores and consider large discrepancies to be clinically meaningful. However, the distribution of discrepancy scores varies across racial/ethnic groups and also across SES levels. Table 3.10 shows the average verbal-performance discrepancy as a function of SES level for Hispanics and African-Americans. Most practitioners have come to expect a significant PIQ > VIQ discrepancy for Hispanic children, and these data show that on average this discrepancy is about 5 1/2 points. However, the magnitude of the average discrepancy for Hispanics decreases as parent education level increases, until no discrepancy is expected for Hispanic children of college-educated parents.

This table also reinforces a point raised earlier about relative verbal-performance scores for African-American children. It is simply not true that African-American children perform better on the performance than the verbal subtests of the WISC-III. In fact, these data suggest the opposite pattern, although mediated by SES. On average, African-Americans score about 2 points higher on verbal than performance IQ scores. However, the difference is larger for African-American children of less educated parents.

Practitioners should be aware of these cultural influences on test scores, and incorporate them into their interpretations as appropriate for each evaluation. As Mattarazzo (1990) indicated in his APA presidential address, psychological assessment is both a science and an art.

PROFESSIONAL ISSUES IN THE USE OF INTELLIGENCE TESTS IN THE U.S.

Questions about the relative appropriateness of various measures of cognitive ability for specific minority populations is at the heart of much professional debate over the use of intelligence tests in the U.S. today. With the complexity of cultural and socioeconomic influences on test scores described above, it is clear that the proper interpretation of test scores must be a professional activity.

TABLE 3.10 Means and Standard Deviations for WISC-III Verbal IQ-Performance IQ and Verbal Comprehension Index-Perceptual-Organization Index Discrepancies in Hispanic and African-American Sample by Parent Education Level and Overall

| | Sample[a,b] | | | |
| | Hispanic | | African-American | |
Parent education level	VIQ-PIQ	VCI-POI	VIQ-PIQ	VCI-POI
<9	−8.6 (10.9) $n = 73$	−8.7 (11.4) $n = 73$	4.7 (11.6) $n = 23$	5.5 (11.9) $n = 23$
9–11	−5.7 (9.4) $n = 57$	−5.3 (9.8) $n = 57$	1.4 (10.8) $n = 78$	2.5 (11.4) $n = 78$
12	−4.7 (13.7) $n = 6.5$	−4.3 (13.7) $n = 65$	2.6 (11.9) $n = 142$	3.4 (11.7) $n = 142$
13–15	−2.6 (8.9) $n = 35$	−1.5 (8.8) $n = 35$	1.8 (12.7) $n = 65$	3.5 (12.5) $n = 65$
>15	0.2 (11.8) $n = 12$	0.2 (13.4) $n = 12$	1.8 (11.1) $n = 30$	2.6 (11.8) $n = 30$
Overall	−5.6 (11.4) $n = 242$	−5.2 (11.7) $n = 242$	2.2 (11.7) $n = 338$	3.3 (11.8) $n = 338$

[a] Negative signs indicate Verbal < Performance (V < P).
[b] VIQ-PIQ, Verbal IQ-Performance IQ; VCI-POI, Verbal Comprehension Index-Perceptual Organization Index.

While technicians may administer and score intelligence tests under supervision, a properly trained and licensed professional is required to interpret the meaning of intelligence test performance in the context of various cultural, medical, educational, and environmental factors. At present, test publishers in the U.S. voluntarily restrict the sale of IQ tests to qualified professionals. The current trend is to qualify an individual based on demonstrated skill sets (relevant course work, supervised internships, etc.), rather than solely on the educational degree obtained. While some test publishers in the U.S. sponsor training workshops for particular test products, they do not typically credential individuals as qualified examiners, but rather review credentials obtained at university-based master's or doctoral programs in psychology. The professional associations of some related disciplines, most notably counselors, have petitioned in state courts to obtain status as qualified users of intelligence tests. At present, requests from professionals in related disciplines are typically handled on a case by case basis with a review of relevant course work and other forms of training.

Apart from the question of who administers and interprets the intelligence test, there are also issues concerning best practice in some settings. In U.S. public schools a great deal of intelligence testing is mandated by the government through important legislation that began with the Education for All Handicapped Children Act of 1975 (Public Law 94-142) and continues in the Individuals with Disabilities Education Act (IDEA) Amendments of 1997. One cornerstone of this wide-ranging legislation is the requirement that both cognitive ability and academic achievement be assessed in evaluations of learning disabled students. If an achievement score (say, reading comprehension) is significantly below the IQ score, then the student is considered eligible to receive special education services for the learning disabled. There are several methods for determining the significance of the ability-achievement discrepancy which vary considerably in statistical rigor. But, many school districts use the simple difference method which identifies students whose achievement score is one standard deviation (15 points) or more lower than their IQ score.

In this author's opinion, there is clinical value in systematically evaluating a child's academic achievement in relation to expectations derived from his or her overall cognitive ability. This is because low achievement scores alone do not necessarily indicate a learning disability. The student may simply be low in ability. The clinical value of this distinction assumes that there are different expectations and remedial strategies for slow learners and learning disabled students. The irony with this legislation is that while the ability-achievement discrepancy method systematically identifies students in need of assistance, strict reliance on this method may also require that some students with learning disabilities fall behind their peers before they become eligible for educational programs that might help them succeed. As a result, school psychologists sometimes search for ways to qualify for services those students whom they believe need assistance even though they do not meet the discrepancy criteria. As we learn more about the precursors of learning disabilities, there may be little reason to wait to provide services for students believed to be at risk. At the same time, knowledge of overall ability is essential to planning the intervention.

Originally, this legislation required a full assessment for all students in special education every 3 years. Today, an evaluation is still required every 3 years but an intelligence test is not a mandated part of the reevaluation. Given the variability of performance in young children, combined with the many factors that can influence test performance on any given administration, it would seem unwise to allow one score to determine a child's educational future without evidence of consistent findings over time.

In conclusion, the complex interaction of cultural and SES issues, combined with legislative requirements for special educational assessments suggests that users of intelligence tests should be highly qualified professionals.

REFERENCES

Angoff, W. H. (1982). Use of difficulty and discriminating indexes for detecting item bias. In R. A. Berk (Ed.), *Handbook of methods for detecting test bias* (96–116). Baltimore, MD: The Johns Hopkins University Press.

Blaha, J., & Wallbrown, F. H. (1996). Hierarchical factor structure of the Wechsler Intelligence Scale for Children—III. *Psychological Assessment, 8,* 214–218.

Flynn, J. R. (1984). The mean IQ of Americans: Massive gains 1932 to 1978. *Psychological Bulletin, 95,* 29–51.

Flynn, J. R. (1987). Massive gains in 14 nations: What IQ tests really measure: *Psychological Bulletin, 101,* 171–191.

Kaufman, A. S., & Doppelt, J. E. (1976). Analysis of WISC-R standardization data in terms of stratification variables. *Child Development, 47,* 165–171.

Konold, T., Kush, J., & Canivez, G. L. (1997). Factor replication of the WISC-III in three independent samples of children receiving special education. *Journal of Psychoeducational Assessment, 15,* 123–137.

Kush, J. C., Watkins, M. W., Ward, T. J., Ward, S. B., Canivez, G. L., & Worrell, F. C. (2001). Construct validity of the WISC-III for white and black students from the WISC-III standardization sample and for black students referred for psychological evaluation. *School Psychology Review, 30,* 70–88.

Logerquist-Hansen, S., & Barona, A. (1994, August). *Factor structure of the Wechsler Intelligence Scale for Children—III for Hispanic and Non-Hispanic white children with learning disabilities.* Paper presented at the meeting of the American Psychological Association, Los Angeles.

Mattarazzo, J. D. (1990). Psychological assessment versus psychological testing: Validation from Binet to the school, clinic, and courtroom. *American Psychologist, 45,* 999–1017.

Neisser, U., Boodoo, G., Bouchard, T. J., Jr., Boykin, A. W., Brody, N., Ceci, S. J., Halpern, D. F., Loehlin, J. C., Perloff, R., Sternberg, R .J., & Urbina, S. (1996). Intelligence: Knowns and unknowns. *American Psychologist, 51,* 77–101.

Prifitera, A., & Saklofske, D. H. (1998). *WISC-III clinical use and interpretation: Scientist-practitioner perspectives.* San Diego, CA: Academic Press.

Prifitera, A., Weiss, L. G., & Saklofske, D. H. (1998). The WISC-III in context. In A. Prifitera & D. H. Saklofske (Eds.), *WISC-III clinical use and interpretation: Scientist-practitioner perspectives* (pp. 1–38). San Diego, CA: Academic Press.

Reynolds, C. R., & Ford, L. (1994). Comparative three-factor solutions of the WISC-III and WISC-R at 11 age levels between 6 1/2 and 16 1/2 years. *Archives of Clinical Neuropsychology, 9,* 553–570.

Reynolds, C. R., & Kaiser, S. M. (1990). Test bias in psychological assessment. In T. B. Gutkin & C. R. Reynolds (Eds.), *The handbook of school psychology* (2nd ed., pp. 487–525). New York: Wiley.

Reynolds, C. R., Willson, V. L., & Jensen, A. R. (1984, April). *Black-white differenced in simultaneous and sequential processing independent of overall ability differences.* Paper presented at the annual meetings of the American Educational Research Association, New Orleans.

Roid, G. H., Prifitera, A., & Weiss, L. G. (1993). Replication of the WISC-III factor structure in an independent sample. *Journal of Psychoeducational Assessment WISC-III Monograph,* 6–21.

Roid, G. H., & Worrall, W. (1996, August). *Equivalence of factor structure in the U.S. and Canada editions of the WISC-III.* Paper presented at the annual meeting of the American Psychological Association, Toronto.

Sattler, J. M. (1992). *Assessment of children* (revised and updated, 3rd ed.). San Diego, CA: Author.

Sattler, J. M. (2001). *Assessment of children: Cognitive applications* (4th ed.). San Diego, CA: Author.

Sattler, J. M., & Saklofske, D. H. (2001). Wechsler Intelligence Scale for Children—III (WISC-III): Description. In J. M. Sattler, (Ed.), *Assessment of children: Cognitive applications* (4th ed., pp. 220–297) San Diego, CA: Author.

Wechsler, D. (1971). Intelligence: Definition, theory, and the IQ. In R. Cancro (Ed.), *Intelligence genetic and environmental influences* (pp. 50–55). New York: Gruene and Stratton.

Wechsler, D. (1991). *Wechsler Intelligence Scale for Children—Third Edition*. San Antonio, TX: The Psychological Corporation.

Weiss, L. G., & Prifitera, A. (1995). An evaluation of differential prediction of WIAT Achievement scores from WISC-III FSIQ across ethnic and gender groups. *Journal of School Psychology, 33,* 297–304.

Weiss, L. G., Prifitera, A., & Roid, G. H. (1993). The WISC-III and fairness of predicting achievement across ethnic and gender groups. *Journal of Psychoeducational Assessment, Monograph Series, Advances in psychological assessment: Wechsler Intelligence Scale for Children—Third Edition* (pp. 35–42).

Wright, B. D., & Stone, M. H. (1979). *Best test design*. Chicago: MESA Press.

4

CANADA

DONALD H. SAKLOFSKE

Department of Educational Psychology and Special Education
University of Saskatchewan
Saskatoon, Saskatchewan, Canada

Following the publication of the Wechsler Intelligence Scale for Children—Third Edition (WISC-III; Wechsler, 1991), it was decided by The Psychological Corporation offices in Canada and the U.S. to undertake a study that would assess the psychometric properties of this test with a sample of Canadian children and publish Canadian norms, if required. While earlier versions of the Wechsler scales were used extensively by Canadian psychologists, the question that had been increasingly heard was: "How well do the Wechsler intelligence tests travel?" At various times over the past 30–40 years, published articles and conference presentations contained suggestions about the need to "Canadianize" the Wechsler tests. These suggestions included changes to the item content, development of culturally sensitive scoring criteria, and the need for and availability of Canadian norms (see Beal, 1988). Although there was every indication that Canadian psychologists were keen to use the WISC-III for assessing children's intelligence, they were also demanding evidence that would fully support the use of this test for assessing the cognitive abilities of Canadian children.

There were two main issues at the core of this more recent call for evidence to support the use of the WISC-III in Canada. First, there had been considerable debate about the appropriateness of the WISC and WISC-R items when used in Canada. Despite the geographical proximity of Canada and the U.S., and the use of a common language (English) by the majority of their populations, Canadian psychologists had questioned whether there may be some cultural bias in particular items that would consequently disadvantage[1] Canadian children who were administered these tests. The second question related to the norms published in the technical manual. Again the question was posed about the accuracy and appropriateness of American norms for representing the intelligence test performance of Canadian children. While these arguments had been raised mainly on face validity grounds, or reflected the unique experiences of individual examiners, these are questions that can and needed to be addressed empirically. Saklofske and Janzen (1990) had previously stated that Canada would likely continue to use tests developed in the U.S., but that they "may be renormed or modified following the accumulation of data from research and clinical use" (p. 9).

ADAPTATION PROCESS

The Canadian standardization study was begun in 1992 following the publication of the WISC-III in the U.S. and was completed with the publication of the WISC-III Manual, Canadian Supplement in 1996 (Wechsler, 1996). Because the Canadian study began after the publication of the WISC-III in the U.S., the decision was made to use the test as published rather than introduce an alternative protocol with some potential substitute items. As Weiss (Chapter 3) reminds us, an item that may be thought even by experts to be potentially biased, may not be so when examined empirically, using various item bias methods. In spite of the earlier efforts to substitute "so-called" Canadian items into the WISC-R Information subtest, there was no evidence to suggest that they were needed, or that they improved the psychometric qualities or clinical utility of the test (Beal, 1996). Furthermore, the item content of the new WISC-III was much more global in focus. Only three items were singled out as having the potential for bias in the Canadian context. As reported in the manual, the means of these three items were higher for Canadian than American children, the item-total correlations were similar to other items on the same scales, and the reliabilities of the scales containing these items were as high as that found for other scales. With so few items identified on *a priori* grounds and without further empirical support (see p. 30 of WISC-III Manual), the development of Canadian norms would in fact take this into consideration. At the same time, it was decided to remain sensitive to more uniquely Canadian responses to test items.

Thus the test was administered to Canadian children in its published form in contrast to using the standardization version which included many additional items that might be used to replace any items that showed bias and affected subtest reliability.

[1] Canada has two official languages. This chapter is limited to the English version of the WISC-III. The development of French-Canadian norms and the translated manual and test for the Échelle Wechsler d' intelligence pour enfants—Troisième édition will not be described here.

SAMPLE CHARACTERISTICS

Much like the U.S., the demographic characteristics of the Canadian population are constantly changing. Such changes are even more evident in a country that has only 10% of the U.S. population. For many years, Canada has been recognized as a multicultural country and this is reflected in the changing census data and ethnic categories used by Statistics Canada to describe the Canadian population. Within Canada, there is some considerable variation between the provinces both in terms of not only population growth but also in the ethnic composition. For example, both Saskatchewan and Manitoba now have Aboriginal populations that comprise more than 10% of the total provincial populations, and with every indication that their numbers are increasing at a significantly greater rate than other defined groups. However, Canada's Aboriginal peoples comprise slightly less than 3% of the Canadian population. At the same time, they are the most impoverished group in Canada, which is further compounded by having the lowest level of educational attainment.

One of the most obvious changes over a relatively short time period is the educational attainment of Canadian adults. For example, in 1976, 25% of Canadians 15 years and older had less than a grade 9 education in contrast to only 12.5% in 1996. Conversely, 30.5% of Canadians 15 years and older had some post-secondary training or completed university degrees in 1976; in 1996 this figure was 47%. Clearly Canada is becoming a more educated nation with each passing decade, with the mean number of years of schooling estimated at 12.3 years in 1996. As noted by Prifitera, Weiss, and Saklofske (1998), education is both highly correlated with intelligence and socioeconomic status (SES) as reflected in a number of published studies (e.g., Emanuelsson & Svensson, 1990; Bouchard & Segal, 1985; Spitz, 1996; see also Sattler, 2001). This advantage will be passed to the youngest generation. Certainly these factors have also been implicated in the observed increases in measured intelligence in developed countries (i.e., Flynn, 1987, 1999) in recent years.

In contrast to the U.S. WISC-III standardization study, where white, African-American, and Hispanic groups comprise about 95% of the population, Canada does not have such clearly demarcated ethnic groupings. The Canadian WISC-III sample defined by data from Statistics Canada 1986 Census was representative of English-speaking Canadian children, aged 6–16 years, 11 months. The variables that defined the sample included gender (boys and girls), geographic region (east, central, west), ethnic origin (British, French or European, multiple origins, other), and parent education level (8th grade or less, grade 9–13, post-secondary courses or diploma, university degree). The stratified random sampling plan was generated to include 100 children at each of the age 11 age groups ($N = 1100$). Fifty boys and fifty girls were included in the sample at each age. Given the population distribution in Canada, 16.3% of the sample was from the east, 45.4% from the central region, and 38.3% from western Canada. While the complete sampling matrix included all of these variables, Table 4.1 presents the age × ethic origin × parent education level for the sample of 1100 children. As can be seen from the bottom of this table, the sample very closely matched the Canadian population demographics.

RELIABILITY

Reliability indices, reported as split-half coefficients, and standard errors of measurement across the age groups and for the total sample are shown in Table 4.2. Average reliability coefficients for the Verbal IQ (VIQ) and Full Scale IQ (FSIQ) were 0.93 and 0.95, respectively, while the Performance IQ (PIQ) coefficient was 0.89, increasing slightly the measurement error associated with this latter score. As expected, slightly lower reliabilities were observed for the four-factor or index scores, ranging from 0.85 for the Freedom from Distractibility Index (FDI) to 0.93 for the Verbal Comprehension Index (VCI). An inspection of Table 4.2 shows that the average reliability coefficients for the subtests generally fell in the 0.70 and 0.80 ranges. Consistent with the findings from the U.S. standardization study, the Object Assembly subtest yielded the lowest reliability coefficient at 0.61.

Test-retest data were not available for the Canadian sample. Given the similarity of psychometric results between the U.S. and Canadian studies, it was argued that the test-retest findings reported in the U.S. technical manual would likely not differ in "any meaningful way" across the two countries (Wechsler, 1996, p. 35).

EVIDENCE OF VALIDITY

At the outset, there was not much reason to expect that the validity of the WISC-III would vary much for Canadian children from that reported in the U.S. technical manual and the studies that were published since 1991. The most critical issue was to ensure a similar pattern of correlations between the subtests and to demonstrate that they loaded on particular factors as was reported in the U.S. standardization study. It is clear from an inspection of Table 4.3 that the correlations between all subtests were positive and further, manifested a pattern that provided support for the IQ and index score clusters. Table 4.4 presents the results of the exploratory factor analysis that clearly support the four factors: Verbal Comprehension (VC), Perceptual Organization (PO), Freedom from Distractibility (FFD), and Processing Speed (PS). This was confirmed by correlating the factor indices, based on the U.S. analyses, with the factors obtained from the Canadian data analyses. The column on the right side of the table supports a general higher order factor reflected in the FSIQ. "The results are completely as expected from the U.S. analyses...the same IQ and index scores can be used with Canadians as are used in the U.S." (Wechsler, 1996, p. 31). Finally, Roid and Worrall (1997) replicated the WISC-III four-factor structure using confirmatory factor analysis.

TABLE 4.1 Demographic Characteristics of the WISC-III Canadian Study: Percentages by Age, Ethnic Origin, and Parent Education Level

Age	n	British				French/European				Multiple origins				Other			
		≤8[a]	9–13	Post-sec.	Univ. degree	≤8[a]	9–13	Post-sec.	Univ. degree	≤8[a]	9–13	Post-sec.	Univ. degree	≤8[a]	9–13	Post-sec.	Univ. degree
6	100	4	10	11	4	4	4	6	2	7	10	17	11	4	2	2	2
7	100	6	8	10	5	4	6	4	2	7	10	18	10	2	3	2	3
8	100	6	9	10	4	4	5	5	2	7	10	18	10	2	2	3	3
9	100	5	9	10	4	4	5	5	2	7	10	17	11	4	2	3	2
10	100	5	8	11	5	5	4	6	2	8	10	16	10	2	2	3	3
11	100	5	9	10	4	4	6	4	2	7	10	18	10	2	3	3	3
12	100	5	9	11	4	5	5	5	1	7	11	16	10	2	2	3	3
13	100	6	9	10	4	5	5	5	2	7	10	18	10	3	2	2	3
14	100	6	8	10	4	4	5	5	2	7	10	17	10	3	2	2	4
15	100	5	9	11	4	4	5	5	2	7	10	17	10	3	2	2	4
16	100	6	8	10	4	4	6	4	2	7	10	17	11	2	2	3	3
Total	1100	5.3	8.7	10.4	4.3	4.3	5.1	5.0	1.9	7.0	10.1	17.3	10.3	2.5	2.3	2.7	2.8
Canadian population[b]		5.4	8.7	10.4	4.3	4.3	5.1	4.9	1.9	7.1	10.1	17.3	10.3	2.5	2.3	2.6	2.8

[a]Numbers are years of parent education which is the average number of years of school completed by the parent or parents living with the child.
[b]Canadian population date for children aged 6–16 are from a crosstabulation analysis by Statistics Canada based on *Census Canada Survey* 1986 by Statistics Canada, 1987, Ottawa: Supply & Services Canada.

TABLE 4.2 Canadian WISC-III Reliability Coefficients[a] and Standard Error of Measurement[b] for the Subtests, IQ Scales, and Factor-Based Scales by Age

Subtest/scale	Age in years											Average r_{xx}^{a}/SEm[b]
	6	7	8	9	10	11	12	13	14	15	16	
Information	0.84	0.79	0.76	0.79	0.80	0.76	0.87	0.83	0.81	0.87	0.90	0.82
(SEm)	1.20	1.37	1.47	1.37	1.34	1.47	1.08	1.24	1.31	1.08	0.95	1.26
Similarities	0.82	0.79	0.81	0.80	0.83	0.77	0.78	0.83	0.82	0.81	0.88	0.81
(SEm)	1.27	1.37	1.31	1.34	1.24	1.44	1.41	1.24	1.27	1.31	1.04	1.29
Arithmetic	0.73	0.62	0.71	0.51	0.74	0.76	0.82	0.78	0.82	0.78	0.76	0.74
(SEm)	1.56	1.85	1.62	2.10	1.53	1.47	1.27	1.41	1.27	1.41	1.47	1.54
Vocabulary	0.75	0.78	0.84	0.83	0.86	0.86	0.91	0.89	0.90	0.92	0.93	0.87
(SEm)	1.50	1.41	1.20	1.24	1.12	1.12	0.90	0.99	0.95	0.85	0.79	1.10
Comprehension	0.79	0.69	0.75	0.72	0.61	0.73	0.69	0.79	0.60	0.67	0.85	0.73
(SEm)	1.37	1.67	1.50	1.59	1.87	1.56	1.67	1.37	1.90	1.72	1.16	1.58
Digit span	0.76	0.73	0.88	0.81	0.85	0.78	0.88	0.86	0.89	0.90	0.90	0.85
(SEm)	1.47	1.56	1.04	1.31	1.16	1.41	1.04	1.12	0.99	0.95	0.95	1.18
Picture completion	0.84	0.85	0.77	0.70	0.75	0.61	0.75	0.70	0.66	0.66	0.70	0.73
(SEm)	1.20	1.16	1.44	1.64	1.50	1.87	1.50	1.64	1.75	1.75	1.64	1.55
Coding	0.75	0.70	0.78	0.78	0.78	0.82	0.82	0.70	0.70	0.90	0.90	0.80
(SEm)	1.50	1.64	1.41	1.41	1.41	1.27	1.27	1.64	1.64	0.95	0.95	1.37
Picture arrangement	0.78	0.74	0.76	0.70	0.72	0.77	0.72	0.54	0.72	0.71	0.76	0.73
(SEm)	1.41	1.53	1.47	1.64	1.59	1.44	1.59	2.03	1.59	1.62	1.47	1.58
Block design	0.80	0.84	0.79	0.70	0.84	0.86	0.88	0.76	0.82	0.84	0.85	0.82
(SEm)	1.34	1.20	1.37	1.64	1.20	1.12	1.04	1.47	1.27	1.20	1.16	1.28
Object assembly	0.53	0.55	0.56	0.67	0.69	0.50	0.55	0.67	0.58	0.72	0.66	0.61
(SEm)	2.06	2.01	1.99	1.72	1.67	2.12	2.01	1.72	1.94	1.59	1.75	1.87
Symbol search	0.69	0.76	0.72	0.72	0.72	0.79	0.79	0.75	0.75	0.82	0.82	0.76
(SEm)	1.67	1.47	1.59	1.59	1.59	1.37	1.37	1.50	1.50	1.27	1.27	1.47
Mazes	0.77	0.76	0.76	0.83	0.77	0.76	0.78	0.64	0.73	0.75	0.72	0.76
(SEm)	1.44	1.47	1.47	1.24	1.44	1.47	1.41	1.80	1.56	1.50	1.59	1.49

Verbal IQ	0.93	0.90	0.93	0.91	0.93	0.92	0.94	0.94	0.93	0.95	0.96	0.93
(SEm)	3.92	4.65	3.94	4.53	3.89	4.12	3.55	3.59	3.83	3.42	2.88	3.85
Performance IQ	0.89	0.89	0.88	0.87	0.88	0.89	0.90	0.83	0.88	0.91	0.92	0.89
(SEm)	4.89	5.07	5.24	5.35	5.12	5.01	4.67	6.10	5.13	4.38	4.30	5.02
Full scale IQ	0.94	0.93	0.94	0.93	0.95	0.94	0.96	0.93	0.94	0.96	0.97	0.95
(SEm)	3.59	3.91	3.57	3.93	3.50	3.63	3.16	3.87	3.52	2.98	2.70	3.49
Verbal comprehension	0.93	0.91	0.93	0.92	0.93	0.92	0.93	0.94	0.92	0.94	0.97	0.93
(SEm)	4.10	4.59	4.08	4.27	4.10	4.32	3.91	3.66	4.28	3.60	2.77	3.97
Perceptual organization	0.88	0.89	0.86	0.86	0.88	0.86	0.88	0.85	0.88	0.89	0.90	0.88
(SEm)	5.14	5.05	5.54	5.58	5.21	5.55	5.09	5.86	5.26	4.90	4.72	5.27
Freedom from distractibility	0.84	0.77	0.84	0.76	0.86	0.82	0.90	0.87	0.90	0.89	0.88	0.85
(SEm)	5.99	7.15	6.02	7.30	5.55	6.28	4.85	5.51	4.68	4.89	5.16	5.76
Processing speed	0.81	0.80	0.86	0.83	0.84	0.88	0.88	0.82	0.82	0.91	0.91	0.86
(SEm)	6.62	6.70	5.70	6.17	5.91	5.26	5.15	6.37	6.35	4.45	4.59	5.75

Note: $N = 100$ for each age group.

[a]The reliability coefficients for all subtests except Coding and Symbol Search are split-half correlations corrected by the Spearman-Brown formula. Coding and Symbol Search raw-score correlations were corrected for the variability of the standardization group (Guilford & Fruchter, 1978). The coefficients for the IQ and factor-based scales were calculated with the formula for the reliability of a composite (Nunnally, 1978); the values for the supplementary subtest (Digit Span, Mazes, and Symbol Search) were not included in these computations. The average r was computed with Fisher's z transformation. For Coding and Symbol Search, reliabilities can only be computed from test-retest data; hence test-retest reliability coefficients from the U.S. WISC-III Technical Manual were used and reported here. The best estimates of the reliability coefficients at an age level for which retesting was not done is the value obtained at the adjacent age level. The exception is for age 8, for which the most reasonable estimate is the value obtained at age 10—the closest age at which Level B of these subtests is administered. (Level A is administered to children younger than age 8.) These "best estimates" for Coding and Symbol Search were used for computing the reliabilities of the composites to which these subtests contribute.

[b]The standard errors of measurement are reported in scaled-score units for the subtests, in IQ units for the Verbal, Performance, and Full Scale scores, and in index units for the Verbal Comprehension, Perceptual Organization, Freedom from Distractibility, and Processing Speed Scores. The reliability coefficients shown in Table 4.2 and the population standard deviations (i.e., 3 for the subtests and 15 for the IQ and index scores) were used to compute the standard errors of measurement. The average SEms were calculated by averaging the sum of the squared SEms for each age group and obtaining the square root of the result. For Coding and Symbol Search, the best estimates of the standard error of measurement at an age level for which retesting was not done is the value obtained at the adjacent age level. The exception is for age 8, as explained above in footnote *a*.

Wechsler Intelligence Scale for Children: Third Edition. Copyright © 1991 by The Psychological Corporation, a Harcourt Assessment Company, USA. Canadian adaptation copyright © 1996 by The Psychological Corporation, USA. Reproduced by permission. All rights reserved.

TABLE 4.3 Intercorrelations of WISC-III Subtest Scaled Scores, IQs and Indexes: Average of All Ages for Canadian Children

Subtest/scale	Inf	Sim	Ari	Voc	Com	DS	PCom	Cd	PA	BD	OA	SS	Mz	VIQ	PIQ	FSIQ	VC	PO	FD	PS
Information														0.83		0.74	0.83			
Similarities	0.63													0.83		0.78	0.85			
Arithmetic	0.54	0.49												0.73		0.71			0.86	
Vocabulary	0.67	0.69	0.49											0.86		0.76	0.88			
Comprehension	0.50	0.53	0.43	0.58										0.76		0.67	0.78			
Digit span	0.34	0.33	0.44	0.34	0.26														0.84	
Picture completion	0.39	0.43	0.38	0.39	0.36	0.21									0.70	0.65		0.74		
Coding (A & B)	0.20	0.24	0.26	0.23	0.26	0.26	0.20								0.57	0.47				0.88
Picture arrangement	0.37	0.41	0.34	0.37	0.30	0.20	0.39	0.26							0.69	0.62		0.71		
Block design	0.38	0.44	0.47	0.37	0.32	0.27	0.46	0.31	0.38						0.78	0.70		0.79		
Object assembly	0.35	0.38	0.33	0.35	0.28	0.18	0.41	0.21	0.35	0.54					0.72	0.63		0.76		
Symbol search (A & B)	0.29	0.34	0.39	0.29	0.32	0.27	0.27	0.55	0.33	0.43	0.31									0.88
Mazes	0.20	0.22	0.25	0.19	0.20	0.15	0.24	0.12	0.20	0.36	0.29	0.20								
Verbal IQ	0.73	0.73	0.58	0.76	0.61	0.43	0.49	0.29	0.45	0.49	0.42	0.40	0.26		0.62	0.91	0.98	0.61	0.69	0.40
Performance IQ	0.48	0.55	0.51	0.49	0.44	0.32	0.51	0.32	0.48	0.61	0.54	0.55	0.35	0.62		0.89	0.59	0.96	0.49	0.64
Full scale IQ	0.66	0.71	0.61	0.69	0.58	0.42	0.56	0.34	0.51	0.60	0.52	0.53	0.34	0.91	0.89		0.88	0.87	0.66	0.57
Verbal comp. Index	0.70	0.73	0.58	0.77	0.61	0.38	0.47	0.28	0.43	0.45	0.41	0.37	0.24	0.98	0.59	0.88		0.58	0.57	0.37
Percep. org. Index	0.49	0.55	0.51	0.49	0.42	0.28	0.54	0.32	0.46	0.60	0.56	0.45	0.36	0.61	0.96	0.87	0.58		0.47	0.44
Free. fr. distr. Index	0.52	0.48	0.44	0.49	0.41	0.44	0.35	0.30	0.32	0.44	0.30	0.39	0.24	0.69	0.49	0.66	0.57	0.47		0.39
Proc. speed Index	0.28	0.33	0.37	0.30	0.33	0.30	0.27	0.55	0.33	0.42	0.30	0.55	0.18	0.40	0.64	0.57	0.37	0.44	0.39	
Mean	10.1	10.0	10.0	10.1	10.0	10.1	10.0	10.0	10.0	10.0	10.1	10.1	10.2	50.2	50.1	100.2	40.2	40.1	20.1	20.1
SD	2.9	3.0	3.0	3.1	3.0	2.9	3.0	3.2	3.2	3.3	3.1	3.2	3.4	12.0	10.9	20.6	10.0	9.5	5.0	5.6

Note: for Tables C.1–C.12 see text (pp. 186–187) in the WISC-III Manual for a description of the procedures used for calculating these values.

TABLE 4.4   Canadian WISC-III Factor Analytic Results

			Factors		
Scale	1	2	3	4	IQ
A. Largest correlations of the factors with the 12 scales					
Information	0.78				0.66
Similarities	0.81				0.69
Arithmetic			0.74		0.66
Vocabulary	0.85				0.68
Comprehension	0.67				0.57
Digit span			0.57		0.45
Picture completion		0.63			0.52
Coding				0.68	0.43
Picture arrangement		0.54			0.49
Block design		0.75			0.61
Object assembly		0.67			0.50
Symbol search				0.75	0.54
Mazes (not in factor analysis)	0.25	0.22	0.34	0.25	0.29
B. Largest correlations with IQ and index scores from U.S. factor analyses					
Verbal IQ	0.92 (0.99)				0.81
Performance IQ		0.84 (0.95)			0.73
Verbal comp.	0.92 (0.99)				0.77
Percep. org.		0.86 (0.98)			0.71
Free fr. distr.			0.77 (0.91)		0.66
Processing speed				0.81 (0.94)	0.55
Full scale IQ					0.86 (0.97)

Note: The value in parentheses is corrected for attenuation due to unreliability of the composite scales and the unreliability of the factors as estimates.

Wechsler Intelligence Scale for Children: Third Edition. Copyright © 1991 by The Psychological Corporation, a Harcourt Assessment Company, USA. Canadian adaptation copyright © 1996 by The Psychological Corporation, USA. Reproduced with permission. All rights reserved.

CULTURAL ISSUES INFLUENCING WISC-III INTERPRETATION IN CANADA

Summarizing the findings of the Canadian WISC-III study, the psychometric properties (e.g., reliability, factor structure) were strongly supported. It was observed that Canadian children, in comparison with the U.S. standardization sample, earned significantly higher IQ and index scores: FSIQ = 3.34, VIQ = 1.40, PIQ = 4.96, VC = 1.67, PO = 4.91, FFD = 1.03, and PS = 2.99.

Significantly higher ($p < 0.05$) subtest scores on all but two subtests (Information and Arithmetic) were also observed for the whole Canadian sample. Furthermore, all subtests except Arithmetic, Digit Span, Block Design, and Symbol Search, showed significant differences between the Canadian and U.S. standardization samples across the IQ range. However, the distributions of scores did not always follow the same trends for Canadian children in comparison to the

American children, with approximately 1% (versus the expected 2%) of Canadian children scoring above an FSIQ of 130 (2 standard deviations above the mean). A related finding occurred in the 70–79 IQ range. Various statistical tests (e.g., sampling error) assured the integrity of the data but did not discover why these differences occurred; of course the study was not designed for the purpose of explaining observed differences. Stated in the manual was the position that "the data are sufficient to conclude that the Canadians did differ somewhat from the U.S. normative sample and consequently new statistical tables would be desirable" (p. 30).

The published Canadian WISC-III norms that resulted from the above findings now permit the comparison of Canadian children to a Canadian national mean. This does result in Canadian children earning slightly lower IQ and index scores when Canadian norms are used. Together with score distribution differences, these findings have important implications when particular scores are used for classification purposes. It is therefore recommended that the Canadian norms be used when assessing children with the WISC-III in Canada. For example, using U.S. norms may yield slightly higher scores in most instances but at the same time, about 1% of Canadian children would fail to be identified in the FSIQ = 130 and above grouping. Of course there are times when the use of U.S. norms may be meaningfully and appropriately used in Canada. These might include instances where the WISC-III has been linked with other tests including the WISC-R and WIAT-II, as well as in longitudinal studies.

Of interest is that while the psychometric properties of the test certainly are in line with those reported for the U.S. WISC-III standardization study, item statistics indicated that all of the items used for the U.S. version were also appropriate for use in Canada. This has been a somewhat controversial issue in Canada, and, in the main, has been based on "armchair speculation." Earlier, Beal (1988) showed that most of the controversy surrounding the Information subtest of the WISC-R had no empirical foundation. At the same time, it was expected that questions about the relevance and position of items such as "senators and congressmen" might be asked by some Canadian psychologists. These data allowed for the following conclusion: "the means of the suspect items for Canadian children were actually higher than they were for the U.S. normative children, the item-total correlations were indistinguishable from the other items on the same scales, and the reliabilities of the scales which had a possible U.S.-biased items were just as high as other scales" (p. 30). However, it was deemed necessary to include an appendix in the manual which contains scoring guidelines for uniquely Canadian responses.

The Canadian manual contains several useful sections that should aid the examiner in administering and scoring the WISC-III when administered to a child in Canada. Lynne Beal's (1996) section on the "importance of Canadian norms to the Canadian school system" and the discussion by Fred French (1996) of "Canadian norms and the assessment of learning disabilities" integrate these Canadian findings into the area of practice. Don Saklofske (1996) described how "using the WISC-III Canadian study results in academic research" will further our understanding of the clinical utility of this test in the Canadian context.

Following the publication of the WISC-III Canadian manual, several more recent publications have provided additional important information of relevance to the Canadian context. It was noted that a number of practical questions were being posed by examiners that related to the differences between Canadian and U.S. norms. Specific questions included how the new Canadian norms would affect the scoring and interpretation of the WISC-III in general, but also in relation to special groups such as children who may be intellectually gifted or who have learning disabilities. While the manual provided considerable technical information, a "questions and answers to the WISC-III manual Canadian supplement" was published in 1997 by The Psychological Corporation. Questions posed by practicing psychologists were gathered and succinctly addressed by Lynne Beal, Don Saklofske, and Richard Gorsuch (1997).

Since then, journal articles of relevance to the Canadian context have appeared, mainly in the *Canadian Journal of School Psychology*. In 1996, a special issue of this journal was devoted to the Wechsler tests and included papers ranging from the development of WISC-III short forms for Canadian children with learning disabilities (Beal, 1996) to a comparison of scoring errors made on the WISC-III and WISC-R (Klassen & Kishor, 1996). Mark, Beal, and Dumont (1998) have proposed a WISC-III short-form for identifying Canadian gifted children, most recently re-examined by Reiter (2001). Weiss, Saklofske, Prifitera, Chen, and Hildebrand (1999) have presented tables for calculating the WISC-III general ability index (GAI) using Canadian norms. This paper stems from earlier work by Prifitera, Weiss, and Saklofske (1998) suggesting that the eight subtests comprising the VC and PO factors could be summarized to estimate FSIQ. The correlation of FSIQ and GAI for the Canadian sample was 0.98. As another example of how the WISC-III has been adapted to the Canadian scene, Kaufman (1994) recommended that Symbol Search be routinely substituted for Coding even though the usual method for calculating PIQ employs the Coding subtest. Canadian norms tables for calculating PIQ and FSIQ scores when Symbol Search replaces Coding were recently published (Saklofske, Hildebrand, Reynolds, & Willson, 1998). Another example of a recent advancement to aid the clinical interpretation of test scores is the use of base rate tables that present the frequency of occurrence of score discrepancies. Table B.2 in the Canadian manual only presented cumulative percentages of VIQ-PIQ and index score discrepancies independent of direction. New tables presenting bi-directional base rates for different ability levels are being made available to Canadian psychologists (Saklofske, Tulsky, Wilkins, & Weiss, 2003).

PROFESSIONAL ISSUES IN THE USE OF THE WISC-III IN CANADA

The purpose of the Canadian WISC-III standardization study was to confirm support for the psychometric integrity of this test, determine if any modifications or changes were required in the item content, and to publish new norms tables as required. At the outset, it was agreed that the most useful normative tables would be based on a national sample of Canadian children rather than on particular sub-groups or based on other demographic variables (e.g., region, parent education level). While demographic-corrected norms can be created for any specific variable (e.g., group membership) two questions immediately come to the fore. What purpose would be served by such norms, and, if item changes were required for various different groups, how would the results from these different versions of the WISC-III within Canada be understood and used?

As stated before, Canada is committed to the ideal of multiculturalism. New immigrants arrive daily, and the shift from mainly immigrants of European heritage to those from third-world countries has been observed in recent years. For example, in 1985 only 84,000 immigrants were admitted to Canada but by 1992, the number increased to 250,000. Prior to 1961, 90% of immigrants arriving in Canada were European-born, but between 1981–1991, this number dropped to 25% (Sorensen & Krahn, 1996). This trend continues such that the population demographics of Canada will continue to change. By the turn of the century, demographic projections indicate that racial and ethnocultural minorities will rise to almost half the populations in some urban areas. Also, within Canada there are unique groups with a long-standing history, but even they show considerable diversity. For example, taking the very narrow category "Indian" within the broader term "aboriginal," Frideres (1993) notes that there are eleven major linguistic Indian groups who live within six recognized cultural regions. While there are clear statistics showing "group" variations in education, income, and other socioeconomic markers, Canadian natives are among the poorest people in Canada with the lowest level of education, and are more often incarcerated than non-Native groups. Previous research using the WISC-R with small samples of Native children have shown lower IQ scores as well as more common VIQ < PIQ discrepancies (e.g., Common & Frost, 1988).

In contrast to the U.S. where the population demographics may still be "roughly" classified according to white, African-American, and Hispanic, this is not the case in Canada, a country that is only 10% the size of the U.S. population. In Canada, studies have not been conducted to examine the effects or interaction between variables such as ethnicity, parent education, and WISC-III scores. The evidence from American studies showing the effects of SES etc., on intelligence, as reported in Chapter 3 would certainly likely hold in Canada. There is compelling and robust data that describes the relationship between SES, parent education, and home and community factors and intelligence test scores (see Sattler, 2001). What these studies tell is that we must be sensitive to effect or influence that such factors have on intelligence test scores for both groups and individuals. It is important to remember that while the scores from the WISC-III or any other intelligence test tell us a child's ability relative to other children, it does not tell us what caused the score. Also if there is reason to believe that a particular child is "unique" relative to the children for whom the test was normed, that information must be factored into the interpretative report. So if we find that a 7-year-old Native child who has lived in a remote area of northern Canada, speaks Cree as a first language, has never been to school, etc., obtains a VIQ of 68 and a PIQ of 97, we should not necessarily be surprised by this VIQ-PIQ discrepancy. More importantly, one would certainly not interpret this VIQ to suggest borderline verbal ability in a "fixed" sense. If, however, this child who obtained the same VIQ and PIQ as above is of Native ancestry, but grew up in a large city, only spoke English, attended both preschool and kindergarten, etc., then our interpretation would be quite different (e.g., verbal learning disability).

The point here is that we can be informed by test scores but they can never be removed from the context of the child and his/her world. It is for this reason that one could say that there are a hundred ways of earning an FSIQ of 100 (e.g., VIQ = 100 and PIQ = 100; VIQ = 120, PIQ = 80) and there are a many reasons for, and ways of interpreting or more appropriately understanding an FSIQ of 100 (pre-head injury FSIQ = 139; extreme test anxiety but with evidence suggesting the child is a gifted musician, and excels in mathematics and science).

Previously published studies with the WISC and WISC-R have suggested that some "unique" groups of Canadian children may show IQ and subtest score differences. This can be expected whenever a subset of a population that does not necessarily share exactly the same characteristics in the same proportions is compared to the population. The *Principles for Fair Student Assessment Practices for Education in Canada* (1993) advises test developers that they have a responsibility to "warn against using published norms with students who are not part of the population. . ." On the other hand, users are expected to "interpret scores taking account of major differences between norm group(s) or comparison groups(s) and the students being assessed. . . (and) examine the need for local norms, and if called for, develop these norms" (p. 18). There is certainly a shared responsibility between test developers and users to ensure that tests such as the WISC-III serve to aid us in understanding individual differences in children.

Finally, a comment is necessary to reflect issues related to test "use" and the test "user." In contrast to the U.S., Canada has not engaged in as much open and direct criticism toward the use of intelligence tests in particular. However, there are certainly strong feelings in both the public and professional sector that can, and do influence assessment practices. Because the Wechsler tests are the most often used measures for assessing the cognitive abilities of children, tests such as the WISC-III are frequently identified when intelligence tests in general are criticized (e.g., "A child was WISC-ed"). For example, it was not uncommon that a simple discrepancy between a WISC-R or WISC-III score and a basic achievement measure served as the basis for a diagnosis of learning disability. Today, we are much more knowledgeable about various kinds of learning disabilities, and the need for a comprehensive assessment, that may include but is not limited to a cognitive measure such as the WISC-III. Or we may hear of a child who was misdiagnosed as having limited intelligence and placed in a class for intellectually challenged children when, in fact, the child was deaf, or non-English speaking.

Both of these examples point as much or more so to issues centered around who can access and use tests.

To address these issues, The Psychological Corporation has clear guidelines for purchasers of tests such as the WISC-III. As well, graduate psychology programs are much more sensitive and responsive to training competency issues related to assessment. Professional associations such as the Canadian Psychological Association (1995, 1996) and the Canadian Association of School Psychologists frequently include opportunities for psychologists to improve and update their assessment skills and knowledge. The Psychological Corporation and other test publishers, also sponsor many workshops related to test administration, scoring, and interpretation. Articles focusing on responsible test use are published in journals and professional associations have developed guidelines for educational and psychological testing. Certainly the ethics codes and professional standards guidelines so carefully crafted by the professional associations provide clear guidance in matters of assessment. Finally, the psychology regulatory bodies in some Canadian provinces now have a section of their regulatory act that describes "who" is deemed professionally competent to diagnose and to communicate the results of a diagnosis. Given our ever increasing knowledge about human intelligence reflected in contemporary tests and their responsible use by highly trained and competent psychologists, the WISC-III and future editions will certainly remain in the forefront of such measures.

REFERENCES

Beal, A. L. (1988). Canadian content in the WISC-R: Bias or jingoism. *Canadian Journal of Behavioural Science, 20*, 154–166.

Beal, A. L. (1996). The importance of Canadian norms to the Canadian school system. In D. Wechsler, *WISC-III Manual Canadian Supplement* (pp. 2–5). Toronto, ON: The Psychological Corporation.

Beal, A. L., Saklofske, D. H., & Gorsuch, R. L. (1997). Questions and answers to the WISC-III manual Canadian supplement. Toronto: ON: The Psychological Corporation.

Bouchard, T. J. Jr., & Segal, N. L. (1985). Environment and IQ. In B. B. Wolman (Ed.), *Handbook of intelligence: Theories, measurements, and applications.* (pp. 391–464). New York: Wiley.

Canadian Psychological Association (1995). *Companion manual to the Canadian code of ethics for psychologists (1991).* Ottawa, ON: Author.

Canadian Psychological Association (1996). *Guidelines for educational and psychological testing.* Ottawa, ON: Author.

Common, R., & Frost, L. (1988). The implications of the mismeasurement of Indian students through the use of standardized intelligence tests. *Canadian Journal of Native Education, 15*, 18–30.

Emanuelsson, I., & Svensson, A. (1990). Changes in intelligence over a quarter of a century. *Scandanivian Journal of Educational Research, 34*, 171–187.

Flynn, J. R. (1987). Massive IQ gains in 14 nations: What IQ testing really measures. *Psychological Bulletin, 86*, 171–191.

Flynn, J. R. (1999). Searching for justice: The discovery of IQ gains over time. *American Psychologist, 54*, 5–20.

Frideres, J. (1993). Native peoples. In P. S. Li, & B. S. Bolaria (Eds.), *Contemporary sociology: Critical perspectives.* Toronto, ON: Copp Clark Pitman.

Kaufman, A. S. (1994). *Intelligent testing with the WISC-III.* New York: John Wiley & Sons.

Klassen, R. M., & Kishor, N. (1996). A comparative analysis of practitioner's errors on WISC-R and WISC-III. *Canadian Journal of School Psychology, 12,* 35–43.

Mark, R., Beal, A. L., & Dumont, R. (1998). Validation of a WISC-III short-form for the identification of Canadian gifted students. *Canadian Journal of School Psychology, 14,* 1–10.

Prifitera, A., Weiss, L. G., & Saklofske, D. H. (1998). The WISC-III in context. In A. Prifitera & D. H. Saklofske (Eds.), *WISC-III clinical use and interpretation: Scientist-practitioner perspective.* San Diego, CA: Academic Press.

Principles for Fair Student Assessment Practices for Education in Canada (1993). Edmonton, Alberta: Joint Advisory Committee.

Reiter, B. A. (2001). *A comparison of WISC-III short forms for the screening of gifted elementary students in Canada.* Unpublished Ph.D. dissertation. University of Calgary.

Roid, G. H., & Worrall, W. (1997). Replication of the Wechsler Intelligence Scale for Children-Third Edition: Four-factor model in the Canadian normative sample. *Psychological Assessment, 9,* 512–515.

Saklofske, D. H. (1996). Using the WISC-III Canadian study results in academic research. In D. Wechsler *WISC-III Manual Canadian Supplement* (pp. 5–13). Toronto, ON: The Psychological Corporation.

Saklofske, D. H., Hildebrand, D. K., Reynolds, C. R., & Willson, V. L. (1998). Substituting symbol search for coding on the WISC-III: Canadian normative tables for performance and full scale IQ scores. *Canadian Journal of Behavioural Science, 30,* 57–68.

Saklofske, D. H., & Janzen, H. L. (1990). School-based assessment research in Canada. *McGill Journal of Education, 25,* 5–23.

Saklofske, D. H., Tulsky, D. S., Wilkins, C., & Weiss, L. G. (2003). Canadian base rates for the WISC-III; Directional differences by ability level. *Canadian Journal of Behavioural Science.* In press.

Sattler, J. M. (2001). *Assessment of children: Cognitive applications* (4th ed.). San Diego, CA: Author.

Sorensen, M., & Krahn, H. (1996). Attitudes toward immigrants: A test of two theories. *The Alberta Journal of Educational Research, XLII,* 3–18.

Spitz, H. H. (1996). Commentary on contributions to this volume. In D. K. Detterman (Ed.), *Current topics in human intelligence: Vol. 5. The environment* (pp. 173–177). Norwood, NJ: Ablex.

Statistics Canada (1986). *Census Canada 1986 Survey.* Ottawa, ON: Supply and Services Canada.

Wechsler, D. (1991). *Wechsler Intelligence Scale for Children—Third Edition.* San Antonio, TX: The Psychological Corporation.

Wechsler, D. (1996). *WISC-III Manual Canadian Supplement.* Toronto, ON: The Psychological Corporation.

Weiss, L. G. (2003). United States. In J. Georgas, L. Weiss, F. J. R. van de Vijver, & D. H. Saklofske (Eds.). *Culture and children's intelligence: Cross-cultural analysis of the WISC-III* (pp. 41–59). San Diego: Academic Press.

Weiss, L. G., Saklofske, D. H., Prifitera, A., Chen, H., & Hildebrand, D. K. (1999). The calculation of the WISC-III general ability index using Canadian norms. *Canadian Journal of School Psychology, 14,* 1–9.

5

UNITED KINGDOM

PAUL MCKEOWN

The Psychological Corporation, Europe
London, United Kingdom

Psychologists in the United Kingdom are in the fortunate position of being able to tap more easily than colleagues in many other countries into the largest and most dynamic test environment in the world—the U.S. A British comedian once commented that one of the key difference between the UK, and the U.S. was that "we speak English." However, in reality, there are such a large number of consistencies in language, culture, values, and educational objectives that tests travel relatively easily from the U.S. to the UK, and the process of "translation," adaptation, and standardization is much more straightforward than in other countries.[1]

Prior to the Wechsler Intelligence Scale for Children—Third Edition (WISC-III), there had been a long history of WISC adaptations in the UK. The WISC^{UK} had been adapted at a fairly superficial level, the WISC-R^{UK} had included a more thorough review and adaptation of items, and provision of "linking" and reliability data for the new items. Both the WISC^{UK} and the WISC-R^{UK} used the U.S. norms for the respective tests. The rationale for this being the perceived links between the two populations (see above), the relatively small number of changes to the test, and the consistency of data, in the case of the WISC-R^{UK} for the changed items when compared with the U.S. original.

---

[1]This chapter is largely based on the examiner's manual for the WISC III^{UK}. Extracts and data are reproduced with permission and must not be reproduced in any format without permission from the publisher. Requests for permission should be directed to The Psychological Corporation Ltd, Harcourt Place, 32 Jamestown Road, London NW1 7BY, United Kingdom.

However, despite this history of acceptable adaptation and use of the test, with the WISC-III development it was argued that it would be necessary to undertake a more thorough adaptation of the test for the UK, with the provision of more substantial UK data. It should be noted that "market" considerations were a major driver in this decision. The UK is one of the few countries where psychologists have a viable local alternative to the WISC series—The British Ability Scales (BAS— published in the U.S. and Denmark as the DAS; Elliot, 1983), first published in the UK in the mid-70s and with full UK standardization. It was apparent by the late 80s that, for the WISC series to compete effectively with the BAS more comprehensive UK data would need to be provided for the WISC-III^{UK}.

The WISC-III^{UK} project began in 1991 with the test being published in March 1992 (Wechsler, 1992). The proximity in time to the U.S. original was an important part of the project. It was important to send a strong message to the UK psychologists that their assessment needs were being taken seriously and that they would have the most up- to-date and widely used instruments available at almost the same time as their U.S. peers. The project was funded by the UK office of The Psychological Corporation. The research project was managed and delivered by Professor Susan Golombok (City University, London) and Dr. John Rust (Goldsmiths College, University of London). They were responsible for managing all phases of the project including review and adaptation of items, training of test examiners, data collection, coordination of examiners, all data analysis, and contributions to the relevant section of the adapted manual for the WISC-III^{UK}. It is a testament to their skill and professionalism that all relevant materials were delivered to The Psychological Corporation on schedule and in budget ready for UK publication in 1992.

ADAPTATION PROCESS

As indicated above, all items were subject to review before inclusion in the WISC-III^{UK}. This process was managed by Professor Golombok and Dr. Rust, and included input from recognized expert practitioners, researchers, and academics in UK Educational Psychology. The UK project had the advantage of not only being very close to the U.S. original, but also the history of adapted items from the WISC-R^{UK}. In some ways the WISC-III^{UK} project was a development from the WISC-R^{UK}, in the same way that the U.S. original developed from the WISC-R. There is also a clear principle in UK adaptation of U.S. tests that as few items as possible are amended in any way. The intention is for the UK version to be as close as possible to the U.S. original. As a result of this approach only 3 of the 13 subtests (Arithmetic, Comprehension, and Information) have notable changes, 1 (Picture Completion) has 2 inconsequential labeling amendments and 9 of the subtests use exactly the same items as the U.S. original.

There are two reasons for this minimalist approach. First, the U.S. Wechsler projects are probably the most thorough and psychometrically sound projects of their type in the world. Tryout and pilot phases in the U.S. frequently exceed the size and scope of the main phase of the projects undertaken in other countries. Sample sizes, the resources allocated to development, and the rigors of the U.S. market result in items, scales, and whole tests which already possess the highest levels of discrimination, reliability, and validity. To paraphrase a UK saying, it is important to avoid re-inventing the wheel. Secondly, changes are likely to result in *more* data collection, expense, and delays. It is clearly in the interests of the potential users of the test that it is delivered in the most timely and cost-effective fashion. Given these factors it was not deemed necessary in the UK to repeat the tryout and pilot phase of the U.S. project. It was accepted if the main adaptation exercise showed reasonably close equivalence—and this had been the experience in previous editions—that much of the original U.S. data could be applied to the UK test. Consequently the project was able to move directly from expert adaptation to main data collection.

As indicated above there were some minor changes to subtests. In Arithmetic U.S. dollars were replaced with UK pounds, cookies became cakes, candy became chocolate, etc. For Comprehension "number plates" was replaced by "license plates," "Senators" became "MPs," ("TDs" for use in the Republic of Ireland). In Information the controversial U.S. claim to the invention of the light bulb (every self-respecting UK student knows it was in fact a chemist in Newcastle-upon-Tyne named Swan—and there are least three other countries which also claim this as their invention) was replaced by the telephone. The major point to note is how few changes there were to the U.S. original. None of the changes could be described as controversial. The items for 10 of the 13 subtests were the same as the U.S. original. Any changes made were also consistent with those which had been used for the WISC-R^{UK}. Because of this approach and the subsequent data, the user of the UK adaptation can be comfortable with the norms from the UK sample— and their interpretation—being supported by the much larger U.S. sample and its excellent reliability and validity.

SAMPLE CHARACTERISTICS

The primary objective of the UK project was to achieve a valid normative frame of reference for the assessment of children in the UK in the 6–16 age range. The accumulated research suggests that any observed differences between U.S. and UK IQ test scores may largely be attributable to time of testing in relation to the date of test standardization—the so-called "Flynn effect." Other possible factors affecting the differences in IQ scores may be associated with differences in the age that schooling begins and typical patterns of school-leaving which differ between the two countries. The UK validation project was designed to clarify the relationship between ability levels in the UK and the U.S. and to generate sufficient additional data to support the preparation of a set of UK transformation tables. As emphasized, the aim was to extract maximum benefit from the extensive

U.S. development and standardization exercise through simultaneous development and to use the power of concurrent U.S. data to underpin the results of a UK validation study.

The U.S. standardization project results confirmed that the WISC-III achieved very high levels of reliability and sound estimates of the standard error of measurement. The UK project team aimed to achieve an additional 800 administrations to provide UK norms that would parallel those derived from the larger U.S. standardization sample.

Participation in the U.S. team from the initial processes of item review was designed to limit the necessity for subsequent revisions to the test that would increase the difference between U.S. and UK editions. The original pool of U.S. items was reviewed to establish their appropriateness in the UK. The attempt to achieve a single set of linguistic and pictorial references having a common cultural value on both sides of the Atlantic presented a significant challenge, particularly when added to all the other constraints involved in the processes of item selection. However, the cultural diversity to be addressed is even more challenging. The difficulty of finding pictorial references culturally appropriate for children from such a variety of locations inevitably involves some compromise. The problem becomes even more complicated when the ethnic demography of each of these societies is so varied. While the majority of items in the final U.S. selection work in the UK and throughout Europe, a small number of artwork changes have been required for the UK edition of the test kit. These changes have subsequently been used as the basis for the WISC-III in the rest of Europe.

The WISC-III^{UK} norms were derived from a validation sample representative of the UK population of children. A stratified random sampling plan was used to ensure that representative proportions of children from each demographic group would be included in the validation sample. Data gathered from the Office of Population Censuses and Surveys (OPCS) and Labour Force Surveys provided the basis for stratification by geographic region, race/ethnicity, and socioeconomic status as measured by parental employment. Within the overall cell structure, equal numbers of children were targeted for each sex and age from 6–16 years inclusive. The following sections present the characteristics of the WISC-III^{UK} validation sample.

The validation sampling targeted 814 cases representing 37 boys and 37 girls for each of 11 age groups ranging from 6–16 years. The categories used, following consultation with the Commission for Racial Equality, were (1) Indian, Pakistani, or Bangladeshi, (2) West Indian or African, (3) White and, (4) Other. Each child in the standardization sample was categorized by his or her parent(s) as belonging to one of these races/ethnic groups. For each age group, the target ratios for ethnic groups were based on the race/ethnicity proportions of adults in the UK population according to the 1985/86 Labour Force Survey (OPCS, 1989) separately for each geographic region. OPCS gives race/ethnicity proportions for the population as a whole and does not provide any breakdown by age, so that there is currently no population data available in the UK on the proportion of ethnic minority children of school age. In light of this the proportion for ethnic minorities as a whole (4.3% in 1984) was adjusted upward to 7% as it was felt preferable to err on the side of over-rather than undersampling for these groups. Figures on race/ethnicity were not available for Northern Ireland. Equal numbers of children from Catholic and Protestant schools were targeted for this region.

The UK was divided into 12 geographic regions: Wales, Scotland, Northern Ireland, and, within England, the North of England, Yorkshire and Humberside, the East Midlands, East Anglia, South East England (excluding Greater London), Greater London, South West England, the West Midlands, and the North East. Children were targeted in accordance with the proportions of all people living in each region in 1989 (OPCS, 1990). Areas of different population density within each region were targeted on the basis of the general density characteristics of that region.

In regard to socioeconomic status, the sample was stratified within each region on the basis of the 1989 Labour Force Survey data on social class of heads of households. The categories used were: Professional, Intermediate, Skilled non-manual, Skilled manual, Partly skilled manual, Unskilled, and Long-term unemployed. Data on heads of household unemployed for less than 3 years were rolled up into the appropriate employment category for their most recent job. Information on employment was obtained from parental consent forms. If both parents lived with the child and were working, then the highest socioeconomic status was used. Where only one parent lived with the child then the occupation of that parent was used.

A matrix of the seven socioeconomic status levels by 12 geographic regions for each combination of sex, age, and race/ethnicity formed the basis of the sampling plan. Expected cell frequencies were generally adjusted to the nearest whole number. Invitations to participate in the WISC-III^{UK} validation were made by letter and telephone to 38 Local Education Authorities (LEAs) chosen to be representative of geographic region, population density (rural, suburban, and urban), and race/ethnic composition. Of these, eight were unable to participate and were replaced by adjacent representative LEAs. Within each LEA, several schools were sampled to include children of both primary and secondary age and to represent the rural/suburban/urban mix of the local authority area. Of the schools approached, eight were unable to participate and were replaced by other representative schools within the same region. In the end 61 schools participated in the study.

In total, 2390 parental consent forms and instructions for distributing these for whole classes of children were mailed to participating schools. The consent form requested the child's date of birth, gender, race/ethnicity, and use of English as well as the parents' occupations.

The validation sample was drawn from state schools in Britain and both Protestant and Catholic schools in Northern Ireland. Children receiving special services in school settings were not excluded from testing. No special schools were involved in the study. Children were tested only if they could speak and understand English.

The returned parental consent forms indicating agreement to participate totaled 2026, representing a response rate of 85%. From these, a database containing demographic information for all children available for participation in the study was compiled. A stratified random sampling approach was then used to select children representative of the population. The lists of selected children within a school were distributed to testers, along with a list of possible "backups" in the event of nonavailability.

Each child was assigned to an examiner, usually an educational psychologist, who had experience in individually administered tests or who had demonstrated proficiency in administering the WISC-R^{UK} or WISC-III^{UK}. Testing for almost all ($N = 740$) examinees was carried out in April and May 1991. Exceptions were a part of Outer London ($N = 19$), who participated in piloting for the overall procedures (November 1990), the Isle of Wight ($N = 22$, March 1991), and some secondary sampling ($N = 43$, July 1991).

Of the 814 children originally targeted, 691 were tested. The 'backup' children accounted for a further 90. The remaining 43 were collected on a secondary sampling from the pool following the withdrawal of one school from the scheme and some limitations on testing in three others. The total sample size was therefore 824.

Table 5.1 summarizes the distribution of parental socioeconomic status for each age group. Table 5.2 gives the breakdown by race/ethnic groups and sex for each age group. Table 5.3 shows the breakdown by geographic region and urban/suburban/rural distribution. These data show that for the stratification

TABLE 5.1   Demographic Characteristics of the UK Validation Sample: Frequencies by Age and Socioeconomic Status

Age	Socioeconomic status							Total
	1	2	3	4	5	6	7	
6	6	25	7	23	3	0	3	67
7	4	19	10	20	10	5	4	72
8	3	21	7	25	10	4	4	74
9	3	21	10	24	10	2	4	74
10	6	19	10	21	5	3	3	67
11	3	27	11	21	12	5	4	83
12	5	19	13	21	10	4	1	73
13	6	25	13	26	9	6	2	87
14	7	20	11	23	11	5	4	81
15	5	21	11	27	14	2	0	80
16	9	15	8	17	12	1	4	66
Total	57	232	111	248	106	37	33	824
UK population	58	234	108	257	109	33	25	

χ^2 for association $= 42.90$; $p = 0.95$.
χ^2 for goodness-of-fit $= 3.51$; $p = 0.75$.
Note: Analysis of variance comparing mean socioeconomic status with age: $F = 0.70$, $p = 0.74$. No significant differences on the Scheffé procedure.

TABLE 5.2 Demographic Characteristics of the UK Validation Sample: Frequencies by Age and Race/Ethnic Group

	Boys					Girls				
	Ethnic group					Ethnic group				
Age	1	2	3	4	Total	1	2	3	4	Total
6	1	1	31	2	35	1	1	29	1	32
7	1	1	32	1	35	1	0	35	1	37
8	1	1	31	0	33	1	1	39	0	41
9	3	1	31	1	36	2	1	34	0	37
10	1	0	33	1	35	2	0	29	0	32
11	3	0	36	2	41	1	2	38	1	42
12	1	1	35	1	38	0	0	36	0	36
13	1	1	37	1	40	1	0	45	1	47
14	0	0	35	3	38	1	0	40	0	43
15	3	2	38	0	43	1	0	36	0	37
16	0	0	31	1	32	0	0	33	1	34
Total	15	8	370	13	406	11	5	394	8	418
UK population	9	5	388	4		9	5	400	4	

χ^2 association test for ethnicity by age for boys 19.71, $p = 0.92$, for girls 20.26, $p = 0.96$.
χ^2 association test for ethnicity by sex $= 3.07, p = 0.38$.
Note: Two-way analysis of variance for years by ethnic group by sex. For ethnic group, $F = 1.00$ ($p = 0.39$), for sex, $F = 0.49$ ($p = 0.48$), for interaction term, $F = 0.45$ ($p = 0.72$). No significant Scheffé comparisons.

TABLE 5.3 Distribution of the UK Validation Sample by Region and by Area (Urban, Suburban, or Rural; Parents, Classification of Home Area)

Region	Urban	Suburban	Rural	Total	Census
North of England	6	19	17	42	44
Yorks and Humberside	14	30	7	51	71
East Midlands	18	49	3	70	58
EastAnglia	0	11	19	30	29
SE England (GLexc.)	21	74	58	153	153
Greater London	39	62	2	103	97
South West England	18	26	39	83	67
West Midlands	36	43	5	84	75
North West England	42	26	3	71	92
Wales	11	15	13	39	41
Scotland	12	30	27	69	74
Northern Ireland	18	10	1	29	23
Total	235	395	194	824	

Note: Under/oversampling in particular regions has been counterbalanced with oversampling from neighboring areas with comparable population densities.

data selected, the WISC-III^{UK} validation sample closely approximates the UK Census data.

A series of WISC-III^{UK} training workshops was held all over the UK to familiarize examiners with the test procedures and the particular requirements of the project. The majority of those participating were experienced test users. In the case of clinical and educational psychologist trainees and practicing psychologists familiar with the WISC-R^{UK}, a full day was devoted to training which concentrated on the clarification of the differences in administration and scoring between the WISC-R^{UK} and the WISC-III^{UK}. In the case of the five qualified teachers who trained, two days were allocated to training with an interval of at least one week during which to carry out practice assignments. Examiners were provided with standardization kits and samples of Record Forms to allow opportunities to practice test procedures. A Project Bulletin provided communication between the project coordinator and the examiners during the period between training and test administration.

RELIABILITY

The split-half reliability for the WISC-III^{UK} is the same as in the U.S. manual and the same regarding the retest reliability.

EVIDENCE OF VALIDITY

Confidence in WISC-III^{UK} score interpretation is based on the extensive U.S. standardization study and the UK validation study, the close correspondence between these two sets of data, and the range of validation data reported in the WISC-III^{UK} Manual.

WISC-III^{UK} norm tables are based on the scores of children in the UK sample. The 824 UK test administrations, combined with the data generated by 2200 concurrent U.S. administrations provide a robust basis from which to establish a set of UK normative reference points. Comparison between U.S. WISC-III means and standard deviations for subtest raw scores for each age band and those derived from the WISC-III^{UK} project demonstrates the close correspondence between the two sets of data. This correspondence is illustrated in Table 5.4 which shows means and standard deviations for UK data using UK scaling and U.S. scaling, respectively. Table 5.5 provides a further comparison by applying U.S. norms to UK raw scores for each age group. The greatest differences are obtained at the lower age groups, where differences in the onset of schooling may be having an effect, and in the top age group where attrition in the UK sample arises from earlier school-leaving patterns. The close correspondence between the two sets of data has provided a basis for the refinement of the UK distributions and establishes a very sound framework for score interpretation.

TABLE 5.4 Means and Standard Deviations with UK Data Using UK Scaling and U.S. Scaling for Scores, Respectively

	UK		U.S.	
	Mean	SD	Mean	SD
Information	10.01	3.08	9.46	3.07
Similarities	10.08	3.08	9.96	3.09
Arithmetic	10.04	3.13	10.20	3.24
Vocabulary	10.14	2.98	10.53	3.10
Comprehension	10.06	3.56	10.17	3.64
Digit span	10.07	3.07	10.51	3.17
Picture completion	10.09	3.12	10.54	3.14
Coding	10.04	3.27	9.81	3.27
Picture arrangement	9.96	3.29	9.50	3.21
Block design	10.14	3.10	11.44	3.29
Object assembly	10.11	3.01	11.08	3.08
Symbol search	9.98	3.19	9.81	3.18
Mazes	10.16	3.14	10.95	3.18
Verbal score	100.3	14.9	100.7	14.5
Performance score	100.4	15.0	103.6	13.7
Full Scale score	100.4	14.8	102.1	13.6
Verbal comp. score	100.1	14.8	100.6	14.7
Percep. org. score	100.1	15.0	104.5	13.8
Free. distr. score	100.4	14.7	102.9	15.0
Proc. speed score	100.2	15.3	100.0	14.2

While WISC-III^{UK} norms are based on the scores of children in the UK sample, reliabilities and standard errors of measurement used to interpret WISC-III^{UK} scores are derived from the larger U.S. study. Therefore the reliability and validity data developed for the original U.S. WISC-III can equally be applied to the UK adaptation.

CULTURAL ISSUES INFLUENCING WISC-III INTERPRETATION IN THE UK

In many ways the structural and ethnic variability and underlying educational and societal values of the UK resemble those of the U.S. What one French government minister described as a "cultural Chernobyl"—the arrival of Disney in France and associated import of American culture—appears to be more readily assimilated by UK society, especially the children. While the odd eco-warrior may well trash a burger bar in London, it would be regarded as bizarre in the extreme if a UK minister chose to comment on the negative influences of Ronald MacDonald, Donald Duck, Bart Simpson *et al.*

TABLE 5.5 UK Data Applying U.S. Norms to UK Raw Scores
(by Age Group)

Age (Years)	Mean verbal 10 (SD)	Mean perf. 10 (SD)	Mean full scale 10 (SD)	N
6	105.8 (13.7)	107.6 (13.6)	107.1 (13.3)	67
7	103.3 (13.0)	108.2 (11.8)	106.0 (11.2)	72
8	98.4 (13.8)	102.4 (13.6)	100.3 (12.9)	74
9	100.9 (13.7)	104.9 (14.2)	103.0 (12.6)	74
10	101.7 (13.7)	106.4 (13.8)	104.1 (13.2)	67
11	99.8 (15.5)	101.8 (13.9)	100.7 (14.3)	83
12	98.0 (13.2)	101.8 (12.4)	99.7 (12.4)	73
13	99.5 (16.7)	102.0 (14.3)	100.6 (15.4)	87
14	101.1 (16.5)	102.7 (13.5)	101.9 (14.7)	81
15	96.7 (13.5)	99.9 (13.0)	97.8 (13.0)	80
16	104.2 (13.9)	103.3 (14.7)	104.0 (13.6)	66

As with the U.S., the ethnic mix and variability of modern UK society is an important feature. A relatively high percentage of the population describe their race/ethnicity as being other than white, and this rises to over 20% in London. Additionally the wide variability in economic and educational outcome within the population more closely resemble the U.S. than European model. These similarities are not just of academic interest; they do seem to have an effect. It is therefore not surprising, as highlighted earlier in this chapter, that the distribution of test scores for the WISC-III was broadly similar for the two countries. This pattern is also repeated in the recent adaptation of the Wechsler Adult Intelligence Scale-III (WAIS-III) in the UK.

Providing, as in all assessment situations, the standardized delivery of the test is followed, there should be few unique considerations when confronted with children from the UK. As there are so many "hyphenated" forms of English (British-English being only one among many) both within the UK and across the world, UK children appear remarkably tolerant of accented and even dialectal English. Examiners should not be too concerned that the children will be biased against them in the testing situation.

It is this linguistic tolerance and variability which is the major challenge to the examiner. Outside of the UK "standard" English is the form routinely taught to non-native speakers. While this form should be understood by all children from the UK, it may not be routinely used. Within the UK there are relatively wide variations, both regionally—sometimes within the same city—and, possibly, between the various ethnic groups. For the verbal scales many UK practitioners will allow for some variability in responses when assessing the child. While it is difficult to be systematic about this issue, it may prove useful to check questionable responses with the parent of the child, i.e., follow basic good practice and do not just rely purely on performance in the test session when assessing the child.

PROFESSIONAL ISSUES IN THE USE OF INTELLIGENCE TESTS IN THE UK

The debate surrounding the use of intelligence tests is, by the nature of psychology, international. It would be surprising if the issues in the UK were more or less controversial, or different, from other countries. The academic debate is appreciated and understood by the UK practitioner community. Issues such as the definition of intelligence, the relationship between the WISC-III and these definitions, environmental influences, the role of socioeconomic status and ethnicity are all the subject of discussion and consideration when assessing children in the UK. However, the predominant mood in the applied UK field is not one of heated controversy but one of pragmatism. UK Psychologists are looking for an acceptable measure of cognitive ability (note, not IQ), adapted for the UK child, with UK norms. Clearly in the WISC-III^{UK} such an instrument exists.

While it is easy to lapse into generalizations, clinical and educational or school psychologists in the UK, who account for 90% of administrations of the WISC-III, were largely anti-testing through the late 1960s, 1970s, and into the 1980s. It is only in the last 15 years that this picture has been transformed. While no one would argue that UK practitioners are currently enthusiastically in favor of testing, it is apparent that test use, from the publisher's perspective, has increased among psychologists and other educational and health professionals.

There are a number of reasons for this apparent increase. First, the perception of testing children was transformed with the introduction by the UK government of national achievement testing in the late 1980s and early 1990s. In some ways related to this, there has been a further need to clearly identify children who have "special educational needs," the so-called "statementing" procedure in the UK. Educational psychologists play *the* leading role in the latter stages of this procedure. Consequently there has been an increasing demand for valid and reliable instruments, as is the case of the WISC-III^{UK}. Secondly, there has been increasing pressure on UK clinical and educational psychologists to justify their role in service provision. One unique aspect of the function of a psychologist (hopefully not the only one), and one which is easily understood by service managers, is the provision of high-level cognitive assessments. Appropriately, psychologists are given access to the WISC-III (in the case of the UK only educational and clinical psychologists, and psychologists with a relevant Ph.D.), and if the service requires this level of assessment then it must employ psychologists. Thirdly, there has been an increasing emphasis in the UK on evidence-based practice. As well-developed tests, including the WISC-III, are a reasonably reliable and valid way in which to provide the necessary "evidence," this has also resulted in growing test use in the UK.

It is worth emphasizing again the essentially pragmatic framework in which the WISC-III^{UK} is deployed. It is expected that psychologists in the UK do not rely solely on the WISC-III^{UK} results in *any* assessment. The results would routinely be interpreted not only in the context of the assessment sessions but also in the context of the wider situational, child, and environment factors. It is widely recognized that while the WISC-III^{UK} is useful as an assessment tool, it will never be sufficient in itself to fully assess the child. It is assumed that the standards and professionalism of test use routinely expected in the UK will also be met in any other country in which the WISC-III is used.

REFERENCES

Elliot, C. D. (1983). *British Ability Scales.* Windsor, Berks: NFER-Nelson.

Office of Population Censuses and Surveys (OPCS) (1989). Population in private households by ethnic group 1985–87. *Regional Trends* 24. London HMSO.

Office of Population Censuses and Surveys (OPCS) (1990). Area and population Table 2.1. Sub-regional statistics. *Regional Trends* 25. London HMSO.

Wechsler, D. (1992). *Wechsler Intelligence Scale for Children–Third Edition UK.* London: The Psychological Corporation.

6

FRANCE AND
FRENCH-SPEAKING
BELGIUM

JACQUES GRÉGOIRE

Faculty of Psychology and Education
The Catholic University of Louvain
Louvain-la-Neuve, Belgium

The French adaptation of the Wechsler Intelligence Scale for Children—Third Edition (WISC-III) began in 1993 and was published in 1996. This adaptation was made by the staff of the French publisher ECPA (Editions du Centre de Psychologie Appliquée, Paris) under the scientific responsibility of Professor Grégoire from the University of Louvain, Belgium. As the previous version of the scale, the WISC-R, was published in France in 1981, it was important to update its norms. The French adaptation of the WISC-III was also important because of improvement of the material (new pictures, enhanced record sheets...) and the clinical information (new subtest, computation of four index scores...) provided by this new U.S. version of the scale.

All the versions of the Wechsler scales have been adapted in France. In addition to the WISC-III, the Wechsler Preschool and Primary Scale of Intelligence—Revised (WPPSI-R) was published in 1995 and the Wechsler Adult Intelligence Scale-III (WAIS-III) in 2000. Therefore, the latest versions of the three Wechsler scales are now available for French psychologists. This French adaptation policy of the Wechsler scales is consistent with the requirements of Standards for Educational and Psychological Testing (AERA, APA, & NCME, 1999).

ADAPTATION PROCESS

The adaptation process concerned only the Verbal scale. The subtests of the Performance scale were kept as they were in the U.S. version. Because of the material, these items are difficult to modify, and any modification is very expensive. However, the Performance subtests were included in a tryout to control the correctness of the item order.

To adapt the items of the Verbal scale, three rules were taken into account: (1) the difficulty level of the French items had to be similar to the U.S. items, (2) the scoring rules of these items had to be easy and obvious to guarantee score reliability, (3) for some subtests, the quality of the answers had to be graduated to permit a scoring with 0, 1, or 2 points.

The French adaptation also concerned the instructions and the scoring rules. It was essential that these rules should be as clear as possible. Testing is always comparing. For fair comparisons, all test procedures have to be identical for each subject. Therefore, it was essential to adapt the instructions and the scoring rules of the verbal items with great care.

Three experts independently adapted the verbal items according to the above rules. For each subtest, more items than required were produced to provide an opportunity for selecting the best ones after tryout. For the Vocabulary subtest, a table of word frequency in the French language was used to help the experts to appraise the item difficulty. For this subtest, the experts also had to balance the number of substantives, adjectives, and verbs.

The items adapted and generated by the experts were discussed and selected. It was decided to keep some anchor items coming from the WPPSI-R, WISC-R and WAIS-III. This rule was used to control the continuity between the Wechsler scales. The number of items generated for each subtest was (in brackets, the number of items required for the final version): Information = 40 (30), Similarities = 22 (19), Arithmetic = 25 (24), Vocabulary = 43 (30), and Comprehension = 21 (18). The Digit Span subtest was kept unchanged and was not included in the tryout.

The adaptation of the U.S. items raised several problems. The first one was the difference in the daily life between France and the U.S. For example, in a French bookshop, customers cannot choose paperback and hardcover books (item 15 of the Comprehension subtest). Consequently, the item referring to such a choice was inappropriate. Another example was the Arithmetic item referring to a girl who sells newspapers (item 14). As, in France, teenagers do not sell newspapers, this content was also inappropriate and had to be modified.

The second problem was the difference of currency and metric system between France and U.S. In the Arithmetic subtest, it was therefore difficult to create items having a similar level of difficulty as the original ones. For example (U.S. item 23), in France, a second-hand bicycle could be about 200 French francs while, in the U.S. item, the price is $28. Using the figure 200, the item would have been more difficult in the French version than in the U.S. one. We chose to substitute "book" for "bicycle" to keep the figure 28 and the same difficulty level in the two versions. We made a similar modification for the U.S. item 21. As 1 mile is equal to 1.6 kilometer, it was difficult to keep 225 as the distance in kilometers covered by a car in 3 hours. The solution was to substitute "motorbike" for "car" to make the situation more plausible and keep the same figure.

Finally, a third problem was the difference of difficulty between the same items in France and U.S. For example, item 20 of Information is more famous in the U.S. than in France. Consequently, keeping the same content, item 20 would have been more difficult in France than in the U.S. For this reason, we substituted another item for the original one. In item 6 of the Arithmetic subtest, the French translation of the question would give the answer to the subject since "to cut in half" should be translated as "couper en deux" (to cut in two). Such an item would have been inappropriate being too easy. Again, another item was substituted for the original one.

A tryout of the five Verbal subtests mentioned above and of four among the seven Performance subtests (Coding, Symbol Search, and Mazes were not included in the tryout) was conducted on two samples (for more details on the tryout results, see Grégoire, Penhouët, & Boy, 1996). A French sample included 220 subjects in 11 age groups ranging from 6–16 years. Since the French adaptation of the WISC-III will also be used in the French-speaking population of Belgium, a Belgian sample, including 120 subjects from 6–16 years, was also used for the tryout. These two samples gave us the opportunity of comparing the item scores between France and Belgium, and the possibility of eliminating biased items. Because of the sample size, the item differential functioning between France and Belgium was analyzed using the Mantel-Haenszel procedure (Holland & Thayer, 1988).

The items were selected referring to the results of three analyses of the tryout data: a classical item analysis, a Rasch analysis, and the Mantel-Haenszel procedure. The scoring problems encountered with some items were also taken into account in the selection procedure.

SAMPLE CHARACTERISTICS

The standardization of the French version of the WISC-III was conducted in 1995. The standardization sample size was 1120 subjects with an age range from 6 to 16. This sample was representative of the French population. It was constructed referring to the results of the general census of the population of 1990. Five stratification criteria were used: age, gender, socioeconomic status, district category, and school system. These data were collected with great care by a team of psychologists trained in the administration of the Wechsler scales.

In France, no information could be collected in the school about the racial/ethnic group of the children. Information about the parent educational level was difficult to collect, and only their occupation was recorded. The occupation was used as information about parents' socioeconomic status according to the INSEE (National Institute of Statistics) categories. These categories are: (1) farmer, (2) shopkeeper and craftsman, (3) manager and higher intellectual occupation, (4) middle manager, technician, and teacher, (5) employee, (6) worker, (7) retired, (8) unemployed. Table 6.1 shows the number of subjects by age and socioeconomic category.

TABLE 6.1   Demographic Characteristics of the Standardization Sample, by Age and Parents'
Socioeconomic Status

Age	Socioeconomic status								Total
	1	2	3	4	5	6	7	8	
6	3	10	14	19	13	42	0	4	105
7	3	9	14	18	13	42	0	3	102
8	3	9	14	18	14	42	0	3	103
9	3	9	15	18	13	42	0	3	103
10	4	9	14	17	13	43	0	2	102
11	3	9	14	18	13	43	0	3	103
12	3	9	13	18	14	37	2	4	100
13	3	9	14	17	14	38	2	3	100
14	3	10	14	19	12	37	1	4	100
15	3	11	14	18	9	39	2	4	100
16	3	9	14	19	12	40	1	4	102
Total	34	103	154	199	140	445	8	37	1120
%	3.0	9.2	13.8	17.8	12.5	39.7	0.7	3.3	100
French popul.	3.0	8.9	13.9	17.9	12.5	39.5	0.9	3.4	100

Note: Socioeconomic categories are: (1) farmer, (2) shopkeeper and craftsman, (3) manager and
higher intellectual occupation, (4) middle manager, technician, and teacher, (5) employee, (6) worker,
(7) retired, and (8) unemployed.

From WISC-III Manual. English version copyright © 1991 and French translation copyright © 1996
by The Psychological Corporation. Adapted and reproduced with permission. All rights reserved.

The percentage of subjects of the standardization sample in each socioeconomic
category is very close to the percentage in the French population.

RELIABILITY

Table 6.2 shows the averages across age groups of the split-half reliability coefficients and standard errors of measurement for each subtest, IQ, and index score.
The average reliability coefficients for the Verbal and the Full Scale IQ scores are
above 0.90. A slightly lower coefficient (0.89) is observed for the Performance
IQ that used to be less reliable than the other IQ scores. The average reliability coefficients of the index scores range from 0.82 to 0.93. As for the subtest
scaled scores, they range from 0.76 (Arithmetic) to 0.84 (Vocabulary) in the Verbal
scale, and from 0.64 (Object Assembly and Mazes) to 0.84 (Block Design) in the
Performance scale.

The corrected test-retest coefficients of the IQ, index, and subtest scores are
presented in Table 6.3 for three age bands. The average coefficients for the three
groups are mentioned in the right-hand column. The average stability coefficients

TABLE 6.2 Reliability Coefficients and Standard Errors of Measurement of the Subtests Scaled Scores, IQ Scores, and Index Scores, by Age[a]

Subtest/scale	Age											Average[c]
	6	7	8	9	10	11	12	13	14	15	16	
Information	0.78	0.56	0.72	0.78	0.79	0.76	0.87	0.75	0.85	0.86	0.84	0.79
(SEm)	1.39	1.99	1.60	1.40	1.37	1.46	1.07	1.51	1.17	1.11	1.21	1.41
Similarities	0.83	0.76	0.74	0.74	0.85	0.84	0.75	0.79	0.82	0.80	0.80	0.80
(SEm)	1.24	1.46	1.54	1.52	1.15	1.22	1.49	1.36	1.26	1.34	1.34	1.36
Arithmetic	0.78	0.74	0.77	0.61	0.74	0.86	0.70	0.77	0.75	0.80	0.72	0.76
(SEm)	1.40	1.52	1.45	1.87	1.53	1.14	1.63	1.45	1.50	1.33	1.57	1.50
Vocabulary	0.76	0.75	0.78	0.82	0.88	0.75	0.85	0.84	0.92	0.90	0.88	0.84
(SEm)	1.47	1.51	1.40	1.26	1.04	1.49	1.17	1.21	0.83	0.97	1.05	1.24
Comprehension	0.72	0.76	0.72	0.76	0.77	0.80	0.78	0.86	0.84	0.81	0.78	0.79
(SEm)	1.59	1.48	1.59	1.46	1.44	1.34	1.40	1.13	1.22	1.30	1.41	1.40
Digit span	0.78	0.75	0.79	0.80	0.76	0.84	0.84	0.87	0.91	0.84	0.90	0.83
(SEm)	1.40	1.49	1.39	1.35	1.45	1.21	1.19	1.08	0.88	1.21	0.96	1.25
Picture completion	0.74	0.73	0.66	0.73	0.68	0.57	0.74	0.70	0.67	0.72	0.74	0.70
(SEm)	1.53	1.56	1.76	1.55	1.71	1.96	1.54	1.64	1.72	1.57	1.54	1.65
Coding	0.83	0.66	—[b]	—[b]	0.73	0.87	—[b]	—[b]	0.76	0.61	—[b]	0.76
(SEm)	1.23	1.75	—[b]	—[b]	1.55	1.08	—[b]	—[b]	1.46	1.87	—[b]	1.52
Picture arrangement	0.77	0.78	0.74	0.71	0.69	0.76	0.82	0.69	0.82	0.75	0.85	0.77
(SEm)	1.43	1.40	1.52	1.61	1.66	1.48	1.29	1.68	1.29	1.49	1.15	1.46
Block design	0.81	0.82	0.80	0.82	0.82	0.87	0.80	0.86	0.86	0.85	0.88	0.84
(SEm)	1.32	1.27	1.35	1.28	1.26	1.07	1.35	1.12	1.12	1.17	1.04	1.22
Object assembly	0.68	0.48	0.64	0.74	0.53	0.70	0.51	0.69	0.63	0.65	0.68	0.64
(SEm)	1.70	2.17	1.81	1.54	2.05	1.65	2.09	1.66	1.82	1.78	1.70	1.83
Symbol search	0.69	0.71	—[b]	—[b]	0.70	0.76	—[b]	—[b]	0.78	0.63	—[b]	0.72
(SEm)	1.68	1.61	—[b]	—[b]	1.64	1.46	—[b]	—[b]	1.42	1.83	—[b]	1.61
Mazes	0.77	0.72	0.71	0.66	0.53	0.68	0.61	0.63	0.51	0.57	0.57	0.64
(SEm)	1.44	1.60	1.62	1.74	2.06	1.69	1.87	1.82	2.09	1.97	1.97	1.82

(*Continues*)

TABLE 6.2 (Continued)

Subtest/scale	Age											Average[c]
	6	7	8	9	10	11	12	13	14	15	16	
Verbal IQ	0.93	0.91	0.92	0.92	0.94	0.94	0.94	0.94	0.96	0.95	0.94	0.94
(SEm)	4.03	4.61	4.37	4.34	3.53	3.72	3.67	3.73	3.14	3.25	3.67	3.85
Performance IQ	0.90	0.86	0.85	0.89	0.87	0.89	0.91	0.91	0.90	0.89	0.89	0.89
(SEm)	4.70	5.53	5.78	5.07	5.31	4.97	4.55	4.52	4.70	5.00	4.96	5.02
Full scale IQ	0.95	0.92	0.93	0.94	0.95	0.94	0.95	0.95	0.96	0.95	0.95	0.95
(SEm)	3.52	4.23	3.99	3.74	3.49	3.53	3.21	3.34	3.06	3.18	3.46	3.54
Verbal compr. I.	0.91	0.89	0.90	0.92	0.94	0.93	0.94	0.94	0.96	0.95	0.94	0.93
(SEm)	4.38	5.07	4.69	4.25	3.72	4.02	3.74	3.80	3.15	3.40	3.66	4.03
Percept. organ. I.	0.89	0.87	0.85	0.87	0.86	0.87	0.89	0.90	0.90	0.90	0.91	0.88
(SEm)	4.89	5.50	5.89	5.31	5.67	5.36	4.95	4.73	4.73	4.70	4.53	5.14
Processing speed I.	0.83	0.77	0.80	0.81	0.80	0.87	0.89	0.86	0.85	0.75	0.78	0.82
(SEm)	6.25	7.22	6.77	6.46	6.63	5.49	5.01	5.68	5.90	7.45	7.02	6.40

[a] N = about 100 for each age group. The reliability coefficients for all subtests, except Coding and Symbol Search, are split-half correlations corrected by the Spearman-Brown formula. For Coding and Symbol Search, raw-score test-retest correlations are presented for six age groups (N = 36 for each group). These coefficients were corrected for the variability of the appropriate group (Guilford & Fruchter, 1978). The coefficients for the IQ and factor-based scales were calculated with the formula for the reliability of a composite (Nunnally, 1978). The values of the supplementary subtests were not included in these computations. The standard errors of measurement are reported in scaled-score units for the subtest, in IQ units for the Verbal, Performance, and Full Scales scores, and in index units for the Verbal Comprehension, Perceptual Organization, and Processing Speed scores.

[b] For Coding and Symbol Search, the best estimates of the reliability coefficients at an age level for which retesting was not done is the value obtained at the adjacent age level. The exception for age 8, for which the most reasonable estimate is the value obtained at age 10, the closest age at which Level B of these subtests is administered (Level A is administered to children younger than age 8). These "best estimates" for Coding and Symbol Search were used for computing the reliabilities of the composites to which these subtests contribute.

[c] The average r was computed with Fisher's z transformation. The average SEMs were calculated by averaging the sum of the squared SEMs for each age group and obtaining the square roots of the results.

TABLE 6.3   Stability Coefficients of the Subtests Scaled Scores, IQ Scores, and Index Scores, by Age

| | Age in years | | | | | | All ages |
| | 6–7 ($n = 60$) | | 10–11 ($n = 59$) | | 14–15 ($n = 61$) | | |
Subtest/scale	r_{12}	r_c^a	r_{12}	r_c^a	r_{12}	r_c^a	Average[b]
Information	0.88	0.89	0.87	0.90	0.88	0.89	0.89
Similarities	0.72	0.72	0.76	0.75	0.85	0.87	0.79
Arithmetic	0.64	0.69	0.67	0.70	0.76	0.78	0.72
Vocabulary	0.72	0.77	0.86	0.86	0.89	0.90	0.85
Comprehension	0.74	0.71	0.84	0.83	0.79	0.82	0.79
Digit span	0.72	0.73	0.74	0.74	0.69	0.72	0.73
Picture completion	0.73	0.83	0.76	0.73	0.84	0.82	0.80
Coding	0.69	0.72	0.80	0.78	0.77	0.67	0.73
Picture arrangement	0.82	0.80	0.77	0.82	0.79	0.66	0.77
Block design	0.81	0.75	0.86	0.84	0.87	0.82	0.81
Object assembly	0.57	0.66	0.70	0.61	0.68	0.70	0.66
Symbol search	0.75	0.68	0.66	0.67	0.72	0.75	0.70
Mazes	0.69	0.62	0.72	0.69	0.38	0.34	0.57
Verbal IQ	0.89	0.91	0.91	0.91	0.93	0.93	0.92
Performance IQ	0.85	0.87	0.88	0.89	0.88	0.87	0.88
Full scale IQ	0.93	0.95	0.92	0.93	0.95	0.94	0.94
Verbal compr. I.	0.90	0.92	0.92	0.92	0.92	0.93	0.92
Percept. organ. I.	0.86	0.88	0.89	0.88	0.90	0.87	0.88
Proc. speed I.	0.79	0.81	0.78	0.81	0.80	0.77	0.80

[a]Correlations were corrected for the variability of WISC-III scores on the first testing (Guilford & Fruchter, 1978).
[b]Weighted average of corrected correlations for ages 6–7, 10–11, and 14–15 were obtained with Fisher's z transformation ($n = 180$).

of the IQ scores range from 0.88 (Performance IQ) to 0.94 (Full scale IQ). For the index scores, these coefficients range from 0.80 (Processing Speed) to 0.92 (Verbal Comprehension). For the subtest scaled scores, the stability coefficients range from 0.57 (Mazes) to 0.89 (Information).

All the reliability coefficients (split-half and test-retest) are close to the U.S. coefficients. The same subtests gave similar coefficients. In most of the cases, the difference between the French and the U.S. coefficients is less or equal to 0.05.

EVIDENCE OF VALIDITY

Several correlations between the WISC-III and other measures were computed and gave criterion-related evidence of validity. Correlations were computed with the WPPSI-R ($n = 60$), WISC-R ($n = 99$), and WAIS-III ($n = 72$). All the correlations between the Full Scale IQ scores were high (respectively, 0.87, 0.88, and 0.99) showing an excellent congruence between the Wechsler scales. Correlations were also computed between the WISC-III and the Kaufman Assessment Battery for Children (K-ABC) ($n = 50$). The correlation between the Full Scale IQ and the Mental Processing Composite as quite high (0.77), indicating a large overlap of the two constructs measured by these scales. A more detailed discussion of these correlations can be found in the French manual of the WISC-III (Wechsler, 1996) and in Grégoire (2000).

The construct validity of the French adaptation of the WISC-III was thoroughly investigated through several factor analyses of the inter-subtest correlation matrix (Table 6.4). The main goal of these analyses was to check the relevance of the computation of the three classical IQ scores and the new factor-based scores. We analyzed the French standardization data with exactly the same method that was used to analyze the U.S. WISC-III standardization sample (Wechsler, 1991). First, an exploratory factor analysis was conducted using the maximum-likelihood method of extraction, followed by a Varimax rotation. The analyses were conducted on the total sample ($N = 1120$) and on the following four age groups: ages 6–7 ($N = 207$), ages 8–10 ($N = 308$), ages 11–13 ($N = 303$), and ages 14–16 ($N = 302$).

In the first analysis, two factors were specified. The results confirmed the validity of the Verbal and Performance IQ scores as measures of two general components of intelligence. But the matching between the subtests and the two scales is far from perfect. All the subtests are also measuring something other than the two

TABLE 6.4   Intercorrelation of Subtest Scaled Scores

Subtest	Inf	Sim	Ari	Voc	Com	DSp	PCo	Cod	PAr	BDi	OAs	SSe	Mz
Information													
Similarities	0.63												
Arithmetic	0.52	0.47											
Vocabulary	0.69	0.70	0.49										
Comprehension	0.55	0.56	0.44	0.66									
Digit span	0.30	0.33	0.36	0.34	0.25								
Picture compl.	0.34	0.34	0.31	0.34	0.35	0.15							
Coding	0.17	0.15	0.23	0.19	0.15	0.19	0.15						
Picture arrang.	0.40	0.40	0.35	0.38	0.35	0.19	0.40	0.21					
Block design	0.38	0.41	0.43	0.39	0.31	0.28	0.43	0.29	0.42				
Object Assembly	0.32	0.33	0.32	0.29	0.25	0.20	0.42	0.21	0.40	0.57			
Symbol search	0.25	0.24	0.29	0.24	0.23	0.21	0.22	0.52	0.30	0.35	0.28		
Mazes	0.21	0.20	0.28	0.24	0.20	0.19	0.27	0.21	0.24	0.36	0.25	0.21	

components, enlarging the aptitude range included in the Total IQ, but also making the interpretation of the Verbal and Performance IQ scores quite tricky.

In a second analysis, three factors were specified. Table 6.5 shows that the Verbal subtests have their highest loading on the first factor and that the Performance subtests have their highest loading on the second factor, except Coding and Symbol Search. These two subtests have their highest loading on the third factor. Similar factor structures were found in all the age groups, except the 8–10 age group.

Most of the studies of the U.S. WISC-III supported a four-factor solution (e.g., Wechsler, 1991; Roid, Prifitera, & Weiss, 1993; Tupa, Wright, & Fristad, 1997). These results led to proposing a clinical use of four factor-based index scores. Unfortunately, the analysis of the French standardization data did not support this four-factor structure. Table 6.6 shows the results of the analysis when four factors were specified. The loadings on the first, second, and third factors are close to those observed with the U.S. WISC-III. On the other hand, the Digit Span subtest is the only one to have its highest loading on the fourth factor, while the Arithmetic subtest has clearly its highest loading on the first factor. Moreover, this factor structure is very unstable across the age range.

A confirmatory factor analysis was conducted with the LISREL 8 program (Jöreskog & Sörbom, 1996) to compare how the different factor solutions fit the data. An improvement of the goodness-of-fit statistics was observed from the one-factor solution to the four-factor solution. The greatest improvement was between the one and two-factor solutions, contrasting with the limited improvement between the three- and four-factor solution. Consequently, the confirmatory analysis did not provide a strong argument in favor of the three- or four-factor solution (for a more detailed presentation of these results, see Grégoire, 2001).

How could the differences between the factor structure of the French and the U.S. WISC-III be explained? Why was a strong *Freedom from distractibility* factor not found with the French data? It seems difficult to explain this phenomenon by sampling bias. The French standardization sample was gathered with great care and its size was adequate for factor analysis. The French adaptation of the subtests does not seem to be implicated. The Digit Span subtest remained identical to the original version and few items of the Arithmetic subtest were slightly modified. Moreover, the reliability of the French subtests is very close to the reliability of the U.S. subtests. The difference between the French and the U.S. factor solutions is not due to poor reliability of the French data.

The more plausible explanation seems related to the meaning of the *Freedom from distractibility* factor. Since it was extracted from the WISC-R data, the exact meaning of this factor has been debated. Recently, Keith and Witta (1997) proposed another interpretation of this factor. As the Arithmetic and Digit Span subtests are essentially linked by a common mental capacity to manipulate numerical data, they suggested naming this factor *Quantitative Reasoning*. This proposal was strongly supported by Carroll (1997). The results of Dowker's research (1998) were congruent with Keith and Witta's suggestion. Dowker analyzed the relationships between arithmetical performances of 6- to 9-year-old children and their results

TABLE 6.5 Maximum-Likelihood Factor Loading (Varimax Rotation) for Three Factors

Subtest	Factor 1: Verbal comprehension				Factor 2: Perceptual organization				Factor 3: Processing speed			
	6–7	8–10	11–13	14–16	6–7	8–10	11–13	14–16	6–7	8–10	11–13	14–16
Information	0.71	0.64	0.75	0.74	0.21	0.19	0.27	0.33	0.06	0.36	0.04	0.14
Similarities	0.61	0.56	0.77	0.79	0.22	0.10	0.31	0.31	−0.04	0.61	0.10	0.10
Arithmetic	0.56	0.47	0.45	0.48	0.41	0.28	0.29	0.42	0.10	0.29	0.19	0.23
Vocabulary	0.83	0.76	0.85	0.87	0.15	0.16	0.13	0.25	0.12	0.36	0.17	0.13
Comprehension	0.67	0.76	0.69	0.74	0.20	0.15	0.21	0.16	0.08	0.07	0.13	0.10
Digit span	0.43	0.18	0.38	0.25	0.35	0.16	0.11	0.16	0.15	0.41	0.21	0.21
Picture compl.	0.24	0.36	0.26	0.31	0.50	0.38	0.58	0.52	0.19	0.05	0.07	0.06
Picture arrang.	0.31	0.35	0.34	0.34	0.43	0.33	0.46	0.56	0.11	0.21	0.19	0.16
Block design	0.19	0.22	0.26	0.27	0.71	0.56	0.74	0.71	0.12	0.39	0.24	0.24
Object assembly	0.18	0.15	0.16	0.13	0.68	0.45	0.71	0.76	0.10	0.32	0.17	0.12
Mazes	0.15	0.19	0.11	0.23	0.53	0.51	0.35	0.23	0.04	0.04	0.28	0.11
Coding	−0.02	0.08	0.13	0.07	0.10	0.55	0.19	0.06	0.99	0.11	0.66	0.90
Symbol search	0.17	0.08	0.17	0.19	0.24	0.61	0.19	0.19	0.37	0.11	0.75	0.64

WISC-III Manual. English version copyright © 1991 and French translation copyright © 1996 by The Psychological Corporation. Adapted and reproduced by permission. All rights reserved.

TABLE 6.6   Factor Loading for the Four-Factor Solution ($N = 1120$)

Subtest	Factor 1	Factor 2	Factor 3	Factor 4
Information	0.72	0.25	0.10	0.16
Similarities	0.71	0.27	0.07	0.20
Arithmetic	0.47	0.30	0.19	0.30
Vocabulary	0.84	0.19	0.11	0.16
Comprehension	0.70	0.20	0.11	0.00
Digit span	0.29	0.12	0.16	0.37
Picture completion	0.29	0.56	0.09	−0.08
Picture arrangement	0.35	0.47	0.19	−0.02
Block design	0.21	0.68	0.21	0.31
Object assembly	0.35	0.47	0.19	−0.02
Mazes	0.14	0.33	0.18	0.16
Coding	0.07	0.14	0.70	0.11
Symbol search	0.15	0.23	0.65	0.07

TABLE 6.7   Arithmetic and Digit Span Loading on the Verbal Comprehension and Freedom

	Verbal comprehension		Freedom from distractibility	
Subtest	U.S. sample	French sample	U.S. sample	French sample
Arithmetic	0.41	0.47	0.73	0.30
Digit span	0.26	0.29	0.34	0.37

on the WISC-III. He observed a correlation of 0.424 ($p < 0.01$) between the Arithmetic subtest and a mental addition test, and a correlation of 0.305 ($p < 0.01$) between the Digit Span subtest and the same mental addition test. These results confirmed that Arithmetic and Digit Span share the ability to keep track of and manipulate numbers into the working memory, which is one of the components of mental arithmetic.

This interpretation is compatible with the content of the two subtests and with empirical data (Table 6.7). Although Arithmetic has its highest loading on the first factor (0.47), its loading on the third factor is significant (0.30) and only slightly smaller than the Digit Span loading on the same factor (0.37). It seems obvious that Arithmetic and Digit Span share a common ability. However, the verbal comprehension ability also plays an important role in the Arithmetic subtest, while its impact in the Digit Span subtest is smaller. Consequently, we hypothesized that the key to understanding the factor structure difference between the French and the American results is the loading of the Arithmetic subtest. The difference of the third factor loading on Arithmetic in France and U.S. could be related by the specificity of mathematical teaching in these two countries. Mathematical teaching in France is much formal than in U.S. Little time is devoted to problem solving in the mathematical curriculum. Problem solving is seen more as an application of mathematical knowledges than a way to develop mathematical skills. Consequently, French children's results to verbal arithmetical problems use is lower than those of the U.S. children (e.g., Van Nieuwenhoven, Grégoire, & Noël, 2001). The kind of problems proposed in the Arithmetical subtest is clearly less familiar to the French children than to those in the U.S. Therefore, the cognitive load of the problem verbal analysis is likely higher for the French children than for those in the U.S. This difference could explain the higher loading of the Verbal Comprehension factor on the Arithmetic subtest in France. Further cross-cultural research should be conducted to control this hypothesis.

CULTURAL ISSUES INFLUENCING WISC-III INTERPRETATION IN FRANCE AND BELGIUM

The adaptations of the Wechsler scales made in France were often considered as "the" French adaptation of these scales, as they could be used in all the French-speaking countries. Such an affirmation is incorrect. The WISC-III, as any normed-referenced test, can only be used in the country where it was developed and standardized. Using this French adaptation in other French-speaking countries, e.g., Quebec, Morocco, or Congo, would lead to important bias in the assessment of children. For these countries, specific norms are needed, but also an adaptation of the content of several subtests. The French-speaking countries do not constitute one homogeneous population. There are numerous differences between these countries. Often, these differences are not obvious and empirical research has to be conducted to spot problematic items. As an illustration, some results are presented from the analysis of the differential item functioning between France and Belgium conducted with five of the WISC-III Verbal subtests.

Belgium is very close to France, sharing a long border with the north of France. Its capital, Brussels, is closer to Paris (about 300 km) than important French cities such as Bordeaux or Marseilles. The language and the way of life in the two countries are very similar. The same books and magazines can be found in the bookshops, and people watch the same TV programs (90% of Belgian households are connected to the TV cable network and receive most of the French channels). The school programs are also similar. Consequently, at first glance, France and Belgium could be considered as one population. Previous adaptations of the Wechsler scales were developed accepting this *a priori*. For the WISC-III adaptation, we decided to control for possible bias between the two countries. This control was done through an analysis of the differential item functioning. "A test item is said to be *unbiased* when probability for success on the item is the same for equally able examinees of the same population regardless of their subgroup membership" (Osterlind, 1989, p. 11). Consequently, for each subtest item, we tested the hypothesis that French and Belgian children were members of the same population.

The differential item functioning was analysis with the data of the tryout conducted on a French sample ($n = 220$) and a Belgian sample ($n = 120$). Both samples answered the items of the five Verbal subtests of the WISC-III adapted in French. The Mantel-Haenszel Chi-square being the best method with small samples (Nandakumar, Glutting, & Oakland, 1993), it was used to test the differential item functioning of the subtest items. Few items were flagged as having a differential functioning: 8 items in Information, 1 item in Similarities, 1 item in Arithmetic, 3 items in Vocabulary, and 4 items in Comprehension. The number of items flagged varied according to the subtest. In some cases, the impact of bias items was limited (e.g., for the Similarities subtest, only 1 item in 21 was flagged as showing a differential functioning). In other subtests, this impact was more important leading to potential bias in the assessment of French and Belgian children. Consequently, problematic items were removed from these subtests. Unfortunately, it was impossible to remove all the items showing a differential functioning because other criteria had to be taken into account in the item selection of the definitive version of the WISC-III.

For example, height items of the Information subtest were flagged as having a different functioning between French and Belgian. Four of theses items were deleted and four were retained in the definitive version of the WISC-III. Some items were retained because we had also to take into account the graduation of the item difficulty and the correlations between the items and the total score. As some bias items had to be retained, we kept two items biased against French children and two items biased against Belgian children, preserving a balance between the two groups. With high-stakes tests (e.g., the Scholastic Aptitude Test), developers used to delete all bias items. Often, this option does not exist when developing clinical tests because it is impossible to conduct tryout of very large sets of items.

Presenting the analysis of bias between French and Belgian, we have seen that even very similar groups items with a differential functioning are flagged. This phenomenon is certainly more important between more distant groups and can lead to very important bias in the assessment of intelligence. Therefore, the French adaptation of the WISC-III should not be used in other French-speaking countries without a careful check of the differential item functioning.

In France and Belgium, for ethical and political reasons, no information is available about the ethnic groups of the children that are currently in the primary and secondary schools. Consequently, no research was conducted on IQ differences between ethnic groups. IQ differences according to socioeconomic status were more debated. Most of the time, the discussion was political, only based on the face validity of the items. Few empirical data are currently available on this topic. Grégoire (1992; 2000) was the only one to conduct statistical analysis of IQ differences on the French WISC-R and on the French WISC-III between children according to their socioeconomic status.

Table 6.8 shows the mean IQ scores (Verbal, Performance and Full scale) of the WISC-III standardization sample according to the eight socioeconomic categories

TABLE 6.8   Mean and Standard Deviation of the Verbal, Performance, and Full Scale IQ Scores of the French Standardization Sample According to Socioeconomic Categories

Socioeconomic categories	N	Full scale IQ		Verbal IQ		Performance IQ	
		Mean	SD	Mean	SD	Mean	SD
1	34	99.53	13.53	98.24	14.20	101.26	14.46
2	103	97.88	14.74	97.43	15.09	98.81	14.70
3	154	109.62	15.21	11.51	14.29	106.13	16.20
4	199	104.70	14.16	104.14	14.56	104.13	13.90
5	140	99.26	14.41	10.06	14.11	98.59	14.38
6	445	96.12	13.97	96.05	14.03	97.26	14.11
7	8	89.63	13.24	97.38	15.15	84.25	14.40
8	37	93.03	11.71	91.78	11.99	95.95	12.26
Total	1120	10.01	15.05	100.04	15.11	99.99	14.85

Note: Socioeconomic categories are: (1) farmer, (2) shopkeeper and craftsman, (3) manager and higher intellectual occupation, (4) middle manager, technician, and teacher, (5) employee, (6) worker, (7) retired, and (8) unemployed.

From Grégoire, J. (2000). *L'évaluation clinique de l'intelligence de l'enfant*, Liège: Mardaga.

used to collect this sample (see Sample Characteristics). Data presented for Categories 7 and 8 should be neglected, the first being too small and the second too heterogeneous. Among the six remaining categories, workers' children have the lower average Full Scale IQ (96.12), while managers' children have the highest average Full scale IQ (109.12). The IQ differences between the six groups were compared using an analysis of variance. For the three IQ scores, no statistical difference was observed between Categories 1, 2, 5, and 6. The Verbal and Full Scale IQ scores of category 3 were statistically higher than those of the other categories. The Performance IQ score of Categories 3 and 4 was statistically higher than the Performance IQ scores of Categories 1, 2, 5, and 6. The Full Scale IQ score of Category 4 was also higher than the Full Scale IQ score of Category 4. The difference between Verbal and Performance IQs was only significant in Category 3 (Manager and higher intellectual occupation) where it reached 4 points in favor of the Verbal IQ. This result is not surprising since verbal performances above average are usually observed in wealthy socioeconomic categories (Mercy & Steelman, 1982).

The average IQ scores according to the socioeconomic status observed on the French WISC-III are similar to those observed on the WISC-R (Grégoire, 1992). Only small differences are observed, and are probably related to sampling errors.

It should be emphasized that the IQ score differences related to the socioeconomic status are relative. The lower average IQ score (workers' children) was only 4 points under 100 (average IQ score of the population). Such a difference cannot be considered as an important sociocultural handicap. Moreover, the IQ score ranges of workers' children and managers' children were similar. For the first, the IQ scores extended from 62–147, while for the second, they extended from 48–149. In other words, a child can obtain a very low or a very high IQ whatever his sociocultural origin.

Even if the average IQ of workers' children was not far from the average IQ of the population, it was about 1 standard deviation from the average IQ of managers' children. Such a difference has to be explained and its clinical consequences have to be drawn.

A first explanation refers to the way intelligence tests, as the WISC-III, are developed. Item contents could reflect the values of the middle class from which test developers come from. Therefore, intelligence tests could be unfair for workers' children since the item content could be less familiar for these children. The empirical evidence of item bias against workers' children in the WISC-III are missing. Most of the time, such judgments come from face validity evidence and, therefore, are inconclusive. Moreover, it is hard to consider all the WISC-III subtests as reflecting middle class values. The content of Block Design or Coding is not typical of a specific social class.

A second explanation of the workers' children's intellectual performances was recently proposed by social psychologists. According to Steel and Aronson (1995), when a subject is in a situation where he thinks that his behavior could conform to a stereotype associated to his membership group, he feels what researchers call "stereotype threat." This perceived threat could influence a subject's thinking and behavior. It could disrupt his cognitive functioning and drive him to protect his self-esteem by avoiding or noninvesting in areas where the stereotype threat is perceived. Two French researchers, Croizet and Claire (1998), have studied the impact of the stereotype threatening on student's intellectual performances according to their socioeconomic background. They asked students whose parents were workers or managers to answer a verbal reasoning test. This was presented as a verbal memory test or as a verbal intelligence test. In the first condition, the scores of the two groups (workers' children versus managers' children) were equivalent. But, in the second condition, students whose parents were workers had significantly lower scores than the students whose parents were managers. Working class students seemed to perceive a threat of fulfillment of the stereotype that workers' children are less intelligent than others. This perceived threat probably caused trouble with the cognitive functioning of these students, lowering their intellectual performances.

Stereotype threat could explain the lower intellectual performances of some subjects, but not account for all differences related to the socioeconomic status. Stereotype threatening probably has a different impact on young children than on students. Moreover, it can hardly explain why shopkeepers and craftsmen's children had IQ scores under the average population, since there are no stereotypes about intelligence of children from this socioeconomic category.

A third explanation referred to the genetic inheritance according to the social class. Herrnstein and Murray (1994) claimed that IQ reflects mostly inherited mental abilities. These abilities would determine professional and social success. According to these authors, workers' children would have a lower IQ than managers' children because they have a less favorable genetic inheritance. Genetic differences would explain intellectual differences that, subsequently, would lead to socioeconomic differences. Therefore, socioeconomic differences would be an effect of intellectual differences, but not the cause.

The Herrnstein and Murray thesis was sharply debated in the media. From a scientific viewpoint, several researches on adopted children strongly moderated this thesis. In particular, Capron and Duyme (1991) used the French WISC-R to test 38 children (average age 14) who were adopted before the age of 6 months. These children were carefully selected according to four categories: (1) biological parents with low socioeconomic status versus adoptive parents with low socioeconomic status; (2) biological parents with low socioeconomic status versus adoptive parents with high socioeconomic status; (3) biological parents with high socioeconomic status versus adoptive parents with low socioeconomic status; and (4) biological parents with high socioeconomic status versus adoptive parents with high socioeconomic status. Each category included 10 children, except Category 3, which included only 8 children. The parents' socioeconomic status was defined by their educational level and their profession. With this research design, it was possible to test the impact of the socioeconomic status of biological parents and adoptive parents on the IQ of adopted children. The influence of adoptive parents can be interpreted as the effect of the cultural environment on the intellectual development. The influence of biological parents can be interpreted as the effect of heredity on intelligence. Statistical analysis showed a statistically significant effect of both adoptive and biological parents on the IQ measured at age 14. These effects are independent and are observed for Full Scale IQ, Verbal IQ, and Performance IQ. Capron and Duyme's study clearly showed an influence of children's socioeconomic status on their IQ measured at age 14. However, this observation does not exclude an influence of genetic factors. From their own data, Duyme and Capron were not able to distinguish between the effect of genotype and the effect of perinatal factors (mother's health during pregnancy, early mother/child relations. . .). Even if the effect of the parent's social class on children's IQ scores cannot be precisely quantified, this influence should be taken into account when interpreting IQ scores on the WISC-III and when using them for school guidance.

The last point of this section emphasizes French cultural features that could influence children's scores on some WISC-III subtests. We already discussed (in Evidence of Validity) the specificity of the mathematical curriculum in France. Mathematical teaching in France is very formal, and little room is devoted to problem solving. Consequently, the kind of items proposed in the Arithmetic subtest is less familiar to the French children than to those in the U.S. Moreover, probabilities are not taught at the primary school, and are only introduced at the end of the high school. For most French children, the content of item 22 does not refer to school learning. Therefore, their answers are only based on their informal mathematical knowledge.

In the first section, Adaptation Process, we described the difficulties we had in adapting some Arithmetic items because of the currency and the metric system used in the U.S. version. Even if there were cents in the French currency (franc), they would be used less than in the U.S. currency because of their low value. Consequently, computation with digits after the decimal point was only introduced at the same time as the metric system, at grade 4. For this reason, the U.S. version of item 18 would have been more difficult for the French children than for those in the U.S. Such an item had to be adapted in order to avoid digits after the decimal point. The introduction of the Euro currency on January 1, 2002 will stimulate changes in school instruction since all the prices are now computed with two digits after the decimal point.

The influence of the specificity of the school curriculum could also be observed in other subtests as Information. Geography and history seem to be more important in the French curriculum than in the U.S. The reverse seems true for sciences. These differences could explain differences of item difficulty in the Information subtest between France and the U.S. However, such an interpretation should be made with caution because empirical data on cultural differences in the WISC-III subtests are currently rather poor.

PROFESSIONAL ISSUES IN THE USE OF INTELLIGENCE TESTS IN FRANCE AND BELGIUM

In a professional context, three questions arise about intellectual testing: When, what, and how. The first question is: When should we use an intelligence test? This question refers to the nature of the psychological problems, and to the legal constraints on the assessment and its consequences. The second question is: What is the most suitable intelligence test for collecting the needed information? The third question is: How should intelligence tests be administered, results be interpreted, and conclusions be communicated to the subject and other professionals?

To answer these questions correctly, some conditions are required. Unfortunately, in France and Belgium, these conditions are far from fulfilled for guaranteeing an appropriate and fair use of intelligence tests (Grégoire, 1999). In the rest of this section, the three main problems related to using intelligence tests in France and Belgium will be discussed: (1) psychologist's competency to use intelligence tests, (2) intelligence test development, and (3) legal issues on intelligence testing.

The current French situation in the area of intelligence testing and assessment is somewhat paradoxical since France is the birthplace of the testing method. In 1905, Binet published the first intellectual test, which had the success we know. Despite this extraordinary success, nobody succeeded Binet who died in 1911 and the testing method remained undeveloped in France, with few exceptions. The use of tests was even strongly criticized after the events of May 1968. Tests were accused of creating a gap in the relationship between psychologist and subject. Psychologists using tests were even described as "armed psychologists." Tests were also accused as being instruments for social classification, stimulating the reproduction of social inequalities. The effect of these criticisms was to dramatically reduce the number of courses on tests in the universities and nearly eliminate research on psychological assessment and psychometrics.

The situation slowly evolved during the nineties. A recent survey on practices in clinical psychology (Castro, Meljac, & Joubert, 1996) showed a new positive attitude on the part of clinical psychologists toward tests. Tests are often perceived as useful instruments for collecting information that could not be collected otherwise. The development of cognitive psychology, neuropsychology, and health psychology has stimulated new interest in measurement instruments, which have now a stronger theoretical background and, consequently, are perceived by practitioners as being more legitimate. Unfortunately, academic training on tests in the French and Belgian universities is still rather poor. Courses on psychometrics are rare and those on testing methods are often insufficient. How could we expect psychologists to take into account validity and reliability of the tests they use if they do not properly understand what these concepts mean? Without a basic knowledge in psychometrics, they are unable to understand the technical sections of test manuals and, consequently, to respect most of the standards for test use (AERA et al., 1999).

The second problem in the use of intelligence tests is related to the French situation of test development. Research on intelligence and psychometric methods fell dramatically during the seventies and eighties. Consequently, few French tests have been developed during the past 30 years. Most of the tests published in France and Belgium are adapted tests, generally from U.S. original tests. As these adaptations are very expensive, the publishers adapt only the best sellers among the U.S. tests. Tests suited for special populations (e.g., people with speech or hearing problems) are not adapted because potential users are limited. Fortunately, as the Wechsler scales are standards for intelligence testing, they were adapted to French soon after their U.S. publication. But, the choice for other intelligence tests is restricted to a very small number of instruments. No recent nonverbal intelligent test battery is currently available to test children with hearing disabilities. The lack of intelligence tests suited to the range of clinical situations leads to bias and nonvalid intellectual assessments.

The third problem in the professional application of intelligence tests is the absence of legal constraints on test use. Without any legal control, many psychologists do not feel responsible for making decisions when they use intelligence test scores. The influence of professional psychological associations is also limited. Only a small number of the French and Belgian psychologists are members of a professional association. They are traditionally individualistic, preferring to organize their professional activity with as little control as possible. Both French and Belgian psychological associations have a Test Commission, but these commissions have a limited influence on testing issues.

In conclusion, the current use of psychological tests in France and Belgium, especially intelligence tests, raises several questions. The most important is the lack of academic training on tests and psychometric methods in the French and

Belgian universities. Psychologists' competency in this area is often insufficient for a proper use of intelligence tests. Information and education should be improved to guarantee an intelligent and fair use of intelligence tests. Testing regulation (e.g., publication of standards for psychological testing) and development of new tests will lead to better psychological assessments only if psychologists are able to understand these rules and correctly use these tests.

REFERENCES

AERA, APA, & NCME (1999). *Standards for educational and psychological testing.* Washington, DC: American Educational Research Association.

Capron, C., & Duyme, M. (1991). Children's IQs and SES of biological and adoptive parents in a balanced cross-frostering study. *European Bulletin of Cognitive Psychology, 11,* 323–348.

Carroll, J. B. (1997). Commentary on Keith and Witta's hierarchical and cross-age confirmatory factor analysis of the WISC-III. *School Psychology Quarterly, 12,* 89–107.

Castro, D., Meljac, C., & Joubert, B. (1996). Pratiques et outils des psychologues cliniciens français. *Pratiques Psychologiques, 4,* 73–80.

Croizet, J.-C., & Claire, T. (1998). Extending the concept of stereotype threat to social class: The intellectual underperformance of students from low socioeconomic backgrounds. *Personality and Social Psychology Bulletin, 24,* 588–594.

Dowker, A. (1998). Individual differences in normal arithmetical development. In C. Donlan (Ed.), *The development of mathematical skills.* Hove, UK: Psychology Press.

Grégoire, J. (1992). *Evaluer l'intelligence de l'enfant.* Liège: Mardaga.

Grégoire, J. (1999). Emerging standards for test application in French-speaking European countries. *European Journal of Psychological Assessment, 15,* 158–164.

Grégoire, J. (2000). *L'évaluation clinique de l'intelligence de l'enfant.* Liège: Mardaga.

Grégoire, J. (2001). Factor structure of the French adaptation of the WISC-III: Three or four factors? *International Journal of Testing, 1,* 271–281.

Grégoire, J., Penhouët, C., & Boy, Th. (1996). L'adaptation française de l'échelle de Wechsler pour enfants, version III. *L'Orientation Scolaire et Professionnelle, 25,* 489–506.

Guilford, J. P., & Fruchter, B. (1978). *Fundamental statistics in psychology and education.* New York: McGraw-Hill.

Herrnstein, R. J., & Murray, C. (1994). *The bell curve. Intelligence and class structure in American life.* New York: Free Press.

Holland, P. W., & Thayer, D. T. (1988). Differential item performance and the Mantel-Haenszel procedure. In H. Wainer & H. Braun (Eds.), *Test validity.* Hillsdale, NJ: Lawrence Erlbaum Associates.

Jöreskog, K. G., & Sörbom, D. (1996). *LISREL 8 user's reference guide.* Chicago, IL: Scientific Software International.

Keith, T. Z., & Witta, E. L. (1997). Hierarchical and cross-age confirmatory factor analysis of the WISC-III: What does it measure? *School Psychology Quarterly, 12,* 89–107.

Mercy, J. A., & Steelman, L. C. (1982). Familial influence on the intellectual attainment of children. *American Sociological Review, 47,* 532–542.

Nandakumar, R., Glutting, J. J., & Oakland, T. (1993). Mantel-Haenszel methodology for detecting item bias. *Journal of Psychoeducational Assessment, 11,* 108–119.

Nunnally, J. C. (1978). *Psychometric theory.* New York: McGraw-Hill.

Osterlind, S. J. (1989). *Test item bias.* Newbury Park, CA: Sage.

Roid, G. H., Prifitera, A., & Weiss, L. G. (1993). Replication of the WISC-III factor structure in an independent sample. *Journal of Psychoeducational Assessment, WISC-III Monograph,* 6–21.

Steele, C. M., & Aronson, J. (1995). Stereotype vulnerability and the intellectual test performance of African-Americans. *Journal of Personality and Social Psychology, 69*, 797–811.

Tupa, D. J., Wright, M., & Fristad, M. A. (1997). Confirmatory factor analysis of the WISC-III with child psychiatric inpatients. *Psychological Assessment, 9*, 302–306.

Van Nieuwenhoven, C., Grégoire, J., & Noël, M.-P. (2001). *TEDI-MATH, Test diagnostique des compétences de base en mathematiques.* Paris: ECPA.

Wechsler, D. (1991). *Manual for the Wechsler Intelligence Scale for Children–Third edition.* San Antonio, TX: Psychological Corporation.

Wechsler, D. (1996). *Manuel de l'échelle d'intelligence de Wechsler pour enfants, troisième édition.* Paris: Editions du Centre de Psychologie Appliquée. (Original work published in 1991.)

7

THE NETHERLANDS AND FLEMISH-SPEAKING BELGIUM

MARK SCHITTEKATTE

Faculty of Psychology and Educational Sciences
University of Ghent
Ghent, Belgium

WILLEM KORT

Department of Research and Development, Dutch Psychological Association Service Center
Amsterdam, The Netherlands

WILMA RESING

Department of Development and Educational Psychology
Leyden University
Leyden, The Netherlands

GRIET VERMEIR

Testing Department, H
Ghent University
Ghent, Belgium

PAUL VERHAEGHE

Testing Department, H
Ghent University
Ghent, Belgium

The Dutch version of the Wechsler Intelligence Scale for Children—Third Edition (WISC-III) has been published recently after a research project of nearly two years (Wechsler, 2002). It concerned a joint adaptation process for the Dutch-speaking population in The Netherlands and in Flanders, the Dutch-speaking part of Belgium. The project has been executed by psychologists of the Research & Development Department of the Dutch Professional Psychologists Association (NIP) in association with researchers from Ghent University, Belgium, and advisers from Leiden University and the Free University Amsterdam.

The first objective was to develop new norms for The Netherlands and Flanders. The last norms dated from 1986 (when the Dutch WISC-R had been published) and due to the well-known Flynn effect (e.g., Flynn, 1984), referring to increases of cognitive scores over generations, we know that regular assessment of children's intelligence to a contemporary cohort is necessary.

The second objective was to develop actual test items, in which new technological and social developments are taken into account (e.g., e-mail, the new European currency Euro, etc.).

Thirdly, attention had to be paid to the factor structure of the WISC-III since research indicated that four factors had been found in the U.S. tests and a new subtest Symbol Search had been added.

ADAPTATION PROCESS

The UK version (WISC-III^{UK}; Wechsler, 1992) served as a basis for translation and adaptation. For eight subtests (the seven Performance tests and Digit Span) it was not necessary to adapt items for the Dutch version. It was considered possible to translate the UK material without danger of finding large differences in test scores as a consequence of cross-cultural differences. Changes were made in five verbal subtests (Information, Similarities, Arithmetic, Vocabulary, and Comprehension). For this purpose a pilot study with 450 subjects had been executed. For each subtest approximately twice as many items as necessary were developed. A considerable amount of these items were newly created or had their origin in the French and German version of the WISC-III. The choice for the items was based on advice from experts (linguists, experimental psychologists, experts in research within ethnic minority groups) or the scientific literature. The new items were combined with items from the UK version. Each item was examined for cultural item-bias with respect to gender, region of the country, and ethnic group. Special attention regarding the Dutch language was given with respect to word frequency, age of acquisition, influence of dialect, differentiation toward word category, etc.

Constructing items for the WISC-III^{NL}, it became clear that the Dutch language is very susceptible to dialects and an extensive study was necessary to find words without alternative meaning in any dialect. It was also difficult to find words that could be used in both countries. Some words had an alternative meaning in the other country. For example, the word "klok" means "a watch" in The Netherlands and "a standing or hanging clock" in Flanders. On the basis of these criteria, many items from the UK version were withdrawn. The following criteria, for each age level and for the total group, were the main focus of the pilot study: level of item difficulty, mean subtest score and variance in scores in the Dutch and Flemish population, homogeneity, and split-half reliability of subtest and scale scores. The pilot study resulted in five revised subtests, adapted to Dutch-speaking children with small regional sensitivities and accurate psychometric qualities.

In these subtests, sometimes the sequence of the items had been completely changed (e.g., the first seven items in the subtest Similarities). In other cases items were replaced because of obvious cultural differences, e.g., in the subtest Comprehension item 13, item 14, or item 17. Those items were replaced by new items like "Why are museums useful?," "What are the advantages of e-mail versus letters?," and "Why is doping in sports forbidden?"

SAMPLE CHARACTERISTICS

Based on the test scores of $n = 1229$ Dutch-speaking children, norms for the WISC-III^{NL} were developed. These 1229 children formed a representative sample from the total population of both Dutch and Flemish children, with a proportion of 2.5:1, in congruence with the population rate. Furthermore, the sample was selected on the basis of gender, age, school type, and several demographic characteristics as indicated by the National Statistics Offices in both countries. There were at least 100 children in each age category. The ratio of boys to girls was evenly distributed (Table 7.1).

The different levels of primary and secondary school (even special education) were adequately represented in the sample for both The Netherlands and for Flanders. To be certain that all children in the sample had opportunities of schooling in the Dutch language at early ages, the criterion was set of at least six years of experience in the Dutch-speaking school system. Information about the educational level of the parents or family was not publicly accessible. We asked,

TABLE 7.1   Amount of Children, Age, Gender, and Country

Age group	Total			Flanders			The Netherlands		
	Boys	Girls	Total	Boys	Girls	Total	Boys	Girls	Total
6	57	54	111	22	21	43	35	38	68
7	46	56	102	6	15	21	40	41	81
8	66	57	123	6	15	21	50	44	94
9	56	53	109	16	13	29	43	37	80
10	58	60	118	13	16	29	42	47	89
11	53	60	113	12	15	27	41	45	86
12	47	57	104	12	16	28	35	41	76
13	48	53	101	17	17	34	31	36	67
14	61	64	125	20	18	38	41	46	87
15	53	56	109	14	19	33	39	37	76
16	54	56	110	20	18	38	34	38	72
Total	599	626	1229[a]	168	181	353	431	445	876
Percentage	49%	51%	100%	48%	52%	100%	49%	51%	100%

[a]The gender was unknown from four children.

however, for the profession of the parents of the children involved in the sample, and post hoc researched this variable. About 8.5% of the children in our sample are children from immigrants from different ethnic groups (mainly Turkish, Moroccan, Surinamese, and Asian).

RELIABILITY

Table 7.2 shows the split-half reliability coefficients and standard errors of measurement across age for the 13 subtests. The reliability for most subtests is satisfying for all age groups, with the exception of the reliabilities for the subtests Object Assembly and Mazes; the small number of items in these subtests might be the main reason for these lower coefficients. This seems to be in accordance to findings in other countries (reliability coefficients for the subtest Mazes are 0.61–0.78 in the UK version and 0.56–0.89 in the German version).

VALIDITY

In this section, three sources of data are reported which are relevant for the validity of the WISC-III^{NL}: (1) the intercorrelations between the subtests and scale scores; (2) the correlations between the test scores, school marks, and achievement test scores; (3) the results of a factor analysis.

Table 7.3 shows the intercorrelations between the subtests. As can be seen a two-factor structure of the Wechsler subtests emerges; we observe correlations between Verbal tests varying from $r = 0.22$–0.63, between Performance tests from 0.15–0.58; the correlations between Verbal and Performance tests ranges from $r = 0.12$–0.45. The clearly lower intercorrelations of Digit Span with other Verbal tests and of Mazes with the other Performance test are notable and point in the direction of the factor structure as reported below.

The relationships between Performance IQ (PIQ), Verbal IQ (VIQ), and Full Scale IQ (FSIQ) and school performance in Dutch language and Arithmetic for primary school pupils are illustrated in Table 7.4. The correlations are in line with previous findings in The Netherlands. For example, Bleichrodt, Resing, Drenth, & Zaal (1987) reported that in general in these analysis values between 0.40 and 0.50 have been found. For the higher correlations of Arithmetic than Dutch language with PIQ and FSIQ but especially with VIQ, we still do not have a clear explanation.

The relationships between school performance and scores on the subtests are shown in Table 7.5. Most striking are the high r's for Information and the lowest r for Mazes with Arithmetic. This last observation is particularly difficult to explain with the construct of Fluid Intelligence in mind (Kaufman, 1994).

We also investigated the relationship between IQ and school level. Given the differences in organization of the school systems between The Netherlands and

TABLE 7.2 Reliability Coefficients and Standard Errors of Measurement of the Subtests Scaled Scores, IQ scores, and Index Scores, by Age[a]

| | Age in years | | | | | | | | | | | |
	6	7	8	9	10	11	12	13	14	15	16	Average
Information	0.71	0.79	0.75	0.81	0.85	0.85	0.57	0.83	0.87	0.79	0.82	0.79
(SEm)	1.80	1.53	1.59	1.41	1.24	1.20	1.90	1.31	1.31	1.37	1.34	1.45
Similarities	0.84	0.74	0.72	0.78	0.77	0.77	0.72	0.83	0.82	0.84	0.77	0.78
(SEm)	1.41	1.56	1.75	1.53	1.50	1.50	1.59	1.37	1.56	1.47	1.56	1.53
Arithmetic	0.89	0.75	0.75	0.82	0.81	0.82	0.80	0.83	0.79	0.74	0.78	0.80
(SEm)	1.31	1.64	1.64	1.56	1.41	1.44	1.62	1.50	1.62	1.56	1.59	1.54
Vocabulary	0.86	0.87	0.85	0.83	0.81	0.84	0.84	0.90	0.83	0.89	0.87	0.85
(SEm)	1.44	1.24	1.34	1.27	1.34	1.24	1.27	1.08	1.34	1.12	1.27	1.27
Comprehension	0.83	0.86	0.79	0.75	0.77	0.69	0.73	0.61	0.65	0.73	0.65	0.73
(SEm)	1.47	1.24	1.34	1.41	1.56	1.56	1.64	1.75	1.85	1.64	1.87	1.58
Digit span	0.79	0.77	0.72	0.67	0.69	0.77	0.76	0.85	0.88	0.91	0.85	0.79
(SEm)	1.92	1.80	1.99	2.08	1.90	1.72	1.77	1.87	1.53	1.41	1.56	1.78
Picture completion	0.75	0.77	0.70	0.70	0.65	0.75	0.71	0.63	0.47	0.69	0.64	0.68
(SEm)	1.53	1.53	1.70	1.85	1.72	1.59	1.80	1.80	2.12	1.90	1.94	1.77
Coding	—	—	—	—	—	—	—	—	—	—	—	—
(SEm)	1.72	1.72	1.50	1.50	1.50	1.34	1.34	1.34	1.16	1.16	1.16	1.40
Picture arrangement	0.78	0.71	0.70	0.83	0.74	0.74	0.73	0.77	0.67	0.78	0.88	0.76
(SEm)	1.53	1.64	1.64	1.50	1.56	1.64	1.64	1.70	1.77	1.50	1.37	1.59
Block design	0.83	0.82	0.82	0.84	0.85	0.89	0.81	0.89	0.88	0.87	0.86	0.85
(SEm)	1.41	1.47	1.37	1.44	1.34	1.27	1.59	1.27	1.27	1.37	1.31	1.37
Object assembly	0.56	0.66	0.36	0.53	0.67	0.60	0.60	0.46	0.51	0.49	0.58	0.55
(SEm)	2.01	2.08	2.32	2.10	2.06	1.99	1.97	2.12	2.20	2.20	1.90	2.09
Symbol search	—	—	—	—	—	—	—	—	—	—	—	—
(SEm)	1.47	1.47	1.47	1.47	1.47	1.47	1.47	1.47	1.47	1.47	1.47	1.47
Mazes	0.78	0.68	0.75	0.63	0.59	0.49	0.66	0.59	59	0.38	0.57	5.92
(SEm)	1.56	1.75	1.75	2.03	2.03	2.24	2.06	1.62	2.08	2.30	2.12	1.96

[a]The reliability coefficients for all subtests except Coding and Symbol Search are split-half correlations corrected by the Spearman–Brown formula. For Coding and Symbol Search, raw-score test-retest coefficients are based on the UK study.

TABLE 7.3   Intercorrelations of Subtest Scaled Scores ($N = 1229$)

Subtest/scale	Inf	Sim	Ari	Voc	Com	DS	PCom	Cd	PA	BD	OA	SS	Mz
Information	—												
Similarities	0.59	—											
Arithmetic	0.57	0.50	—										
Vocabulary	0.63	0.62	0.50	—									
Comprehension	0.46	0.53	0.39	0.62	—								
Digit span	0.34	0.28	0.35	0.33	0.22	—							
Picture completion	0.30	0.36	0.33	0.34	0.32	0.16	—						
Coding	0.23	0.24	0.26	0.21	0.19	0.22	0.16	—					
Picture arrangement	0.34	0.34	0.35	0.34	0.26	0.22	0.38	0.22	—				
Block design	0.38	0.37	0.45	0.35	0.30	0.28	0.40	0.28	0.39	—			
Object assembly	0.28	0.31	0.29	0.28	0.25	0.24	0.38	0.18	0.37	0.55	—		
Symbol search	0.28	0.27	0.34	0.27	0.20	0.25	0.22	0.58	0.30	0.36	0.26	—	
Mazes	0.14	0.13	0.19	0.16	0.12	0.17	0.16	0.15	0.19	0.31	0.22	0.18	

TABLE 7.4   Correlations Between IQs and School Results for Dutch and Arithmetic for Primary School Pupils in The Netherlands and Flanders ($N = 203$)

	Dutch	Arithmetic	Performance IQ	Verbal IQ	Total IQ
Dutch		0.72[a]	0.37[a]	0.43[a]	0.46[a]
Arithmetic	0.72[a]		0.45[a]	0.48[a]	0.53[a]

[a] Significant at $p = 0.01$.

TABLE 7.5   Correlations between Subtests Scores and School Results for Dutch and Arithmetic for Primary School Students in The Netherlands and Flanders ($N = 203$)

	PC	Inf	Cd	Sim	PA	Arith	BD	Voc	OA	Com	SS	DS	Mz
Dutch	0.20[b]	0.40[b]	0.30[b]	0.34[a]	0.17[a]	0.43[a]	0.33[a]	0.32[a]	0.23[a]	0.20[a]	0.31[a]	0.31[a]	0.20[a]
Arithmetic	0.28[a]	0.45[a]	0.30[a]	0.37[a]	0.21[a]	0.56[a]	0.42[a]	0.32[a]	0.29[a]	0.18[a]	0.37[a]	0.30[a]	0.09

[a] Significant at $p = 0.05$.
[b] Significant at $p = 0.01$.

Flanders, analyses for children from both countries were executed separately. The levels in FSIQ, VIQ, and PIQ appeared to be different, all significant ($p < 0.01$) between the school levels in both regions. It was clear in each analysis that the higher the school level the higher the IQ with regular differences of more than 10 points in IQ score between children from different school levels.

Factor analyses were performed for both the total sample ($n = 1229$) and for subdata sets of 4 age groups: 6–7 years ($n = 212$), 8–10 years ($n = 351$), 11–13 years ($n = 321$), and 14–16 years ($n = 345$). The methods that were used were principal component analysis with maximum likelihood extraction and Varimax rotation. Two other methods were applied also (with PC extraction and Varimax rotation and with ML extraction and Oblimin rotation).

In all analyses, a three-factor solution was dominant. Most striking was the absence of the so-called factor Freedom of Distractibility (subtests Arithmetic, Digit Span, and Coding). In the UK version the explained percentage variance for this factor is only 2–3%. A "new" factor, Processing Speed (subtests Coding and Symbol Search) does emerge very clearly (explained variance nearly 10%; in the UK version only 4–5%). The Verbal Comprehension factor explained about 20% of the variance and the Perceptual Organization factor explained 15%. Omitting the subtest Symbol Search in the analysis did not have any effect. The results from the explorative three-factor solution are shown in Table 7.6. It is only for children in the youngest age group that Processing Speed is not a dominant factor. For these youngest children the high loading (0.70) of Arithmetic for the Verbal Comprehension factor is also remarkable.

CULTURAL ISSUES INFLUENCING WISC-III INTERPRETATIONS IN THE NETHERLANDS AND FLANDERS (BELGIUM)

In this section a summary of some differences is given between two cultural groups which both speak Dutch: The Netherlands and Flanders. The differences between both groups should be interpreted as differences between subpopulations. That was the main reason to create common norms.

The variance in scores for the subtests Vocabulary and Comprehension was different for both countries. Dutch children mostly scored 1 point and Flemish children were more likely to score 0 or 2 points. The mean score is almost the same for both populations. A combination of qualitative and quantitative differences seems to be responsible for this phenomenon. Flemish children gave more short but also more correct answers, while in The Netherlands children tended to give a more extensive and illustrated, but incomplete answer. Furthermore, Flemish children often gave answers as, "I don't know" if they were not sure and Dutch children tended to give an answer anyway, even if they did not understand the question completely. Dutch children were more verbally expressive than Flemish children for whom shyness is more dominant.

There were some clear differences between the scores of both groups on the subtest Information; Flemish children scored significantly higher than Dutch children. These differences most certainly are a reflection of the different educational systems in each country. Generally speaking, in Flanders the school system emphasizes factual knowledge. Therefore, e.g., much attention is paid to correct writing and spelling. In the Dutch educational system, however, it is important for a child to know where to find information and not merely "assessing" that information. Time pressure is less important; and pupils are stimulated to express their opinions. As a consequence they tend to be more assertive.

TABLE 7.6 Maximum-Likelihood Factor Loadings (Varimax Rotation) for Three Factors

Subtest/scale	Factor 1: Verbal comprehension				Factor 2: Perceptual organization				Factor 3: Processing speed			
	Ages				Ages				Ages			
	6–7	8–10	11–13	14–16	6–7	8–10	11–13	14–16	6–7	8–10	11–13	14–16
Information	**0.59**	**0.72**	**0.69**	**0.67**	0.11	0.19	0.32	0.25	**0.49**	0.21	0.12	0.20
Similarities	**0.50**	**0.65**	**0.71**	**0.77**	0.20	0.22	0.27	0.29	**0.41**	0.14	0.13	0.13
Vocabulary	0.21	**0.83**	**0.86**	**0.80**	0.18	0.13	0.18	0.22	**0.90**	0.12	0.10	0.21
Comprehension	0.32	**0.70**	**0.66**	**0.65**	22	0.15	0.13	0.20	**0.57**	0.08	0.04	0.06
Picture completion	0.04	0.41	0.31	0.18	**0.49**	**0.42**	**0.48**	**0.57**	0.29	0.10	0.01	0.14
Picture arrangement	0.24	0.35	0.30	0.24	0.28	**0.33**	**0.40**	**0.41**	0.12	0.16	0.21	0.15
Block design	0.31	0.27	0.16	0.31	**0.72**	**0.71**	**0.73**	**0.60**	0.18	0.22	0.22	0.24
Object assembly	0.13	0.19	0.15	0.22	**0.64**	**0.69**	**0.71**	**0.58**	0.06	0.17	0.03	0.15
Mazes	0.21	0.06	0.09	0.09	**0.46**	**0.50**	0.19	0.14	0.12	0.05	0.10	0.20
Arithmetic	**0.70**	0.54	0.52	0.53	0.20	0.28	0.25	0.27	0.28	0.34	0.19	0.18
Digit span	0.46	0.24	0.30	0.38	0.19	0.13	0.12	0.22	0.17	0.16	0.24	0.25
Coding	0.30	0.17	0.09	0.15	0.13	0.13	0.10	0.14	0.05	**0.66**	**0.78**	**0.79**
Symbol search	0.40	0.17	0.11	0.17	0.30	0.30	0.34	0.39	0.11	**0.81**	**0.80**	**0.64**

Knowing this, it is not surprising that children score in a different way on the WISC-III[NL]. Flemish children score better on Information, Arithmetic, Coding, and Symbol Search. Dutch children score better on Comprehension, Vocabulary, and Picture Completion.

Finally, Dutch children tend to do better than Flemish children on the subtest Mazes. Literature indicates that environmental factors may influence task results in intelligence testing. In The Netherlands, there are large concentrations of the population in areas around big cities (more than 40% versus only 11% in Flanders). Possibly, children in big cities are more familiar with complex tasks such as mazes, because of the daily experience of living in a complex environment.

PROFESSIONAL ISSUES IN THE USE OF INTELLIGENCE TESTS IN THE NETHERLANDS AND FLANDERS (BELGIUM)

We restrict our comments in this section on following topics: how is IQ testing with children typically used in educational and clinical evaluations in our regions, some main issues currently focused by the professional associations, and a search for unity toward classifications according to different IQ levels.

In The Netherlands and Flanders intelligence tests for children are used for different goals. Intelligence tests are widely used for both placement of children with severe learning and/or behavioral problems in special education and for diagnosing the specific problems of the child, including advice about their treatment. Further applications are for the purposes of determining class level of the child, choices of treatment, adaptation of the educational program for the child, etc. (e.g., de Leeuw & Resing, 1985).

First, these tests have predictive value and, consequently, can support the choice of an optimal educational type for each child in trouble and also the prediction of school grades or professional achievement. Secondly, these tests have a significant (and still rising) diagnostic function: correct use of the test[1] will allow evaluation and description of cognitive (dys)functioning of the child. Another goal might be improvement of performance of the child in school. In this case the test has a diagnostic and prescriptive function, whose goal is guided choices for children with difficulties at school.

A third function of intelligence tests concerns screening, but for this purpose tests such as the WISC-III and the RAKIT (Bleichrodt, Drenth, Zaal, & Resing, 1984) are almost never used. We are, in these cases, very careful when evaluating test results. On the one hand we do not want to emphasize the IQ as long as there is no problem situation; on the other hand we do not want to spread the test material "gratuitously" into the public.

[1] Recently in Flanders in this context the question was raised from clinical policy makers: When is it useful to retest children with Wechsler tests and when is this not the case. This resulted in a Dutch article accessible on the Internet (Schittekatte, 2000).

The WISC-III serves a useful and specific purpose for the assessment process. In The Netherlands, the system "Back to School Together" is adopted by educators, whose purpose is to keep as many children as possible in elementary school. If this is not possible the child goes to a school with a special education program or to a school within cluster 1 (blind children, etc.); cluster 2 (deaf children, etc.; language and speech disorders); cluster 3 (mental retardation; serious physical retardation, or a combination of the two) or cluster 4 (psychological disorders). A child enters cluster 3 if the IQ is below 70. Children with a slightly higher IQ and without major problems regarding clusters 1, 2, or 4, will be placed in special elementary school, as will children with serious learning difficulties. It is obvious that in this assessment procedure, measuring intelligence necessarily plays an important role. When the conclusion for a particular child is that his or her IQ reaches below 70, always other aspects of personality, behavior, and social skills will be evaluated. Resing and Evers, *et al.* (2002) stated,

> ... in order to diagnose a person as mentally retarded, three conditions have to be fulfilled. These conditions are based on recommendations of the American Psychiatric Association and the American Association for Mental Retardation, both accepted in The Netherlands. Not only the IQ has to be below 70, there has to be a significant problem on at least two of the following areas: communication, self-care, living independently at home, social skills, self-control/self-discipline, health and safety, functional school skills, effort, and work. The third demand is that the mental retardation needs to be determined before the 18th birthday ...

Second, it is important to report that in both the Dutch and Belgian professional associations of psychologists, the question of the qualifications of the examiners is a hot topic. The main issue is the correct evaluation of the importance of level of education, competence, and experience from the users on the one hand and the kind of test and the test use (e.g., assessing, scoring, interpretation, etc.) on the other hand. The debates are inconclusive for the moment but clear points of view are expected in the near future. Furthermore, the standards for correct test use are focused. Also, the need for more research on intelligence and ethnic minorities is in the center of their discussions. With respect to this last issue Resing and Hessels (2001) conclude that in elementary schools in The Netherlands more and more pupils from ethnic minorities are overrepresented in special education, a tendency also noted in Flanders. These researchers also looked in the available manuals of Dutch intelligence tests for information about scores from children of ethnic minorities. Social economic standard and length of stay seem the most important variables. Whether the norms can be used for these groups of children remains a question. Supplementary intelligence-research with ethnic minority groups is strongly indicated, preferably in relation with learning potential. Special attention is necessary for the scores of children from the second and third generation of the immigrant population. A first analysis of our WISC-III data of the scores of ethnic minorities is hopeful; statistically controlling for the effects of Socioeconomic status (SES) we see the differences between the scores of autochthons and immigrants decrease compared with analyses in the past decade. These differences even fade away for the children with highly educated parents. An important reason that might underlie this evolution is an increasing acculturation of the immigrant population. As a result, among other things, cognitive testing becomes less "unusual" and parents emphasize more cognitive skills early in the development.

Finally, regarding the issue of classification recently a major step forward was made with the publication of a proposition for standard classification for different IQ levels (Resing & Blok, 2002). They propose that every psychologist, when measuring the intelligence of children, adolescents, or adults, will use the same vocabulary when describing the intelligence level in their reports.

REFERENCES

Bleichrodt, N., Drenth, P. J. D., Zaal, J. N., & Resing, W. C. M. (1984). *Revisie Amsterdamse Kinder Intelligentie Test*. Lisse: Swets and Zeitlinger.

Bleichrodt, N., Resing, W. C. M., Drenth, P., & Zaal, J. N. (1987). *Measuring intelligence with children* [Intelligentie-meting bij kinderen: empirische en methodologische verantwoording van de geReviseerde Amsterdamse Kinder Intelligentie Test]. Lisse: Swets and Zeilinger.

Flynn, J. R. (1984). Massive IQ gains in 14 nations: What IQ tests really measure. *Psychological Bulletin, 95*, 29–51.

Kaufman, A. S. (1994). *Intelligent testing with the WISC-III*. New York: Wiley.

Leeuw, L. de, & Resing, W. C. M. (1985). Research on intelligence at school [Intelligentie-onderzoek op school]. In H. P. M. Creemers, P. J. D. Drenth, & D. B. P. Kallen (Eds.), *Losbladig onderwijskundig lexicon*, IO 2100-1-22. Alphen aan den Rijn: Samson.

Resing, W. C. M., & Blok, J. B. (2002). Classification of intelligence scores: Proposition of an univocal system [De classificatie van intelligentiescores. Voorstel voor een eenduidig systeem]. *De Psycholoog, 37*, 244–249.

Resing, W. C. M., Evers, A., Koomen, H. M. Y., Pameijer, N. K., Bleichrodt, N., & Boxtel, H. van (2002). *Assessment for indications: conditions and instrumentarium* [Indicatiestelling: Condities en Instrumentarium]. Amsterdam/Meppel: NDC/Boom.

Resing, W. C. M., & Hessels, M. G. P. (2001). The assessment of cognitive abilities of minority children [Het testen van cognitieve vaardigheden bij allochtone kinderen]. In N. Bleichrodt & F. J. R. van de Vijver (Eds.), *Het gebruik van psychologische tests bij allochtonen: problemen en remedies*. Lisse: Swets and Zeitlinger.

Schittekatte, M. (2000). *Retesting intelligence with children* [Het hertesten van intelligentie bij kinderen: een literatuurstudie]. Significant, published on http://users.skynet.be/vsig.

Wechsler, D. (1992). *Manual for the Wechsler Intelligence Scale for Children—Third Edition UK*. London: The Psychological Corporation.

Wechsler, D. (2002). *Wechsler Intelligence Scale for Children, derde editie NL. Handleiding*. (W. Kort, M. Schittekatte, E. L. Compaan, M. Bosmans, N. Bleichrodt, G. Vermeir, W. C. M. Resing, & P. Verhaeghe, Trans.). London: The Psychological Corporation. (Original work published in 1991.)

8

GERMANY

UWE TEWES

Institute of Medical Psychology
Hannover Medical School
Hannover, Germany

The Hamburg Wechsler Intelligence Test for Children (HAWIK-III) (Wechsler, 1999) is an adaptation of the WISC-III for the German-speaking countries of Europe. Nearly 50 years ago a first German version of the Wechsler Intelligence Scale for Children (WISC) was published, which has been widely used in clinical and educational settings (HAWIK; Hardesty & Priester, 1956). This test remained unchanged for over two decades, although it was increasingly criticized with regard to the validity of numerous items and the reliability of some scales. In addition, it was questioned whether the norms for the test's scales were up to date. With the financial support of the German Research Foundation (Deutsche Forschungs-gemeinschaft) it was possible to develop a revised version, the HAWIK-R in 1983 (Tewes, 1983). Although this version was based on the basic concept of the WISC-R (Wechsler, 1974), a number of marked differences in test items and scoring procedures existed. In the 1990s, several factors contributed to the need for a new adaptation, including the fact that a completely revised English language version had been published (the WISC-III; Wechsler, 1991). In addition, after the reunification of East and West Germany (i.e., the Federal Republic of Germany and the German Democratic Republic), it could no longer be assumed that the norms of the HAWIK-R were representative, in part because the populations from the two parts came from very different educational systems. Since then, adaptations for other German-speaking cultures of other countries have been made (Schallberger, Gysin, Mattes, & Siegrist, 1981), and it was decided to make an adaptation of the WISC-III for the entire area of German-speaking parts of Europe (i.e., Germany,

Culture and Children's Intelligence:
Cross-Cultural Analysis of the WISC-III

121

Austria, and parts of Switzerland). This new version was published in 1999 by
Tewes, Rossmann, & Schallberger (see Wechsler, 1999).

ADAPTATION PROCESS

The details regarding the adaptation for Austria and Switzerland are discussed
in a separate chapter by Rossmann & Schallberger (see Chapter 9). As specified
by the American publisher, the German version was to resemble the UK WISC-III
as closely as possible. Therefore, the scales of the Performance section remained
largely unchanged, and from the subtest Picture Completion only the phone was
eliminated because the device shown is no longer typical for the everyday experience of children with phones. On the other hand, a larger number of changes had
to be made in the Verbal section. For the subtests Information, Similarities, Arithmetic, Vocabulary, and Comprehension, the original items were initially translated
into German. Additional items of little, moderate, and high difficulty were then
added from the HAWIK-R (i.e., six items for Vocabulary and three items for the
remaining scales). Examples for Vocabulary are "to participate," "interrogation,"
"hierarchy," for Comprehension, "Why do things and persons in larger distance
look smaller?," and for Information, "Which metal is fluid in normal temperature?" The items from the Verbal section were chosen so that regional differences
in language utilization would have no influence. More details regarding this issue
can be found in Chapter 9. The new scales of the Verbal section were initially
tested in a sample of 326 German children. Since no important shortcomings were
found, the new scales were used as a basis to create the new norms. The scales
were then reduced to the length of the American original by eliminating those
items with the lowest discriminatory power. This reduction did not decrease the
internal consistency of the scales.

However, it was necessary to make substantial modifications of the contents
of the Arithmetic subtest. A large proportion of the arithmetic problems on the
original American test included calculations with monetary currencies. This posed
problems because the currencies in the three German-speaking European countries were radically different, and in Austria and Germany the introduction of the
Euro was imminent. Therefore, the arithmetic problems were transformed into calculations with other measuring units without, however, altering the calculations
themselves. A later comparison revealed that item difficulties ranked similarly in
the three participating European countries.

SAMPLE CHARACTERISTICS

The norms were based exclusively on data from children who were native
German speakers. The entire sample consisted of $N = 1570$ children (Table 8.1).
In Germany 990 children were included. The Austrian and Swiss populations are

TABLE 8.1   Description of the German Sample

| Age | n | Gender | | Educational level | | | | |
		Boys (%)	Girls (%)	Kindergarten/ preschool (%)	Special school (%)	Primary school (%)	Secondary school (%)	High school (%)
6	90	50	50	40.0	1.1	58.9		
7	90	50	50		6.7	93.3		
8	90	50	50		8.9	91.1		
9	90	50	50		10.0	90.0		
10	90	50	50		10.0	86.7		3.3
11	90	50	50		10.0	86.7		3.3
12	90	50	50		8.9	58.9	21.1	11.1
13	90	50	50		6.7	10.0	62.2	21.1
14	90	50	50		4.4	2.2	72.2	21.1
15	90	50	50		3.3		76.7	20.0
16	90	50	50		6.7		73.3	20.0
Total	990	50	50	3.6	7.0	52.5	27.8	9.1

described in Chapter 9. The composition of the German sample was made according to school types, based on percentages from the German Statistical Yearbook (Statistisches Bundesamt, 1995).

These data were gathered in all regions of Germany. One critique concerning the composition of the sample was that no further subdivision according to socioeconomic criteria was carried out. In regards to this, one should note that Germany has very strict protection of privacy laws with regard to the storage of personal data. Comparison of the results from Germany, Austria, and Switzerland revealed no significant differences of means, and the distribution of raw values showed a large degree of concordance with the data from the U.S. and UK standardization. Hence, systematic errors are very unlikely. However, the German sample showed a greater variation than the Austrian and Swiss samples.

RELIABILITY

Table 8.2 shows the split-half reliability coefficients and standard errors of measurement for the individual subtests. In addition, the IQ and index values are shown both separately for each age group and for the entire sample. These data suggest a slightly higher reliability of the HAWIK-III compared to the WISC-III, although the differences are minimal. Retest reliability coefficients have thus far not been computed for the HAWIK-III, but doing so for tests which can be easily recognized appears problematic.

TABLE 8.2 Reliability Coefficients and Standard Errors of Measurement of the Subtests Scaled Scores, IQ Scores, and Index Scores, by Age

Subtest/scale	Age in years											Average
	6	7	8	9	10	11	12	13	14	15	16	
Information	0.70	0.80	0.79	0.83	0.88	0.84	0.86	0.87	0.87	0.89	0.90	0.85
(SEm)	1.64	1.34	1.37	1.24	1.04	1.20	1.12	1.08	1.08	0.99	0.95	1.20
Similarities	0.78	0.75	0.77	0.83	0.79	0.82	0.76	0.81	0.84	0.78	0.78	0.80
(SEm)	1.41	1.50	1.44	1.24	1.37	1.27	1.47	1.31	1.20	1.41	1.41	1.37
Arithmetic	0.84	0.88	0.81	0.80	0.86	0.82	0.90	0.82	0.86	0.76	0.88	0.84
(SEm)	1.20	1.04	1.31	1.34	1.12	1.27	0.95	1.27	1.12	1.47	1.04	1.20
Vocabulary	0.77	0.75	0.81	0.88	0.89	0.91	0.91	0.91	0.92	0.91	0.93	0.88
(SEm)	1.44	1.50	1.31	1.04	0.99	0.90	0.90	0.90	0.85	0.90	0.79	1.07
Comprehension	0.70	0.75	0.77	0.82	0.86	0.79	0.82	0.81	0.79	0.87	0.85	0.81
(SEm)	1.64	1.50	1.44	1.27	1.12	1.37	1.27	1.31	1.37	1.08	1.16	1.33
Digit span	0.83	0.76	0.88	0.88	0.85	0.87	0.88	0.87	0.88	0.86	0.91	0.88
(SEm)	1.24	1.47	1.41	1.04	1.16	1.08	1.04	1.08	1.04	1.12	0.90	1.15
Picture completion	0.70	0.80	0.75	0.83	0.79	0.73	0.77	0.71	0.48	0.68	0.77	0.74
(SEm)	1.64	1.34	1.50	1.24	1.37	1.56	1.44	1.62	2.16	1.70	1.44	1.56
Coding	—	0.86	—	—	—	0.83	—	—	—	—	—	0.85
(SEm)	—	1.12	—	—	—	1.24	—	—	—	—	—	1.18
Picture arrangement	0.71	0.69	0.77	0.80	0.82	0.73	0.74	0.76	0.73	0.68	0.74	0.75
(SEm)	1.62	1.67	1.44	1.34	1.27	1.56	1.53	1.47	1.56	1.70	1.53	1.52
Block design	0.84	0.87	0.86	0.89	0.91	0.90	0.89	0.91	0.87	0.85	0.88	0.88
(SEm)	1.20	1.08	1.12	0.99	0.91	0.90	0.99	0.91	1.08	1.16	1.04	1.04
Object assembly	0.75	0.68	0.62	0.74	0.71	0.60	0.76	0.63	0.65	0.62	0.59	0.68
(SEm)	1.50	1.70	1.85	1.53	1.62	1.90	1.47	1.82	1.77	1.85	1.92	1.73

Symbol search	—	0.80	—	—	—	0.77	—	—	—	—	—	0.79
(SEm)	—	1.34	—	—	—	1.44	—	—	—	—	—	1.39
Mazes	0.82	0.89	0.69	0.69	0.71	0.60	0.68	0.63	0.56	0.58	0.66	0.69
(SEm)	1.27	0.99	1.67	1.67	1.62	1.90	1.70	1.82	1.99	1.94	1.75	1.69
Verbal IQ	0.91	0.92	0.93	0.95	0.96	0.95	0.95	0.95	0.96	0.95	0.96	0.95
(SEm)	4.50	4.24	3.79	3.35	3.00	3.35	3.35	3.35	3.00	3.35	3.00	3.53
Performance IQ	0.90	0.90	0.91	0.94	0.94	0.92	0.93	0.91	0.89	0.89	0.90	0.91
(SEm)	4.74	4.74	4.50	3.67	3.67	4.24	3.97	4.50	4.97	4.97	4.74	4.45
Full scale IQ	0.94	0.95	0.95	0.97	0.97	0.96	0.97	0.96	0.95	0.95	0.96	0.96
(SEm)	3.67	3.35	3.35	2.60	2.60	3.00	2.60	3.00	3.35	3.35	3.00	3.10
Verbal comp. index	0.89	0.90	0.92	0.94	0.95	0.95	0.94	0.95	0.95	0.95	0.96	0.94
(SEm)	4.97	4.74	4.24	3.67	3.35	3.35	3.67	3.35	3.35	3.35	3.00	3.78
Percept. organ. index	0.89	0.89	0.89	0.93	0.93	0.90	0.92	0.90	0.87	0.87	0.89	0.90
(SEm)	4.97	4.97	4.97	3.97	3.97	4.74	4.24	4.74	5.41	5.41	4.97	4.79
Freed. distract. index	0.89	0.88	0.86	0.90	0.91	0.89	0.92	0.89	0.90	0.83	0.92	0.89
(SEm)	4.97	5.20	5.61	4.74	4.50	4.97	4.24	4.97	4.74	6.18	4.24	4.97
Proc. speed index	0.86	0.88	0.87	0.87	0.88	0.87	0.87	0.87	0.87	0.88	0.87	0.87
(SEm)	5.61	5.20	5.41	5.41	5.20	5.41	5.41	5.41	5.41	5.20	5.41	5.37
n	129	142	143	141	151	160	147	147	135	147	128	1570

Note: The reliability coefficients for all subtests except Coding and Symbol Search are split-half correlations corrected by the Spearman-Brown formula. For Coding and Symbol Search the scores for the first minute were correlated with the scores for the second minute, and the correlations were corrected by the Spearman-Brown formula.

EVIDENCE OF VALIDITY

As the WISC-III, the HAWIK-III represents a revision of an established tool rather than a new test. As is pointed out in Chapter 1 about the American version, few tests exist that have been researched as well as the Wechsler scales. It would certainly not be practical to reinvent the wheel and replicate all previous validity studies for the new version. For the HAWIK-III, thus far results exist concerning the construct validity and some results regarding the criterion validity.

The intercorrelations of the subtests differed only very slightly from those of the U.S. and UK versions (see Table 8.3). In addition, factor analyses based on the Maximum Likelihood Method with Varimax rotation were carried out to reveal two factors demonstrating the difference between the Verbal and Performance sections and to reveal four factors for the representation of the four index scores (see Tables 8.4 and 8.5). The construct validity of the concept of four index scores developed in the American version was replicated.

With regard to criterion validity, differences between school types and correlations with school performance were evaluated, based on the samples from Germany, Austria, and Switzerland. As expected, children from more advanced types of school had better test scores (e.g., college preparatory schools) than children of the same age group from less academically demanding schools (Table 8.6).

Correlations with school performances were evaluated for the Austrian and Swiss samples (see Tables 8.7 and 8.8). It was found that the correlation between

TABLE 8.3 Intercorrelation of Subtest Scale Scores

Subtest/scale	Inf	Sim	Ari	Voc	Com	DS	PCom	Cd	PA	BD	OA	SS	Mz
Information													
Similarities	0.64												
Arithmetic	0.56	0.50											
Vocabulary	0.66	0.65	0.48										
Comprehension	0.52	0.54	0.37	0.65									
Digit span	0.38	0.35	0.43	0.36	0.33								
Picture completion	0.45	0.46	0.34	0.45	0.41	0.28							
Coding	0.27	0.27	0.30	0.30	0.25	0.33	0.21						
Picture arrangement	0.44	0.41	0.40	0.43	0.33	0.29	0.45	0.33					
Block design	0.45	0.46	0.45	0.43	0.36	0.36	0.47	0.34	0.46				
Object assembly	0.38	0.33	0.34	0.31	0.29	0.30	0.43	0.32	0.48	0.59			
Symbol search	0.31	0.30	0.34	0.32	0.23	0.35	0.29	0.54	0.37	0.42	0.38		
Mazes	0.25	0.21	0.24	0.24	0.21	0.23	0.30	0.18	0.25	0.39	0.30	0.20	

TABLE 8.4 Maximum-Likelihood-Factor Loadings (Varimax-Rotation) for Two Factors

Subtest/scale	Verbal					Performance				
	6–7	8–10	11–13	14–16	Total	6–7	8–10	11–13	14–16	Total
Information	0.68	0.75	0.72	0.70	0.71	0.21	0.35	0.32	0.39	0.33
Similarities	0.58	0.71	0.74	0.75	0.72	0.23	0.32	0.33	0.32	0.31
Arithmetic	0.51	0.60	0.51	0.41	0.49	0.38	0.36	0.40	0.45	0.41
Vocabulary	0.71	0.79	0.84	0.86	0.82	0.20	0.26	0.25	0.25	0.24
Comprehension	0.64	0.60	0.67	0.75	0.66	0.24	0.36	0.18	0.10	0.22
Digit span	0.44	0.48	0.36	0.16	0.34	0.36	0.40	0.40	0.31	0.39
Picture completion	0.42	0.40	0.40	0.41	0.41	0.46	0.51	0.45	0.44	0.47
Coding	0.14	0.25	0.26	0.15	0.20	0.29	0.47	0.54	0.44	0.47
Picture arrangement	0.31	0.41	0.36	0.33	0.36	0.44	0.56	0.56	0.55	0.54
Block design	0.24	0.40	0.33	0.25	0.31	0.75	0.67	0.72	0.70	0.71
Object assembly	0.29	0.18	0.19	0.08	0.17	0.65	0.76	0.71	0.71	0.71
Symbol search	0.22	0.27	0.21	0.16	0.20	0.44	0.50	0.59	0.57	0.54
Mazes	0.11	0.25	0.12	0.16	0.17	0.57	0.36	0.43	0.34	0.41
Eigenvalue	2.67	3.35	3.18	2.97	3.01	2.46	2.91	2.99	2.74	2.83
% of variance	20.51	25.70	24.44	22.84	23.17	18.95	22.36	23.01	21.10	21.75

school performance and the HAWIK-III test scores was slightly higher in the Swiss sample compared to the Austrian sample. Tests scores were more highly correlated with the teacher's estimation of the student's intelligence than with school performance.

German children with learning disabilities showed markedly decreased test scores for all scales (see Table 8.9). However, a divergence of test scores as large as that reported for American children with learning disabilities (Rourke, 1998) was not found in the German sample. Similar to the American findings, German children with learning disabilities showed the largest deficits in the index score for Verbal Comprehension.

In addition, a clinical sample of children with attention deficit hyperactivity disorder (ADHD) was evaluated (see Table 8.10). A comparison of these data with those from various earlier studies on the validity of the WISC-III (Prifitera & Dersh, 1993; Schwean, Saklofske, Yackulic, & Quinn, 1993; Anastopoulos, Spisto, & Maher, 1994; Saklofske, Schwean, Yackulic, & Quinn, 1994) reveals similar results, although the scores from the German ADHD sample shows clearer divergence in certain areas. As in previous studies, the German sample shows more pronounced deficits in the Verbal IQ than in the Performance IQ. Smallest deficits were found for the index scores of both the HAWIK-III and the WISC-III, and similar to the American sample, German children with ADHD had the best scores in the Picture Completion subtest.

TABLE 8.5   Maximum-Likelihood Factor Loadings (Varimax Rotation) for Four Factors

Subtest/scale	Factor 1: Verbal comprehension				Factor 2: Perceptual organization				Factor 3: Freedom from distractibility				Factor 4: Processing speed			
	Ages				Ages				Ages				Ages			
	6–7	8–10	11–13	14–16	6–7	8–10	11–13	14–16	6–7	8–10	11–13	14–16	6–7	8–10	11–13	14–16
Information	0.61	0.39	0.76	0.64	0.19	0.34	0.29	0.35	0.27	0.51		0.35	0.06	0.17	0.16	10
Similarities	0.55	0.29	0.62	0.71	0.19	0.28	0.27	0.26	0.16	0.29	n	0.30	0.15	0.11	0.24	13
Vocabulary	0.72	0.86	0.67	0.85	0.15	0.27	0.21	0.21	0.13	0.27	o	0.16	0.15	0.17	0.21	18
Comprehension	0.68	0.41	0.35	0.77	0.23	0.38	0.15	0.09	0.05	0.28		0.02	0.09	0.15	0.15	12
Picture completion	0.44	0.26	0.33	0.38	0.49	0.56	0.55	0.46	0.06	0.17	s	0.16	0.05	0.13	0.07	10
Picture arrangement	0.26	0.23	0.28	0.30	0.38	0.48	0.54	0.51	0.20	0.22	o	0.16	0.23	0.34	0.21	28
Block design	0.23	0.17	0.26	0.21	0.74	0.68	0.63	0.60	0.09	0.28	l	0.23	0.21	0.19	0.29	23
Object assembly	0.29	0.09	0.13	0.05	0.64	0.72	0.68	0.79	0.13	0.13	u	0.04	0.13	0.25	0.20	25
Mazes	0.09	0.21	0.13	0.15	0.52	0.42	0.43	0.31	0.13	0.13	t	0.14	0.17	0.05	0.07	09
Arithmetic	0.32	0.18	0.56	0.30	0.24	0.23	0.27	0.28	0.90	0.68	i	0.63	0.18	0.24	0.16	21
Digit span	0.37	0.24	0.31	0.12	0.28	0.31	0.19	0.14	0.29	0.49	o	0.23	0.21	0.28	0.30	29
Coding	0.10	0.10	0.17	0.13	0.16	0.14	0.24	0.13	0.09	0.14	n	0.02	0.34	0.90	0.84	72
Symbol search	0.12	0.11	0.15	0.11	0.19	0.29	0.28	0.29	0.08	0.23		0.19	0.97	0.55	0.62	65

TABLE 8.6   Educational Level

Subtest/scale	Germany		Austria		Switzerland (Sekundarstufen)	
	HauptRealsch.	Gymnasium	Hauptschule	AHS	Grundansprüche	Erweiterte Ansprüche
	$n = 140$	$n = 48$	$n = 93$	$n = 44$	$n = 20$	$n = 66$
Information	9.0	11.5	9.8	11.8	7.7	10.7
Similarities	9.3	13.1	8.9	10.1	9.3	11.1
Arithmetic	9.6	11.9	9.4	11.3	9.6	12.0
Vocabulary	9.7	12.2	8.8	10.7	8.1	9.5
Comprehension	10.8	12.1	8.0	9.4	8.2	8.8
Digit span	10.3	11.3	8.6	11.1	8.8	9.3
Picture completion	9.8	11.2	9.1	10.0	9.5	10.9
Coding	9.8	11.4	9.9	11.3	9.6	10.3
Picture arrangement	9.7	11.1	9.5	10.9	9.7	11.1
Block design	9.5	11.8	8.9	10.3	9.0	11.9
Object assembly	9.8	11.1	10.1	11.5	9.1	10.6
Symbol search	9.7	11.3	10.2	10.7	9.8	11.1
Mazes	9.9	10.7	9.8	10.5	10.6	10.9
Verbal IQ	99.2	114.5	94.6	104.3	91.7	102.8
Performance IQ	98.8	110.2	97.4	106.5	96.6	107.4
Full scale IQ	98.8	114.0	95.2	106.0	93.2	105.7
Verbal comprehension index	99.5	114.1	94.5	103.5	90.9	100.5
Percept. organization index	99.1	109.4	97.2	105.3	96.4	108.2
Freedom-distract. index	100.4	110.1	94.8	107.8	95.7	104.6
Processing speed index	98.7	107.8	100.5	105.6	98.7	104.0

TABLE 8.7 Correlations between IQ Scales, Grades, and Intelligence Rating by Teachers (Switzerland)

Age groups	Year	n	Scale	Mathematics	German	Notendurchschnitt	Intelligence rating by teachers
Young Children	1–3	84	Verbal IQ	0.40	0.40	0.46	0.39
			Performance IQ	0.25	0.31	0.32	0.33
			Full scale IQ	0.37	0.41	0.45	0.41
Old Children	4–6	82	Verbal IQ	0.44	0.44	0.50	0.58
			Performance IQ	0.32	0.33	0.38	0.49
			Full scale IQ	0.45	0.46	0.52	0.64
Total	1–6	166	Verbal IQ	0.42	0.40	0.47	0.49
			Performance IQ	0.28	0.30	0.33	0.40
			Full scale IQ	0.40	0.41	0.47	0.52

TABLE 8.8 Correlations between IQ Scales, Index Scores, and Grades (Austria)

Scale	Volksschule ($N = 119$)			Hauptschule ($N = 93$)		
	Mathematics	German	Mean	Mathematics	German	Mean
Verbal comprehension index	0.39	0.27	0.35	0.44	0.32	0.43
Percept. organization index	0.35	0.28	0.33	0.14	0.13	0.16
Freedom-distractibility index	0.39	0.23	0.33	0.33	0.31	0.36
Processing speed index	0.26	0.16	0.23	0.17	0.25	0.24
Verbal IQ	0.40	0.26	0.35	0.44	0.31	0.43
Performance IQ	0.36	0.29	0.35	0.15	0.19	0.19
Full scale IQ	0.43	0.31	0.40	0.35	0.30	0.37

CULTURAL ISSUES INFLUENCING THE WISC-III INTERPRETATION IN GERMANY

The German-language version of the WISC-III (i.e., the HAWIK-III) has been commercially available for 2 years. Empirical findings concerning possible cultural influences on the test results and their interpretation are therefore not yet present for the German-language areas. However, similar considerations were made for the HAWIK-R (WISC-R), which are likely to apply at least in part to the HAWIK-III.

TABLE 8.9   Means for IQ, Factor Index, and Subtest for Normal Children and Children with Learning Disabilities

Subtest/scale	Children with learning disabilities (grades 1–6) n = 42		Normal children (grades 1–6) n = 456	
	Mean	Standard deviation	Mean	Standard deviation
Information	5.2	2.9	10.4	3.0
Similarities	5.1	2.6	10.4	3.0
Arithmetic	5.7	2.1	10.4	2.9
Vocabulary	5.2	2.8	10.2	3.2
Comprehension	5.0	3.0	10.9	3.1
Digit span	5.7	2.8	10.5	3.0
Picture completion	6.5	3.9	10.4	3.0
Coding	6.7	3.0	10.3	3.0
Picture arrangement	5.6	3.0	9.8	3.0
Block design	4.9	3.2	10.0	3.3
Object assembly	6.6	3.4	10.2	2.9
Symbol search	6.2	3.0	10.3	3.2
Mazes	7.4	3.2	10.2	3.3
Verbal IQ	75.0	10.9	103.7	14.7
Performance IQ	77.8	14.9	101.7	14.8
Full scale IQ	75.2	11.4	103.1	14.9
Verbal comprehension index	75.7	11.3	103.8	14.6
Percept. organization index	78.6	14.9	101.6	14.9
Freedom-distractibility index	76.9	11.2	103.6	14.7
Processing speed index	81.4	14.1	101.8	15.0

In regard to possible cultural factors, one must differentiate between two different influences. First, it is conceivable that individual items or subtests measure different things in different countries. However, this potential problem would normally be solved by the use of country-specific norms. A problem would only arise if a child was tested within a different culture and his or her test results were interpreted based on those different culture-specific norms. Secondly, because tests results are influenced by culture experiences, it is possible that within one country, children from a specific ethnical background would have advantages or disadvantages.

For the HAWIK-III and its previous versions (HAWIK-R, HAWIK) there are no empirical studies to support any such effects. This may be attributed primarily to the fact that the proportion of citizens of foreign descent is still very small in Germany and that these tests' norms were therefore exclusively made for children whose native language is German.

TABLE 8.10   Means for IQ, Factor Index, and Subtest for Children with ADHD

Subtest/scale	Mean	Standard deviation
Information	7.6	2.1
Similarities	8.6	2.7
Arithmetic	8.2	3.0
Vocabulary	7.4	2.7
Comprehension	8.8	2.9
Digit span	8.8	2.2
Picture completion	12.7	2.5
Coding	8.3	2.8
Picture arrangement	7.7	2.7
Block design	9.1	3.2
Object assembly	9.4	2.5
Symbol search	8.2	3.2
Mazes	11.1	2.9
Verbal IQ	88.6	12.3
Performance IQ	97.8	12.6
Full scale IQ	92.9	10.7
Verbal comprehension index	87.9	12.8
Percept. organization index	98.1	11.9
Freedom-distractibility index	91.7	13.5
Processing speed index	90.4	15.0

The debate over possible cultural influences is therefore largely based upon intuition rather than empirical data. The following exemplary arguments are at the center of this discussion:

1. Unlike those subtests which enter into the Performance IQ, the tasks and subtests for the Verbal IQ are more strongly influenced by education and learning experience, and hence also cultural influences (Zimbardo & Gering, 1999).
2. Tasks and norms of the Verbal section are based primarily on experiences of the middle class, and this holds particularly true for the Comprehension and Information subtests (Legewie & Ehlers, 1992).
3. Numerous items of the Performance subtest, in particular Picture Completion, Picture Arrangement, and Object Assembly, are based on objects or contents which are typical for the experiences and background of North American children, and their contents may cease to be up-to-date more quickly than the norms can be renewed (Guthke, Böttcher, & Sprung, 1991). It was additionally criticized that some children may be put at a disadvantage by the presence of stereotypes which are influenced by socioeconomic status in the subtest Picture Arrangement (Sühring & Sühring, 1984).

The discussion about the validity of these arguments constitutes the contents of this book. Clearly, these issues should not be answered based on the data of one single country, but one should nevertheless mention some experiences regarding intercultural comparisons of the test results. The adaptation of the WISC-R for Germany involved marked alterations in items and scales in both the Verbal and Performance sections. In contrast, the German adaptation of the WISC-III was much more closely based on the American original. The Performance sections were unchanged except for a minor modification in the Picture Completion subtest, and in the Verbal section close attention was paid to ensure an optimal distribution of item difficulties. Since the translation into German of some of the English originals affected the degree of difficulty for some items, some of the original items were replaced by new constructions. For the HAWIK-R it was noted that some children tended to give a political rather than factually correct answer. For example, the answer to the question why oil swims on top of water was in some cases answered by suggesting that the industries had drained the oil into the water. In those cases one would then have to ask why it is that the oil swims on top after being drained into the water. In the Performance section of the WISC-III, most of the above-mentioned limitations and difficulties were solved. The contents and presentation forms were kept neutral such that there were no difficulties regarding the adaptation to circumstances in German. However, in the German adaptation of the Picture Completion subtest, the item "phone" was eliminated, although it had revealed the highest discriminatory power for the entire sample. The children were supposed to recognize that the phone cord was missing. However, due to the increasing use of cordless phones, the difficulty and validity of this item are likely to change very quickly. The high discriminatory power of this item in the entire sample probably simply reflects an effect of age, reflecting different everyday experiences of older and younger children. Older children have more experiences than younger children with phones with an attached cord. For the remaining subtests there was no evidence that individual items posed particular problems for German compared to American children. It is noteworthy, however, that German children of all age groups received higher raw scores in the subtest Block Design than American children. This type of task appears to be easier for German than American children.

An interesting side finding should also be mentioned. The variance of the subtest scores was higher in the German than the Austrian and Swiss samples. That may be an effect of the larger N in the German sample, or one could conclude that Germany has both more highly intelligent and less gifted children. However, an empirically based explanation does not exist. The German school system, which is more hierarchically structured, may also play a role in this finding. The sample of children tested for the creation of the norms was representative with regard to percentage of children in each school form, and it has been shown that children from different school forms do in fact have different test results (see Table 8.6). These results are also in accordance with those of the Program for International Student Assessment (PISA) study which compared the basic knowledge and abilities of students in the larger industrial nations. In addition to the finding that

German scores were below the mean, it was also found that there was a greater variance in German students' scores compared to those of students from other nations (Baumert, 2001).

PROFESSIONAL ISSUES IN THE USE OF INTELLIGENCE TESTS IN GERMANY

In recent years, the opinion has spread among diagnostic experts that in the interest of effective quality control in the field of psychological diagnostics it is necessary for all diagnostic tools to adhere to the modern standards of test development, and that these tools should be exclusively applied and interpreted by qualified experts.

Unfortunately the development of obligatory guidelines is problematic because of the diverging viewpoints of different interest groups. For example, professional organizations, scientific societies, and publishers argue about the contents of such guidelines and about the issue of quality control. In particular, a current debate over whether a bottom-up quality management, which could be established fairly quickly in the various application fields of psychological diagnostics would be preferable to a top-down management which would be more difficult and time-consuming to organize (see Tewes, 1998).

In Germany, intense debate is ongoing with regards to which test-theoretical basis intelligence tests should be constructed upon. Some test authors reject the approach based on the classical model and argue that intelligence tests should be developed based upon the Rasch model instead. In the meantime, a German version of the WISC, based on probabilistic theory, has been published and is being used as an adaptive measurement tool (Kubinger & Wurst, 1985).

The German-language version of the WISC has been used predominantly in clinical and special-educational diagnostics (Tewes & Titze, 1983). In clinical diagnostics it had been used primarily in the fields of neurology, child and youth psychiatry, and in clinical psychology. Since the HAWIK (WISC) remained unchanged for a long time, a shift in the norms took place. In addition, the content of numerous items was no longer up-to-date. The HAWIK-R (WISC-R) received positive resonance from the field of clinical diagnostics, while it remained disputed among users in educational diagnostics, much like its predecessor (i.e., the HAWIK) had been. Although the test had been certified by the responsible governmental agencies as an officially approved tool, numerous educators and psychologists strongly opposed its use. In part, this was due to the opposition by a large group of professionals regarding the use of intelligence tests in general, arguing that the determination of the IQ in less talented children would lead to a stigmatization. In addition, it was feared that the assessment of the IQ could be abused for selection purposes. Followers of this group prefer tools based on dynamical assessments as an approach to evaluating learning potential. However, in the past years, the use of intelligence tests for the diagnosis of highly and less talented children have been viewed less critically, and it seems that intelligence tests including the German versions of the Wechsler Tests are used increasingly, not only in routine diagnostics but also in scientific investigations.

REFERENCES

Anastopoulos, A. D., Spisto, M. A., Maher, M. C. (1994). The WISC-III freedom from distractibility factor: Its utility in identifying children with attention deficit hyperactivity disorder. *Psychological Assessment, 6*, 368–371.

Baumert, J. (Ed.) (2001). *Basiskompetenzen von Schülerinnen und Schülern im internationalen Vergleich*. Leverkusen: Leske & Budrich.

Guthke, J., Böttcher, H. R., & Sprung, L. (1991). *Psychodiagnostik*. Berlin: Verlag Deutscher Wissenschaften.

Hardesty, F. P., & Priester, H. J. (1956). *Hamburg-Wechsler-Intelligenztest für Kinder (HAWIK)*. Bern: Hans Huber.

Kubinger, K. D., & Wurst, E. (1985). *Adaptives Intelligenzdiagnostikum*. Weinheim: Beltz.

Legewie, H., & Ehlers, W. (1992). *Knaurs moderne Psychologie* (2nd ed.). München: Droemer Knaur.

Prifitera, A., & Dersh, J. (1993). Base rates of WISC-III diagnostic subtest patterns among normal, learning-disabled an ADHD samples. *Journal of Psychoeducational Assessment, WISC-III Monograph Series*, 43–55.

Rourke, B. P. (1998). Significance of verbal-performance discrepancies for subtypes of children with learning disabilities—opportunities for the WISC-III. In A. Prifitera & D. H. Saklowske (Eds.), *WISC-III clinical use an interpretation: Scientistic-practitioner perspectives* (pp. 139–156). San Diego, CA: Academic Press.

Saklofske, D. H., Schwean, V. L., Yackulic, R. A., & Quinn, D. (1994). WISC-III and SB:FE performance of children with Attention Deficit Disorders. *Canadian Journal of School Psychology, 10*, 167–171.

Schallberger, U., Gysin, H. R., Mattes, W., & Siegrist, M. (1981). *Die Anwendung des HAWIK bei deutschschweizer Kindern. Mit einer Normierung für dass 9. bis 12.* Lebensjahr. Bern: Huber.

Schwean, V. L., Saklofske, D. H., Yackulic, R. A., & Quinn, D. (1993). *WISC-III performance of ADHD children*. Journal of Psychoeducational Assessment, WISC-III Monograph, 56–70.

Statistisches Bundesamt (1995). *Statistisches Jahrbuch 1995*. Stuttgart: Metzler & Poeschel.

Sühring, H., & Sühring, S. (1984). Die Bildergeschichten des Subtests Bilderordnen im HAWIK-R. Eine kritische Betrachtung. *Zeitschrift für Heilpädagogik, 35*, 725–731.

Tewes, U. (Ed.) (1983). *Hamburg-Wechsler-Intelligenztest für Kinder (HAWIK-R)*. Bern: Hans Huber.

Tewes, U. (1998). Qualitätsmanagement in der Psychologischen Diagnostik. *Zeitschrift für Medizinische Psychologie, 7*, 114–120.

Tewes, U., & Titze, I. (1983). Untersuchungen zur Anwendung des HAWIK in der klinischen und sonderpädagogischen Diagnostik. *Zeitschrift für Differentielle und Diagnostische Psychologie. 4*, 179–201.

Wechsler, D. (1974). *Wechsler Intelligence Scale for Children—Revised*. San Antonio, TX: The Psychological Corporation.

Wechsler, D. (1991). *Wechsler Intelligence Scale for Children—Third Edition*. San Antonio, TX: The Psychological Corporation.

Wechsler, D. (1999). *Hamburg-Wechsler-Intelligenztest für Kinder (HAWIK-III)* (U. Tewes, P. Rossmann, & U. Schallberger, Trans.). Bern, Switzerland: Hans Huber. (Original work published in 1991.)

Zimbardo, P. G., & Gering, R. J. (1999). *Psychologie* (7th ed.). Berlin, Heidelberg: Springer.

9

AUSTRIA AND SWITZERLAND

PETER ROSSMANN

Institute of Education
Karl-Franzens University of Graz
Graz, Austria

URS SCHALLBERGER

Department of Applied Psychology
University of Zurich
Zurich, Switzerland

The German-language version of the Wechsler Intelligence Scale for Children (WISC-III); (see Chapter 8) has been adapted by a joint working group from Germany, Austria, and Switzerland and was published as the HAWIK-III by Tewes, Rossmann, & Schallberger (Wechsler, 1999). The abbreviation "HAWIK" stands for "Hamburg Wechsler Intelligenztest für Kinder" (Hamburg Wechsler Intelligence Test for Children), which traditionally was the name of the German WISC adaptations (Hardesty & Priester, 1956; Tewes, 1983). The third edition of the HAWIK accordingly is based on the third edition of the WISC. But the HAWIK-III project was new in several respects. Most important is the fact that the adaptation and standardization of the test was intended from the very beginning to be valid for the whole German-speaking area. The HAWIK-III was adapted and standardized not only for West Germany (which in the past was the rule for most of the tests that have been published in German) but for all the major German-speaking regions of modern Europe. These regions are: (1) the reunited Germany, with inclusion of the former East Germany, the so-called "new federal countries," which are part of the Federal Republic of Germany since 1990, (2) Austria, and (3) the German-speaking regions of Switzerland. This geographical area together comprises a total population of more than 90 million inhabitants, which is an enormous number of inhabitants for European standards. However, the cultural and linguistic diversity in this area is enormous as well, and high cultural diversification does not facilitate the development and standardization of mental tests, as every professional knows.

In this chapter the discussion will be centered on the extent that the new HAWIK-III is equivalent in Germany, Austria, and Switzerland with regard to the distribution of Scaled Scores at the subtest level as well as with regard to IQ and index scores. Data on the equivalence of reliability of subtests and the full scale will also be reported.

ADAPTATION PROCESS

Austria, Switzerland, and Germany are three countries differing widely in their historical and cultural development. In this respect even within each of the three countries there are remarkable regional differences. Germany, for example, originally emerged out of nearly 300 small states and cities, which were still relatively independent a few centuries ago. The situation in Austria and Switzerland is very similar. Both countries are federal republics composed of relatively small federal states and cities, which are not only units of administration, but also show notable differences, especially with regard to the regional variants of the German language spoken. Everybody who has learned German at school and who ever had the opportunity to travel through some of the northern and southern German-speaking regions in Europe understands these differences. Even for German native speakers it is sometimes impossible to understand the language of Austrians and Swiss, though they are considered to and consider themselves to speak "German." In Switzerland the differences between the regional dialects are of such an extent that in some places people from different Swiss regions, which are no more than 20–30 km apart from each other (linear distance, with high mountains in between), can hardly understand each other. Also it has been said that German is literally a kind of foreign language for the Swiss, which is learned like other foreign languages in school. In everyday life, as well as in radio and TV, local dialects are spoken, which have very little resemblance to the official German language. Under these circumstances the project of adapting a single test of intellectual functioning for the use in all three German-speaking countries is a delicate and challenging enterprise.

Thus it was very important to pay special attention to the adaptation of the verbal subtests (see also the account given by Tewes in Chapter 8). With regard to the translation of the original (UK version) WISC-III items there were in principle two pathways followed. The first was, wherever possible, to try to find one single translation that was understood and had the same meaning in all the geographic regions mentioned above, thus resulting in comparable item difficulty and item-total correlations in Germany, Austria, and Switzerland. In case such a single translation or adaptation could not be achieved, the second possible solution was to find several regional translations for an item, which were also expected to result in comparable estimates of the major psychometric item characteristics. This procedure was necessary with regard to some items and scoring directions that had to be adapted to local linguistic variants or national differences. So, for example, "Members of Parliament" are called "Bundestagsabgeordnete" in Germany, "Nationalratsabgeordnete," in Austria and "Nationalräte" in Switzerland. The respective translations of "number plates" in the three countries are "Nummernschilder," "Nummerntafeln," and "Autonummern." "Ice cream" is called "Eistüte" in Germany and Austria, but "Glace" in Switzerland; "cake" translates as "Keks (*m*)" in Germany, "Keks (*n*)" in Austria, and "Guetzli" in Switzerland. Altogether in the German WISC-III there are 22 items with a special adaptation for at least one of the three countries. Most of these items belong to the Information (9 items), Arithmetic (6), and Comprehension (4) subtests. The "national" adaptations of items are explicitly described in the directions for administration and scoring section of the HAWIK-III manual.

Although every effort was made to achieve an optimal solution, some compromise in item translation and selection was inevitable. Some of the original WISC-III items had to be discarded from the very beginning because it was evident that a translation or adaptation of the kind mentioned above could never work. Therefore some new items had to be constructed in order to replace the discarded ones and some additional items were necessary in order to have enough items in reserve for item analysis (for details see also Chapter 8).

Special problems arose with regard to some items of the Arithmetic subtest which require numerical operations with money (pounds and pence in the UK version). The difficulties with these items were twofold. First, at the time of test adaptation there were three different currencies in Germany, Austria, and Switzerland (German mark, Austrian schilling, and Swiss franc) with substantially differing values. And second, soon after the publication of the test two of the three countries, Germany and Austria, were expected to adopt the Euro as their new official currency. As a result of this complicated situation none of the original items referring to money seemed acceptable for the German language version. In rewriting the items of the Arithmetic subtest it was therefore primarily attempted to maintain the nature of the logical and numerical operations that had to be performed in order to solve the original problems.

The translation of the original WISC-III items and the construction of new ones were carried out in several rounds of a stepwise feedback process of proposal, correction, and new suggestions by the leaders of the working groups and their co-workers. Then the process of data collection was started and separate item analyses in each of the three countries were carried out. On the basis of item difficulty estimates and part-whole correlations all items were eliminated, whose psychometric characteristics were unsatisfactory in at least one country. In this way it was intended to achieve a single set of items with comparable "national" characteristics.

SAMPLE CHARACTERISTICS

The following analyses are based on the data of the German, Austrian, and Swiss subsamples which together form the HAWIK-III standardization sample of 1570 children and adolescents. The probands have been selected to be representative for the population of 6- to 16-year-olds of both genders in each country. The German subsample is the largest, consisting of 990 cases (for a closer description of the sample characteristics see Chapter 8); the Austrian and Swiss subsamples comprise 300 and 280 cases, respectively. The three subsamples do not differ with regard to their mean age (11.5 years), nor do they differ with regard to the distribution of the sexes (half of the S's in each sample were girls, half boys).

The Austrian subsample was obtained by means of stratified random sampling of 6- to 16-year-olds in the Austrian school system. Because of the high correlation between levels of education and measures of intelligence, a careful stratification procedure was indispensable. Stratification was done on the basis of regional school statistics which give detailed reports of the distribution of students in the different types of Austrian schools and the age distribution in the classes of the schools. The number of Austrian children attending schools in urban and in rural areas is also reported. Within each type of school and area a number of schools were selected for sampling. Within the selected schools a random selection of classes and a random selection of students in each class was made. Thus, the Austrian subsample seems to be a relatively good sample of the distribution of pupils in Austrian schools.

The Swiss subsample fulfills the requirements of stratified random sampling to an even better extent. The Swiss sample was also obtained by stratified random sampling in the school system. The sample was stratified with regard to type of area, type of school, classes, and gender on the basis of sociodemographic statistical information. Eighty municipal districts in Switzerland were randomly selected for sampling and within each of these areas stratified random sampling was performed by means of a very sophisticated procedure, insuring that not more than one child was tested per community and class. Thus the formation of every kind of "lump" in the sample has effectively been avoided. More detailed information on the distribution of age, sex, and type of school in the Austrian and Swiss subsamples can be found in Tables 9.1 and 9.2. However, it should be noted that children who apparently had problems understanding the German language spoken in their environment have not been included in any of the three samples.

RELIABILITY

Table 9.3 provides a cross-national comparison of estimates of reliability at the subtest level as well as at higher levels of aggregation. In order to be able to compare the coefficients of the three national subsamples, split-half coefficients with the

TABLE 9.1 Characteristics of the Austrian Standardization Subsample by Age, Sex, and Educational Level

	Gender		Education level				
Age	Boys (f)	Girls (f)	Primary school (%)	Secondary school (%)	Higher schools (%)	Apprenticeship (%)	Other schools (%)
6	8	11	100.0				
7	11	10	100.0				
8	18	14	100.0				
9	11	12	100.0				
10	18	14	71.9	15.6	12.5		
11	19	19	2.6	81.6	15.8		
12	17	12		58.6	41.4		
13	11	21		65.6	34.4		
14	11	9		75.0	10.0		15.0
15	14	16		13.3	26.7	10.0	50.0
16	12	12			4.2	45.8	50.0
Total	150	150					

TABLE 9.2 Characteristics of the Swiss Standardization Subsample by Age, Sex, and Educational Level

	Gender		Education level				
Age	Boys (f)	Girls (f)	Kindergarten (%)	Primary school (%)	Secondary basic level (%)	Secondary advanced level (%)	Other schools (%)
6	9	11	90	10.0			
7	16	15		100.0			
8	9	12		100.0			
9	16	12		100.0			
10	15	14		100.0			
11	16	16		100.0			
12	11	17		89.3		10.7	
13	11	14		8.0	28.0	60.0	4.0
14	10	15			12.0	80.0	8.0
15	15	12			18.5	77.8	3.7
16	7	7			35.7	50.0	14.3
Total	135	145					

Spearman-Brown correction were calculated for all subtests, except for the two speed tests Coding and Symbol Search. The usual way of computing separate split-half coefficients in 11 different age groups has not been viable due to the relatively small size of the Austrian and Swiss subsamples. Therefore the computations were

TABLE 9.3   Reliability Coefficients of Subtests and IQ Scales by Country and Two Age Bands

	Germany		Austria		Switzerland		
	6–10 $(n = 450)$	11–16 $(n = 540)$	6–10 $(n = 127)$	11–16 $(n = 173)$	6–10 $(n = 129)$	11–16 $(n = 151)$	Average (Manual)
Information	0.89	0.92	0.83	0.82	0.89	0.85	0.85
Similarities	0.85	0.84	0.71	0.70	0.78	0.81	0.80
Arithmetic	0.91	0.88	0.84	0.82	0.89	0.83	0.84
Vocabulary	0.91	0.94	0.89	0.91	0.84	0.87	0.88
Comprehension	0.87	0.86	0.74	0.71	0.79	0.68	0.81
Digit span	0.91	0.89	0.72	0.82	0.85	0.86	0.88
Picture completion	0.84	0.75	0.81	0.71	0.82	0.59	0.74
Picture arrangement	0.85	0.76	0.78	0.67	0.85	0.69	0.75
Block design	0.92	0.91	0.85	0.85	0.88	0.86	0.88
Object assembly	0.74	0.67	0.78	0.71	0.78	0.69	0.68
Mazes	0.80	0.68	0.81	0.61	0.77	0.49	0.69
Verbal IQ	0.96	0.96	0.94	0.94	0.95	0.94	0.95
Performance IQ	0.94	0.91	0.93	0.89	0.93	0.87	0.91
Full scale IQ	0.97	0.96	0.96	0.95	0.96	0.94	0.96

done separately for only two age bands, thus securing a sample size of more than 100 cases in all groups.

The pattern of coefficients for the subtests given in Table 9.3 was analyzed further, after transformation into Fisher's z scores, by means of a $2 \times 2 \times 3$ factorial analysis of variance (Verbal/Performance, 2 age bands, 3 countries) with repeated measurements in the last two factors. The results of the computations indicated that on the average, the coefficients for the subtests in the German sample tended to be higher than those of the two other samples, $F(2, 18) = 18.4$, $p < 0.01$, and the reliability of the subtests seems to be slightly better in the younger than in the older groups, $F(1, 9) = 11.9$, $p < 0.01$.

Finally the split-half coefficients at higher levels of aggregation were computed by means of the method described by Lienert and Raatz (1994, p. 330). For the composite of the five Verbal regular subtests, the composite of the five available Performance subtests, and at last, for the combination of both, the differences between the three national coefficients were essentially nonsignificant. Moreover, the coefficients for the Verbal, Performance, and Full Scales computed in each of the relatively small national subsamples were nearly exactly the same as the respective average split-half reliabilities of the HAWIK-III, which are reported in the manual (Tewes, Rossmann, & Schallberger, 2002, p. 98) and are also given in Table 9.3.

Summarizing the above, on the subtest level the estimates of reliability computed in the German sample tended consistently to be a little bit higher than in the two other samples. But at higher levels of aggregation (Verbal, Performance,

Full Scale IQ), the differences between the three national coefficients were too
small to be of any practical significance.

EVIDENCE OF VALIDITY

Table 9.4 shows the means and standard deviations for IQs, index scores, and
subtest scaled scores in the German, Austrian, and Swiss subsamples, beginning
with Full Scale IQs, Verbal IQs, and Performance IQs. In each row the differences
between means were tested for significance by a one-way analysis of variance.
The results of ANOVAs and of post hoc Scheffé comparisons are given in the
table. Neither mean Full Scale IQs nor mean Verbal IQs differed significantly in
the three national samples. This is a very encouraging result with respect to the
efforts of verbal subtest adaptation described above. Interestingly enough, there
is a small but significant difference in mean Performance IQs, the mean of the

TABLE 9.4   IQs, Index Scores, and Subtest Scaled Scores by Country: Means, Standard
Deviations, ANOVA, and Post-Test Results

| | Germany ($n = 990$) | | Austria ($n = 300$) | | Switzerland ($n = 280$) | | |
	M	SD	M	SD	M	SD	p
Information	9.6a	3.6	10.7b	2.6	9.7a	2.7	$p < 0.01$
Similarities	9.9a,b	3.4	9.6a	2.2	10.4b	2.5	$p < 0.01$
Arithmetic	9.7	3.2	10.2	2.6	10.3	3.1	n.s.
Vocabulary	9.8	3.6	9.4	2.8	10.0	2.4	n.s.
Comprehension	10.4b	3.4	8.6a	2.7	9.1a	2.1	$p < 0.01$
Digit span	10.0	3.3	9.6	2.6	9.4	2.6	$p < 0.01$
Picture completion	9.9	3.2	9.7	2.8	10.4	2.5	n.s.
Coding	9.8a	3.2	10.6b	2.8	9.7a	3.0	$p < 0.01$
Picture arrangement	9.4a	3.3	10.3b	2.9	10.3b	2.9	$p < 0.01$
Block design	9.5a	3.5	9.6a	3.0	11.0b	2.9	$p < 0.01$
Object assembly	9.7a	3.1	10.6b	3.0	9.8a	2.8	$p < 0.01$
Symbol search	9.8	3.3	10.4	2.7	10.0	2.9	n.s.
Mazes	9.7a	3.4	9.6a	3.2	10.6b	3.1	$p < 0.01$
Full scale IQ	99.5	16.8	100.5	11.5	101.4	11.0	n.s.
Verbal IQ	100.2	16.9	99.1	11.1	100.2	11.0	n.s.
Performance IQ	98.7a	16.1	102.0b	13.2	102.4b	12.0	$p < 0.01$
Verbal comp. index	100.5	17.0	98.6	10.9	99.7	10.5	n.s.
Percept. org. index	98.7a	16.0	101.3a,b	13.5	103.2b	11.9	$p < 0.01$
Freedom dist. index	100.0	16.2	100.3	12.1	99.8	13.5	n.s.
Process. speed index	99.3a	15.8	103.0b	12.8	99.4a	13.8	$p < 0.01$

$p < 0.01$; means sharing a common letter are *not* significantly different from one another according
to post hoc Scheffé comparisons.

German children being a little bit lower than those of the Swiss and Austrian children. However, the observed differences in mean Performance IQs seem to be too small to be of any practical relevance.

A comparable pattern emerges with respect to the index scores. No significant differences were found with regard to the Verbal Comprehension Index or with regard to the Freedom from Distractibility Index, both scores reflecting performance in verbal subtests. In the Perceptual Organization Index the Swiss children scored best whereas the Austrians scored best in Processing Speed.

It is hardly surprising that similar results can be seen in the comparisons of mean scaled scores for each subtest. In the Verbal subtests there are some significant differences but again these differences were minor and moreover, there was no consistent trend in any direction. In the Performance subtests there is a more pronounced trend for the German probands to have the lowest mean scores, but this trend is not very strong.

However, there is one aspect of these data that is puzzling. The scores (Table 9.4) of the German sample had greater variance than Switzerland and Austria in all of the test variables. Variances are unequal in all rows ($p < 0.01$) except for four of the Performance subtests: Coding, Picture Arrangement, Object Assembly, and Mazes. But even there, the standard deviations of the Germans are numerically the largest. On IQ level these differences in standard deviations sum up to a considerable extent. The causes for this effect are not yet known. However, after re-analyzing the German data it can be said that the heightened variability of scores in the German subsample is not due to differences between former East Germany and West Germany. It is also unlikely that the observed differences in variability of scaled scores are due to a statistical artifact in the calculation of the norms, because there are also similar effects in the variability of raw scores. But there are some other potential explanations. The first possibility is that the differences in variability are the results of differences in the sampling procedures used in the three countries. However, the sampling procedures employed in the three countries were virtually the same: representative samples of the child and adolescent population of each country by stratified random sampling in the school system. Perhaps the Swiss sample came closest to ideal of a stratified random sample, nonetheless, it showed relatively low variability of scores. Moreover, effects of this kind have already been observed earlier in connection with attempts to adapt and standardize previous German WISC versions for Switzerland. For example Bründler and Schallberger (1988) reported comparable results for the Swiss adaptation of the HAWIK-R.

So, if the three national samples in the present analysis are considered to be representative samples of the respective populations, then the reported differences in variability must be taken for granted, which leads to the conclusion that there is really greater variability in the test performance of German children compared to Swiss and Austrian children. Again this effect is not easy to explain. Perhaps there is greater than expected cultural (e.g., linguistic) diversity within Germany compared to the two other countries, or the effect could be due to a comparably greater diversification of the German educational system together with a greater percentage of children from different ethnic groups. Work on this aspect is still in progress. Some problems in connection with these facts will still have to be resolved and some of the open questions can only be answered in cross-cultural validation studies. Interesting parallels to our observations have recently been reported in connection with the results of the Program for International Student Assessment (PISA) conducted by the Organization for Economic Cooperation and Development (OECD, 2001). In this cross-cultural study large samples of 15-year-old students from 32 countries were assessed with regard to their reading skills, mathematic skills, and scientific literacy. The variability of reading scores in the German sample was the highest of all 32 nations that participated in the study (including the U.S.). For mathematic skills and scientific literacy the standard deviations of scores in the German sample were the third and fourth largest of the 32 participating countries.

Summarizing, in regard to mean Full Scale IQs, Verbal IQs, and Performance IQs, the differences between the national samples were either statistically insignificant or practically irrelevant. Regarding mean subtest scores, significant differences between Germany, Austria, and Switzerland were found, but no conclusive pattern emerged. However, the German sample in general tended to have the highest standard deviations in all measures. Additional information concerning the validity of the German WISC-III (e.g., intercorrelations of subtests, results of factor analyses, correlations with teacher ratings and grades, data on clinical groups) is presented by Tewes in Chapter 8.

CULTURAL ISSUES INFLUENCING WISC-III INTERPRETATIONS IN AUSTRIA AND SWITZERLAND

As described above, the most important cultural variable that could significantly influence the results of intelligence testing in the German-speaking countries is the local dialect or variant of the German language. In order to guarantee fair conditions for all German-speaking children it is an important precondition that the wording, especially of the items in the Verbal subtests, is carefully adapted to the linguistic and cultural environment of the tested child. In the HAWIK-III manual a special translation for Austrian and/or Swiss children is given for each of the items that have been considered during test adaptation to be critical in this sense. The proper wording of the questions, however, is only one part of the job of the professional who administers the test. In order to be able to evaluate the answers of the child correctly it is of critical importance that the tester him/herself is also able to fully understand the local variant of the German language spoken by the probands. This, in our opinion, is a good example for the necessity of a regionalized approach within a common European cultural framework. But even when these necessary preconditions for the assessment of German-speaking children are fulfilled, a number of questions remain unresolved in connection with the test administration in minority groups. Over the last decades the number of immigrants has steadily been rising in Austria as well as in Switzerland. Today, especially in the larger cities, a considerable proportion of schoolchildren belong to different ethnic groups and come from homes in which German is not the primary language. According to our experience, many of these children are poorly prepared for school and are at high risk of academic and behavioral problems. This situation is well recognized and discussed among practitioners. Nevertheless up until now the problem of testing in minority groups has not received very much attention by researchers. As all European states, especially those in the European Union, clearly seem to be on their way toward multicultural societies, this attitude will probably have to be changed very soon. We are convinced that in this connection the availability and comparability of adaptations of the same mental test in different European languages (and the availability of professionals who are able to administer them) will become a more important issue for practitioners as well as for researchers.

PROFESSIONAL ISSUES IN THE USE OF INTELLIGENCE TESTS IN AUSTRIA AND SWITZERLAND

In Austria the legal situation concerning the use of intelligence tests is a little bit confusing and contradictory. On the one hand, since the enactment of the Austrian Psychologist's Act (Psychologengesetz) in 1991 the title "psychologist" is protected by law. The right of practicing psychology in the health services is reserved to licensed clinical psychologists or to licensed health service psychologists who must have successfully completed a course of postgraduate professional training also regulated by the law (see Kierein, Pritz, & Sonneck, 1991; Kryspin-Exner, 2001). Even reimbursement of the costs of psychodiagnostic assessment (including the use of intelligence tests when necessary) by medical insurance programs is possible when the assessment is made by a licensed clinical psychologist and has been prescribed by a physician or a psychotherapist. This relatively well-defined situation is perhaps one of the reasons why in Austria at the moment there is not very much pressure from nonpsychological professionals to enter the field of clinical psychodiagnosis.

On the other hand, the use of psychological tests in general and intelligence tests in particular by nonpsychological professionals in other fields (e.g., psychiatrists, psychotherapists, pedagogues, special education teachers, or even economists working as personnel managers. . .) is neither forbidden nor restricted by law. On the contrary, some laws implicitly seem to encourage the use of tests by nonpsychology professionals. For example, the 1993 amendment of the School Attendance Act regulates the definition and assessment of a child's special educational needs in the Austrian school system on the basis of an expert opinion that has to be delivered by a special education teacher. Also in the field of personnel management and selection nonpsychology professionals form a large if not the largest group of practitioners.

In Switzerland a federal commission was constituted in 2001 with the mandate to prepare a bill for the training and occupation of psychologists. The nature of the final law cannot be predicted at the present time. Presently there are no legal regulations concerning the field of psychology or psychodiagnosis on a national level. Perhaps this is one of the reasons that the discussion about minimum standards for psychological testing among Swiss psychologists seems to be more pronounced than in Austria (see Hänsgen, 1997; Hänsgen & Bernasconi, 2000). In 1997 the Federation of Swiss Psychologists founded a Test Commission and together with the professional associations from Austria, Germany, and Liechtenstein a center called Test Consult was initiated in order to promote quality standards for psychological testing. As in other European countries the discussion centers around three main issues: (1) what are the minimum standards for a good test and on which basis should a certification of tests be done; (2) who is authorized to employ a "good test"; and (3) how should the certification of practitioners be regulated? So far no final and conclusive answers to these questions have been given and no legal regulations of this matter have been achieved in Switzerland and Austria. In the opinion of the present authors it is neither very likely nor desirable that regulations concerning psychological testing will be made on the basis of national law alone. As proponents of a multinational test project we would prefer rules that are well embedded in an international perspective of quality control in psychological and educational testing.

Given the rather unclear and complex situation of psychological testing in Switzerland and in Austria the professional psychological associations for the time being at least try to restrict the selling of psychological test materials to academically trained psychologists and properly trained professionals from related disciplines only.

REFERENCES

Bründler, M., & Schallberger, U. (1988). *HAWIK-R, Ergänzungsband zum Handbuch mit Testanweisung und Normentabelle für die deutschsprachige Schweiz.* Bern: Huber.

Hänsgen, K. D. (1997). Psychodiagnostik und Qualitätssicherung—Aufgaben und Probleme in der Schweiz. *Psychoscope, 18,* 17–19.

Hänsgen, K. D., & Bernasconi, M. (2000). Wachstumsmarkt Diagnostik. Daten und Fakten zur aktuellen Lage in der Schweiz. *Psychoscope, 21,* 17–19.

Hardesty, F. P., & Priester, H. J. (1956). *Hamburg-Wechsler-Intelligenztest für Kinder (HAWIK).* Bern: Huber.

Kierein, M., Pritz, A., & Sonneck, G. (1991). *Psychologen-Gesetz, Psychotherapie-Gesetz: Kurzkommentar.* Wien: Orac.

Kryspin-Exner, I. (2001). Psychotherapy and Clinical Psychology in Austria. *European Psychotherapy, 2,* 20–24.

Lienert, G. A., & Raatz, U. (1994). *Testaufbau und Testanalyse* (5. Aufl.). Weinheim: Beltz.

OECD (Ed.) (2001). *Knowledge and skills for life. First results from PISA 2000*. Paris: OECD.

Tewes, U. (1983). *Hamburg-Wechsler-Intelligenztest für Kinder, Revision 1983 (HAWIK-R)*. Bern: Huber.

Tewes, U., Rossmann, P., & Schallberger, U. (2002). *HAWIK-III Manual* (3. überarbeitete und ergänzte Aufl.). Bern: Huber.

Wechsler, D. (1999). *Hamburg-Wechsler-Intelligenztest für Kinder (HAWIK-III)* (U. Tewes, P. Rossmann, & U. Schallberger, Trans.). Bern, Switzerland: Hans Huber. (Original work published in 1991.)

1 O

SWEDEN

KARIN SONNANDER

Department of Neuroscience
Uppsala University
Uppsala, Sweden

BENGT RAMUND

Department of Education
Uppsala University
Uppsala, Sweden

The Swedish version of the Wechsler Intelligence Scale for Children (WISC) available up to 1999 was developed in the mid-1960s (Wechsler, 1969) and based on the WISC published in the U.S. in 1949 (Wechsler, 1949). The following revised version WISC-R (Wechsler, 1974) was never adapted for use in Sweden. Several studies have shown that norms of intelligence tests become dated over time (Flynn, 1984, 1985; Emanuelsson, 1987; Kaufman, 1990; Sonnander, 1990). In particular, over a period of several decades, average performance on items included in intelligence tests has been increasing. Long and justified professional dissatisfaction with the available Swedish version of WISC together with empirical evidence (Sonnander, 1990) of an upward drift of the test score distribution presented an urgent need of a new version of WISC adapted for use in a Swedish setting.

The Swedish version of WISC-III was published (Wechsler, 1998) following 7 years of work on adaptation and norms.[1] The Swedish-speaking area is small and

---

[1] A Swedish version of the WISC-III has been made possible by the untiring involvement and contributions from several authorities and individuals. The Psykologiförlaget AB, Stockholm, the National Board of Health and Welfare, the Stockholm County Council, the Federation of Swedish County

consequently it has always been difficult to find the funds and resources necessary for test standardization in general as well as periodic updating of norms.

ADAPTATION PROCESS

The work on the Swedish version of WISC-III is based on the version developed in the UK (Wechsler, 1992), as there was reason to believe that the cultural differences between Sweden and the UK might be smaller than those between Sweden and the U.S.

The performance items have not been substituted or adapted (apart from minor revision and scoring in a few cases). Because of the material, these items are difficult to modify, and any modification is very expensive.

The Verbal subtests have, on the other hand, been thoroughly revised and adapted and tried out in several steps (as were the Performance subtests). First, the UK version was translated into the Swedish language by an experienced psychologist followed by an independent translation check by two experienced psychologists. Second, the Vocabulary and Information subtests were thoroughly revised by substituting items considered not to function well in a Swedish setting by items selected from lists of synonyms employed in research at the Department of Education, University of Gothenburg as well as consulting the existing Swedish version of the WISC. Further, it was decided to include 40 items in these two Verbal subtests in the tryout version as compared to 30 items in the British final version. The reason for this was to have an ample selection of items to choose from, when selecting which and how many items to include in the standardization and the final version of the Swedish WISC-III. It was also important to be able to establish the number of failures preceding an interruption of the test.

A third step included a pilot study with 175 children and adolescents. The objective was to check the new items compiled, to establish the consecutive order of items by item analysis for the coming standardization, and to check the

Councils, Uppsala University, and the Swedish Psychological Association (through Stiftelsen för Tillämpad Psykologi) provided major funds. Associate Professor Lars Kebbon, Department of Neuroscience, Psychiatry Ulleråker, Uppsala University; Licensed Psychologist Ingela Palmér, The Swedish Psychological Association, and Licensed Psychologist Katarina Forssén, the Psykologiförlaget AB formed an executive group, which supervised the work. Associate Professor Karin Sonnander, Department of Neuroscience, Psychiatry Ulleråker, Uppsala University directed the Swedish project. Associate Professor Bengt Ramund, Department of Education, Uppsala University carried out the important task of statistical analysis and norms development. Licensed Psychologist Kjerstin Hemmingsson, Department of Neuroscience, Psychiatry Ulleråker, Uppsala University acted as project coordinator and recruited local authorities, schools, and families and supervised those professional psychologists and psychology students who carried out the Swedish testing. Ann Jacobson, B.Sc., Department of Psychology, Stockholm University coordinated the testing carried out in the Stockholm area and was also editor of the Swedish technical manual. Associate Professor Ann-Charlotte Smedler, Department of Psychology, Stockholm University provided expertise in the early stages of the adaptation process and contributed a chapter in the Swedish technical manual on issues related to clinical application as well as the interpretation of individual test results.

applicability of the protocol, scoring procedure, and manual. The scored protocols were obtained from experienced psychologists who tested children and adolescents and also commented on test item content and testing procedure. In a fourth step, the standardization version of the Swedish WISC-III was modified according to the outcomes of the pilot study. Items in the subtests Comprehension and Similarities were retained as were the items in the subtest Arithmetic, to which one extra item was added during the standardization process, but the final version of Arithmetic has 24 items. In the Arithmetic subtest personal names, some objects, and currency were replaced by equivalent content better suited to the Swedish context, without changing the calculations. The Vocabulary subtest was comprised of 40 items and the Information subtest 32 items in the modified standardization version. This modified version formed the basis for the standardization of the Swedish WISC-III.

A number of items in the UK version of the WISC-III were considered culture biased and were consequently substituted by Swedish items. For example, the unit of measurement "dozen" is not frequently employed today. Thus, item 11 (UK version) in the Information subtest was substituted by, "How many centimeters make up a decimeter?" Another example is item 29 which was substituted by, "Who was Carl von Linné?" Naturally, item 28, was substituted by, "How far is it from (two cities)?" or for children and adolescents living north of Gävle, two other cities were substituted. In the Vocabulary subtest item 17 was substituted by "emigrate" since the UK word is a highly technical word in the Swedish language, not commonly used.

Following the standardization the final sets of items were established in a fifth step. The statistical analyses and reported experiences from testers formed the basis for the final selection of test items. It was considered important that items of each subtest were placed in order of difficulty and that it was established when to discontinue, i.e., after how many consecutive failures. When two items were considered equal in terms of order of difficulty that item which repeatedly had proven either difficult to score or showed lower construct equivalence with the other items was excluded. The Swedish version of WISC-III includes the same number of items in each subtest as in the UK version.

SAMPLE CHARACTERISTICS

The Swedish standardization sample was comprised of 1036 children and adolescents ages 6 years 0 months to 15 years 11 months with a minimum of 50 individuals in each 6-month period across the age span, corresponding to the ages of the Swedish compulsory school system (grade 1–9). The sample distribution across chronological ages and gender is presented in Table 10.1.

Testing was done by experienced psychologists and by psychology students in collaboration with the Department of Psychology at Uppsala University and Department of Psychology at Stockholm University. Therefore, children and adolescents were sampled from school districts in these areas. Socioeconomic status based on occupation and educational level of the adult population in these

TABLE 10.1 Standardization Sample: Age (Year, Month) and Gender
($n = 1036$)

Age	Gender		Total sample
	Girls	Boys	
6:0–6:5	25	25	50
6:6–6:11	29	25	54
7:0–7:5	27	25	52
7:6–7:11	26	25	51
8:0–8:5	31	28	59
8:6–8:11	26	26	52
9:0–9:5	25	25	50
9:6–9:11	24	26	50
10:0–10:5	25	25	50
10:6–10:11	25	25	50
11:0–11:5	24	26	50
11:6–11:11	34	17	51
12:0–12:5	26	24	50
12:6–12:11	25	25	50
13:0–13:5	20	30	50
13:6–13:11	24	26	50
14:0–14:5	26	28	54
14:6–14:11	25	25	50
15:0–15:5	25	25	50
15:6–15:11	33	30	63
Total sample	525	511	1036

areas was obtained from local government offices. Equivalent information is available on a national level. A sample of school districts was drawn from all the school districts in the area and in a second step a sample of schools was drawn from each school district. School principals were informed by letter describing the project and invited to participate in the project. Schoolteachers concerned were individually informed about the project and invited to participate. Pupils from 19 municipality schools, 14 in Uppsala and 5 in Stockholm, formed the sampling base for the standardization. No special schools were involved in the study. Children receiving remedial education in school settings were not excluded from testing. Parents or guardians of pupils in school classes finally included in the project were informed and asked to give their informed consent by letter. The consent form requested the parents' occupation and level of education as well as use of the Swedish language at home. Children were tested only if they could understand and speak Swedish. The rates of acceptance varied between 51% (grade 9, 15 year olds) to 77% (grade 4, 10 year olds). The mean rate of parental acceptance to participate was 65%.

The rate of children whose parents reported that the home language was Swedish comprised 87% of the total sample. According to Swedish national statistics the corresponding rate for the country 1995/1996 was 88% (Official Statistics of Sweden, 1998). In addition, children who spoke Swedish adequately and a second language at home were included in the sample. More than 20 non-Swedish languages were reported for the standardization sample. Of those parents who agreed to participate in the standardization 95% provided information concerning occupation and educational level. Education is generally considered a proxy variable for socioeconomic status. Test scores were more strongly related to level of education than to occupation. The correlations between subtest scores and parental education ranged from $r = 0.19$ to 0.26, $r = 0.41$ for Verbal IQ, $r = 0.27$ for Performance IQ, and $r = 0.39$ for Full Scale IQ. Consequently, the representativeness of the standardization sample was checked using level of education as a basis for comparison. It was found that in the standardization sample 70% of the parents had a higher education (post gymnasium). The corresponding rate in the Swedish population (Official Statistics of Sweden, 1998) of persons aged 25–45 years was 30%. Persons in this age group were likely to be the parents of children in the Swedish WISC-III standardization sample. Therefore, raw score means of every subtest were proportionally adjusted according to the difference between means of children with parents of higher education and means of children with parents of lower education. In order to obtain a more reliable measure of this education-related difference, these calculations were based on three pooled age groups: 6–8 years, 9–12 years, and 13–15 years, instead of 20 smaller groups of 50 persons each.

As the number of girls and boys was not exactly equal in certain age groups, a corresponding adjustment of subtest means was performed according to the subtest mean difference between boys and girls in these age groups. Finally, for every subtest the twenty half-year group means were plotted against age. These development curves were found to be uneven—an expected and inevitable effect of sampling fluctuations. Moreover, they were more or less nonlinear in shape. The overall pattern of development was considered to be more reliable than the single mean value of any half-year group, influenced by sampling error. The smoothing procedure therefore was accomplished by adjusting the means to the most suitable mathematical function of age. For most subtests this function was of the second degree. Only two subtests, Coding and Symbol Search, were adjusted to linear functions of age (means for the ages 6 and 7 were adjusted with other coefficients than higher ages). The deviations from linear development were rather slight in most subtests. The coefficient for the quadratical term of the second degree function was less than ± 0.05 for Information, Similarities, Digit Span, and Vocabulary and 0.05 to 0.10 for Arithmetic, Picture Completion, and Comprehension. In four subtests, Picture Arrangement, Object Assembly, Mazes, and Block Design, a coefficient exceeding 0.10 was found. In order to get the Mazes means increasing even in the highest age groups, despite the ceiling effect, this curve was further modified. A similar smoothing was carried out for the subtest standard deviations. All of them, except Arithmetic, were found to increase by age, especially Vocabulary and Picture Completion.

RELIABILITY

Table 10.2 shows split-half reliability coefficients and standard errors of measurement (SEM) for the subtests, IQ, and index scores, by age, and over-all. The subtest mean reliabilities ranged from $r = 0.56$ for Object Assembly to $r = 0.85$ for Block Design. Reliability coefficients for all subtests, except for Coding and Symbol Search, were calculated with the split-half Spearman-Brown formula. As this method is not suited for items with equal level of difficulty which depend on speed, the reliabilities of Coding and Symbol Search were estimated by coefficients of stability yielded from a test-retest procedure. The stability coefficients for these two tests were based on a sample with 47 ten-year-old children and 41 twelve-year-old children retested after 2–3 weeks. These stability coefficients were used as reliability estimates. For Coding, they were $r = 0.80$ for the younger age group and $r = 0.87$ for the older group; for Symbol Search, they were $r = 0.48$ and $r = 0.82$, respectively. Retest correlations for the other subtests were not produced in the Swedish standardization.

The reliability coefficients of the Swedish standardization sample scores were in most cases lower than the coefficients presented in the UK manual. In addition to sampling fluctuations the reason for this might be ceiling effects which influenced the variation of scores in the older age groups; when the variation of obtainable scores is limited, measurement error will play a more important part for the score. If the Swedish sample is more homogenous than the U.S. and UK samples, this would give the same effect on the reliabilities, since limited variation causes lower correlation and consequently lower reliability coefficients. Additionally, the statistical analyses of the Swedish material included calculation of differences between factor index scores, subtest scores, minimum differences required for statistical difference (all at 0.10 and 0.05 level of confidence) and frequency of intersubtest scatter. Thus the aim was fulfilled to make the Swedish version of the manual as similar as possible to the UK manual.

EVIDENCE OF VALIDITY

The Swedish version of WISC-III included factor analyses in order to investigate internal validity. The procedures applied in the U.S. and UK analyses were employed (maximum likelihood factor analysis followed by varimax rotation). Analyses were based on total sample scores ($n = 1036$) as well as across the following three age groups: 6–8 years ($n = 305$), 9–12 years ($n = 393$), and 13–15 years ($n = 311$).

The intercorrelations of subtest scaled scores are presented in Table 10.3. Additionally, maximum likelihood factor loadings for four factors are reported in Table 10.4.

The factor analyses showed that the Swedish version of WISC-III will function as a homogenous measure of g, since a common factor explained 36% of the total

TABLE 10.2 Reliability Coefficients and Standard Errors of Measurement of the Subtests Scaled Scores, IQ Scores, and Index Scores by Age

Subtest/scale	6	7	8	9	10	11	12	13	14	15	Average
Information	0.77	0.79	0.66	0.77	0.84	0.80	0.74	0.82	0.73	0.82	0.78
(SEm)	1.44	1.37	1.75	1.44	1.20	1.34	1.53	1.27	1.56	1.27	1.43
Similarities	0.85	0.75	0.75	0.87	0.85	0.76	0.82	0.74	0.62	0.74	0.78
(SEm)	1.16	1.50	1.50	1.08	1.16	1.47	1.27	1.53	1.85	1.53	1.42
Arithmetic	0.71	0.76	0.69	0.68	0.77	0.83	0.81	0.77	0.78	0.74	0.76
(SEm)	1.62	1.47	1.67	1.70	1.44	1.24	1.31	1.44	1.41	1.53	1.49
Vocabulary	0.71	0.67	0.70	0.80	0.84	0.85	0.85	0.90	0.83	0.89	0.82
(SEm)	1.62	1.72	1.64	1.34	1.20	1.16	1.16	0.95	1.24	0.99	1.33
Comprehension	0.73	0.76	0.60	0.71	0.75	0.72	0.71	0.76	0.69	0.73	0.72
(SEm)	1.56	1.47	1.90	1.62	1.50	1.59	1.62	1.47	1.67	1.56	1.60
Digit span	0.69	0.64	0.76	0.77	0.76	0.81	0.83	0.83	0.86	0.86	0.79
(SEm)	1.67	1.80	1.47	1.44	1.47	1.31	1.24	1.24	1.12	1.12	1.40
Picture completion	0.66	0.78	0.72	0.78	0.77	0.69	0.76	0.66	0.57	0.50	0.70
(SEm)	1.75	1.41	1.59	1.41	1.44	1.67	1.47	1.75	1.97	2.12	1.67
Coding	0.80	0.80	0.80	0.80	0.80	0.87	0.87	0.87	0.87	0.87	0.84
(SEm)	1.34	1.34	1.34	1.34	1.34	1.08	1.08	1.08	1.08	1.08	1.22
Picture arrangement	0.80	0.73	0.79	0.57	0.77	0.83	0.82	0.82	0.76	0.64	0.76
(SEm)	1.34	1.56	1.37	1.97	1.44	1.24	1.27	1.27	1.47	1.80	1.49
Block design	0.87	0.84	0.86	0.83	0.79	0.80	0.89	0.88	0.89	0.84	0.85
(SEm)	1.08	1.20	1.12	1.24	1.37	1.34	0.99	1.04	0.99	1.20	1.16
Object assembly	0.46	0.60	0.62	0.58	0.56	0.61	0.64	0.45	0.59	0.44	0.56
(SEm)	2.20	1.90	1.85	1.94	1.99	1.87	1.80	2.22	1.92	2.24	1.99
Symbol search	0.48	0.48	0.48	0.48	0.48	0.82	0.82	0.82	0.82	0.82	0.69
(SEm)	2.16	2.16	2.16	2.16	2.16	1.27	1.27	1.27	1.27	1.27	1.77
Mazes	0.78	0.75	0.68	0.70	0.36	0.58	0.57	0.53	0.58	0.20	0.60
(SEm)	1.41	1.50	1.70	1.64	2.40	1.94	1.97	2.06	1.94	2.68	1.96
Verbal IQ	0.92	0.91	0.88	0.92	0.94	0.94	0.94	0.93	0.91	0.93	0.92
(SEm)	4.24	4.50	5.20	4.24	3.67	3.67	3.67	3.97	4.50	3.97	4.24
Performance IQ	0.84	0.87	0.89	0.87	0.89	0.90	0.92	0.88	0.90	0.83	0.88
(SEm)	6.00	5.41	4.97	5.41	4.97	4.74	4.24	5.20	4.74	6.18	5.20
Full scale IQ	0.92	0.93	0.93	0.94	0.95	0.95	0.96	0.94	0.93	0.93	0.94
(SEm)	4.24	3.97	3.97	3.67	3.35	3.35	3.00	3.67	3.97	3.97	3.67
Verbal comp. index	0.91	0.90	0.87	0.92	0.93	0.93	0.93	0.93	0.90	0.93	0.92
(SEm)	4.50	4.74	5.41	4.24	3.97	3.97	3.97	3.97	4.74	3.97	4.24
Perc. organ. index	0.86	0.89	0.89	0.87	0.84	0.88	0.89	0.87	0.85	0.76	0.86
(SEm)	5.61	4.97	4.97	5.41	6.00	5.20	4.97	5.41	5.81	7.35	5.61
Freedom distr. index	0.68	0.71	0.69	0.72	0.74	0.87	0.85	0.84	0.87	0.85	0.79
(SEm)	8.49	8.08	8.35	7.94	7.65	5.41	5.81	6.00	5.41	5.81	6.87
Process. speed index	0.74	0.74	0.75	0.77	0.76	0.89	0.90	0.90	0.91	0.89	0.84
(SEm)	7.65	7.65	7.50	7.19	7.35	4.97	4.74	4.74	4.50	4.97	6.00

TABLE 10.3   Intercorrelation of Subtest Scaled Scores ($n = 1036$)

Subtest/scale	Inf	Sim	Ari	Voc	Com	DS	PCom	Cd	PA	BD	OA	SS	Mz
Information													
Similarities	0.60												
Arithmetic	0.47	0.42											
Vocabulary	0.63	0.62	0.41										
Comprehension	0.47	0.53	0.32	0.57									
Digit span	0.26	0.28	0.36	0.27	0.19								
Picture completion	0.35	0.37	0.24	0.35	0.32	0.16							
Coding	0.14	0.10	0.23	0.13	0.14	0.13	0.09						
Picture arrangement	0.33	0.34	0.30	0.36	0.32	0.15	0.35	0.23					
Block design	0.40	0.39	0.39	0.35	0.33	0.24	0.38	0.23	0.37				
Object assembly	0.28	0.31	0.30	0.24	0.28	0.15	0.37	0.21	0.37	0.52			
Symbol search	0.22	0.18	0.30	0.21	0.21	0.20	0.21	0.49	0.26	0.36	0.34		
Mazes	0.21	0.21	0.23	0.21	0.15	0.18	0.19	0.10	0.25	0.32	0.26	0.21	

variance, which justifies the use of a Full Scale IQ in the interpretation of test results. Moreover, a solution of four factors was confirmed: Verbal Comprehension, Perceptual Organization, Freedom of Distractibility, and Processing Speed. The subtests included in the four factors corresponded to the subtest distribution obtained in the analyses of the UK and U.S. samples. A first factor, Verbal Comprehension, was clearly identified in the scores of the total sample as well as in the three age groups analyzed. A second factor, Perceptual Organization, was also clearly identified in the total sample as well as in two age groups. However, in the 9–12 age group the subtests Mazes and Symbol Search were also included in the second factor. A third factor, Processing Speed, was identified in all age groups as well as in the total sample. Finally, Freedom of Distractibility, a fourth factor, was clearest in the oldest age group (13–15 years) and in the total sample. The outcome of confirmatory maximum-likelihood factor analyses showed that the structure of the Swedish version of WISC-III is best described by the four factors identified in the exploratory analyses performed, which are the same as the U.S. sample. The Swedish standardization of WISC-III did not include any analyses of validity evidence based on internal structure of the test across groups of children other than the total standardization sample. It was suggested that, as the overall results of the factor analyses applied corresponded well to the U.S. and UK results, analyses on scores from special groups from these countries may serve as interpretation guidelines in clinical-practical work also for Swedish users. An account of these non-Swedish studies is given in the Swedish technical manual. The Swedish version of WISC-III is useful for gifted children in the lower and middle age levels, but not for the gifted children in the older age spans as ceiling effects are notable in certain performance subtests, e.g., Mazes. However, in Sweden, the WISC-III is predominantly applied in the assessment of younger children for which diagnostic evaluations are more frequently demanded by providers of health care and education.

TABLE 1O.4 Maximum-Likelihood Factor Loadings (Varimax Rotation) for Four Factors

Subtest/scale	Factor 1: Verbal comprehension Ages			Factor 2: Perceptual organization Ages			Factor 3: Freedom from distractibility Ages			Factor 4: Processing speed Ages		
	6–8	9–12	13–15	6–8	9–12	13–15	6–8	9–12	13–15	6–8	9–12	13–15
Information	0.56	0.65	0.76	0.15	0.24	0.18	0.47	0.41	0.23	0.12	0.06	0.01
Similarities	0.62	0.71	0.68	0.34	0.22	0.26	0.17	0.31	0.31	0.05	0.00	0.00
Vocabulary	0.71	0.79	0.83	0.16	0.17	0.14	0.18	0.28	0.20	0.15	0.04	0.07
Comprehension	0.64	0.70	0.56	0.21	0.25	0.21	0.13	0.08	0.09	0.16	0.11	0.04
Picture completion	0.25	0.42	0.36	0.51	0.47	0.42	0.07	0.05	0.03	0.03	0.06	0.03
Picture arrangement	0.33	0.38	0.28	0.48	0.42	0.44	-0.11	0.12	0.12	0.27	0.20	0.16
Block design	0.15	0.26	0.28	0.56	0.50	0.60	0.40	0.25	0.32	0.15	0.17	0.22
Object assembly	0.03	0.17	0.14	0.54	0.71	0.79	0.24	0.13	0.11	0.19	0.15	0.12
Mazes	0.22	0.11	0.08	0.47	0.31	0.26	0.11	0.19	0.30	0.01	0.05	0.20
Arithmetic	0.31	0.28	0.38	0.18	0.28	0.18	0.30	0.61	0.65	0.36	0.14	0.09
Digit span	0.17	0.24	0.15	0.13	0.14	0.06	0.35	0.37	0.52	0.09	0.13	0.09
Coding	0.07	0.03	0.06	0.01	0.16	0.11	0.04	0.12	0.04	0.69	0.98	0.70
Symbol search	0.17	0.12	-0.03	0.27	0.41	0.17	0.21	0.21	0.20	0.53	0.47	0.71

The previous Swedish version of the WISC (Wechsler, 1969) included separate norms for children in remedial classes for underachievers in the compulsory comprehensive school. Those norms were considered helpful and frequently employed by clinical psychologists. Remedial classes for underachievers or their equivalent are not found in the Swedish compulsory comprehensive school today, which complicated sample selection. However, there was a need among clinicians for a test for adults with intellectual disabilities. Therefore, norms were developed with the WISC-III based on test scores obtained with informed consent from 141 adult persons with a diagnosed intellectual disability (15–64 years). The factor analysis procedures applied were identical to those employed in the Swedish standardization and the outcome showed a corresponding structure with four factors and an identical distribution of subtests across factors (Sonnander & Ramund, 2000).

CULTURAL ISSUES INFLUENCING WISC-III INTERPRETATIONS IN SWEDEN

Sweden, a monarchy with a democratic constitution and situated between the Baltic Sea and the North Sea, is the fifth largest country in Europe. In terms of area its size is similar to Spain, Thailand, or the state of California. Sweden has 8.9 million inhabitants. Its population has remained stable over the last decade. Approximately 85% of the population lives in urban areas, mostly in Stockholm, Gothenburg, and Malmö. Compared to most European Union (EU) countries, its population density is low, averaging 19 inhabitants per square kilometer.

For many years Sweden was ethnically very homogenous. An exception is the Saami people, one of the indigenous peoples of the Fennoscandian area (Scandinavia, Finland, Eastern Karelia, and the Kola Peninsula) of which 17,000 live in Sweden. During the 1960s and 1970s more than half a million immigrants moved to Sweden to work, mainly from Finland, but also from the Balkans and other countries. In addition, Sweden has received refugees in need of protection from many troubled corners of the world. Eighty-seven percent of the population of Sweden are members of the Church of Sweden, which is Lutheran. Approximately 1.8% of the population are Catholics, and 1.7% are Muslims.

Svenska is the language of Sweden, and is also spoken by 300,000 inhabitants in Finland and by around 77,000 Swedish immigrants in the U.S. (U.S. Census Bureau, 2002). The Swedish language belongs to the Indo-European language family to which almost all European languages belong (with the exception of Finnish-Ugrian, Basque, and Caucasian languages) and has many features in common with all of these. It belongs to the North-Germanic subgroup which includes Danish, Norwegian, Icelandic, and Faroese. The English language belongs to the West-Germanic subgroup within the Indo-European language family. Swedish is very similar to Danish and Norwegian, especially in written form. Its grammar and syntax is very similar to English, more so than German or French.

Many Swedish words are easily recognizable by English speakers, and even more so by German speakers.

The Swedish public school system is composed of the comprehensive compulsory school (9 years) and upper secondary school (3 years). Education is compulsory for 9 years, and it should be noted that even though upper secondary school is voluntary education 73% of adolescents complete an upper secondary school program (2001). Compulsory education includes comprehensive compulsory school, including school for the Saami people of northern Sweden, school for children with impaired sight, hearing, or speech, and school for children with intellectual disabilities. Tuition in the state schools is free. Neither pupils nor their parents usually incur any costs for teaching materials, school meals, health care, school transport, etc. Parliament and the government define curricula, national objectives, and guidelines for state schooling in Sweden. The National Agency for Education (Skolverket) has the task of developing, evaluating, following up, and supervising state schooling in Sweden. The national budget includes grants to the municipalities for their various activities. Most children attend a municipal school near their homes, but pupils and their parents have the right to select another municipal school, a school independent of the local authority, or a private school. Independent schools must be approved by the National Agency for Education to receive municipal grants. The curricula are the same, but the school may have a distinct profile. They may be, for example, schools with a special religious profile, or schools based on special educational methods such as Montessori or Waldorf. Approximately 2% of pupils in comprehensive compulsory schools attend approved independent schools (1995). In addition, there are a number of international schools in Sweden. These are partly state-aided and are primarily intended for the children of foreign nationals who reside in Sweden for a short period.

The standardization sample of the Swedish WISC-III was recruited from municipal schools. Children were tested only if they could understand and speak Swedish. No further analyses comparing different groups based on, e.g., language spoken at home in the Swedish standardization sample, have up to now been made.

To apply the Swedish version of WISC-III is not advisable in a number of circumstances, one of them being when a child originates from another culture and masters the Swedish language imperfectly. In such cases, the test hardly functions as intended. Naturally, the verbal subtests are especially sensitive to cultural differences. A test result obtained in such circumstances provides information of how a child performs in relation to Swedish peers. This may be informative, but does not provide an account of the cognitive abilities of the child tested. For several reasons, information concerning the size of the difference between Verbal and Performance subtests total score in the standardization sample is needed.

When testing a child who migrates from Sweden into another country, it is naturally preferable to use the now available Swedish version of the WISC-III including norms and that the child is tested by a Swedish-speaking psychologist. A professional in another country who is to make a culturally sensitive evaluation of a Swedish child should know that all items in the Performance subtests (from the UK version) are retained in the Swedish version and found to function adequately. However, item 16 in Picture Completion is culturally biased as a Swedish bathtub typically comes with a shower. Most children thus report the shower as missing. This required a change in scoring instructions in the Swedish version. In the Verbal Scale the Information and Vocabulary subtests were found to be especially culture biased. Consequently, several items were substituted. Thus, these two subtests are not applicable when directly translated. The subtests Similarities and Comprehension are composed of the same items as the UK version, however, the order of items is modified. Arithmetic items are identical, but for personal names, some objects, and of course currency. It should be noted that the unit of measurement "dozen" is not common in Sweden today. In conclusion, the Performance Scale is overall useful with few modifications. A professional must refrain from using any version but the Swedish version of WISC-III of the Verbal Scale.

PROFESSIONAL ISSUES IN THE USE OF INTELLIGENCE TESTS IN SWEDEN

Measures of cognitive ability and particularly IQ scores were strongly criticized by academic psychology as well as by professional psychologists beginning in the late 1960s and continuing for several decades. A major concern was the appropriateness and usefulness of the IQ test as a valid measure of human intelligence. Another concern was test bias, as available tests were considered to favor middle class children rather than children from less affluent backgrounds and children with a non-Swedish background. As a consequence, the anti-test climate influenced both academic curricula and clinical practice. Academic courses on test theory and the administration and interpretation of intelligence test results were no longer regarded a necessity. Following the requirement put forward by psychologists in clinical practice, the manual of the Swedish version of WISC (Wechsler, 1974) did not include norm tables presenting IQ scores. Instead the manual provided stanine scores (standardized scores in a nine-point scale format), thus avoiding the illusory exactitude associated with the IQ concept. The use of tests of cognitive ability, however, was not abandoned completely by Swedish psychologists and was subsequently resumed in the last decade. There has been a renewed interest in intelligence testing as an important part of diagnostic casework propelled by, e.g., advances in neuropsychological research and an increasing demand from professions in different settings. In Sweden the WISC is used exclusively by licensed psychologists. The test publisher voluntarily restricts the sale of intelligence tests to qualified professionals and/or their employers, e.g., schools, children's hospitals, child health centers.

Intelligence testing in Sweden is in general applied when the objective is to obtain a basis for intervention, treatment, and the provision of services. Child and adolescent psychiatric clinics, rehabilitation and early intervention clinics, children's hospitals, primary child health care, and schools are examples of settings where testing of general cognitive ability is an essential part of individual comprehensive multidisciplinary assessment.

The original purpose and the current principal use of intelligence tests was and is to identify children with developmental disabilities in need of special education programs. Such testing is usually based on teacher referral with individual pupils and requires parental consent. "Developmental disabilities" is a broad concept within which children with intellectual disabilities and children with learning disabilities represent large groups with cognitive impairment in common. The criteria for identification of intellectual disabilities, an intellectual limitation of an $IQ \leq 70$ that coexists with related limitations in adaptive skills (Luckasson et al., 1992) are similar to those employed in most countries. A below-average IQ score is a necessary but not sufficient criterion for a child to be eligible for education in a special school for children with intellectual disabilities. In addition, a comprehensive evaluation must also indicate that the pupil will benefit from special education. Also, parents or guardians themselves have to apply for special school education. The prevalence rate of school-age children in special education in Sweden has generally been estimated at 0.60–0.70% (Sonnander, Emanuelsson, & Kebbon, 1993). As a consequence of the recent increase of referrals to special schools during the 1990s, just over 1% of all pupils in the Swedish compulsory school are enrolled in special schools at present (Skolverket, 1998). It is claimed by school psychologists in special schools (for pupils with intellectual disabilities) that the ability of WISC to differentiate in a clinical meaningful way at lower levels of test performance ($IQ \leq 70$) is limited.

School psychologists also evaluate pupils in order to obtain a basis for educational support (other than placement in a special school) and/or specialist referral. Such pupils typically have school achievement problems due to specific learning difficulties, e.g., writing and reading, arithmetic difficulties, and learning disabilities. Learning disabilities, i.e., significant problems in one or more school subjects indicated by remedial education of some kind within the comprehensive compulsory school, is estimated to comprise around 35% of all pupils in an age cohort (Persson, 1998). It should be noted that Swedish school authorities do not provide remedial education or other educational support exclusively to pupils with learning difficulties caused by physical or cognitive impairment, but to those children who need help with learning tasks. An evaluation of cognitive ability is not a prerequisite for remedial education in Swedish schools. School children without observed school problems (or gifted children) are not tested on a regular basis in Sweden.

The WISC and the other members of the Wechsler test family are widely used by Swedish professional psychologists. The WISC has been for a long time and is still the only available test of general cognitive ability for Swedish children in the comprehensive compulsory school. For children with multiple disabilities or those who are not fluent in Swedish or come from a non-Swedish cultural background the Leiter International Performance Scale is a suggested nonverbal alternative.

One of the problems associated with the period of questioning of IQ testing was limited training in testing and psychometrics offered in the undergraduate curriculum. The interpretation of test results and the hypotheses generated from IQ test profiles are areas that demand knowledge and skills. The application of IQ tests in Sweden is not indiscriminate. However, the need to take into consideration errors of measurement and confidence intervals, as well as supporting test profile interpretation with data from multiple sources cannot be pointed out often enough to students.

The influence of cultural, socioeconomic, as well as general and specific test situations on test scores, is generally accepted by the professional community. Consequently, the use of tests only by qualified examiners is a self-evident requirement. To maintain their reliability and validity, tests must be administered and interpreted by psychologists who have been well trained and supervised in their correct usage. Appropriate training ensures that the psychologist is aware of the many factors that can affect test performance and is competent to appraise the relative weaknesses and strengths of available methods. Besides the necessary qualifications of the person who administers tests and interprets test results the application of intelligence tests also requires knowledge among those professionals who refer children and adolescents for evaluation including IQ tests. This is an important aspect of test usage more often than not overlooked.

REFERENCES

Emanuelsson, I. (1987). Longitudinal Studies of Mental Development. *Uppsala Journal of Medical Sciences, Supplement 44*, 58–69.
Flynn, J. R. (1984). The mean IQ of Americans: Massive gains 1932 to 1978. *Psychological Bulletin, 95*, 29–51.
Flynn, J. R. (1985). Wechsler intelligence tests: Do we really have a criterion of mental retardation? *American Journal of Mental Deficiency, 90*, 236–244.
Kaufman, A. S. (1990). *Assessing adolescent and adult intelligence*. Boston: Allyn and Bacon.
Luckasson, R., Coulter, D., Polloway, E., Reiss, S., Schalock, R., Snell, M. *et al.* (1992). (Eds.), *Mental retardation: Definition, classification and systems of support*. Washington, DC: American Association of Mental Retardation.
Official Statistics of Sweden (1998). Statistical Yearbook of Sweden 1997, 83, Vol. 83. Örebro: Statistics Sweden, Publication Service.
Persson, B. (1998). *Specialundervisning och differentiering. En studie av grundskolans användning av specialpedagogiska resurser*. Göteborgs universitet: institutionen för pedagogik, rapport nr 10 (in Swedish).
Skolverket (1998). *Skolan. Jämförelsetal för skolhuvudmän. Organisation—resurser—resultat*. Skolverket: rapport nr 97, Stockholm, Sverige (in Swedish).
Sonnander, K. (1990). Prevalence of mental retardation—An empirical study of an unselected school population. In W. Fraser (Ed.), *Key issues in mental retardation research*. Proceedings of the Eighth Congress of the International Association for the Scientific Study of Mental Deficiency. London: Routledge.
Sonnander, K., Emanuelsson, I., & Kebbon, L. (1993). Pupils with mild mental retardation in regular Swedish schools: Prevalence, objective characteristics and subjective evaluations. *American Journal of Mental Retardation, 97*, 692–701.

Sonnander, K., & Ramund, B. (2000). *Specialnormering av WISC-III. Manual* (in Swedish). Psykologiförlaget AB: Stockholm, Sweden.

U.S. Census Bureau (2002). *Census of population and housing*. Washington, DC: United States Department of Commerce.

Wechsler, D. (1949). *Manual for the Wechsler Intelligence Scale for Children*. New York: The Psychological Corporation.

Wechsler, D. (1969). *Manual till WISC*. Stockholm: Skandinaviska Testförlaget AB.

Wechsler, D. (1974). *Manual for the Wechsler Intelligence Scale for Children—Revised*. San Antonio, TX: The Psychological Corporation.

Wechsler, D. (1992). *Wechsler Intelligence Scale for Children—Third Edition UK*. London: The Psychological Corporation.

Wechsler, D. (1998). *Wechsler Intelligence Scale for Children—Third edition (WISC-III)*, svensk version (K. Sonnander, B. Ramund, & A.-Ch. Smedler, Trans.) Stockholm, Sweden: Psykologiförlaget AB. (Original work published in 1991.)

11

LITHUANIA

GRAŽINA GINTILIENĖ

Department of General Psychology
Vilnius University
Vilnius, Lithuania

SIGITA GIRDZIJAUSKIENĖ

Department of Social Work
Vilnius University
Vilnius, Lithuania

At the time of writing the Wechsler Intelligence Scale for Children—Third Edition (WISC-III) was in the process of publication in Lithuania following four years of adaptation research by a group of researchers of the Psychological Testing Center at the Laboratory of Special Psychology of Vilnius University. The WISC-III will be the first intelligence test standardized in Lithuania in about 70 years. The history of intelligence testing in Lithuania can be traced back to the beginning of the last century when the Binet-Simon Intelligence Scale was translated into Lithuanian in 1927 and used in the educational system until the Soviet occupation. Testing was forbidden in the USSR for many years. This arrested the development of psychological testing in Lithuania for a half century and partially determined the situation of the construction and adaptation of psychological and psychoeducational tests today. On one hand, the use of tests and other standardized techniques is regulated by the Rules of Standardized Psychological Assessment Techniques adopted by the Lithuanian Psychological Association in 1997. It forbids use of assessment techniques that have not been verified scientifically and that are not valid or reliable. On the other hand, keeping in mind that answering referral questions about students' learning abilities occupies a very important place in the practice of school and clinical psychologists, it is difficult to imagine how they are going to perform the assessment of learning problems without using intelligence and achievement tests. These two reasons were the main purpose of beginning the project of the WISC-III standardization in Lithuania pursuant to the agreement with the Psychological Corporation in 1997.

ADAPTATION PROCESS

The main goal of the Lithuanian project was the development of the WISC-III Lithuanian version (Wechsler, 2002) available for the assessment of Lithuanian children's intellectual abilities. The first phase of the project envisaged a translation of the WISC-III^{UK} Manual (Wechsler, 1992) into Lithuanian. A panel was established of four psychologists with good knowledge of English and practice in the field of the psychological assessment. They translated Chapter 6 of the UK manual. In the case of disagreement between translators regarding back translation of some Vocabulary and Comprehension items, including UK sample responses, a further check for translation was conducted with the help of American psychologists using Wechsler scales in their practice and having a good knowledge of Lithuanian.

A pilot project of the translated WISC-III was carried out in 1998 by the Lithuanian standardization group. The representative sample of 381 children was stratified by random choice technique based on four demographic categories: age, gender, place of residence, and parent education. The main goal of this project was to compare the results of the UK standardization with the Lithuanian representation sample and to analyze variables that contributed to potential differences between Lithuanian and UK samples.

Based on UK norms to score the Lithuanian data, significant differences ($p \leq 0.05$) in means were found on all WISC-III subtests, with Lithuanian children scoring lower than the UK standardization sample. Lithuanians ranged below the UK sample from 2.7 points for Similarities and Comprehension to 0.2 points for Arithmetic. The pilot study also determined that even translated subtests with high split-half reliabilities had items with different order of difficulty than the UK items, and low item discrimination (Gintiliene, Cerniauskaite, Draguneviciene, & Girdzijauskiene, 1999). Most of these items were found in the Information, Similarities, Vocabulary, and Comprehension subtests of the Verbal Scale. Different order of difficulty and low item-discrimination were also found in the Picture Completion subtest of the Performance scale. Examples of correct and incorrect responses, different from those in the UK WISC-III Manual (Wechsler, 1992) for the Similarities, Vocabulary, and Comprehension subtests were added, based on responses of Lithuanian children and according to the scoring criteria given in the WISC-III Manual. The children's responses to the Verbal subtest items were evaluated by two independent experts in accordance with the Lithuanian response examples and the translated examples from the UK Manual. In the case the scoring of these two experts differed, the final decision was made by the panel of experts: researchers of the Laboratory of Special Psychology at Vilnius University and school psychologists from the Vilnius Psychological-Pedagogical Service. Item substitution according to the results of item analysis were made in the Information and Vocabulary subtests. The order of item difficulty also changed in Information, Similarities, Arithmetic, Vocabulary, Comprehension, and Picture Completion.

Before the pilot study the item "London" in the Information subtest was changed to "Vilnius" and 13 items in the Arithmetic subtest were slightly modified, changing the names, currency, units of length, and names of commodities according to our situation. The name of one item, 17, was changed in the Comprehension subtest to correspond to the Lithuanian system of government, without changing the meaning of the question.

The pilot study identified three items (19, 24, and 30 of the UK version) in the Information subtest that were too difficult: less than four percent of our sample passed each of them and they did not discriminate with Lithuanian children. One Vocabulary item did not meet the demands of these two criteria. Item 13 was passed by only one percent of Lithuanian children. This word in the Lithuanian language has been used as a chemical term "soak." We also found six other items (19, 20, 25, 26, 28, and 30) that did not discriminate because of the peculiarities of Lithuanian language. For example, the word in Lithuanian "*pasakėčia*," has the same root as the words "say," "tell," "fairy-tale," "story" (in Lithuanian, respectively, "*pasak*yti," "*pasak*oti," "*pasak*a," "*pasak*ojimas"). So this item was one of the disadvantages for reaching objectivity in scoring children's answers. As discussed above we found changes of item difficulty in the Picture Completion subtest of the Performance scale also. For example, Lithuanian children were more alert to the details of home accessories than their British peers (item 17 to order of difficulty 9 and 20 to order of difficulty 15). However, nobody from the Lithuanian sample was able to answer item 26 correctly.

The substitution of the Information and Vocabulary items was based on the results of item analysis. For example, we changed item 30 to "amber" as they both are minerals and because we lacked Information items with difficulty level clustering around 0.40. In the Vocabulary subtest item 19 was substituted with a similar level of difficulty but with better discriminating power.

This adapted Lithuanian WISC-III version was used in the second, standardization stage for establishing WISC-III norms in Lithuania carried out in 2000 (Wechsler, 2002).

SAMPLE CHARACTERISTICS

During the last decade in Lithuania, political, economic, and social changes proceeded at a rapid rate. These changes have altered the demographic characteristics of the population of Lithuania. In Lithuania, as in the other post-communist countries, the same tendencies can be observed: decline in birthrate, rising social differentiation, etc. A standardization sample of 453 Lithuanian children with ages ranging from 6–16 years was selected by means of a stratified random choice technique. The selection of the examinees for the standardization group was 84.7% of the population of Lithuanian children attending schools and kindergartens. This sample group excluded non-Lithuanian-speaking children attending Russian or Polish schools and kindergartens. Children receiving special education services in mainstreaming school settings were included in the sample. Each child in the sample was given a parent consent form and was categorized by his or her parents as belonging to one of three language groups. In 93% of the homes, the only language spoken was Lithuanian, 5.3% used two languages (one of which was Lithuanian), and 1.7% of the sample spoke other languages, usually Russian and Polish.

The selection of the Lithuanian sample was based on four demographic categories: age, gender, place of residence, and parent or foster parent education. These demographic data were compared to statistics provided by the Statistic Yearbook of Lithuania (1998). The children were tested in the schools and kindergartens.

As shown in the Table 11.1 the percentage of children in the Lithuanian standardization sample matched those of the population values for level of parent education and residence at each age level. It was difficult to select a representative sample for the age 6 group because children in Lithuania usually start school at age 7. The percent of 6 year olds attending kindergarten or preschool classes is 60.7, while 12% attend first grade and 27.3% of 6 year olds do not attend either school or kindergarten. Data about the latter group's parent education according to place of residence are available in medical settings only. As the Ministry of Health was not involved in this project it was not possible to provide perfect representativeness of the 6-year-old group.

TABLE 11.1 Demographic Characteristics of the Lithuanian Standardization Sample: Percentages by Age, Parent Educational Level, and Residence Place

Age	n	Parent educational level (years)				Residence place		
		≤ 10	11–12	13–15	≥ 16	Rural	Town	Urban
6	36	—	27.7	41.7	30.6	13.9	19.4	66.7
7	41	7.2	28.6	45.2	19.0	26.2	33.3	40.5
8	42	4.8	31.0	42.8	21.4	23.8	33.3	42.9
9	42	4.8	35.4	42.9	16.9	23.8	33.3	42.9
10	44	4.8	33.3	40.5	21.4	23.8	33.3	42.9
11	44	2.4	40.5	33.3	23.8	23.8	38.1	38.1
12	43	2.4	38.1	40.5	19.0	19.0	38.1	42.9
13	41	4.9	34.1	41.5	19.5	19.5	36.6	43.9
14	40	9.5	35.7	33.4	21.4	21.4	35.7	42.9
15	40	4.9	34.1	34.1	26.9	19.5	36.6	43.9
16	40	7.3	31.7	43.9	17.1	19.5	36.6	43.9
Total	453	4.9	34.1	40.0	21.0	21.4	34.2	44.4
Lithuanian population		5.0	34.5	40.5	20.0	23.0	31.5	45.5

Note: Lithuanian population data of children aged 6–16 are from *Training of Children and Schoolchildren in Educational Institution, 1997*, by Department of Statistics to the Government of the Republic of Lithuania and survey of Laboratory of Special Psychology Vilnius University, 1997.

Data copyright © 2001 by the Laboratory of Special Psychology Vilnius University.

RELIABILITY

Table 11.2 shows the average (across age) split-half reliability coefficients and standard errors of measurement (SEM) for the subtests, IQ, and index scores by age and overall. As shown in the table, the average reliabilities for the IQ scores are all above 0.90. The average of the index scores ranged from $r = 0.85$ for Freedom from Distractibility Index (FDI) and Processing Speed Index (PSI) to $r = 0.93$ for Verbal Comprehension Index (VCI). The average subtest reliabilities ranged from $r = 0.71$ for Object Assembly to $r = 0.87$ for Vocabulary.

Table 11.3 shows the average of the uncorrected retest correlations for the subtest's overall age group ($n = 45$). These ranged from $r = 0.55$ for Object Assembly to $r = 0.94$ for Block Design. Due to the small sample we did not separate the ages into groups.

EVIDENCE OF VALIDITY

Experts in psychoeducational measurement agree that direct translations of the tests into a foreign language cannot be assumed to have the same properties as the original (Aiken, 1987; Geisiner, 1994; Reynolds & Kaiser, 1990). Whereas the Lithuanian version has some adapted items and new normative data, evidence regarding the validity of the scale is required. The WISC-III is the first intelligence scale standardized in Lithuania so the comparison of WISC-III^{LT} with other intelligence tests is not possible. Therefore, some evidence of criterion validity indicates correlations between WISC-III^{LT} scales and school grades. School marks assigned by teachers were obtained for 234 children ages 7–16.

All the correlations between school grades in Lithuanian language, Mathematics and Nature Science and the Full Scale as well as Verbal and Performance scales and Index scores for the most part are in the $r = 0.40$s ($p < 0.001$). The Full Scale IQ (FSIQ) score correlates moderately with the grades in Lithuanian (0.45) and Natural Science (0.42) as well as with the school grades average (0.49) and high (0.53) with the Mathematics. For Mathematics the correlations ranged from a low of 0.38 for PSI to 0.53 for FSIQ. The correlations of Mathematics were slightly higher than those of the Lithuanian language (range of 0.29 for Perceptual Organization Index, POI to 0.48 for Verbal IQ, VIQ) and Natural Science average (range of 0.26 for PSI to 0.44 for VIQ).

Inspection of the intercorrelations between WISC-III^{LT} subtests and scales (see Table 11.4) indicates that in the total group correlations between the 13 subtests ranged from low (and nonsignificant) $r = 0.07$ (Mazes and Coding) to high of $r = 0.65$ (Vocabulary and Similarities). It would appear that the Verbal Scale subtests correlated more highly with each other (Mdn $r = 0.46$) than the Performance Scale subtests (Mdn $r = 0.31$). Correlations between the Verbal subtests and Verbal Scale ranged from 0.40 to 0.78 (Mdn $r = 0.62$), and those between the Performance subtests and Performance Scale ranged from $r = 0.30$ to 0.60 (Mdn $r = 0.50$).

TABLE 11.2 Reliability Coefficients and Standard Errors of Measurement of the Subtest Scaled Scores, IQ Scores, and Index Scores by Age

Subtest/scale	6 n = 36	7 n = 41	8 n = 42	9 n = 42	10 n = 44	11 n = 44	12 n = 43	13 n = 41	14 n = 40	15 n = 40	16 n = 40	Average
Information	0.76	0.69	0.85	0.84	0.88	0.91	0.91	0.84	0.74	0.82	0.92	0.83
(SEm)	1.47	1.67	1.16	1.2	1.04	0.90	0.90	1.2	1.53	1.27	0.85	1.23
Similarities	0.89	0.76	0.80	0.77	0.79	0.78	0.66	0.75	0.86	0.82	0.82	0.79
(SEm)	0.99	1.47	1.34	1.44	1.37	1.41	1.75	1.5	1.12	1.27	1.27	1.37
Arithmetic	0.80	0.61	0.80	0.64	0.71	0.85	0.76	0.82	0.85	0.84	0.82	0.77
(SEm)	1.34	1.87	1.34	1.8	1.62	1.16	1.47	1.27	1.16	1.2	1.27	1.43
Vocabulary	0.89	0.84	0.92	0.84	0.90	0.92	0.86	0.82	0.86	0.82	0.91	0.87
(SEm)	1.20	1.20	0.85	1.20	0.95	0.85	1.12	1.27	1.12	1.27	0.90	1.10
Comprehension	0.84	0.76	0.81	0.77	0.77	0.86	0.73	0.78	0.86	0.80	0.82	0.80
(SEm)	1.2	1.47	1.31	1.44	1.44	1.12	1.56	1.41	1.12	1.34	1.27	1.34
Digit span	0.71	0.78	0.73	0.78	0.81	0.86	0.78	0.87	0.88	0.88	0.64	0.79
(SEm)	1.62	1.41	1.57	1.41	1.31	1.13	1.41	1.08	1.03	1.03	1.80	1.37
Picture completion	0.78	0.79	0.84	0.63	0.68	0.67	0.77	0.66	0.78	0.73	0.82	0.74
(SEm)	1.41	1.37	1.20	1.82	1.70	1.72	1.44	1.75	1.41	1.56	1.27	1.53
Coding	—[b]	—[b]	—[b]	—[b]	—[b]	—[b]	—[b]	—[b]	—[b]	—[b]	—[b]	0.80
(SEm)	—[b]	—[b]	—[b]	—[b]	—[b]	—[b]	—[b]	—[b]	—[b]	—[b]	—[b]	1.39
Picture arrangement	0.91	0.80	0.85	0.85	0.86	0.83	0.86	0.80	0.82	0.85	0.88	0.84
(SEm)	0.90	1.34	1.16	1.16	1.12	1.24	1.2	1.34	1.27	1.16	1.04	1.18
Block design	0.84	0.88	0.88	0.78	0.88	0.79	0.76	0.86	0.76	0.87	0.73	0.82
(SEm)	1.20	1.04	1.04	1.41	1.04	1.37	1.47	1.12	1.47	1.08	1.56	1.27

Age in years

170

Object assembly	0.72	0.48	0.75	0.79	0.68	0.73	0.68	0.76	0.75	0.80	0.70	0.71
(SEm)	1.59	2.16	1.50	1.37	1.70	1.56	1.70	1.47	1.50	1.34	1.64	1.61
Symbol search	—b	—b	—b	—b	—b	—b	—b	—b	—b	—b	—b	0.76
(SEm)	—b	—b	—b	—b	—b	—b	—b	—b	—b	—b	—b	1.48
Mazes	0.84	0.87	0.77	0.73	0.80	0.68	0.59	0.68	0.64	0.68	0.58	0.71
(SEm)	1.20	1.12	1.44	1.56	1.34	1.70	1.92	1.70	1.80	1.70	1.94	1.68
Verbal IQ	0.93	0.90	0.95	0.90	0.94	0.94	0.93	0.94	0.95	0.95	0.96	0.94
(SEm)	4.09	4.09	3.37	4.77	3.7	3.62	3.83	3.75	3.33	3.42	3.13	3.7
Performance IQ	0.89	0.87	0.91	0.88	0.92	0.92	0.91	0.90	0.91	0.93	0.93	0.91
(SEm)	4.86	4.86	4.44	5.2	4.27	4.15	4.52	4.63	4.58	3.85	4.00	4.51
Full scale IQ	0.91	0.89	0.94	0.89	0.93	0.93	0.92	0.92	0.93	0.94	0.94	0.93
(SEm)	4.45	4.45	3.82	4.97	3.98	3.93	4.14	4.17	3.92	3.61	3.55	4.08
Verbal comp. index	0.90	0.90	0.94	0.91	0.93	0.96	0.93	0.93	0.94	0.94	0.95	0.93
(SEm)	4.74	4.74	3.54	4.44	3.84	3.16	4.05	4.09	3.6	3.81	3.19	3.85
Percept. organ. index	0.90	0.87	0.92	0.89	0.92	0.92	0.89	0.90	0.91	0.92	0.92	0.90
(SEm)	4.83	4.83	4.15	5.08	4.30	4.36	4.93	4.81	4.60	4.30	4.34	4.69
Freedom-distract. index	0.78	0.76	0.84	0.70	0.82	0.89	0.84	0.90	0.90	0.91	0.82	0.85
(SEm)	7.04	7.04	5.98	8.24	6.36	4.94	6.00	4.66	4.70	4.59	6.36	5.89
Processing speed index	—b	—b	—b	—b	—b	—b	—b	—b	—b	—b	—b	0.85
(SEm)	—b	—b	—b	—b	—b	—b	—b	—b	—b	—b	—b	5.84

[a]The reliability coefficients for all subtests except Coding and Symbol Search are split-half correlations corrected by the Spearman-Brown formula.

[b]For Coding and Symbol Search the estimates of reliability was not done.

Data Copyright © 2001 by the Laboratory of Special Psychology Vilnius University.

TABLE 11.3   Stability Coefficients of the Subtests, IQ
Scales, and Factor-Based Scales

Subtest/scale	Z
Information	0.87
Similarities	0.90
Arithmetic	0.62
Vocabulary	0.78
Comprehension	0.70
Digit span	0.74
Picture completion	0.70
Coding	0.80
Picture arrangement	0.65
Block design	0.94
Object assembly	0.55
Symbol search	0.76
Mazes	0.60
Verbal IQ	0.91
Performance IQ	0.80
Full scale IQ	0.86
Verbal comprehension index	0.93
Perceptual organization index	0.81
Freedom from distractibility index	0.75
Processing speed index	0.81

Data copyright © 2001 by the Laboratory of Special
Psychology Vilnius University.

Thus, the Verbal subtests have more in common with each other than the Performance subtests. Furthermore, the Verbal subtests correlate more highly with
each other than with Performance subtests and Performance subtests correlated
with each other more highly than with the Verbal subtests and followed the same
pattern as in the UK sample (Wechsler, 1992). These results support evidence
of the convergent and discrimination validity of the WISC-III (Cicchetti, 1994;
Rogers, 1995).

Despite the fact that comparison of the patterns of intercorrelations between
WISC-III subtests and scales of the UK and Lithuanian samples showed very
similar tendencies (the absolute differences ranged from 0.00 to 0.17 with a mode
of 0.01 and median of 0.03), exploratory common factor analyses in order to
extract factors from the Lithuanian data were used. The results in Table 11.5 are
solutions based on maximum-likelihood factor analysis (iterated Squared Multiple
Correlation communalities, Varimax rotations).

The results of the exploratory analysis confirm two major factors and two
smaller supplementary factors that account for approximately 63.6% of the variance. The first two factors are familiar, Verbal Comprehension and Perceptual
Organization, and account for approximately 48.6% of the variance. Factor 3,

TABLE 11.4 Intercorrelation of Subtest Scaled Scores

Subtest/scale	Inf	Sim	Ari	Voc	Com	DS	PCom	Cd	PA	BD	OA	SS	Mz
Information													
Similarities	0.59^b												
Arithmetic	0.51^b	0.50^b											
Vocabulary	0.62^b	0.65^b	0.46^b										
Comprehension	0.45^b	0.48^b	0.36^b	0.60^b									
Digit span	0.30^b	0.37^b	0.43^b	0.31^b	0.24^b								
Picture completion	0.41^b	0.39^b	0.32^b	0.43^b	0.36^b	0.27^b							
Coding	0.20^b	0.19^b	0.27^b	0.19^b	0.17^b	0.27^b	0.21^b						
Picture arrangement	0.41^b	0.28^b	0.36^b	0.36^b	0.31^b	0.28^b	0.41^b	0.25^b					
Block design	0.45^b	0.34^b	0.46^b	0.37^b	0.29^b	0.28^b	0.42^b	0.27^b	0.40^b				
Object assembly	0.36^b	0.31^b	0.30^b	0.26^b	0.29^b	0.27^b	0.41^b	0.25^b	0.39^b	0.52^b			
Symbol search	0.30^b	0.35^b	0.32^b	0.34^b	0.23^b	0.26^b	0.31^b	0.45^b	0.32^b	0.41^b	0.31^b		
Mazes	0.11^a	0.14^a	0.20^b	0.11^a	0.18^a	0.10^a	0.24^b	0.07	0.21^b	0.23^b	0.23^b	0.09	

[a] $p < 0.05$.
[b] $p < 0.001$.
Data copyright © 2001 by the Laboratory of Special Psychology Vilnius University.

TABLE 11.5 Maximum–Likelihood Factor Loadings (Varimax Rotation) for Four Factors

Subtest/scale	Factor 1: Verbal comprehension	Factor 2: Perceptual organization	Factor 3: Freedom from distractibility	Factor 4: Processing speed
Information	0.60	0.32	0.29	0.12
Similarities	0.65	0.18	0.30	0.18
Vocabulary	0.86	0.15	0.16	0.14
Comprehension	0.63	0.23	0.10	0.07
Picture completion	0.37	0.50	0.08	0.16
Picture arrangement	0.26	0.47	0.17	0.18
Block design	0.22	0.58	0.26	0.27
Object assembly	0.16	0.66	0.10	0.16
Mazes	0.06	0.32	0.11	0.02
Arithmetic	0.34	0.25	0.72	0.15
Digit span	0.19	0.23	0.41	0.16
Coding	0.08	0.21	0.19	0.41
Symbol search	0.19	0.16	0.09	0.96

Data copyright © 2001 by the Laboratory of Special Psychology Vilnius University.

labeled Freedom from Distractibility and composed of the Arithmetic and Digit Span, accounted for about 6.6% of the variance. Factor 4, labeled Processing Speed and composed of Coding and Symbol Search, accounted for about 8.4% of the variance.

Maximum-likelihood factor analyses were conducted for two, three, four, and five factors. Subsequent rotations of five factors showed the presence of a weak fifth factor with low loadings (maximum loading 0.22).

Correlation matrixes for the 13 subtests were computed for the total sample and used in a series of confirmatory factor analyses to test five models of WISC-III^{LT}. Successive factor models were evaluated according to a variety of goodness-of-fit indices. Table 11.6 presents the comparative results of various goodness-of-fit analyses of the following five models for the total sample. The goodness-of-fit of the whole model was judged by means of four measures of overall fit: chi-square (χ^2); chi-square fit statistic divided by degrees of freedom; adjusted goodness-of-fit index (AGFI); and root mean square residual (RMSR) (Jöreskog & Sörbom, 1996).

Statistically, none of the models fit the data very well except for the four-factor model. The four-factor model advocated by Wechsler (1992), Roid, Prifitera, and Weiss (1993), and Kamphaus, Benson, Hutchinson, and Platt (1994) is supported by our analysis.

In spite of the fact that confirmatory analysis of the results of the Lithuanian standardization sample confirmed the advantage of the four-factor model, the significance of singled out factors and their diagnostic value are usually corroborated by research with different clinical groups.

TABLE 11.6   Goodness-of-Fit Statistics for Confirmatory Maximum-Likelihood Factor Analysis (LISREL 8) of 13 Subtests ($n = 453$)

Model	χ^2	df	χ^2/df	AGFI	RMSR
One-factor[a]	369.99	65	5.69	0.818	0.067
Two-factor[b]	230.31	64	3.60	0.893	0.054
Three-factor[c]	185.32	62	3.00	0.909	0.048
Three-factor[d]	195.85	62	3.16	0.911	0.049
Four-factor[e]	138.86	59	2.35	0.956	0.038

[a]Model 1: One general factor. All 13 subtests as one factor (Wechsler, 1992; Weiss, Prifitera, & Roid., 1993).

[b]Model 2: Two factors (Verbal and Performance)—6 Verbal subtests and 7 Performance subtests (Wechsler, 1992; Weiss, Prifitera, Roid, 1993).

[c]Model 3A: Three factors (Verbal, PO, and PS)—6 Verbal subtests, 5 Perceptual Organization subtests and Coding and Symbol search on the Processing Speed factor (Wechsler, 1992; Weiss, Prifitera, & Roid, 1993).

[d]Model 3B: Three factors (as in the WISC-R)—VC, PO (including Symbol Search) and FD (Arithmetic, Digit Span, and Coding) (Weiss, Prifitera, & Roid, 1993).

[e]Model 4: Four factors (VC, PO, FD, PS) found in the exploratory analyses.

Data copyright © 2001 by the Laboratory of Special Psychology Vilnius University.

CULTURAL ISSUES INFLUENCING WISC-III
INTERPRETATION IN LITHUANIA

An issue relating to culture test bias is a disputed issue in intelligence tests. Such discussions are also inevitable in the practice of researchers measuring children's intellectual abilities with the Wechsler scales. Representatives of ethnic minorities who usually receive lower IQ scores than whites (Prifitera, Weiss, & Saklofske, 1998; Sattler, 1992; Tanner-Halverson, Burden, & Sabers, 1993; Weiss, Prifitera, & Roid, 1993) have been an important issue in the U.S. However, cultural issues may be important not only when ethnic minority groups are investigated within countries, but also when the norms of a separate country in which the standardization of test was carried out are interpreted.

The WISC-III[LT] norm tables are based on the scores of children in the Lithuanian sample. However, as discussed above, Lithuanian children scored lower on all IQ and index scores when employing the UK standardization norms ($p < 0.05$). Full Scale IQ mean differences showed that Lithuanians were 6.8 points below the UK sample. The greatest differences between samples were obtained in Verbal Comprehension (9 points) and Freedom from Distractibility (8.4 points) scores. The smallest (1 point) difference was found in Processing Speed. This result might imply that Lithuanian children are worse at performing WISC-III tasks. However, Information, Similarities, Vocabulary, and Comprehension subtests composing VCI are deemed to be more culturally determined.

During the adaptation phase, the order of items was changed in all five subtests of the Verbal Scales. However, employing the norms of the Lithuanian standardization sample with the adapted items increased the means of the Information and Vocabulary subtests, which had the effect of substantially reducing item bias for these subtests. Similarities item bias could be explained by the peculiarities of the Lithuanian language. The dictionary of modern Lithuanian language presents the primary mean of the word "similar" as "having the same features and peculiarities." Traditionally in our country the word "similar" is used for the description of similarities between parents and children. So in the Lithuanian language, questions about similarities are more oriented toward attaining answers about outside features than generalizing about similarities. Therefore it was recommended that examiners presenting example items of the Similarities subtest for children to stress the word "both" ("They *both* are xxx"). Cultural bias of Comprehension is directly related to social norms and conventional standards existing within the society. It was interesting to observe that Lithuanian children's answers revealed their relatively good understanding of how to behave in situations with the "ball" but provoked confusing feelings in the situation with the "wallet." The answers to the latter item indicated that considerable numbers of Lithuanian children knew the right answer but some part of them would not practice this, and they openly talked about this to the examiners. Lithuanian children's answers also showed relatively good understanding of the importance of "meat" but sought adults' help when facing a "fight" situation.

The difference in Freedom from Distractibility scores was mainly determined by low scores of Lithuanian children on the Digit Span subtest (score mean according to UK norms is 8.4). It was unexpected for us to learn about the importance of the situation context in the Digit Span subtest. At first glance Digit Span seemed to be free of any cultural influence. However, Lithuanian children found it more difficult to hear and memorize similar sounding three-syllable names of digits than their English-speaking peers who are asked to hear and memorize one-syllable digits. One example is the perception of three digits in item 2 of Digits Backward. This item is more difficult for Lithuanians because of the longer time it take to pronounce digits in Lithuanian (pen-ki—sep-ty-ni—ke-tu-ri) and of the more complicated recognition of three-syllable digits "seven" and "four" sounding similar to "nine" and "eight."

The development of cognitive abilities reflects the interaction of many factors. Hence the lower result achieved might be determined not only by lower abilities but by a different context, that is by different experiences of subjects (Laboratory of Comparative Human Cognition, 1990). The important factor that may have influenced the results of Lithuanian children is the testing situation itself. Most of the children participating in the standardization of the WISC-III had never been tested before. Moreover, they had never met a psychologist in their lives. Many rural and even some small town schools hosted a psychologist for the first time in their history. The children were inclined to treat the testing situation as an assessment of their academic achievement or even as a check of their knowledge. So, in the course of research one could observe how children not only did their best to cope with the tasks but also to produce a very neat piece of work. This was observed particularly with items of the Picture Arrangement, Block Design, and Object Assembly subtests.

It is important to be aware of subcultural differences influencing WISC-III interpretation in Lithuania. The variable ethnic minority was in fact eliminated in the Lithuanian standardization because Lithuanian-speaking children only were included in the sample. In the future it may also be necessary to standardize the WISC-III for the other ethnic groups who do not speak Lithuanian.

Other factors affecting WISC-III results are place of child's residence and level of parent education. Both factors were found to be closely related to socioeconomical status (SES). Education is highly correlated with intelligence (Sattler, 1992). Lithuanian children from homes whose parents have the highest level of education (university degree) also had scores considerably higher than groups with secondary and less than 11 grades of education. The correlation between the years of school completed by the child's parents and FSIQ was $r = 0.32$ ($p < 0.01$) for the total standardization sample. We obtained a progressive increase in FSIQ means according to years of parent education: 10 or fewer years of education FSIQ—94.0; 11–12 years of FSIQ—95.97; 13–15 years FSIQ—101.2, and 16 or more years—106.9. Minimal mean differences were found with PSI scores for the entire Lithuanian standardization sample; for the four educational levels from lowest to highest, means are 97.1, 98.1, 100.9, and 103.8, respectively.

Another proximate variable for SES in Lithuania is place of residence. According to the data for household income and expenditure research of the Department of Statistics of the Government of the Republic of Lithuania (2000), the rural population is 1.6 and town population is 1.3 times poorer than the urban population. In order to investigate the differences among groups of children living in different areas we examined the WISC-III IQ and index scores. The means of scores of children groups living in rural, town, and urban areas showed scale and index score differences between children groups living in different areas. Means of all indicators of rural children were lower than those of children living in towns, who in their turn showed lower means than urban children. All three groups showed statistically significant differences on FSIQ, VIQ, and VCI scores. It is not clear why the intellect assessment scores of rural and town children were lower than those of urban children. Several hypotheses can be suggested. Lower scores shown by rural children may be determined not by poorer abilities but by the novelty of material or the unusual testing situation (Groth-Marnat, 1997). Second, as is indicated by many authors, the difference may be determined by SES (Sattler, 1992; Puente & Salazar, 1998; Groth-Marnat 1997; Snaw & Yalow, 1990). The Lithuanian sample was stratified by parent education level as one of the important indicators of the SES. A larger percentage of children whose parents have higher or college-type education can be found in urban, not in rural areas. Therefore a simple comparison of means between groups according to their place of residence will yield scores that do not take into account the impact of variables that may affect scores. For further investigation of the relationship between these two SES variables with IQ scores, we matched samples of children groups living in rural, town, and urban areas on age, sex, and parent education.

Even if the FSIQ score differences between children from rural and urban areas are reduced from 13.5 to 10.4 points when taking into account education they remain statistically significant. The same occurs with VIQ, PIQ, and index scores with the exception of POI scores. However, IQ differences between children living in rural areas and towns as well as IQ differences between children groups living in towns and urban areas are substantially reduced when samples are matched. These data suggest looking at other variables in the home and school environment that may affect the opportunity to develop child's cognitive abilities. Low family income often determines poorer nourishment, worse health care, and limited chances of many-sided development. Children studying in rural schools in Lithuania have limited chances for learning as compared to their urban cohorts. Though the above-mentioned environmental variables are directly related to the development of intellectual abilities, not a single one of them, according to Sattler (1992), has a decisive impact on intellect. When assessing each child individually, intellect rates should not be viewed as final or invariable.

PROFESSIONAL ISSUES IN THE USE OF
INTELLIGENCE TESTS IN LITHUANIA

As discussed above, psychological testing in Lithuania during the past generations did not follow the same course as in the U.S., Europe, and other countries. The WISC-III will be the first intelligence test standardized in Lithuania. The appearance of this scale will give Lithuanian psychologists a chance to carry out a reliable and valid assessment of intellectual abilities of Lithuanian children. The Education Act of July 25, 1991 and the Law on Special Education of December 15, 1998, and other laws of the Republic of Lithuania ensure the right of Lithuanian children to qualified psychological services. The WISC-III has been expected by Lithuanian psychologists working in Pedagogical-Psychological Services and Mental Health Centers. Only the members of the Lithuanian Psychological Association, those with at least a master's degree level in psychology, will be entitled to use the WISC-III. The Lithuanian Psychological Association has 235 members and is a member of the European Federation of Psychologists' Associations (EFPA) and of the International Test Commission (ITC). Lithuanian psychologists who work in the area of psychological assessment are regulated by the Rules of Standardized Psychological Techniques adopted by the Lithuanian Association of Psychologists in 1997 and International Guidelines for test use adopted by the ITC in 1999. However, our psychologists as a part of an interdisciplinary team did not play an essential role in the evaluation of special needs of exceptional children until now. Professionals have tended to develop an attitude that expensive intelligence testing cannot provide as exhaustive an amount of information about a child's strengths and weaknesses in the learning process as Curriculum Based Assessment, or other techniques of educational assessment. Taking this attitude into account and seeking to ensure a high professional level of psychologists who will perform intelligence testing in school and clinical settings, WISC-III publishers in Lithuania plan to organize relevant course work and supervised internships.

We hope that WISC-III standardization in Lithuania and subsequent research studies will show advantages of intelligence testing in answering referral questions about children's learning abilities and increasing their educational opportunities. In the authors' opinion, when responding to the issues of intelligence testing it is important to pool the forces of all psychologists, both scientists and practitioners.

REFERENCES

Aiken, L. R. (1987). *Assessment of intellectual functioning*. Boston: Allyn and Bacon.

Cicchetti, D. V. (1994). Guidelines, criteria, and rules of thumb for evaluating normed and standardized assessment instruments in psychology. *Psychological Assessment, 6*, 284–290.

Geisiner, K. F. (1994). Cross–cultural normative assessment: translation, adaptation issues influencing the normative interpretation of assessment instruments. *Psychological Assessment, 8*, 304–312.

Gintiliene, G., Cerniauskaite, D., Draguneviciene, R., & Girdzijauskiene, S. (1999). Analysis of WISC III results based on a Lithuanian children representative sample (in Lithuanian). *Psychology: Research papers, 20,* 5–18.

Groth-Marnat, G. (1997). *Handbook of psychological assessment.* 3rd ed. New York: John Wiley & Sons.

Jöreskog, K. G., & Sörbom, D. (1996). *LISREL 8: User's reference guide.* Chicago, IL: Scientific Software.

Kamphaus, R. W., Benson, J., Hutchinson, S., & Platt, L. O. (1994). Identification of factor models for the WISC-III. *Educational & Psychological Measurement, 54,* 174–187.

Laboratory of Comparative Human Cognition (1990). Culture and intelligence. In R. J. Sternberg (Ed.), *Handbook of human intelligence* (pp. 642–722). Cambridge: Cambridge University Press.

Prifitera, A., Weiss, L. G., & Saklofske, D. H. (1998). The WISC-III in context. In A. Prifitera & D. H. Saklofske (Eds.), *WISC-III clinical use and interpretation: Scientist-practitioner perspectives* (pp. 1–38). San Diego, CA: Academic Press.

Puente, A. E., & Salazar, D. G. (1998). Assessment of minority and culture diverse children. In A. Prifitera & D. H. Saklofske (Eds.), *WISC-III clinical use and interpretation: Scientist-practitioner perspectives* (pp. 227–248.) San Diego, CA: Academic Press.

Reynolds, C. R., & Kaiser, S. M. (1990). Bias in assessment of aptitude. In C. R. Reynolds & R. W. Kamphaus (Eds.), *Handbook of psychological and educational assessment of children: Personality, behavior and context.* New York: The Guilford Press.

Rogers, T. B. (1995). *The psychological testing enterprise: An introduction.* Pacific Grove, CA: Brooks/Cole.

Roid, G., Prifitera, A., & Weiss, L.G. (1993). Replication of the WISC-III factor structure in an independent sample. *Journal of Psychoeducational Assessment WISC-III Monograph,* 6–21.

Sattler, J. M. (1992). *Assessment of children* (3rd ed.). San Diego, CA: Author.

Snaw, R. E., & Yalow, E. (1990). Society, culture, and intelligence. In R. J. Sternberg (Ed.), *Handbook of human intelligence* (pp. 493–585). Cambridge: Cambridge University Press.

Tanner-Halverson, P., Burden, T., & Sabers, D. (1993). WISC-III normative data for Tohono O'Odham Native-American children. *Journal of Psychoeducational Assessment WISC-III Monograph,* 125–133.

Wechsler, D. (1992). *Wechsler Intelligence Scale for Children—Third Edition.* London: The Psychological Corporation.

Wechsler, D. (2002). *Wechslerio intelekto skalė vaikams—trečias leidimas. Vadovas* (G. Gintilienė, S. Girdzijauskienė, D. Černiauskaitė, & R. Dragūnevičienė, Trans.). Vilnius, Lithuania: Vilniaus universiteto Specialiosios psichologijos laboratorija. (Original work published in 1991.)

Weiss, L. G., Prifitera, A., & Roid, G. (1993). The WISC-III and the fairness of predicting achievement across ethnic and gender groups. *Journal of Psychoeducational Assessment WISC-III Monograph,* 35–42.

12

SLOVENIA

DUŠICA BOBEN

Center for Psychodiagnostic Resources
Ljubljana, Slovenia

VALENTIN BUCIK

Department of Psychology
University of Ljubljana
Ljubljana, Slovenia

Quality adaptations of psychological tests like the Wechsler Intelligence Scale for Children—Third Edition (WISC-III) known throughout the world mean more than valid measurement techniques to Slovenian psychologists and to a country that has been independent only since 1991. They mean possibilities for professional applications and high level research, equivalent to those of colleagues worldwide. An adaptation of old and inadequate items and the necessity of new norms were needed, as the first standardization of the WISC was done in the former Yugoslavia 30 years ago (Šali, 1972).

The adaptation and standardization of the WISC-III (Wechsler, 2001) took four years, from 1997–2001. Responsible for the project was the Center za psihodi-agnosticna sredstva (Center for Psychodiagnostic Resources) under the direction of Dušica Boben, and was supported by state institutions such as the Education Development Unit of the Ministry of Education, Science, and Sports, the University of Ljubljana, and numerous primary and secondary schools throughout Slovenia. More than 80 psychologists from educational and medical institutions participated in this project. It can be said that the final result was accomplished with teamwork and many people volunteered their time and effort for the success of the project.

Culture and Children's Intelligence:
Cross-Cultural Analysis of the WISC-III
181

ADAPTATION PROCESS

The UK version was chosen rather than the U.S. version, because we believed that the European context is closer to Slovenia that of the U.S. The first step was the translation of instructions and items by an expert in the English language. These translations were then reviewed by a group of five psychologists with clinical experience in testing with children. These expert psychologists were all fluent in English. They did not back-translate the Slovene translation into English to find out whether the meaning of the translation is the same as the meaning of the original, as it is usually done. Instead of that, the content of the items and of the directions was reviewed from the aspects of language, method, understanding of directions, and of course clinical child psychology. Thus, several changes were made in verbal subtests.

Based on our experience, culturally biased items were corrected so that the original UK item and its Slovenian counterpart had the same construct. These corrections were made in the Information, Similarities, and Arithmetic subtests. For example, item 3 from the Similarities subtest was changed so that the correct answer would be the same. This was done because in Slovene, shoes are not considered to be an item of clothing, but footwear and are named with two distinctive words "oblačila" (clothing) and "obutev" (footwear). Items of the Arithmetic subtest that had monetary unit content were changed into the Slovene monetary unit "tolar," so that the contents of the items were changed but the calculations were the same.

The names of the children were all changed into Slovene names. New items for the Information and Vocabulary subtests based on the Slovenian culture were added with the purpose of potentially replacing culture-biased items from the UK version. The Information and Vocabulary subtests were treated especially carefully. For these tests, the order of items and the discontinue rule were slightly modified.

Slovenian criteria for scoring and typical examples of answers for Information, Similarities, Vocabulary, and Comprehension subtests were determined by five psychologists, each of them individually reviewing the criteria and, subsequently, all five reviewing and deciding upon the final criteria and typical examples of answers. Care was taken with the Verbal subtests, so that regional expressions found in dialects were not a biased factor in the wording of the instructions and the items.

Children aged from 6 years and 5 months to 16 years and 11 months ($n = 1080$) were tested with these new items. (See also the Sample Characteristics section.) Item analysis followed. The statistical analysis of data included item difficulty and reliability across the age groups (i.e., the sample was divided in 11 groups, according to chronological age). These data provided information for choosing adapted items based on the Slovenian culture, if the UK items appeared biased, for the Information and Vocabulary subtests. For example, in the Information subtest, the item, "Who wrote the first Slovenian book?" was substituted for item 20, and "Who was Jurij Vega?" was substituted for item 28. In the Vocabulary subtest, seven items were substituted by new ones.

The order of items was changed on the Picture Completion, Information, Similarities, Arithmetic, and Vocabulary subtest. For example, the Information item 18 was more difficult in the UK version than for Slovenian children (item 12), probably because the Slovene verb for "sun set"—"zahajati"—denotes the western direction of the sunset.

The data file with data collected from 1080 children was then corrected in terms of the changes made in the Information and Vocabulary subtests. This was the only way to collect data on a large sample and still stay within the financial capabilities of the project.

SAMPLE CHARACTERISTICS

Slovenia is a small country with fewer than 2 million inhabitants. The population has been slightly but steadily decreasing during the past 20 years and the number of children per generation is approximately 22,000–27,000. Slovenia is divided into 12 regions that differ in population and living standards. The population is composed of 87% Slovenes and approximately 12% with Slovenian citizenship but of other ethnic groups. The ethnic groups are Croats (2.8%), Serbs (2.4%), Muslims (1.4%), Hungarians (0.4%), Macedonians (0.2%), Montenegrins (0.2%), Albanians (0.2%), Italians (0.2%), and 0.1% Romany. The ethnic groups from the nations from the former Yugoslavia live in all regions of Slovenia: 99% of Hungarians live in the Northeastern Pomurska region, 90% of Italians live in the Southwestern Obalno-kraška region and 94% of Romany live in the Pomurska, Podravska, Dolenjska, and Osrednjeslovenska regions. Italians and Hungarians are recognized national minorities and their language is official in the territories where they live. That means they use their own language in all areas of life. There are also primary and secondary schools in which teaching is in Italian or Hungarian. The WISC-III has not been specially adapted for them, as the Italian and Hungarian versions of WISC-III are probably more appropriate for them.

The Slovenian language belongs to the Slavic languages and has as a literary language since the 16th century. Slovenian uses the Latin script and its special characteristics are declinations and duals, the latter unusual among Slavic languages. Apart from two grammatical numbers also known in English, singular and plural, Slovenian also has dual, used whenever two things are in question: for example, en pes—one dog (singular), trije psi—three dogs (plural), and dva psa—two dogs (dual). Regarding declination, in Slovenian the inflection denotes not only the number form (as it does in the English language) but also the relationship of individual words in the sentence, which in English with some exceptions (cf. the Saxon genitive) is expressed by the use of prepositions.

During the period of data collection for the WISC-III, the Slovenian school system was undergoing a period of educational reforms. At the time of testing the majority of children in Slovenia entered elementary school at 7 years of age. Children younger than seven attended one year of compulsory "little school," which is a transition from kindergarten to primary school, which will be changed to the first year of the nine-year primary educational system upon the complete introduction of the new reforms. The duration of the elementary school system at the time of testing was 8 years. Elementary school is compulsory. The duration of secondary school education is not compulsory, but 97–98% of school children continue their education for 2–4 more years depending on the type of secondary school they choose to attend.

The 1080 children aged from 6 years and 5 months to 16 years and 11 months were included in the standardization sample, which represents 0.4% of the population. They were proportionally chosen from different regions, age groups, and gender. The age groups have values in the interval of one year, i.e., so that a full year is in the middle of an interval, e.g., age 8 includes children from 7 years and 7 months to 8 years and 6 months at the time of testing. The structure of the standardization sample in relation to the general population is shown in Table 12.1.

The sampling was done as follows. First, we determined the percent of the child population according to regions, using the data from the Statistical Office of the Republic of Slovenia (Rapid Reports, 1992, 1997). We decided to sample using stratums: region, school, grade, and child. Second, a random sample of schools was chosen from each geographical location. Our criteria were regions and urban-rural residence, and a random distribution of socioeconomic status of families of the children. We did not collect data on their socioeconomic status or educational level from parents. Thus 100 schools were chosen: 62 primary and 38 secondary. Two children from each grade were chosen from every school. The following system of sampling children was employed. The school counselor chose one class from each grade level and in each of these classes, the seventh pupil according to alphabetical order of the name was the first student tested; the second pupil chosen was of the opposite gender, again according to alphabetical order. The students were tested before noon. No additional information was collected from them.

Support and permission for testing was obtained from the Education Development Unit at the Ministry of Education, Science, and Sports, primary and secondary schools, and the parents of the children chosen. The psychologists who collected the standardization data were experienced in testing children with the WISC and trained in the use of the WISC-III. The collection of data took place from December 1999 to June 2000.

No significant gender differences in intelligence were found. Small and non-significant differences between the east, central, and western parts of Slovenia were found. The central part includes the capital city of Ljubljana and the surrounding area, the eastern part includes some rural regions, among them some less developed, and the western part is situated near the Alps and the Adriatic Sea.

RELIABILITY

While preparing the Slovene translation/adaptation of WISC-III the alpha coefficients of reliability were calculated first to show the internal consistency as

TABLE 12.1 Demographic Characteristics of the Standardization Sample: Frequencies (Percentages) by Gender, Age, and Region

Age[b]	n	Gender		Region[a]											
		M	F	1	2	3	4	5	6	7	8	9	10	11	12
7	60	27	33	5	9	1	12	3	6	4	8	3	3	2	4
	(5.6)	(45.0)	(55.0)	(8.3)	(15.0)	(1.7)	(20.0)	(5.0)	(10.0)	(6.7)	(13.3)	(5.0)	(5.0)	(3.3)	(6.7)
8	103	53	50	4	16	6	15	3	4	5	26	10	3	5	6
	(9.5)	(51.5)	(48.5)	(3.9)	(15.5)	(5.8)	(14.6)	(2.9)	(3.9)	(4.9)	(25.2)	(9.7)	(2.9)	(4.9)	(5.8)
9	125	65	60	6	21	8	17	4	2	7	27	16	4	4	9
	(11.6)	(52.0)	(48.0)	(4.8)	(16.8)	(6.4)	(13.6)	(3.2)	(1.6)	(5.6)	(21.6)	(12.8)	(3.2)	(3.2)	(7.2)
10	112	53	58	6	13	5	19	3	5	10	23	11	5	3	9
	(10.4)	(47.7)	(52.3)	(5.4)	(11.6)	(4.5)	(17.0)	(2.7)	(4.5)	(8.9)	(20.5)	(9.8)	(4.5)	(2.7)	(8.0)
11	117	65	52	6	18	7	15	5	3	8	34	10	3	3	5
	(10.8)	(55.6)	(44.4)	(5.1)	(15.4)	(6.0)	(12.8)	(4.3)	(2.6)	(6.8)	(29.1)	(8.5)	(2.6)	(2.6)	(4.3)
12	128	60	68	7	20	6	19	3	5	8	28	15	3	5	9
	(11.9)	(46.9)	(53.1)	(5.5)	(15.6)	(4.7)	(14.8)	(2.3)	(3.9)	(6.3)	(21.9)	(11.7)	(2.3)	(3.9)	(7.0)
13	114	58	56	5	18	4	14	4	3	8	26	15	4	4	9
	(10.6)	(50.9)	(49.1)	(4.4)	(15.8)	(3.5)	(12.3)	(3.5)	(2.6)	(7.0)	(22.8)	(13.2)	(3.5)	(3.5)	(7.9)
14	124	59	65	5	13	7	22	7	5	8	27	13	6	2	9
	(11.5)	(47.6)	(52.4)	(4.0)	(10.5)	(5.6)	(17.7)	(5.6)	(4.0)	(6.5)	(21.8)	(10.5)	(4.8)	(1.6)	(7.3)

(Continues)

TABLE 12.1 (Continued)

Age[b]	n	Gender		Region[a]											
		M	F	1	2	3	4	5	6	7	8	9	10	11	12
15	104	61	43	8	22	6	15	3	1	4	18	11	2	8	6
	(9.6)	(58.7)	(41.3)	(7.7)	(21.2)	(5.8)	(14.4)	(2.9)	(1.0)	(3.8)	(17.3)	(10.6)	(1.9)	(7.7)	(5.8)
16	93	47	46	6	6	6	16	2	4	8	14	17	2	4	8
	(8.6)	(50.5)	(49.5)	(6.5)	(6.5)	(6.5)	(17.2)	(2.2)	(4.3)	(8.6)	(15.1)	(18.3)	(2.2)	(4.3)	(8.6)
Total	1080	548	531	58	156	56	164	37	38	70	231	121	35	40	74
	(100)	(50.8)	(49.2)	(5.4)	(14.4)	(5.2)	(15.2)	(3.4)	(3.5)	(6.5)	(21.4)	(11.2)	(3.2)	(3.7)	(6.9)
M	548	—	—	31	78	27	84	19	20	34	118	60	18	22	37
	(50.8)	—	—	(53.4)	(50.0)	(49.1)	(51.2)	(51.4)	(52.6)	(48.6)	(51.1)	(49.6)	(51.4)	(55.0)	(50.0)
F	531	—	—	27	78	28	80	18	18	36	113	61	17	18	37
	(49.2)	—	—	(46.6)	(50.0)	(50.9)	(48.8)	(48.6)	(47.4)	(51.4)	(48.9)	(50.4)	(48.6)	(45.0)	(50.0)
SLO Population[c]		(51.2)	(48.8)	17.5	43.1	11.1	37.9	6.5	10.6	15.6	73.2	29.3	7.2	17.4	13.4
				(6.2)	(15.3)	(3.9)	(13.4)	(2.3)	(3.7)	(5.5)	(25.9)	(10.4)	(2.5)	(6.1)	(4.7)

[a]Region: 1 = Pomurska, 2 = Podravska, 3 = Koroška, 4 = Savinjska, 5 = Zasavska, 6 = Spodnjeposavska, 7 = Dolenjska, 8 = Osrednjeslovenska, 9 = Gorenjska, 10 = Notranjsko-kraška, 11 = Goriška, and 12 = Obalno-kraška.

[b]The age of n years meaning the age from n − 1 years 7 months to n year 6 months.

[c]Children aged from 6 years 0 months to 16 years 11 months in thousands (Rapid Report 1994, 1997).

reliability of the test. The alpha coefficient, which is an average of all possible coefficients of division, has a number of advantages in comparison to other coefficients, especially to those in which the method of splitting the test into two halves is used (Cronbach, 1990). Namely, it excludes the error that occurs due to the influence of systematic factors at the division of the group of measures into two or more parts. That is why the alpha coefficient is an estimate of the lower limit of internal consistency of a group of measures, meaning that the actual reliability is probably higher.

However, due to the comparison of the measuring characteristics of WISC-III to the older Wechsler intelligence scales, split-half coefficients of internal consistency of the individuals' answers to a row of items in a certain subtest were also calculated, although a relatively small number of items in certain subtests in which the items' difficulty grows from the beginning to the end of the subtest, presenting us with a problem of correct division of items into two reliably comparable halves. It is well known that alpha coefficients in average give us the information on the lower limit of reliability, and split-half coefficients tend to be slightly higher, which has to be considered when interpreting the coefficients of reliability. Split-half coefficients of reliability are presented in Table 12.2. In the manual of the Slovene adaptation/translation of the WISC-III test, alpha coefficients of internal consistency can also be read from Table 4.3b (Wechsler, 2001). In comparison with the split-half coefficients of reliability and standard errors of measurement that can be found in the UK manual in Tables 4.3 and 4.4 (Wechsler, 1992), split-half coefficients from Slovene samples presented in Table 12.2 are surprisingly similar as are the standard errors of measurement.

It should be noted that the coefficients of reliability for three IQ scales and four-factor based scales were calculated following a form proposed by Nunnally (Nunnally & Bernstein, 1994) for calculating the reliability of a composite of tests. For the Coding subtest, data from the American study have been taken, whereas the best evaluations of reliability coefficients for an age group, on which retest has not been performed, are the values of the next age group. These "best evaluations" for Coding have been used to calculate the reliability of the IQ scales and factor-based scales in which the Coding test plays a part.

Retest reliability was not estimated in the standardization study, but is planned for the future.

EVIDENCE OF VALIDITY

Data on external validity were not collected for the Slovenian WISC-III. The internal validity of WISC-III can be assessed by comparing the intercorrelations of the subtest scaled scores of the Slovenian standardization with those of the UK and U.S. version (see Table 12.3). The correlations are virtually the same, with few exceptions in the sense that on the average, some correlations in Slovenian

TABLE 12.2 Split-Half Reliability Coefficients and Standard Errors of Measurement of the Subtest Scaled Scores, IQ Scores, and Index Scores by Age

Subtest/scale[c]	Age in years[a]										Average[b]
	7	8	9	10	11	12	13	14	15	16	
Information[c]	0.83	0.85	0.76	0.75	0.83	0.75	0.82	0.79	0.78	0.76	0.79
(SEm)	1.24	1.16	1.47	1.50	1.24	1.50	1.27	1.37	1.41	1.47	1.37
Similarities	0.75	0.69	0.81	0.57	0.81	0.70	0.77	0.71	0.64	0.72	0.72
(SEm)	1.50	1.67	1.31	1.97	1.31	1.64	1.44	1.62	1.80	1.59	1.59
Arithmetic	0.84	0.77	0.90	0.90	0.79	0.83	0.88	0.73	0.87	0.93	0.86
(SEm)	1.20	1.44	0.95	0.95	1.37	1.24	1.04	1.56	1.08	0.79	1.12
Vocabulary	0.86	0.77	0.81	0.79	0.83	0.80	0.85	0.76	0.83	0.85	0.82
(SEm)	1.12	1.44	1.31	1.37	1.24	1.34	1.16	1.47	1.24	1.16	1.27
Comprehension	0.72	0.66	0.73	0.65	0.77	0.64	0.57	0.54	0.54	0.69	0.66
(SEm)	1.59	1.75	1.56	1.77	1.44	1.80	1.97	2.03	2.03	1.67	1.75
Digit span	0.62	0.79	0.75	0.75	0.85	0.82	0.85	0.86	0.82	0.88	0.81
(SEm)	1.85	1.37	1.50	1.50	1.16	1.27	1.16	1.12	1.27	1.04	1.31
Picture completion	0.83	0.74	0.78	0.76	0.75	0.74	0.70	0.72	0.65	0.61	0.73
(SEm)	1.24	1.53	1.41	1.47	1.50	1.53	1.64	1.59	1.77	1.87	1.56
Coding	—[d]	0.70	—[d]	0.78	0.82	—[d]	—[d]	0.70	0.90	—[d]	0.80
(SEm)	—[d]	1.64	—[d]	1.41	1.27	—[d]	—[d]	1.64	0.95	—[d]	1.34
Picture arrangement	0.79	0.87	0.81	0.86	0.79	0.85	0.88	0.85	0.86	0.86	0.84
(SEm)	1.37	1.08	1.31	1.12	1.37	1.16	1.04	1.16	1.12	1.12	1.20
Block design	0.63	0.83	0.74	0.76	0.77	0.82	0.81	0.83	0.81	0.82	0.79
(SEm)	1.82	1.24	1.53	1.47	1.44	1.27	1.31	1.24	1.31	1.27	1.37
Object assembly	0.71	0.54	0.69	0.47	0.43	0.34	0.38	0.54	0.45	0.41	0.51
(SEm)	1.62	2.03	1.67	2.18	2.26	2.44	2.36	2.03	2.22	2.30	2.10
Symbol search	0.84	0.87	0.59	0.73	0.71	0.81	0.71	0.81	0.80	0.87	0.79
(SEm)	1.20	1.08	1.92	1.56	1.62	1.31	1.62	1.31	1.34	1.08	1.37
Mazes	0.76	0.72	0.79	0.62	0.76	0.51	0.62	0.65	0.78	0.81	0.71
(SEm)	1.47	1.59	1.37	1.85	1.47	2.10	1.85	1.77	1.41	1.31	1.62

Verbal IQ	0.94	0.92	0.93	0.91	0.94	0.92	0.94	0.90	0.91	0.93	0.94
(SEm)	3.67	4.24	3.97	4.50	3.67	4.24	3.67	4.74	4.50	3.97	3.67
Performance IQ	0.88	0.91	0.90	0.90	0.89	0.90	0.90	0.90	0.90	0.92	0.92
(SEm)	5.20	4.50	4.74	4.74	4.97	4.74	4.74	4.74	4.74	4.24	4.24
Full scale IQ	0.95	0.95	0.95	0.94	0.95	0.94	0.95	0.93	0.94	0.95	0.96
(SEm)	3.35	3.35	3.35	3.67	3.35	3.67	3.35	3.97	3.67	3.35	3.00
Verbal comp. index (VCI)	0.93	0.91	0.92	0.88	0.93	0.90	0.92	0.89	0.89	0.91	0.93
(SEm)	3.97	4.50	4.24	5.20	3.97	4.74	4.24	4.97	4.97	4.50	3.97
Percept. comp. index (POI)	0.87	0.90	0.89	0.88	0.86	0.88	0.88	0.89	0.86	0.88	0.91
(SEm)	5.41	4.74	4.97	5.20	5.61	5.20	5.20	4.97	5.61	5.20	4.50
Freedom distr. index (FDI)	0.80	0.85	0.87	0.88	0.87	0.85	0.90	0.84	0.89	0.92	0.88
(SEm)	6.71	5.81	5.41	5.20	5.41	5.81	4.74	6.00	4.97	4.24	5.20
Process. speed index (PSI)	0.83	0.88	0.80	0.83	0.84	0.89	0.82	0.84	0.91	0.92	0.87
(SEm)	6.18	5.20	6.71	6.18	6.00	4.97	6.36	6.00	4.50	4.24	5.41
n	60	103	125	112	117	128	114	124	104	93	1,080

Note: $N = 1080$. The coefficients of the IQ scale and of the factor based scales have been calculated following the form for reliability of a composite (Nunnally & Bernstein, 1994); the values for additional subtests (Digit Span, Labyrinth, Symbol Search) have not been included in these calculations. The standard errors of measurement are expressed in units of balanced scores for subtests, in units of IQ for Verbal, Performance, and Full Scale and in index units for VCI, POI, FDI, PSI. Reliability coefficients and standard deviations of population (i.e., 3 for subtests and 15 for IQ and index scores) have been used for the calculation of SEm.

[a] The age of *n* years meaning the age from *n* − 1 years 7 months to *n* year 6 months.

[b] Average r_{xx} has been computed with Fisher's *z* transformation. Average SEm has been calculated using the average sum of square SEm for an individual age group and square root of the result.

[c] Reliability coefficients are calculated as split-half coefficients of internal consistency.

[d] For the Coding subtest, data from the American study have been taken, whereas the best evaluations of reliability coefficients for an age group, on which retest has not been performed, are the values of the next age group. The age of 8 is an exception. The most appropriate value for it is the value of the age of 10—this is the nearest age group for which level B has been used. (Level A is used for children under the age of 8.) These "best evaluations" for Coding have been used to calculate the reliability of the composite, composed by this subtest.

TABLE 12.3   Intercorrelation of Subtest Scaled Scores

Subtest/scale	Inf	Sim	Ari	Voc	Com	DS	PCom	Cd	PA	BD	OA	SS	Mz
Information													
Similarities	0.59												
Arithmetic	0.45	0.33											
Vocabulary	0.64	0.61	0.37										
Comprehension	0.44	0.46	0.24	0.57									
Digit span	0.32	0.27	0.27	0.31	0.23								
Picture completion	0.36	0.37	0.24	0.35	0.34	0.18							
Coding	0.15	0.16	0.12	0.18	0.12	0.20	0.08						
Picture arrangement	0.33	0.29	0.26	0.31	0.26	0.14	0.32	0.17					
Block design	0.37	0.30	0.31	0.32	0.26	0.23	0.37	0.23	0.37				
Object assembly	0.31	0.30	0.22	0.31	0.26	0.15	0.38	0.10	0.30	0.44			
Symbol search	0.21	0.22	0.16	0.22	0.18	0.22	0.16	0.50	0.32	0.28	0.19		
Mazes	0.14	0.11	0.13	0.15	0.06	0.15	0.20	0.11	0.13	0.27	0.20	0.05	

and UK validation samples are a bit lower than in the U.S. standardization sample. However, the pattern of the correlation is very similar in all three correlation matrices.

The four-factor structure is also reported (Table 12.4). The factor structure has been determined through exploratory factor analysis with maximum likelihood extraction, where the evaluations of communalities represented squared multiple correlations and rotations were with Varimax rotations. Factor analysis was performed on the total sample and on three subsamples: age groups 7–9 years, 10–13 years, and 14–16 years. The Kaiser-Guttmann criterion and Cattell's Scree-test suggested a four-factor solution. All factors had eigenvalues greater than 1, and the total variance explained by the four factors was approximately 62% in all four analyses.

Confirmatory factor analysis (ML algorithm, LISREL 8 program; Jöreskorg & Sörbom, 1996) was employed to confirm or reject the internal factor structure of the subtests. Five alternative models were tested: a one-factor model (a representation of a general intelligence factor); a two-factor model with six verbal and seven performance subtests; a three-factor model with six verbal subtests, five performance subtests, and with the Coding and Symbol Search subtests; the four-factor model determined by the exploratory factor analysis; and a five-factor model, identical to that suggested by Woodcock (1990) with a Verbal Comprehension factor, Perceptual Organization factor, Processing Speed factor, Memory factor (consisting of Digit Span) and Numerical Ability factor (consisting of Arithmetic). According to χ^2, χ^2/df, AGFI and RMSR goodness-of-fit indexes and the Tucker-Lewis index (TLI), showing the improvement of fit regarding to zero-model (Table 12.5), the

TABLE 12.4 Maximum-Likelihood Factor Loadings (Varimax Rotation) for Four Factors Across Ages

Subtest/scale	Factor 1: Verbal comprehension				Factor 2: Perceptual organization				Factor 3: Freedom from distractibility				Factor 4: Processing speed			
	Ages			Total sample	Ages			Total sample	Ages			Total sample	Ages			Total sample
	7–9	10–13	14–16		7–9	10–13	14–16		7–9	10–13	14–16		7–9	10–13	14–16	
Information	0.59	0.70	0.61	0.59	0.19	0.18	0.36	0.24	0.41	0.22	0.26	0.49	0.01	0.13	0.08	0.10
Similarities	0.53	0.71	0.67	0.64	0.16	0.23	0.34	0.21	0.43	0.07	0.06	0.29	0.08	0.13	0.08	0.12
Vocabulary	0.73	0.81	0.80	0.75	0.21	0.21	0.16	0.19	0.40	0.12	0.14	0.29	0.01	0.12	0.19	0.12
Comprehension	0.76	0.62	0.53	0.66	0.13	0.26	0.17	0.18	0.19	0.03	0.03	0.04	0.04	0.12	0.07	0.10
Picture completion	0.37	0.32	0.22	0.36	0.42	0.52	0.62	0.49	0.22	0.10	0.00	0.05	-0.03	0.06	0.07	0.06
Picture arrangement	0.32	0.19	0.22	0.24	0.42	0.43	0.37	0.41	0.21	0.12	0.12	0.11	0.19	0.27	0.23	0.25
Block design	0.24	0.17	0.13	0.15	0.61	0.52	0.61	0.65	0.23	0.45	0.20	0.22	0.06	0.25	0.22	0.20
Object assembly	0.16	0.22	0.17	0.24	0.56	0.61	0.61	0.58	0.21	0.09	0.08	0.05	0.09	0.07	0.07	0.10
Mazes	0.02	0.05	0.06	0.01	0.48	0.27	0.25	0.35	0.07	0.36	0.01	0.16	-0.03	0.00	0.05	0.08
Arithmetic	0.12	0.41	0.24	0.25	0.34	0.13	0.19	0.24	0.48	0.38	0.94	0.46	0.01	0.11	0.13	0.10
Digit span	0.18	0.30	0.28	0.22	0.25	0.02	0.03	0.14	0.39	0.40	0.22	0.32	0.10	0.19	0.28	0.19
Coding	-0.03	0.17	0.14	0.02	0.02	0.09	0.17	0.10	-0.03	0.24	0.05	0.13	0.55	0.50	0.52	0.53
Symbol search	0.11	0.14	0.06	0.12	0.08	0.18	0.18	0.13	0.17	-0.02	0.03	0.04	0.92	0.95	0.91	0.91

TABLE 12.5   Goodness-of-Fit Statistics for Confirmatory Maximum-Likelihood Factor Analysis of 13 Subtests

Model	χ^2	d.f.	χ^2/df	AGFI	RMSR	χ^2	d.f.	TLI[a]
Total ($N = 1080$)								
One-factor	797.88	65	12.28	0.84	0.66	—	—	—
Two-factor	489.02	64	7.64	0.90	0.52	308.86[a]	1	0.41
Three-factor	254.02	62	4.10	0.95	0.36	235.00[a]	2	0.73
Four-factor	222.92	59	3.78	0.95	0.32	31.10[a]	3	0.74
Five-factor	209.01	57	3.67	0.95	0.31	19.91	2	0.76
Ages 7–9 ($n = 288$)								
One-factor	298.13	65	4.59	0.80	0.68	—	—	—
Two-factor	247.40	64	3.87	0.84	0.65	50.73[b]	1	0.20
Three-factor	155.82	62	2.51	0.88	0.46	91.58[b]	2	0.58
Four-factor	143.54	59	2.43	0.89	0.44	12.28[b]	3	0.60
Five-factor	141.28	57	2.47	0.89	0.44	2.23	2	0.59
Ages 10–13 ($n = 471$)								
One-factor	376.56	65	5.79	0.83	0.68	—	—	—
Two-factor	214.72	64	3.36	0.90	0.50	161.84[b]	1	0.51
Three-factor	134.43	62	2.17	0.94	0.39	80.29[b]	2	0.76
Four-factor	123.94	59	2.10	0.94	0.36	10.49	3	0.77
Five-factor	139.51	57	2.45	0.93	0.38	−15.57	2	0.70
Ages 14–16 ($n = 321$)								
One-factor	299.51	65	4.61	0.81	0.58	—	—	—
Two-factor	201.23	64	3.14	0.87	0.58	98.28[b]	1	0.41
Three-factor	139.82	62	2.15	0.94	0.38	61.41[b]	2	0.68
Four-factor	123.33	59	2.09	0.95	0.32	16.49[b]	3	0.70
Five-factor	133.87	57	2.35	0.94	0.36	−10.54	2	0.63

Columns grouped under **Goodness-of-fit index** (χ^2, d.f., χ^2/df, AGFI, RMSR) and **Improvement** (χ^2, d.f., TLI[a]).

[a]The Tucker-Lewis index (TLI) expresses the difference between the first, so-called zero model (χ^2_0 at df_0) and the concurrent evaluated model (χ^2_i at df_i) like this: TLI = $\{[(\chi^2_0 \div df_0) - (\chi^2_i \div df_i)] \div [(\chi^2_0 \div df_0) - 1]\}$. These indexes are lower as they would be if we had calculated the difference between the truly independent (zero) model, where all variables are independent, and the concurrent model.

[b]$p < 0.01$ (d.f. = 1) = 6.63; $p < 0.01$ (d.f. = 2) = 9.21; $p < 0.01$ (d.f. = 3) = 11.30. AGFI: adjusted goodness-of-fit index; RMSR: root mean square residual.

four-factor model that was extracted from exploratory factor analysis provided the best fit. Thus, the factor structure was identical to that of the U.S. test for the total sample and for the three age subsamples. A more detailed analysis of the comparison of the U.S. and the Slovenian factor structures is described in the Slovene WISC-III-SI Manual (Wechsler, 2001).

    Now that the WISC-III has been adapted and standardized to the Slovenian population, we expect that Slovene psychologists and researchers will soon conduct studies with various clinical and school groups in order to present information on the validity of WISC-III-SI.

CULTURAL ISSUES INFLUENCING WISC-III INTERPRETATIONS IN SLOVENIA

As described in the Sample Characteristics section, Slovenia is a small country, where 87% of the population is of Slovene origin and 12% of Slovene citizens are of other ethnic groups, mostly from other republics of the former Yugoslav Federation. Children of these ethnic groups attend Slovenian schools and there are few significant cultural differences between them and other children. The small Italian minority in the southwest and the Hungarian in the northeast, attend schools in which the curriculum is in their own language; thus, the WISC-III-SI is not appropriate for use with them. The Italian or Hungarian versions of the WISC-III would be more appropriate here. There is a larger cultural difference between Slovenian and other Slavic children and Romany children. Future studies are necessary to investigate the potential cultural bias of the WISC-III results with these children, so results of testing with Romany children must be interpreted carefully. Psychologists in other countries who will test Slovenian immigrants with the WISC-III-SI should be advised to first check his/her nationality origin. In some countries, Slovenian children have been mistakenly identified as Slovak or Slavonian because of the similarity in the names of the two countries.

An important cultural issue related to the administration and scoring of the items is the language competency of the child and the tester. Because the Slovenian language is grammatically complicated, an inadequate test performer and child language skills could be a cause of errors in scoring and interpretation. In general, the child's level of answers should not be spoiled because of poor use of grammar and syntax. We wish to call to the attention of Slovenian-speaking psychologists from other countries whose language fluency is not excellent some specific characteristics of our language. We have found that even in Slovenia, lower language skills of children have hampered children's performance on the test and the evaluation of the IQ. That is why we have added definitions of words from the *Dictionary of Slovene Literary Language* (1994) to the Vocabulary subtest in WISC-III-SI. Some of the words have several meanings of which some are less important. Some of them are less known, perhaps because of our low knowledge of the language or because of differences between dialects in different regions.

The result of the testing may not express the actual situation (e.g., we may get a very low result) albeit the high professional quality of the test and of its performer. In such cases, Slovenian psychologists agree with Wechsler and other experts' opinions that one should interpret in a more responsible, whole, global, and deepened way—different causes have to be considered, from actual low mental ability to motivational, social, medical, and economical factors.

PROFESSIONAL ISSUES IN THE USE OF
INTELLIGENCE TESTS IN SLOVENIA

There are three institutions directly related to psychological tests in general and to tests of intelligence in Slovenia: the Department of Psychology at the Faculty of Arts of the University of Ljubljana, the Slovenian Psychological Association (SPA), and the main publishing company of psychological tests Center za psihodiagnosticna sredstva in Ljubljana.

The educational program of the Department of Psychology has a very important role in the use of intelligence tests. Approximately 50 young psychologists graduate every year and they obtain, in comparison to curricula in other European countries, a strong statistical and psychometric basis for the use of different psychological tests. The psychology program also has courses for the use of some basic psychological instruments from different psychological fields (developmental, educational, clinical, social, and work psychology). Young psychologists get a relatively broad education during the study of psychology. In addition, they specialize in different fields of applied psychology in postgraduate programs.

The SPA has approximately 400 members which is approximately one-fourth of all active psychologists. The SPA is a member of the European Federation of Professional Psychologists' Associations (EFPPA) and of the International Test Commission (ITC). The psychological association has had, since 1973, a commission for psychodiagnostics, and prepared the first code of ethics in 1985, and has defined the categories of tests and the procedure of classification. Psychologists in Slovenia have always respected the agreement that psychological tests may only be used by a graduate in psychology. A representative of the SPA has participated in the work of a Standing (formerly task force) Commission for tests and testing in EFPPA. In recent years the association has invested considerable energy into passing a law of psychological activity at the parliament, which would, among other things, regulate licenses, qualification, and control over tests.

The publishing company Center za psihodiagnosticna sredstva has close connections to the SPA, where it actively cooperates in the work of the Commission for Psychodiagnostic Instruments as well as with the faculty and researchers who participate in its projects. The Center is a member of the ITC. There are also other institutions in Slovenia who publish tests, but this is not their main activity.

After the independence of the country, the opening of the borders and the approaches to the European Union (EU), the situation concerning the test and testing has changed in Slovenia. Slovenian psychologists can also buy psychological tests from other countries. The limitations and competencies of the users are different in different countries and there are no universal rules on competent use of these instruments.

Nevertheless, in this chapter we describe mostly the situation inside psychology, where use of intelligence tests is allowed according to Slovene norms and the situation as seen by the Slovene psychologists. In Slovenia, the WISC-III has been classified as a test that can be competently used only by a professional graduate in psychology.

Also in Slovenia, very wide definitions of intelligence can be found as entire palettes of skills, knowledge, sets of learning, and tendencies of generalizing (which are deemed as intellectual) that are available at any given time (Humphreys, 1989), or as capabilities or skills of problem solving or designing of a product that is valuable within one or more cultural environments (Gardner, 1983), or as an experience-independent capability of fast, precise, and effective information processing (Bucik, 1997; Pogačnik, 1995). Wechsler's conceptualization of intelligence is also popular in Slovenia, saying that intelligence should be operatively defined as an aggregate or a global ability of an individual to act resolutely, to think rationally, and to cooperate with his or her environment efficiently. It is global or common as it is composed of elements or capabilities, which are—although not completely independent—quantitatively distinguishable. But intelligence is not only equal to a sum of these capabilities, it joins them into a whole. Wechsler also claimed that one must count on a number of so-called "nonintellectual" factors when assessing intelligence.

The measurement of intelligence in Slovenia does have not a long tradition as in, e.g., the U.S. The discussions on differences in intelligence have also never been polemic. On the contrary, there is a belief, that can sometimes be sensed, that there are not many differences between people in terms of their intelligence, and if there are, they are not very important. Perhaps this is a legacy of the near past that has favored social equality. But as the question of intelligence in the U.S. has been connected to racial differences, the measurement of intelligence and the search for differences in intelligence of people has also always been a socially delicate subject in Slovenia.

The main problem in Slovenia is the lack of standardized and modern intelligence tests. This is also true for psychological instruments in general, or measures of other psychological characteristics of an individual. There are tests for measuring general intelligence, e.g., the Raven's Progressive Matrices (Raven, Raven, & Court, 1999) and also an original Slovenian test by Pogačnik (1994), but the situation is worse in the field of tests of specific intelligence and test series, that tell more about the hierarchical structure of intelligence. Among the most frequently used (Boben & Pogačnik, 2000) psychological tests for the measurement of intelligence were in 1999, WISC (Šali, 1972), Wechsler-Bellevue (W.B-II) (Šali, 1970), and the Multifactor Test Battery (MFBT) (1992). The latter is used by psychologists in school counseling services or at the Bureau of Employment to counsel primary school children in vocational and educational and professional counseling. The psychodiagnostics of intelligence of young, pre-school children is especially weak.

Such a poor situation can be comprehended if one understands that all tests have to be in Slovenian, which is a very specific language; translations, adaptations, or development of Slovenian tests, but also current updating of norms are financially demanding, and a population of more than two million Slovenians does not offer a basis for a large market. To be able to get a satisfying series of quality and modern psychological tests (for the field of intelligence also) realistically soon, a state-supported effort would be needed, but cannot be expected at the present time.

That is why the WISC-III-SI, which was translated and adapted in a relatively large project, comes as an infrequent but welcome improvement in the field of child assessment. We expect to adapt other important worldwide intelligence tests slowly, but reliably.

One of the more important problems in the field of psychological testing in Slovenia is thus, the fact that psychological activity and within it, psychological testing, is not regulated. Other standards, rules, and agreements have been established and harmonized with Europe more intensively in recent years. Professional rules are linked to the Code of Professional Ethics (1985) today, but this document is obligatory only to the members of the SPA. A code, harmonized with the European Metacode of Psychologists' Professional Ethics (1995), is in preparation. As we are actively joining the work of the EFPPA Standing Committee on Tests and Testing and ITC, a translation of the International Guidelines for test use is in preparation, and we are also working on European test review criteria. We will also have to either adopt foreign (e.g., American or EFPPA) standards for psychological and educational testing, or to build our own, following these examples. We have found that both psychological tests as well as translations of tests, imported from other countries are sometimes used, without knowledge of under which conditions these tests have been constructed (Bartram & Coyne, 1998; Boben, 1997). Slovene psychologists who responded to a survey have expressed their attitudes on the usefulness of tests, the need for the legal regulation of test-related work, the control over use and distribution of tests, the need for test-related information, and different test-related problems (Boben & Pogačnik, 2000; Muñiz et al., 2001). We were able to compare the Slovene results to those from other European countries and discovered that there are not many differences. From the results of this survey, it can be concluded that Slovene psychologists miss quality and accessible education on tests and new and objective test-related information. They also stated that because of different reasons psychological testing should remain under psychologists' control.

It can be concluded that with the help of psychological tests like the WISC-III, a quality, sensible, and client-fair assessment of intelligence could be applied in Slovenia. However, one should consider factors other than just intelligence test results in psychological assessment, such as social environment in which the test user lives, development possibilities, level of education, etc. The opinion of Slovenian psychologists is that psychological assessment should be performed by highly qualified, competent experts, who are aware of advantages, weaknesses, and limits of their diagnostic practice.

REFERENCES

Bartram, D., & Coyne, I. (1998). *Testing and test use within Europe*. Report. London: EFPPA Task Force on Test and Testing and ITC.

Boben, D. (1997). *Evropska raziskava o testih in testiranju* [European research on tests and testing]. Paper presented at the 2nd Congress of Slovenian Psychologists, Portoroz, Slovenia.

Boben, D., & Pogačnik, V. (2000). Mnenje psihologov o uporabi psiholoških testov [Slovenian psychologists about the use od psychological tests]. *Psihološka obzorja/Horizons of Psychology, 9,* 79–94.

Bucik, V. (1997). *Osnove psihološkega testiranja* [Essentials of psychological testing]. Ljubljana: Univerza v Ljubljani, Oddelek za psihologijo.

Cronbach, L. J. (1990). *Essentials of psychological testing* (5th ed.). New York: Harper Collins.

Gardner, H. (1983). *Frames of mind: The theory of multiple intelligences.* New York: Basic.

Humphreys, L. G. (1989). Intelligence: Three kinds of instability and their consequences for policy. In R. L. Linn (Ed.), *Intelligence* (pp. 154–172). Urbana: University of Illinois Press.

Jöreskog, K. G., & Sörbom, D. (1996). *LISREL 8. User's reference guide.* Chicago, IL: Scientific Software International.

Kodeks poklicne etike psihologov Slovenije [Code of professional ethics of Slovenian Psychologists] (1985). Ljubljana: Društvo psihologov Slovenije.

Meta-Code of Ethics (1995). Athens: EFPPA General Assembly.

Multifaktorska baterija testov—MFBT: Priročnik [Multifactor test battery—MFBT: Manual]. (1992). Ljubljana: Republiški zavod za zaposlovanje.

Muñiz, J., Bartram, D., Evers, A., Boben, D., Matesic, K., Glabeke, K., Fernández-Hermida, J. R., & Zaal, J. N. (2001). Testing Practices in European Countries. *European Journal of Psychological Assessment, 17,* 201–211.

Nunnally, J. C., & Bernstein, I. H. (1994). *Psychometric theory* (3rd ed.). New York: McGraw-Hill.

Pogačnik, V. (1994). *Test nizov—TN: priročnik* [Series test—TN: Manual]. Ljubljana: Produktivnost, d.o.o., Center za psihodiagnostična sredstva.

Pogačnik, V. (1995). *Pojmovanje inteligentnosti* [The concept of intelligence]. Radovljica: Didakta.

Rapid Reports (1992). Ljubljana: Statistical Office of the Republic of Slovenia.

Rapid Reports (1997). Ljubljana: Statistical Office of the Republic of Slovenia.

Raven, J., Raven, J. C., & Court, J. H. (1999). *Priročnik za Ravnove progresivne matrice in besedne lestvice. Splošni pregled.* [Manual for Raven's Progressive Matrices and Vocabulary Scales. General Overview]. Ljubljana: Center za psihodiagnosticna sredstva, d.o.o.

Slovar slovenskega knjižnega jezika [The Dictionary of Slovenian Literary Language] (1994). Ljubljana: DZS.

Šali, B. (1970). *WB-II: Priročnik* [WB-II: Manual]. Ljubljana: Zavod SR Slovenije za produktivnost dela.

Šali, B. (1972). *WISC—Wechslerjev test inteligentnosti za otroke: Priročnik* [WISC—Wechsler intelligence scale for children: Manual]. Ljubljana: Zavod SR Slovenije za produktivnost dela.

Wechsler, D. (1992). *Wechsler Intelligence Scale for Children—Third Edition UK, Manual.* London: The Psychological Corporation.

Wechsler, D. (2001). *Wechslerjeva lestvica inteligentnosti za otroke—tretja izdaja SI: Priročnik* (D. Boben & V. Bucik, Trans.). Ljubljana, Slovenia: Center za psihodiagnostična sredstva, d.o.o. (Original work published in 1991.)

Woodcock, E. W. (1990). Theoretical foundations of the WJ-R measures of cognitive ability. *Journal of Psychoeducational Assessment, 8,* 231–258.

13

GREECE

JAMES GEORGAS

Department of Psychology
The University of Athens
Athens, Greece

IOANNIS N.
PARASKEVOPOULOS

Department of Psychology
The University of Athens
Athens, Greece

ELIAS BESEVEGIS

Department of Psychology
The University of Athens
Athens, Greece

NIKOLAOS GIANNITSAS

Department of Psychology
The University of Athens
Athens, Greece

KOSTAS MYLONAS

Department of Psychology
The University of Athens
Athens, Greece

The standardization of the Hellenic Wechsler Intelligence Scale for Children—Third Edition (WISC-III) began in 1993 and was completed in 1997 by the Psychometric Laboratory of the Department of Psychology of the School of Philosophy of the University of Athens (Wechsler, 1997). Psychologists have employed the WISC-R and the WISC for many years in Greece, but these versions were based mostly on translations by individual psychologists from the U.S. WISC without authorization. The norms employed were based on the U.S. sample and not on a representative sample of Greece. As expected, the evaluation of cognitive functioning and computation of IQs and Scaled Scores with the U.S. version of the WISC based on American norms led to questionable diagnoses and prognostic decisions.

The standardization of the WISC-III in Greece was subsequently necessary in order to provide a reliable and valid measure of children's intelligence.

Intelligence and aptitude tests standardized in Greece in the past were an Intelligence Test for Children (Georgas, 1971, 1972), for children ages 6–12 and the Greek adaptation of the Illinois Test for Psycholinguistic Abilities (Paraskevopoulos, 1973). There has been an increase of adaptations and construction of Greek psychological tests during the past 10 years, primarily personality scales, but also tests of learning disabilities (Paraskevopoulos, Kalantzi-Azizi, & Giannitsas, 1999).

ADAPTATION PROCESS

The UK version of the WISC-III (Wechsler, 1992) was employed in the standardization of the Hellenic WISC-III. The adaptation process began with an examination of primarily the verbal items for cultural bias. History of use of the WISC test in Greece indicated that Greek children did not have problems with the nonverbal items. Thus, they appeared to be valid for use in Greece. A panel of experts, including the authors, examined the items of the verbal scales for potential cultural bias. Items from the Greek culture were added as parallel items to those UK items which appeared to be culturally biased, with the intention of making a final decision which items to select for the standardization after the pilot study. Greece has a special problem in terms of item bias. Because many scientific or technical terms have Greek roots, some difficult items in the English language are very simple in Greek. For example in the Information subtest, "hieroglyphics" is not a difficult item in Greek. Also, "capital of Greece" could obviously not be employed and the capital of Portugal was substituted.

Thus, in addition to items from the UK version, items from the Greek culture were also added to the pilot test version. The number of items employed for the pilot study was 30 for Information, 26 for Similarities, and 80 Vocabulary items split into two forms. For Comprehension, an initial study with 40 children indicated that one item, paperback books and hardcover books, was not appropriate since in Greece hardcover books are expensive and most printed books are paperback and school books are all paperback, etc. An item comparing phonograph records and cassettes was substituted.[1] These 18 items were employed for the pilot study and the standardization. The 24 Arithmetic items were maintained, with changes in content. That is, because in some items, differences in monetary value between the pound sterling and the drachma were so great, e.g., 1 pound equaled over 500 drachmas at the time of the standardization, the question was framed differently, without money, but maintaining the same calculations. For example, an item such as, "Phil was paid 25 pounds. He was paid 5 pounds an hour. How many hours

[1] In the meantime, cassettes have been replaced by CDs, and it appears that the replacement of CDs with flexible discs which resemble phonograph records is only a matter or time. This appears to be the danger of employing items based on current technology, which changes so rapidly, in these tests.

did he work?" was changed to "Eleutheria solved 25 problems. She solved 5 problems an hour..."

The pilot study had four goals: (1) to select the items to be employed in the standardization of the WISC-III; (2) to evaluate the adequacy of the Greek translation of the examiner instructions and the syntax of the questions; (3) to add to the sample responses of the UK items which would be retained, and to generate sample responses to the substituted Greek items; and (4) to try out the procedure of administration of the tests and scoring of the responses in order to identify problems requiring further modification for the standardization. The pilot study sample consisted of 216 children ages 5–17, half males and half females, from the greater Athens area. The specific age groups chosen were 5, 6, 8, 10, 12, 14, 16, and 17. The age groups 5 and 17 were chosen so as to provide wider variation of scores in lower and upper age levels of each scale necessary for determining the degree of item differentiation at ages 6 and 16.

Item selection was based on three criteria. The first criterion was cultural bias. If the UK item was not culturally appropriate for Greece, the parallel Greek item was chosen. The second criterion was the degree of item discrimination according to age level and the difficulty level of the item in terms of percent of children passing at a specific age level. First, the percent of children passing each item was plotted according to age levels 5–17. The item was potentially useful if an S curve indicated discrimination between lower and higher age levels. Second, a horizontal line at the point where 50% of the sample correctly answered the question was drawn to the curve, and a vertical line from that point indicated the age level of the item. This enabled selection of the item on the basis of its order of difficulty, but also ensured that items were equally spaced across all age levels. The third criterion was to estimate the biserial correlation of the school marks of each student with pass or failure on each item, as well as the correlation of school marks of each student with total score on each subtest.

In choosing the items for the standardization version, the criterion was employed of maintaining as many items as possible of the UK version in order to minimize changes in the content of each subtest which might have the effect of changing the constructs of the subtests. The final number of items chosen for each Verbal subtest was the same as in the UK version. Of the 30 items of the Information subtest, 20 were identical with the UK version, content appropriate to the Greek culture was substituted for 7 UK version items, e.g., "the distance between two Greek cities," and 3 items were directly from the Greek culture, e.g., "Who was a famous Greek poet?" Nineteen of the twenty items of the UK revision were maintained from Similarities. The computations of all Arithmetic items were maintained, but the content was changed on items with currency. Vocabulary had the most changes. Nineteen items of the UK version were maintained, and 11 Greek items were substituted. Only one item was changed in Comprehension. All the items of the Performance tests of the UK version were appropriate for the Greek context and were maintained.

SAMPLE CHARACTERISTICS

Greece is a homogeneous country in which at the time of the standardization, approximately 98% of the population was ethnically Greek. Approximately 2% of the population of Greece is Moslem and lives in northeastern Greece, although Greek speaking. The standardization sample consisted of 956 children, 482 males and 474 females, with the number of children in each age group ranging from $n = 81$ to 96. The proportions of children from each geographical area of Greece were based on demographic data of 1991 from the National Statistical Service of Greece. These were separated into urban, semi-urban, and towns. Greater Athens is in Attica, and includes the city of Athens, a relatively small area, the port of Piraeus, urban municipalities, suburban areas, and rural towns comprising approximately 45% of the population of Greece; the sample tested in this region was 47% of the total sample. Thessalonike is the second largest city in Greece and the sample tested was 10% of the total, which corresponds to approximately the same percent of the general population. The remainder of the sample was drawn from 14 cities and small towns near the cities, representing all geographical areas in Greece. A special problem were the hundreds of inhabited islands in Greece. Two relatively large islands, Crete and Rhodes, were chosen.

The 127 schools in these areas taking part in the standardization were chosen randomly from the catalog of schools of the Ministry of Education. School marks from the previous year were obtained, as well as information on parent education (Table 13.1). Children were chosen for testing in the following manner. The tester opened a book at random and pointed to the first letter of the first word on left-hand side of the page. The tester then employed the class record of students, and if there was a student whose last name began with that letter, selected the first student with that letter, that is, a boy and a girl from each grade in the school, e.g., one boy and one girl from grade 1, one boy and one girl from grade 2, etc.

The WISC-III was administered by 45 psychologists and graduate students in clinical psychology and school psychology programs. In order to ensure similarity of administration, they attended a specially prepared seminar which presented the details of the method of sample selection, administration procedures, and other aspects of the WISC-III test.

RELIABILITY

The split-half reliability coefficients and standard errors of measurement across ages, for the subtests, IQ, and index scores are presented in Table 13.2. The split-half reliabilities for the Verbal IQ (VIQ) scores ranged between $r = 0.92$ and $r = 0.97$ across the age span, with average $r = 0.96$; the Performance IQ (PIQ) reliabilities ranged from $r = 0.94$ to $r = 0.97$ with average $r = 0.95$; Full Scale IQ (FSIQ) reliabilities ranged from $r = 0.87$ to $r = 0.94$ with average $r = 0.91$. These split-half reliabilities were all above 0.90 and similar to those of the American and UK samples. The average reliability for the Index scores were $r = 0.98$

TABLE 13.1 Demographic Characteristics of the Standardization Sample: Percentages by Age and Parent Education Level

Age	n	Parent education (years)				
		≤6	7–11	12	13–15	≥16
6	96	14.6	8.3	35.4	16.7	25.0
7	88	32.0	14.0	16.0	12.0	26.0
8	86	18.2	12.7	29.1	14.5	25.5
9	83	33.3	27.1	16.7	12.5	10.4
10	85	19.3	29.8	19.3	8.8	22.8
11	87	16.4	20.0	25.5	10.9	27.3
12	96	20.3	20.3	24.3	24.3	10.8
13	81	12.3	29.2	21.5	23.1	13.8
14	90	20.8	13.9	26.4	15.3	23.6
15	81	17.1	18.6	12.9	37.1	14.3
16	83	20.9	14.9	28.4	17.9	17.9
Total	956[a]	20.10	19.10	23.10	18.30	19.40
Greek population ($N = 9,039,479$)	57.10	10.77	20.65	4.83	6.65	
Greek adults (25–60 years old; $N = 3,956,049$)		53.07	7.33	25.33	3.82	10.46

Note: The large differences of the population percentages for education level of 11 years or less may be explained in regard to the census data (1991). The 1991 census conveys information selected from people who did not receive any education at all, or received just the basic education, because compulsory education (9 years) was established a few decades ago. Also, young parents have received more years of education than the census data imply, thus the highest categories (13 years or more) are represented by larger percentages in the Greek standardization data.

[a] For the parent education level, $n = 661$.

for Processing Speed Index (PSI), $r = 0.97$ for Perception Organization Index (POI), and $r = 0.96$ for Verbal Comprehension Index (VCI) (identical to that of the Verbal IQ scores, since as will be discussed below, three factors were found in the Greek standardization). The average subtest reliabilities ranged from $r = 0.71$ for Object Assembly to $r = 0.87$ for Block Design.

The stability coefficients were determined by $n = 200$ children retested after a period of between 8 and 16 weeks. Pearson r correlations for the subtests, IQ, and index scores for age groups 6, 8, 12, and 16 and the average correlations across age groups are presented in Table 13.3. The average correlations for the subtests ranged from $r = 0.71$ for Object Assembly to $r = 0.85$ for Information. The average correlation for VIQ was $r = 0.92$, for PIQ was $r = 0.87$, and $r = 0.91$ for FSIQ. As expected, the retest correlations were lower for the 6 year olds as compared to the older age groups.

EVIDENCE OF VALIDITY

The intercorrelations of subtest scaled scores are presented in Table 13.4. The pattern of intercorrelations between the four Verbal subtests, Vocabulary,

TABLE 13.2 Reliability Coefficients and Standard Errors of Measurement of the Subtests Scaled Scores, IQ Scores, and Index Scores by Age[a]

	Age in years											
Subtest/scale	6	7	8	9	10	11	12	13	14	15	16	Average[c]
n	96	88	86	83	85	87	96	81	90	81	83	
Information	0.69	0.79	0.78	0.88	0.89	0.83	0.85	0.87	0.88	0.79	0.77	0.83
(SEm)	1.67	1.37	1.41	1.04	0.99	1.24	1.16	1.08	1.04	1.37	1.44	1.12
Similarities	0.68	0.65	0.56	0.65	0.84	0.75	0.85	0.84	0.85	0.75	0.73	0.76
(SEm)	1.70	1.77	1.99	1.77	1.20	1.50	1.16	1.20	1.16	1.50	1.56	1.23
Arithmetic	0.87	0.89	0.88	0.73	0.84	0.8	0.88	0.76	0.75	0.77	0.72	0.82
(SEm)	1.08	0.99	1.04	1.56	1.20	1.34	1.04	1.47	1.50	1.44	1.59	1.14
Vocabulary	0.69	0.67	0.81	0.84	0.88	0.86	0.83	0.83	0.09	0.79	0.86	0.82
(SEm)	1.67	1.72	1.31	1.20	1.04	1.12	1.24	1.24	0.95	1.37	1.12	1.13
Comprehension	0.81	0.83	0.67	0.79	0.8	0.78	0.74	0.73	0.78	0.81	0.47	0.76
(SEm)	1.31	1.24	1.72	1.37	1.34	1.41	1.53	1.56	1.41	1.31	2.18	1.22
Digit span	0.77	0.82	0.8	0.8	0.85	0.86	0.84	0.8	0.87	0.87	0.88	0.84
(SEm)	1.44	1.27	1.34	1.34	1.16	1.12	1.20	1.34	1.08	1.08	1.04	1.10
Picture completion	0.74	0.85	0.74	0.78	0.81	0.86	0.82	0.78	0.73	0.74	0.68	0.78
(SEm)	1.53	1.16	1.53	1.41	1.31	1.12	1.27	1.41	1.56	1.53	1.70	1.19
Coding	0.77	—[b]	—[b]	0.46	—[b]	—[b]	0.62	—[b]	—[b]	—[b]	0.94	0.72
(SEm)	1.44	—[b]	—[b]	2.20	—[b]	—[b]	1.85	—[b]	—[b]	—[b]	0.73	1.29
Picture arrangement	0.79	0.78	0.62	0.82	0.84	0.82	0.76	0.81	0.85	0.78	0.80	0.79
(SEm)	1.37	1.41	1.85	1.27	1.20	1.27	1.47	1.31	1.16	1.41	1.34	1.17
Block design	0.82	0.83	0.09	0.83	0.87	0.88	0.88	0.83	0.89	0.92	0.88	0.87
(SEm)	1.27	1.24	0.95	1.24	1.08	1.04	1.04	1.24	0.99	0.85	1.04	1.04
Object assembly	0.68	0.73	0.7	0.69	0.75	0.77	0.8	0.65	0.69	0.76	0.55	0.71
(SEm)	1.70	1.56	1.64	1.67	1.50	1.44	1.34	1.77	1.67	1.47	2.01	1.27
Symbol search	0.75	—[b]	—[b]	0.8	—[b]	—[b]	0.68	—[b]	—[b]	—[b]	0.67	0.73

	[b]	[b]		[b]	[b]		[b]	[b]	[b]	[b]	
(SEm)	1.50	1.72	1.75	1.34	1.31	1.50	1.70	2.20	1.85	1.27	1.72	1.25
Mazes	0.78	0.67	0.66	0.75	0.81	0.75	0.77	0.46	0.62	0.82	0.77	0.73
(SEm)	1.41	1.72	1.75	1.50	1.31	1.50	1.44	2.20	1.85	1.27	1.44	1.26
Verbal IQ	0.94	0.95	0.95	0.96	0.97	0.96	0.97	0.97	0.97	0.95	0.92	0.96
(SEm)	3.61	3.22	3.29	3.07	2.64	2.85	2.64	2.64	2.42	3.22	4.22	1.75
Performance IQ	0.94	0.95	0.94	0.94	0.96	0.96	0.96	0.95	0.96	0.97	0.96	0.95
(SEm)	3.70	3.32	3.64	3.58	3.15	3.07	3.15	3.49	3.11	2.60	2.92	1.80
Full scale IQ	0.87	0.90	0.90	0.90	0.92	0.93	0.93	0.92	0.94	0.93	0.88	0.91
(SEm)	5.41	4.84	4.74	4.79	4.24	4.11	3.85	4.27	3.79	4.11	5.15	2.12
Percept. organ. index	0.96	0.97	0.96	0.97	0.97	0.97	0.97	0.96	0.97	0.97	0.96	0.97
(SEm)	3.00	2.72	3.07	2.81	2.55	2.46	2.60	2.85	2.81	2.72	3.11	1.67
Processing speed index	0.98	0.982	0.972	0.971	0.97	0.972	0.971	0.972	0.972	0.984	0.984	0.98
(SEm)	2.12	2.01	2.51	2.55	2.60	2.51	2.55	2.51	2.51	1.90	1.90	1.53

[a]N varies with group. The reliability coefficients for all subtests except Coding and Symbol Search are split-half correlations corrected by the Spearman-Brown formula. For Coding and Symbol Search, raw-score test-retest correlations are presented for four age groups; these coefficients, which are based on samples of 50 children tested twice, were corrected for the variability of the appropriate standardization group (Guilford & Fruchter, 1978). The coefficients for the IQ and factor-based scales were calculated with the formula for the reliability of the composite (Nunnally, 1978); the values for the supplementary subtests (Digit Span, Mazes, and Symbol Search) were not included in these computations. The standard errors of measurement are reported in scaled-score units for the subtests, in IQ units for the Verbal, Performance, and Full Scale scores, and in index units for the Perceptual Organization, and Processing Speed scores. For the Freedom from Distractibility Index no coefficients are reported since this factor does not emerge in the Greek data. Also, for the Verbal Comprehension Index, no coefficients are reported since the respective first factor in the Greek data is the same with the Verbal IQ index.

[b] For Coding and Symbol Search, the best estimates of the reliability coefficient at an age level for which retesting was not done is the value obtained at the adjacent age level. These "best estimates" for Coding and Symbol Search were used for computing the reliabilities of the composites to which these subtests contribute. For ages 14 and 15 the reliability coefficient of age 16 was used as the best possible estimate.

[c] The average r was computed with Fisher's z transformation. The average Standard Errors of Measurement (SEms) were calculated by averaging the sum of the squared SEms for each age group and obtaining the square root of the results.

TABLE 13.3   Stability Coefficients of the Subtests and IQ Scales by Age ($n = 200$)

Subtest/scale	Ages								Average[b]
	6 ($n = 50$)		8 ($n = 50$)		12 ($n = 50$)		16 ($n = 50$)		
	r_{12}	r_c^a	r_{12}	r_c^a	r_{12}	r_c^a	r_{12}	r_c^a	
Information	0.69	0.74	0.89	0.83	0.86	0.91	0.89	0.86	0.85
Similarities	0.60	0.45	0.83	0.69	0.76	0.80	0.90	0. 88	0.74
Arithmetic	0.42	0.54	0.71	0.79	0.87	0.88	0.75	0.76	0.77
Vocabulary	0.55	0.44	0.80	0.72	0.90	0.93	0.83	0.81	0.78
Comprehension	0.70	0.80	0.83	0.80	0.58	0.67	0.61	0.77	0.77
Digit span	0.66	0.85	0.57	0.57	0.63	0.68	0.76	0.90	0.78
Picture completion	0.75	0.75	0.81	0.69	0.89	0.90	0.93	0.91	0.83
Coding	0.65	0.77	0.55	0.55	0.75	0.62	0.93	0.94	0.77
Picture arrangement	0.67	0.67	0.73	0.60	0.78	0.64	0.86	0.84	0.70
Block design	0.56	0.61	0.62	0.62	0.87	0.85	0.92	0.94	0.80
Object assembly	0.64	0.77	0.76	0.71	0.77	0.79	0.57	0.53	0.71
Symbol search	0.53	0.75	0.74	0.80	0.70	0.68	0.72	0.67	0.73
Mazes	0.63	0.64	0.73	0.72	0.78	0.72	0.76	0.83	0.74
Verbal IQ	0.79	0.84	0.92	0.94	0.91	0.95	0.93	0.93	0.92
Performance IQ	0.83	0.91	0.83	0.75	0.88	0.84	0.94	0.93	0.87
Full scale IQ	0.87	0.93	0.92	0.88	0.90	0.91	0.94	0.93	0.91

[a] Correlations were corrected for the variability of WISC-III scores on the first testing (Guilford & Fruchter, 1978).
[b] Weighted averages of corrected correlations for all ages were obtained with Fisher's z transformation ($n = 200$).

Similarities, Arithmetic, and Comprehension was high, ranging from $r = 0.33$ between Arithmetic and Comprehension to $r = 0.60$ between Information and Vocabulary. On the other hand, the intercorrelations between the Performance subtests were lower than the Verbal subtests. In general, the patterns are similar with those of the U.S. test.

The construct validity of the Greek adaptation of the WISC-III was tested through several factor-analytic models, both on the exploratory and on the confirmatory levels. The methods employed were the same as in the U.S. and the UK standardizations. For the exploratory factor analysis models the maximum likelihood method was employed followed by orthogonal rotation of the axes. Oblique rotations resulted in similar factor structures, thus the orthogonal factor solutions were explored further. These exploratory factor analyses were performed for all age groups ($n = 956$) and for four age-bands: 6–7 years ($n = 185$), 8–10 years ($n = 253$), 11–13 years ($n = 264$), and 14–16 years ($n = 254$). At the first stage of exploratory factor analysis it appeared that for the Greek data there was no

TABLE 13.4 Intercorrelations of Subtest Scaled Scores ($n = 956$)

Subtest/scale	Inf	Sim	Ari	Voc	Com	DS	PCom	Cd	PA	BD	OA	SS	Mz
Information													
Similarities	0.60												
Arithmetic	0.50	0.40											
Vocabulary	0.59	0.58	0.44										
Comprehension	0.37	0.40	0.33	0.43									
Digit span	0.28	0.30	0.35	0.30	0.21								
Picture completion	0.31	0.33	0.27	0.27	0.27	0.12							
Coding	0.24	0.28	0.26	0.24	0.15	0.24	0.22						
Picture arrangement	0.38	0.30	0.36	0.35	0.31	0.18	0.36	0.24					
Block design	0.39	0.38	0.38	0.35	0.26	0.27	0.39	0.32	0.41				
Object assembly	0.29	0.29	0.26	0.28	0.20	0.21	0.37	0.24	0.37	0.59			
Symbol search	0.28	0.29	0.34	0.28	0.24	0.23	0.20	0.44	0.31	0.39	0.30		
Mazes	0.20	0.20	0.27	0.20	0.14	0.18	0.24	0.15	0.29	0.38	0.35	0.23	

clear-cut four factor solution. Arithmetic was not closely linked to Digit Span, neither for the four age-bands nor for the total sample. In addition, there were strong indications that Arithmetic was closely linked to the other verbal subscales and that Digit Span did not emerge on any factor.

At a second stage, a three-factor solution was attempted which resulted in the factor loadings presented in Table 13.5. These factor structures also indicated the existence of three factors, a Verbal Comprehension factor (Vocabulary, Information, Similarities, Arithmetic, and Comprehension), a Perceptual Organization factor (Picture Completion, Picture Arrangement, Block Design, and Object Assembly), and a Processing Speed factor (Coding, and Symbol Search). For the Processing Speed factor a discrepancy was observed for the age group of 6–7 years, for which this third factor did not appear. For the Perceptual Organization Index the Mazes subscale also loaded highly on the factor, but the supplementary nature of the subscale led to the decision not to include it in the final POI index (after having employed the methods followed in the WISC-III[UK] standardization, as well, as described in the UK standardization manual) (Wechsler, 1992, p. 82).

The exploratory factor analyses structures were tested through successive confirmatory factor analysis models as well. The null model was tested followed by unifactorial, two-, three-, four-, and five-factor models. These models were tested for all 956 cases and for each age-band separately. Improvement for goodness-of-fit and other criteria (root mean square error of approximation and χ^2 significance levels) favored a three-factor solution, but also indicated a possibility for a four-factor solution for two age-bands (8–10 and 14–16), although the improvement from the three-factor structures was not very high. Also, for the

TABLE 13.5 Maximum-Likelihood Factor Loadings (Varimax Rotation) for Three Factors

Subtest/scale	Factor 1: Verbal comprehension				Factor 2: Perceptual organization				Factor 3: Processing speed			
	Ages				Ages				Ages			
	6–7	8–10	11–13	14–16	6–7	8–10	11–13	14–16	6–7	8–10	11–13	14–16
Information	0.68	0.80	0.73	0.80	0.24	0.26	0.26	0.26	0.31	0.24	0.12	0.10
Similarities	0.73	0.71	0.75	0.72	0.23	0.27	0.23	0.23	0.00	0.20	0.19	0.29
Arithmetic	0.73	0.49	0.52	0.43	0.25	0.24	0.48	0.36	0.87	0.37	0.14	0.16
Vocabulary	0.69	0.68	0.82	0.76	0.19	0.30	0.17	0.20	0.19	0.31	0.17	0.25
Comprehension	0.54	0.57	0.56	0.49	0.22	0.21	0.22	0.17	0.20	0.26	0.06	0.09
Picture completion	0.23	0.42	0.38	0.21	0.46	0.51	0.40	0.51	0.13	0.21	0.15	0.01
Picture arrangement	0.20	0.45	0.38	0.31	0.60	0.39	0.41	0.51	0.16	0.26	0.13	0.19
Block design	0.26	0.37	0.28	0.21	0.69	0.66	0.71	0.75	0.09	0.25	0.26	0.33
Object assembly	0.17	0.19	0.13	0.16	0.68	0.81	0.70	0.72	-0.04	0.18	0.09	0.24
Coding	0.16	0.27	0.19	0.27	0.34	0.25	0.21	0.18	0.15	0.69	0.96	0.58
Symbol search	0.30	0.24	0.26	0.17	0.38	0.24	0.41	0.24	0.19	0.66	0.41	0.72
Digit span	0.33	0.34	0.28	0.33	0.30	0.18	0.19	0.19	0.16	0.38	0.17	0.23
Mazes	0.09	0.18	0.20	0.16	0.58	0.46	0.46	0.45	0.12	0.20	0.09	0.13

age group of 6–7 years, a two-factor solution seemed to fit the subscale covariance matrix quite well, which verified the discrepancy observed in the exploratory phase. However, for the total standardization sample the improvement from the three- to the four-factor model was not large. For these reasons and also due to the results of the exploratory factor analyses, we concluded that the three-factor solution was the more appropriate for the Hellenic WISC-III standardization data.

Most of the studies of the U.S. WISC-III supported a four-factor solution (e.g., Roid, Prifitera, & Weiss, 1993; Tupa, Wright, & Fristad, 1997; Wechsler, 1991). One possible explanation for the three-factor outcome for the Greek standardization might be that the Greek school curriculum emphasizes formal arithmetic teaching instead of problem solving techniques, mainly addressed by the Arithmetic subscale. Thus, Arithmetic items might be addressed more "formally" by Greek students and less as a way of implementing mathematical knowledge for problem solving. As a consequence, it is possible that Arithmetic loads better on a Verbal-Cognitive factor rather than forming a Freedom from Distractibility Index together with Digit Span.

An indication of external validity was the correlations between father's and mother's education and performance on the subtests, IQ scores, and index scores (Table 13.6). Low correlations were found on all the subtests, an average of $r = 0.20$ on the Verbal subtests and somewhat lower on the Performance subtests. The correlations between father's and mother's education and VIQ were $r = 0.36$ and $r = 0.33$, respectively; with PIQ, $r = 0.24$ and $r = 0.19$; and with FSIQ, $r = 0.22$ and $r = 0.30$. The correlations between father's and mother's education and the VCI were $r = 0.22$ and $r = 0.19$, respectively; and with the POI, $r = 0.18$ and $r = 0.13$. In an intelligence test for children constructed and standardized by Georgas (1971, 1972) over 30 years ago, the correlations between a vocabulary test and three nonverbal tests with parental education and socioeconomic status were much higher, in the 0.60s for the verbal test. The lower correlations found with the WISC-III would be very likely due to greater homogeneity in education and socioeconomic status; increased percents of students attend high school and the economic level of Greece has increased during these past three decades.

Another measure of external validity was the correlation between school marks and performance on the WISC-III. The average correlations across all ages were $r = 0.31$ for VIQ, $r = 0.31$. $r = 0.22$ for PIQ, and $r = 0.30$ for FSIQ. The correlations ranged from a low of $r = 0.23$ for ages 11–13 for VIQ to $r = 0.50$ for ages 14–16 for VIQ.

CULTURAL ISSUES INFLUENCING WISC-III
INTERPRETATION IN GREECE

Greece forms the base of the Balkan peninsula in the Eastern Mediterranean. Its geographic features are a spine of mountains that extends from north to south, a few fertile plains, and the hundreds of islands scattered throughout the Ionian,

TABLE 13.6 Correlations of Subscale Scores with Education Level of Father and Mother

Age	Educ. level	Inf	Sim	Ari	Voc	Com	DS	PCom	Cd	PA	BD	OA	SS	Mz	VIQ	PIQ	FSIQ	POI	PSI
6	Father	0.18	0.32	0.23	0.20	0.02	0.38	-0.09	-0.14	0.17	0.22	0.03	0.03	0.06	0.27	0.04	0.17	0.02	-0.11
	Mother	0.13	0.21	0.13	0.19	-0.08	0.29	-0.19	-0.25	0.05	0.34	-0.04	0.20	0.26	0.21	0.03	0.14	0.19	-0.09
7	Father	0.50	0.31	0.35	0.55	0.35	0.32	0.11	0.04	0.12	0.24	0.11	0.24	0.06	0.57	0.21	0.52	0.20	0.13
	Mother	0.42	0.29	0.32	0.40	0.24	0.26	0.20	-0.05	0.19	0.37	0.22	0.19	0.17	0.46	0.34	0.52	0.37	0.05
8	Father	0.18	0.17	0.09	0.17	-0.05	0.18	0.14	0.17	-0.13	-0.05	0.14	0.09	0.29	0.14	0.08	0.12	-0.01	0.19
	Mother	0.27	0.29	0.16	0.22	0.05	0.23	0.03	0.18	-0.14	0.00	0.05	0.14	0.03	0.29	0.05	0.19	-0.04	0.20
9	Father	0.25	0.36	0.10	0.30	0.28	0.24	0.32	0.20	0.11	0.11	0.09	0.13	0.02	0.31	0.22	0.30	0.15	0.17
	Mother	0.42	0.45	0.07	0.29	0.38	0.15	0.19	0.06	0.13	-0.03	0.00	0.09	0.03	0.39	0.09	0.29	0.06	0.07
10	Father	0.60	0.43	0.31	0.52	0.44	0.29	0.33	0.34	0.39	0.49	0.43	0.34	0.21	0.62	0.52	0.63	0.52	0.35
	Mother	0.50	0.47	0.30	0.42	0.29	0.31	0.25	0.37	0.31	0.37	0.37	0.27	0.15	0.54	0.45	0.55	0.43	0.34
11	Father	-0.01	0.36	0.10	0.15	0.30	0.00	0.30	0.20	0.11	0.14	0.20	-0.07	0.14	0.23	0.33	0.31	0.24	0.11
	Mother	0.25	0.26	0.31	0.09	0.15	0.08	0.22	0.12	0.29	0.30	0.18	-0.07	0.27	0.29	0.35	0.35	0.32	0.04
12	Father	0.16	0.20	0.32	0.26	0.36	0.37	0.15	0.24	0.28	0.19	0.07	0.26	0.06	0.34	0.27	0.33	0.25	0.27
	Mother	0.17	0.15	0.30	0.30	0.23	0.28	0.07	0.09	0.25	0.07	0.11	0.16	0.04	0.29	0.16	0.25	0.18	0.11
13	Father	0.24	0.38	0.21	0.25	0.10	0.07	0.31	-0.03	0.01	0.26	0.24	0.10	-0.07	0.30	0.21	0.30	0.24	0.21
	Mother	0.34	0.42	0.19	0.37	0.36	0.21	0.29	0.21	0.17	0.21	0.17	0.31	-0.01	0.40	0.31	0.41	0.15	0.22
14	Father	0.34	0.24	0.25	0.39	0.25	0.00	0.04	0.20	0.24	0.16	0.12	0.17	0.21	0.39	0.27	0.38	0.24	0.21
	Mother	0.29	0.22	0.11	0.38	0.24	0.02	0.05	0.24	0.18	0.12	0.06	0.17	0.06	0.32	0.21	0.31	0.15	0.22
15	Father	0.33	0.44	0.25	0.27	0.18	0.36	0.13	0.26	0.27	0.13	0.15	0.25	0.12	0.38	0.24	0.35	0.14	0.21
	Mother	0.11	0.16	0.07	0.03	0.09	0.27	0.16	0.00	0.12	-0.03	0.03	0.07	0.03	0.12	0.07	0.11	0.05	0.04
16	Father	0.40	0.37	0.11	0.34	0.27	0.00	0.04	0.18	0.01	0.14	0.17	0.22	-0.14	0.42	0.17	0.34	0.14	0.21
	Mother	0.27	0.27	0.13	0.33	0.35	0.15	0.05	0.04	0.00	0.06	-0.01	0.03	-0.17	0.37	0.06	0.24	0.04	0.04
All ages	Father	0.19	0.26	0.17	0.22	0.19	0.18	0.14	0.16	0.15	0.17	0.15	0.17	0.10	0.36	0.24	0.35	0.22	0.18
	Mother	0.20	0.21	0.15	0.19	0.17	0.17	0.12	0.10	0.14	0.14	0.12	0.12	0.08	0.33	0.19	0.30	0.19	0.13

Aegean, and Cretan seas. The population of Greece is approximately 10,500,000, with almost half living in the greater Athens region. Greece is a homogeneous country with approximately 98% of the population Greek and its religion is Greek Orthodox. Its ethnic composition has changed somewhat during the past 10 years with an influx of refugees from Albania and Middle East countries which represent perhaps 4% of the population at the present time.

One source of bias in psychological tests is a result of cultural influences. Language is both a cultural product and the means of communication of cultural ideas, products, behavior, values, etc. The modern Greek language has evolved from ancient Greek. An important feature of the Greek language within the geographical context of Europe, the Middle East, and North Africa is that no language in these countries, except for Cyprus, is directly related to Greek. French, Italian, and Spanish, for example, are derived from Latin, countries in the Balkans speak variations of Slavic languages, English has Anglo-Saxon roots, and there are the Germanic languages, the Scandinavian languages, in addition to Arabic, Turkish, and other languages. Thus, the Greek language is unique in this context, in addition to its employment of the Greek alphabet.

On the other hand, Greek words have been incorporated into many other languages. It has been estimated that approximately 30% of the words in the English language have Greek roots. They include common terms such as "airplane," "taxi," "new," many scientific terms such as, "therapy," "geography," "arithmetic," "physics," terms in political science such as "democracy," "hegemony," "ideology," "technological," and "cybernetics." Approximately 20% more words are required to express the same sentence in Greek as compared to English. In addition, Greek syntax differs from that in English and other languages.

The decision to administer the Hellenic WISC-III to an ethnic Greek child or adolescent in another country or the version of that country depends upon the number of years of residence and the language facility in the Greek or host country language. The above aspects of the Greek language are important in evaluating the cognitive abilities on the Verbal subtests. If the language facility in Greek is not high, it may be preferable to employ the host country version. In borderline situations of language competence, it might be possible to employ a combination of both versions of the WISC-III.

Because of the uniqueness of the Greek language and the necessity for communication of Greeks with other member-states of the European Union, students begin studying foreign languages at an early age. The proportion of young people in Greece who are bilingual and trilingual is among the highest in the European Union. This foreign language facility can be reflected in performance on the Vocabulary subtest.

As indicated above, Arithmetic is part of the VCI. Its high correlations with Information (0.50), Vocabulary, (0.44) and Similarities (0.40) are in fact higher than the correlations between Comprehension and these same three Verbal subtests, suggesting closely related cognitive processes of mathematical thinking with these verbal tests.

Because of the homogeneity of the Greek culture, differences in intelligence test performance associated with socioeconomic status, parent education, and, particularly, rural-urban residence, have lessened during the past 30 years. The marginal increase in refugees and immigrants during recent years, particularly ethnic Greeks from the former Soviet Union, does raise an issue of evaluation of their intellectual functioning with the WISC-III. But the small numbers in each ethnic group do not warrant the high costs of standardization for each ethnic group. One of the desirable consequences of this book is that the comparisons of the standardizations of the WISC-III in different cultures will permit psychologists to make better judgments regarding the intellectual functioning of ethnic groups based on the degree of variability of the subtests in different cultures, for example, certain Performance tests as compared to Verbal tests.

PROFESSIONAL ISSUES IN THE USE OF INTELLIGENCE TESTS IN GREECE

Psychology has had a long history but only a brief presence in modern psychology in Greece. The history of psychology begins with the systematic study of psychological phenomena in the 7th century B.C. by Hellenic philosophers. The etymology of the term philosophy is the love of wisdom, and is characteristic of the belief of the ancient Greek philosophers that observation and logic are methods for understanding social and physical phenomena in contrast to the animistic beliefs of the cultures of that period. The term "psychology" denotes both psyche and logic. The precursors of many theories in modern psychology are of Hellenic origin. Locke's empiricism was originally discussed by Democritus, Epicouros, and Aristotle, and the term agraphos pinax was employed by Aphrodiseas many centuries before tabula rasa. The recent rise of cognitive psychology with its challenge to behaviorism and to psychoanalysis had its antecendents in the skepticism of the reality of the senses and its belief in rationalism as exemplified by Pythagoras, Heraclitos, Democritus, Anaxagoras, Socrates, Plato, and Aristotle. Plato discussed the relationship of nature and nurture, and his treatment of the role of dreams in the psyche antedates Freud's unconscious. Aristotle was the most eminent in defining and systematically studying the phenomena of psychology. He wrote about the senses and perception, about the nature of the psyche, about sleep and alertness, about dreams, about youth and old age. His writings on the phenomena of memory and recollections were precursors of the law of association by the British associationists. In social psychology, Holland's theory of attitude change has its precursors in Aristotle's Rhetorics.

The science of modern psychology in Greece begins with Theophilos Voreas, who wrote his Ph.D. under Wundt in 1897, and established the first Psychological Laboratory at the University of Athens in 1926. The first Greek book, *Child Psychology,* was written by G. Sakellariou in 1922, who also standardized the Binet-Simon intelligence test, and went on to establish the Psychological Laboratory of the University of Thessalonike in 1937. However, the first programs issuing degrees in psychology were established in Greece beginning in the late 1980s. At the present time, there are four departments of psychology: at the Aristotelian University of Thessalonike, the University of Crete, the University of Athens, and Panteion University. The title of the degree is the Ptychion. Graduate programs (Metaptychiako diploma) are in areas such as clinical psychology, school psychology, organizational and economic psychology, and cognitive science. Programs leading to the Ph.D., Didaktoriko Diploma, by research, are offered in a variety of fields in psychology. Both the certification and licensing of psychologists was mandated by law in 1979 and in 1993, respectively.

There are two psychological associations in Greece. The Association of Greek Psychologists (AGP) was established in 1963. It is currently primarily an association of professional psychologists and membership is based on at least a Masters level degree in psychology. The AGP is a member of the European Federation of Psychologists' Associations (EFPA). The Hellenic Psychological Society was established in 1990. It is an association of university faculty and psychologists at research institutions, and the requisite for full membership is a Ph.D. in psychology. There is a code of ethics regulating teaching, research, and practice of psychology, including issues related to the use of psychological testing, and Greece is also bound by the code of ethics of EFPA. The sale of the WISC-III by the publisher is restricted to members of the AGP, to members of the Hellenic Psychological Society, and to university departments in psychology, mental health, and other institutions which have qualified psychologists on their staff. Intelligence tests are administered only by psychologists and the AGP has played an important role in monitoring the attempts to administer psychological tests by other professionals.

REFERENCES

Georgas, J. (1971). *Test Noemosynis gia paedia*. [Intelligence test for children]. Athens: Kedros.

Georgas, J. (1972). A children's intelligence test for Greece. In L. J. Cronbach & P. J. D. Drenth (Eds.), *Mental tests and cultural adaptation*. (pp. 217–222). The Hague, The Netherlands: Mouton.

Georgas, J., Paraskevopoulos, I. N., Besevegis, E., & Giannitsas, N. D. (1997). *The Hellenic WISC-III*. Athens: Psychometric Laboratory, University of Athens.

Guilford, J. P., & Fruchter, B. (1978). *Fundamental statistics in psychology and education*. Sixth Edition. New York: McGraw-Hill.

Nunnally, J. C. (1978). *Psychometric theory*. New York: McGraw-Hill.

Paraskevopoulos, J. (1973). *The Illinois Test of Psycholinguistic Abilities*. Ioannina: Psychological and Educational Laboratory of the University of Ioannina.

Paraskevopoulos, J., Kalantzi-Azizi, A., & Giannitsas, N. D. (1999). *Athena Test diagnosis dyskolion matheses* [Athena Test of diagnosis of learning difficulties]. Athens: Ellinika Grammata.

Roid, G. H., Prifitera, A., & Weiss, L. G. (1993). Replication of the WISC-III factor structure in an independent sample. In B. A. Bracken & R. S. McCallum (Eds.), *Wechsler Intelligence Scale for Children: Third Edition. Journal of Psychoeducational Assessment, Advances in psychoeducational assessment* (pp. 6–21). Brandon, US: Clinical Psychology Publishing Co.

Tupa, D. J., Wright, M., & Fristad, M. A. (1997). Confirmatory factor analysis of the WISC-III with child psychiatric inpatients. *Psychological Assessment, 9*, 302–306.

Wechsler, D. (1991). *Manual for the Wechsler Intelligence Scale for Children—Third Edition*. San Antonio, TX: The Psychological Corporation.

Wechsler, D. (1992). *Wechsler Intelligence Scale for Children—Third Edition UK*. London: The Psychological Corporation.

Wechsler, D. (1997). *To Helleniko WISC-III* (J. Georgas, I. N. Paraskevopoulos, E. Besevegis, & N. D. Giannitsas, Trans.). Athens: Psychometric Laboratory, University of Athens. (Original work published in 1991.)

14

JAPAN

KAZUHIKO UENO

Tokyo Gakugei University
Tokyo, Japan

ICHIRO NAKATANI

Japan Institute of Psychological Aptitude
Nihon Bunka Kagakusha
Tokyo, Japan

All the Wechsler Intelligence tests have been standardized and used in Japan. The original Wechsler Intelligence Test for Children (WISC) was first published in 1953, the WISC-R was published in 1978, and the WISC-III in 1998 (Wechsler, 1998). As for other Wechsler intelligence tests, the Wechsler Preschool and Primary Scale of Intelligence (WPPSI) was published in 1969, the Wechsler Adult Intelligence Scale (WAIS) in 1958, the WAIS-R in 1990, and the WAIS-III is in process of standardization. The WISC-R has been used extensively in Japan, mainly at schools and hospitals for screening children with mental disabilities. The Conference for the Learning Disabilities started with an investigation in the Ministry of Education in 1990. As a result, the utilization needs of WISC-III as a diagnosis test in the educational sector are expanding further today.

The Japan Institute of Psychological Aptitude, which has played a major role in the dissemination of the WISC-R, established a special team to translate and adapt the Japanese version of the WISC-III in 1991 (Wechsler, 1991). Our team completed the translation and standardization of the Japanese version in 1998 (Wechsler, 1998).

ADAPTATION PROCESS

The procedures followed in the translation and adaptation of the WISC-III in Japan were based on the rich experiences of the adaptation and standardization of the Wechsler tests in the past. The items were translated into Japanese and back-translated into English and checked for equivalence of meaning. Before the standardization, we conducted two case studies, one as pilot test and the other as tryout test to select the items for each subtest. The number of subjects involved with the pilot test were $n = 330$ including the group tests, and the tryout test was based on $n = 160$. When selecting items, we calculated the passing rate and the point biserial correlation coefficient in each age group. Then, eliminating the items of the same level of difficulty, we selected items that were highly correlated with the score of each subtest. Consequently, 50% of items in Information, 40% in Picture Completion, and 25% in Comprehension were replaced with new items.

What was always challenging in the process of developing Japanese versions of the WISC-R and WAIS-R was the great difference in language, culture, and history between the U.S. and Japan. A number of U.S. items were culturally biased and Japanese items were substituted. For example, in Picture Completion, for consideration of people with disabilities, the missing parts on the body in people and animals were replaced with those on things. For example, "animal ear" and the "animal foot," and parts of the human body were replaced with "vehicle tire" and "stockings." On the Information subtest, historical persons, scientists, authors, and geographic questions were replaced with those familiar to Japanese people. As a result, many of the items were replaced with new items that have no relation to U.S. items.

The Japanese Vocabulary items were selected anew and were not dependent on the translation of the existing U.S. items. In developing the items for Vocabulary, we divided the developmental phase into four phases; the infant phase (4–6 years old), the elementary school phase (7–12 years old), the junior high phase (13–15 years old), and the high school phase (16 years old and above). In selecting items for Vocabulary in each phase, the results from previous studies were used. The references for the infant phase are from Okubo and Kawamata (1982), Vocabulary for Under School Age, Report of the National Institute for Japanese Language 71, The National Institute for Japanese Language, and Report of the National Institute for Japanese Language (1980), Vocabulary of Infants, Tokyo-shoseki. The references for the elementary school phase are the *Journal of Japan Educational Research Institute 35* (1985), Studies on the Basic Vocabulary in School Learning I, Kyoiku-shuppan, and Sakamoto (1959), Shin Kyoiku Kihon Goi (New Basic Vocabulary in Education), Gakugei-tosho. The references for the junior high and high school phases are Hayashi (1971), Vocabulary Research and Basic Vocabulary, Report of the National Institute for Japanese Language 39, the National Institute for Japanese Language.

The number of vocabulary items selected for the pilot test was 6 for the infant phase, 20 for the elementary school phase, 12 for the junior high, and 6 for the high school, totaling 44 potential items. For the data from the pilot and preliminary tests, we calculated the degree of difficulty and the point biserial correlation coefficient in each age group and finalized the items of selection. As a result, only two U.S. items were retained.

SAMPLE CHARACTERISTICS

The Japanese WISC-III norms are based on a standardization sample representative of the Japanese population of children and adults. An analysis of data gathered in 1995 by the Basic Survey of Schools of the Ministry of Education provided the basis for stratification across the following variables: age, gender, and geographic region. For the standardization sample, the actual ages of the target groups were subdivided into 12 age groups by every 12 months starting from ages 5 years 0 months 0 days to 16 years, 11 months and 30 days. We set a target number of 1200 children in total 100 for each age group. Concerning gender, 50 children in each age group were used as targets in order to make the sampling of both genders even. The number of children in the final standardization sample was $n = 1125$, which was 94% of what we had expected and enough data for statistical analysis. It is generally acknowledged that there are no cultural differences in different localities in Japan. However, in this standardization sample we were careful to avoid sampling bias regarding geographical location. Therefore, we first divided Japan into eight geographic areas and allocated the target number of samples to each area. Then, we further divided Japan into two major areas, east and west, to collect data in accordance with the ratios of the Census of Japan. The census indicates the population ratio between east and west Japan to be 3 to 2 (Statistics Bureau of the Management and Coordination Agency, 1992). As Table 14.1 shows, the proportions of children sampled in these geographical areas were a similar ratio to those in the population based on census statistics.

Testers who had completed training at the WISC-R Skill Seminar held by the Japan Institute of Psychological Aptitude were asked to administer the WISC-III for the standardization phase. In selecting subjects, we picked children randomly from classrooms to avoid selection bias.

RELIABILITY

Table 14.2 presents the split-half reliability coefficients and standard errors of measurement for the subtests, IQs, and index scores by age and overall. As shown in the table, the average reliability for the three IQ scores was above 0.90. The average reliabilities for the index scores ranged from $r = 0.81$ for Processing Speed Index (PSI) to $r = 0.89$ for Perceptual Organization Index (POI). The average subtest reliabilities ranged from $r = 0.64$ for Object Assembly to $r = 0.87$ for Digit Span. The Standard Errors of Measurement (SEms) were correlated with the reliabilities in that those subtests with the highest reliabilities had the smallest standard errors.

TABLE 14.1   Demographic Characteristics of the Standardization Sample: Percentages by Age

Age	n	Geographic region	
		East Japan	West Japan
5	96	58.3	41.7
6	93	61.3	38.7
7	94	69.1	30.9
8	88	59.1	40.9
9	102	67.6	32.4
10	82	67.1	32.9
11	114	62.3	37.7
12	87	59.8	40.2
13	82	63.4	36.6
14	81	58.0	42.0
15	106	69.8	30.2
16	100	53.0	47.0
Total	1125	62.5	37.5
Japan population		60.9	39.1

Table 14.3 shows the average corrected retest correlations for the subtests, IQs and index scores. The retest intervals are between 2 weeks to 6 months (average 76.2 days), and age ranged between 6 years 2 months and 15 years 10 months (average 10 years 7 months). These data were based on 84 children. The retest correlations for the IQ scores ranged from $r = 0.83$ for Performance IQ (PIQ) to $r = 0.93$ for Verbal IQ (VIQ) and Full Scale IQ (FSIQ). The retest correlations for the index scores ranged from $r = 0.78$ for PSI to $r = 0.91$ for Verbal Comprehension Index (VCI). The retest correlations for the subtests ranged from $r = 0.54$ for Picture Arrangement to $r = 0.89$ for Information.

EVIDENCE OF VALIDITY

The WISC-III was compared to other major intelligence tests, including the Tanaka-Binet Intelligence Scale, the Kaufman Assessment Battery for Children (K-ABC), and Illinois Test of Psycholinguistic Abilities (ITPA). Because of space limitations, we describe the correlation between the WISC-III FSIQ score and the Tanaka-Binet IQ score. The WISC-III and the Tanaka-Binet were administered to a sample of 38 children. The FSIQ correlation with Tanaka-Binet IQ is $r = 0.74$. The results suggested that the WISC-III has a strong relationship with the Tanaka-Binet.

The result of the WISC-III intercorrelations averaged across all age groups is presented in Table 14.4. The Verbal subtests had higher intercorrelations with the other Verbal subtests than the Performance subtests. The Performance subtests had higher intercorrelations with other Performance subtests than the Verbal subtests.

TABLE 14.2 Reliability Coefficients and Standard Errors of Measurement of the Subtests Scaled Scores, IQ Scores, and Index Scores by Age[a]

Subtest/scale	5	6	7	8	9	10	11	12	13	14	15	16	Average[b]
Information	0.56	0.67	0.78	0.80	0.76	0.81	0.85	0.78	0.88	0.85	0.90	0.90	0.81
(SEm)	1.99	1.73	1.39	1.35	1.48	1.30	1.16	1.40	1.03	1.15	0.95	0.97	1.30
Similarities	0.76	0.79	0.55	0.70	0.70	0.68	0.68	0.64	0.61	0.72	0.79	0.57	0.69
(SEm)	1.46	1.36	2.01	1.63	1.63	1.69	1.71	1.81	1.88	1.59	1.36	1.96	1.67
Arithmetic	0.87	0.73	0.81	0.80	0.85	0.77	0.77	0.62	0.81	0.84	0.85	0.82	0.80
(SEm)	1.08	1.55	1.32	1.34	1.17	1.45	1.43	1.85	1.29	1.21	1.14	1.26	1.33
Vocabulary	0.84	0.72	0.69	0.77	0.74	0.80	0.87	0.73	0.88	0.92	0.91	0.90	0.83
(SEm)	1.21	1.60	1.68	1.45	1.52	1.36	1.07	1.55	1.05	0.87	0.92	0.96	1.25
Comprehension	0.73	0.65	0.62	0.67	0.77	0.86	0.84	0.82	0.82	0.74	0.88	0.80	0.78
(SEm)	1.55	1.77	1.85	1.73	1.43	1.10	1.22	1.27	1.26	1.53	1.04	1.34	1.41
Digit span	0.82	0.86	0.82	0.81	0.89	0.88	0.85	0.90	0.88	0.88	0.90	0.90	0.87
(SEm)	1.28	1.13	1.27	1.31	0.99	1.06	1.16	0.97	1.04	1.03	0.95	0.93	1.09
Picture completion	0.87	0.73	0.84	0.89	0.80	0.80	0.77	0.72	0.69	0.83	0.74	0.77	0.80
(SEm)	1.07	1.55	1.20	1.01	1.36	1.34	1.43	1.57	1.66	1.25	1.52	1.44	1.36
Coding	0.75	0.75	0.75	0.88	0.88	0.88	0.88	0.88	0.67	0.67	0.67	0.67	0.78
(SEm)	1.51	1.51	1.51	1.03	1.03	1.03	1.03	1.03	1.73	1.73	1.73	1.73	1.40
Picture arrangement	0.68	0.63	0.85	0.74	0.72	0.76	0.72	0.58	0.54	0.79	0.73	0.68	0.71
(SEm)	1.70	1.84	1.14	1.53	1.58	1.45	1.58	1.94	2.03	1.38	1.56	1.69	1.61
Block design	0.76	0.84	0.81	0.79	0.89	0.83	0.88	0.86	0.86	0.88	0.89	0.90	0.85
(SEm)	1.46	1.21	1.32	1.38	1.01	1.24	1.05	1.10	1.11	1.04	1.02	0.95	1.15
Object assembly	0.58	0.58	0.58	0.67	0.54	0.50	0.49	0.43	0.70	0.75	0.84	0.78	0.64
(SEm)	1.94	1.94	1.94	1.71	2.04	2.13	2.15	2.27	1.64	1.49	1.19	1.39	1.80

(Continues)

TABLE 14.2 (Continued)

Subtest/scale	Age in years												Average[b]
	5	6	7	8	9	10	11	12	13	14	15	16	
Symbol search	0.73	0.73	0.73	0.57	0.57	0.57	0.57	0.57	0.59	0.59	0.59	0.59	0.64
(SEm)	1.56	1.56	1.56	1.96	1.96	1.96	1.96	1.96	1.92	1.92	1.92	1.92	1.81
Mazes	0.73	0.74	0.81	0.76	0.74	0.55	0.71	0.65	0.80	0.73	0.61	0.65	0.71
(SEm)	1.55	1.53	1.31	1.48	1.53	2.00	1.61	1.79	1.35	1.55	1.86	1.77	1.60
Verbal IQ	0.91	0.89	0.90	0.92	0.92	0.94	0.94	0.90	0.94	0.94	0.96	0.94	0.93
(SEm)	4.40	4.94	4.85	4.37	4.26	3.78	3.68	4.79	3.77	3.57	2.81	3.54	4.02
Performance IQ	0.89	0.87	0.91	0.91	0.91	0.90	0.88	0.87	0.88	0.92	0.91	0.90	0.90
(SEm)	4.99	5.34	4.61	4.43	4.46	4.63	5.09	5.38	5.11	4.20	4.42	4.68	4.77
Full scale IQ	0.94	0.93	0.94	0.95	0.95	0.95	0.95	0.92	0.95	0.96	0.97	0.96	0.95
(SEm)	3.67	4.11	3.71	3.43	3.50	3.25	3.44	4.18	3.45	3.03	2.69	3.13	3.44
Verbal comp. index	0.89	0.87	0.87	0.90	0.90	0.93	0.93	0.90	0.93	0.93	0.96	0.93	0.84
(SEm)	5.07	5.47	5.46	4.80	4.72	4.01	3.85	4.85	4.01	3.95	3.09	3.96	6.09
Percept. organ. index	0.87	0.85	0.90	0.90	0.89	0.88	0.86	0.83	0.88	0.93	0.92	0.90	0.89
(SEm)	5.36	5.87	4.73	4.74	4.99	5.27	5.70	6.09	5.30	3.99	4.27	4.78	4.99
Freed. distract. index	0.89	0.86	0.88	0.86	0.91	0.86	0.86	0.81	0.90	0.91	0.92	0.91	0.88
(SEm)	4.93	5.53	5.27	5.56	4.60	5.61	5.56	6.52	4.68	4.45	4.21	4.56	5.09
Process. speed index	0.83	0.83	0.84	0.83	0.83	0.83	0.82	0.82	0.77	0.75	0.77	0.76	0.81
(SEm)	6.24	6.27	6.05	6.19	6.18	6.23	6.34	6.36	7.20	7.44	7.27	7.37	6.58

[a] N = between 81–114. The reliability coefficients for all subtests except Coding and Symbol Search are split-half correlations corrected by the Spearman-Brown formula. For Coding and Symbol Search, raw-score test-retest correlations are presented for three age-bands. The coefficients for the IQ and factor-based scales were calculated with the formula for the reliability of the composite (Guilford, 1954); the values for the supplementary subtests (Digit Span, Mazes, and Symbol Search) were not included in these computations. The standard errors of measurement are reported in scaled-score units for the subtests, in IQ units for the Verbal, Performance, and Full Scale scores, and in index units for the Verbal Comprehension, Perceptual Organization, Freedom from Distractibility, and Processing Speed scores.

[b] The average r was computed with Fisher's z transformation. The average SEms were calculated by averaging the sum of the squared SEms for each age group and obtaining the square root of the results.

TABLE 14.3 Stability Coefficients of the Subtests, IQ Scales, and Factor-Based Scales ($N = 84$)

Subtest/scale	r_{12}	Averages[a]
Information	0.87	0.89
Similarities	0.65	0.71
Arithmetic	0.72	0.77
Vocabulary	0.84	0.82
Comprehension	0.65	0.78
Digit span	0.85	0.82
Picture completion	0.67	0.74
Coding	0.76	0.83
Picture arrangement	0.56	0.54
Block design	0.71	0.84
Object assembly	0.55	0.69
Symbol search	0.65	0.75
Mazes	0.56	0.58
Verbal IQ	0.89	0.93
Performance IQ	0.76	0.83
Full scale IQ	0.88	0.93
Verbal comprehension index	0.86	0.91
Perceptual organization index	0.77	0.84
Freedom from distractibility index	0.84	0.81
Processing speed index	0.68	0.78

[a] Correlations were corrected for the variability of WISC-III scores on the first testing (Guilford & Fruchter, 1978).

TABLE 14.4 Intercorrelation of Subtest Scaled Scores

Subtest/scale	Inf	Sim	Ari	Voc	Com	DS	PCom	Cd	PA	BD	OA	SS	Mz
Information													
Similarities	0.54												
Arithmetic	0.54	0.46											
Vocabulary	0.62	0.60	0.49										
Comprehension	0.51	0.52	0.44	0.62									
Digit span	0.39	0.33	0.45	0.36	0.29								
Picture completion	0.39	0.40	0.33	0.35	0.38	0.23							
Coding	0.30	0.31	0.34	0.29	0.29	0.27	0.22						
Picture arrangement	0.38	0.32	0.36	0.33	0.33	0.20	0.39	0.31					
Block design	0.40	0.39	0.49	0.36	0.35	0.37	0.43	0.38	0.40				
Object assembly	0.34	0.29	0.34	0.32	0.31	0.24	0.43	0.27	0.34	0.52			
Symbol search	0.34	0.31	0.39	0.31	0.31	0.32	0.31	0.55	0.36	0.44	0.30		
Mazes	0.20	0.19	0.25	0.17	0.17	0.18	0.21	0.22	0.23	0.37	0.22	0.22	

TABLE 14.5   Maximum-Likelihood Factor Loadings (Varimax Rotation) for Four Factors

	Factor 1: Verbal comprehension	Factor 2: Perceptual organization	Factor 3: Freedom from distractibility	Factor 4: Processing speed
Information	0.64	0.25	0.15	0.31
Similarities	0.63	0.25	0.17	0.18
Vocabulary	0.79	0.16	0.13	0.20
Comprehension	0.66	0.24	0.17	0.10
Picture completion	0.35	0.57	0.11	0.02
Picture arrangement	0.29	0.43	0.26	0.08
Block design	0.17	0.64	0.26	0.38
Object assembly	0.21	0.58	0.13	0.14
Arithmetic	0.42	0.28	0.21	0.52
Digit span	0.27	0.16	0.19	0.48
Coding	0.18	0.18	0.70	0.14
Symbol search	0.18	0.28	0.63	0.20
Mazes	0.06	0.32	0.16	0.21

This pattern of correlations provided evidence of convergent validity. Lower correlations between Verbal subtests and Performance subtests are evidence of discriminant validity.

For the factor analysis, the principal factor method was employed using data from all 1125 subjects of the standardization sample. The results indicated that for all subtests except Mazes, loadings for each factor with the one-factor solution were at least 0.51. A second factor analysis was conducted with four factors and a Varimax rotation. Table 14.5 presents the maximum-likelihood factor loadings with Varimax rotation for the four factors. Analyses for the total sample ($N = 1125$) justify a four-factor structure. Factor 1, composed of the Information, Similarities, Vocabulary, and Comprehension subtests, is the Verbal Comprehension factor. Factor 2, composed of the Picture Completion, Picture Arrangement, Block Design, and Object Assembly subtests, is the Perceptual Organization factor. Factor 3, composed of the Cording and Symbol Search, is the Processing Speed. Factor 4, composed of the Arithmetic and Digit Span, is Freedom from Distractibility. Thus, the Japanese version obtains the same four-factor structure as the U.S. test.

CULTURAL ISSUES INFLUENCING THE WISC-III IN JAPAN

Japan is a highly homogeneous culture. For example, conditions, such as the standardized language of Japanese, cultural homogeneity influenced by the development of mass media, the unified educational system (including the national curriculum, the commonly used textbooks, and the nationwide teachers' training standardization), create the nationwide cultural homogeneity with few ethnic groups within the country.

The items used in Vocabulary, Information, and Comprehension and in Picture Completion had to be substituted or added from the point of view of content valid to Japanese education, history, and culture. Therefore, they are not necessarily the same items as those used in the U.S. test. As the factor analysis shows, however, the construct validity of index scores in WISC-III Japanese version indicates that its structure is the same as the U.S. test.

Though this is an important chapter in which to examine the cultural differences in WISC-III, unfortunately there are not many cross-cultural studies of these differences at the present time. It is known, however, that Japanese children show high test performances on the speed tests, including Coding, Symbol Search, Picture Arrangement, Block Design, and Mazes. Therefore, there appeared to be a ceiling effect in item response and few items with high degree of difficulty. Thus, the time limit for some subtests and some items were shortened (e.g., Coding and Symbol Search, which were originally 120 seconds were shortened to 90 seconds), and more difficult items were added to some subtests (e.g., Block Design).

In developing the Japanese version of the WISC-III, we found a very interesting cultural difference. Japanese show a much higher rate of performance in Coding, which is a performance subtest that measures the amount of performance within a certain period of time. Therefore to avoid the ceiling effect, the operation time was shortened from 120 seconds to 90 in standardizing WISC-R. In the standardization of the WISC-III, the same method was adopted for Coding and Symbol Search. Therefore, we should not compare the results of these tests simply in terms of international comparison. Since Japanese are characterized by better performance on these speed-type tests in the performance subtests, the comparative analysis should be done considering that the operation time was revised and shortened.

PROFESSIONAL ISSUES IN THE USE
OF INTELLIGENCE TESTS IN JAPAN

Concerning the educational use of psychological tests in Japan, especially intelligence tests, we have experienced some difficultly. In 1979, the Education for All Handicapped Children Act came into effect. On the one hand, in the U.S. the educational measures for children with first-degree disabilities, especially with learning disabilities, were rapidly provided and disseminated, while in Japan attention was focused mostly on support for the very disabled. Special education in the required curriculum was limited to children with second-degree and heavier disabilities, which limited the rate of school attendance of these children to 1.3% of the total number of students. Under such conditions, psychological tests were mainly used in medical clinics, and schools showed adverse attitudes toward the tests.

Sakamoto, I. (1959). *Shin Kyoiku Kihon Goi* (New basic vocabulary in education). Tokyo, Japan: Gakugei-tosho.

Statistics Bureau of the Management and Coordination Agency (1992). *Population census of Japan.* Tokyo, Japan: Japan Statistical Association.

Wechsler, D. (1991). *Wechsler Intelligence Scale for Children—Third Edition.* San Antonio, TX: The Psychological Corporation.

Wechsler, D. (1998). *Wechsler Intelligence Scale for Children—Third Edition; Japanese Edition.* (H. Azuma, K. Ueno, K. Fujita *et al.*, Trans.). Tokyo, Japan: Nihon Bunka Kagakusha. (Original work published in 1991.)

15

SOUTH KOREA

KEUMJOO KWAK

Department of Psychology
Seoul National University
Seoul, South Korea

The Korean version (K-WISC) of the original Wechsler Intelligence Scale for Children (WISC) was initially standardized in 1974. The Korean Wechsler Intelligence Scale for Children-Revised (KEDI-WISC) was standardized in 1991 and has been used for assessing the intelligence of children of ages 5 through 15, instead of 6 through 16 as in the original version. This was created because the Wechsler Preschool and Primary Scale of Intelligence (WPPSI), which is for younger children, was not yet developed in Korea. Since the Korean WPPSI for children ages 3 through 7 was published in 1996 by Choi, Kwak, & Park, it became necessary to readjust the lowest age limit of the WISC to 6 and to extend it to 16. Therefore, in the case of K-WISC-III, the ages were readjusted back to 6 through 16 and the items were selected in order to reflect the original items. Nonetheless some items necessarily had to be corrected or substituted to suit the Korean-speaking children and the order of items was also somewhat changed due to the cultural differences. In the case of pictorial materials, the race of persons depicted was changed into Asian and any English word presented in the background was replaced with the equivalent Korean word. The translation of the test material, the pilot study, and the standardization of the Korean WISC-III began in 1998, publishing in 2001 by Kwak, Choi, and Kim (Wechsler, 2001).

ADAPTATION PROCESS

Three psychologists who received their training in the U.S. together with five research assistants translated the manual and the items of the WISC-III into Korean. The next step was a back-translation into Korean. The third step was to correct the items, discrepant from the original English.

In order to construct the materials for the standardization, a pilot study (Kwak, Choi, & Kim, 2001) was conducted with 220 children ages 6–16. In the process of translating the WISC-III into Korean, due to differences between the two cultures and the characteristics of the pilot group, some of the WISC-III items were corrected and other Korean items were substituted for the U.S. items. For example, some U.S. Vocabulary items with high order of difficulty were at a lower level of difficulty in Korean language, and some Arithmetic items with high level of difficulty were at a lower level in the Korean pilot study. As mentioned before, additional items were constructed and added in the pilot study. Items were added to the Verbal subtests, sensitive to Korean cultural characteristics, as well as some items from the K-WPPSI (Choi *et al.,* 1996), KEDI-WISC (KEDI, 1991), and K-WAIS (Division of Clinical Psychology of KPA, 1990). A total of 56 items were added; 1 to Picture Arrangement, 12 to Information, 8 to Similarities, 16 to Arithmetic, 12 to Vocabulary, and 7 to Comprehension. According to the pilot study, the final items were selected for the standardization study. The bases for the selection were: (1) to include as many items as possible from the U.S. WISC-III, (2) to exclude those items with low internal-consistency, items with point biserial correlations with the total subtests scores less than 0.30, and (3) to select items with level of difficulty across the age groups. The decisions regarding which items would be included in the final questionnaire for the standardization were contingent on their fulfilling these three criteria.

The selected items based on the pilot study above were used in the standardization study. In Picture Completion, the order of items was switched in the K-WISC-III from the original ordering of WISC-III. The rearrangement was made considering the level of difficulty according to the age, whereby two-thirds of the items were presented in a different order of difficulty. Moreover among the pictures, the labels on the cans in the picture of a "supermarket" were all switched from English to Korean to increase familiarity with the children. Besides somewhat modifying the faces of the characters in the pictures to make them look more Asian, the pictures of the original material were used without modifications.

In Information, the order of the presentation was also changed and the original items were either excluded, substituted, or modified. For example, in items 6 "coins," could not be used because of the difference in Korean currency system. Item 29 also sounded rather unfamiliar and distant for Korean children, so the cities were substituted with Seoul and Tokyo. In Similarities, almost the same items were used with some modification in the order. Picture Arrangement and Block Design were used with only a little modification in order of difficulty; the order of five items and one item, was changed. In Vocabulary and Comprehension, the order of presentation was changed and four items and three items were substituted with other items. This modification was necessary since those items were found to have no discriminatory validity in the pilot study due to the changes in the meaning that occurred in the process of translating them into Korean. In Arithmetic, the items were modified because of differences in the unit of currency (in Korea, it is "won"), whereby adjustments were made according to the Korean currency. The order of presentation was also changed. In addition, since many items were relatively easy for Korean high school students, they were replaced with somewhat more difficult problems based on the pilot study. Hence, in the process of modification, the same number of items was maintained, while the total subtest score was changed to 33, instead of 30.

Compared to the Verbal Subtests, the Performance Subtests were used with relatively few modifications in the items and in their ordering. Therefore, items in Coding, Object Assembly, Symbol Search, and Mazes were identical from those in the original material. Modification was made only with Digit Span, where children had difficulty in understanding the task in Digits Forward. A sample item (8-2) was also added and in the case of the second item (3-8-6), because these numbers hold a special cultural meaning to Korean children, it was changed to 3-7-6.

SAMPLE CHARACTERISTICS

Since Korea is a homogeneous country in terms of ethnicity, the ethnic composition of the sample was not a significant factor in the standardization process. A stratified sampling frame based on the 1995 population census of Korea separated the geographical areas into 8 regional sectors. The number of children sampled from these sectors were: Seoul ($n = 524$), Busan ($n = 207$), Taegu ($n = 128$), Kyunggi-do ($n = 486$), Jeolla-do ($n = 259$), Choongchung-do ($n = 230$), Kangwon-do ($n = 92$), and Kyungsang-do ($n = 300$), for a total of $n = 2231$ children, ages 6–16. In the pilot study, it was found that the intelligence of the child was significantly related to the level of the parents' education, especially that of the mother. IQ scores of children were found to differ according to the mother's education ($F = 7.82$, $p < 0.01$). The mean score of children's IQ was 83.86 ($SD = 11.38$), 90.65 ($SD = 11.70$), 100.08 ($SD = 14.53$), and 107.80 ($SD = 13.31$), according to the level of mother's education: below 6 years, 7–9 years, 10–12 years, 13–17 years, and above 18 years, respectively.

Table 15.1 shows the distribution of children, included in the standardization according to their age and geographical regions. In the pilot study, it was found that the intelligence of the child was significantly related to the level of the parents' education, especially that of the mother. Therefore, the mother's educational background was divided into two, and the sample was obtained from two groups of children, i.e., below 12 years and 13 or above and the stratified sample was obtained according to the level of the education of the mother. The Frequency of the distribution according to the parents' education level is presented on Table 15.2. Table 15.3

TABLE 15.1   Demographic Characteristics of the Standardization Sample: Percentages by Age and Region

Age	N	Seoul	Busan	Taegu	Kyunggi	Jeolla	Choongchung	Kangwon	Kyungsang
6	208	21.0	8.3	5.4	26.3	10.2	11.2	3.9	13.7
7	202	24.7	9.9	6.4	19.3	12.4	10.4	4.0	12.9
8	207	25.1	8.2	5.8	22.2	11.1	10.1	3.8	13.5
9	203	22.7	10.8	5.4	22.2	11.8	10.3	3.5	13.3
10	199	22.6	9.6	5.0	23.1	12.1	10.5	4.0	13.1
11	198	23.4	10.2	6.6	20.8	11.2	10.1	4.0	13.7
12	197	22.8	9.1	6.1	20.8	13.2	10.7	4.6	12.7
13	206	24.4	10.2	5.9	21.0	11.2	10.2	3.9	13.2
14	208	25.0	8.2	4.8	20.2	11.5	10.6	4.8	14.9
15	202	24.3	8.9	5.9	20.8	11.4	9.9	5.0	13.8
16	201	22.9	9.0	6.0	23.4	11.9	9.4	4.0	13.4
Total	2231	23.6	9.3	5.8	21.8	11.6	10.3	4.1	13.5

TABLE 15.2   Demographic Characteristics of the Standardization Sample: Percentages by Parent Education Level

Parent education level	Father		Mother	
	Frequency	Percent	Frequency	Percent
6	28	1.25	30	1.34
9	90	4.03	141	6.32
12	999	44.78	1504	67.41
13–15	11	0.49	7	0.32
16	773	34.65	463	20.75
18	99	4.44	31	1.39
Total	2231	100	2231	100
Missing	231	10.36	55	2.47

is the distribution of gender and age of the children according to the two levels of education of the mothers. Table 15.4 shows the distribution of parents' occupation.

RELIABILITY

Table 15.5 shows the mean (across age) split-half reliability coefficients and standard errors of measurement for the subtests, IQ, and index scores by age and overall. The average reliability was $r = 0.89$ for Verbal Comprehension Index (VCI), $r = 0.80$ for Perceptual Organization Index (POI), and $r = 0.78$ for Freedom from Distractibility Index (FDI), with Processing Speed Index (PSI) showing relatively low reliability of $r = 0.51$. The reliability coefficient of $r = 0.90$ was

TABLE 15.3 Demographic Characteristics of the Standardization Sample: Percentages by Age and Mother's Education Level

		Boy		Girl		
		6–12	Above 13	6–12	Above 13	Total
Age	N	%	%	%	%	%
6	208	37.8	13.4	38.8	10.0	100.0
7	202	38.9	11.9	38.3	10.9	100.0
8	207	37.9	10.6	36.9	14.6	100.0
9	203	39.7	11.8	36.6	11.8	100.0
10	199	38.3	7.3	41.4	13.0	100.0
11	198	39.9	10.9	36.3	12.9	100.0
12	197	36.2	14.0	37.8	11.9	100.0
13	206	37.6	11.2	41.0	10.2	100.0
14	208	40.0	10.3	38.0	11.7	100.0
15	202	37.5	12.0	38.5	12.0	100.0
16	201	41.7	9.5	37.2	11.6	100.0
Total	2231	38.7	11.2	38.3	11.8	100.0

TABLE 15.4 Demographic Characteristics of the Standardization Sample: Percentages by Parent Job

	Father		Mother	
	Frequency	Percent	Frequency	Percent
Skilled professional	228	10.22	88	3.94
Administrative/managerial	175	7.84	42	1.88
Office worker	464	20.80	138	6.19
Sales/retail	242	10.85	192	8.60
Services	183	8.20	200	8.97
Farming/fishing/forestry	35	1.57	11	0.49
Production/manufacturing	142	6.36	39	1.75
Transportation/distribution	105	4.70	0	0
Simple manual labor	30	1.34	6	0.27
Others	466	20.90	1376	61.68
Missing	161	7.22	139	6.23
Total	2231	100	2231	100

found for Verbal IQ (VIQ), $r = 0.60$ for Performance IQ (PIQ), and $r = 0.79$ for Full Scale IQ (FSIQ).

The test-retest reliability was based on a sample of $n = 121$ children, ages from 6–9 ($n = 63$), 10–13 ($n = 27$), 14–16 ($n = 31$), and the time of the test-retest varied from 8–119 days with the mean of 24 days. The results are presented in Table 15.6. For the overall sample, the reliabilities ranged from $r = 0.91$ for VIQ and PIQ to $r = 0.93$ for FSIQ. The index scores ranged from $r = 0.88$ for PSI to $r = 0.91$ for

TABLE 15.5 Reliability Coefficients and Standard Errors of Measurement of the Subtests Scaled Scores, IQ Scores, and Index Scores, by Age

					Age in years							
Subtest/scale	6	7	8	9	10	11	12	13	14	15	16	Average
Information	0.58	0.74	0.74	0.82	0.81	0.87	0.87	0.87	0.85	0.87	0.80	0.81
(SEm)	1.95	1.54	1.54	1.28	1.30	1.08	1.07	1.09	1.17	1.07	1.33	1.34
Similarities	0.66	0.69	0.71	0.67	0.76	0.79	0.79	0.76	0.75	0.72	0.62	0.72
(SEm)	1.76	1.68	1.60	1.72	1.46	1.38	1.38	1.46	1.49	1.60	1.85	1.59
Arithmetic	0.68	0.69	0.71	0.75	0.76	0.78	0.76	0.80	0.73	0.79	0.69	0.74
(SEm)	1.69	1.67	1.63	1.51	1.48	1.40	1.46	1.36	1.55	1.38	1.67	1.53
Vocabulary	0.61	0.74	0.82	0.87	0.85	0.87	0.87	0.86	0.84	0.82	0.81	0.82
(SEm)	1.88	1.54	1.26	1.10	1.16	1.09	1.09	1.13	1.21	1.27	1.31	1.30
Comprehension	0.72	0.74	0.72	0.73	0.68	0.74	0.71	0.74	0.81	0.66	0.68	0.72
(SEm)	1.58	1.54	1.59	1.56	1.70	1.52	1.61	1.53	1.31	1.75	1.70	1.59
Digit span	0.67	0.69	0.70	0.76	0.79	0.83	0.79	0.80	0.81	0.78	0.76	0.77
(SEm)	1.71	1.66	1.64	1.45	1.36	1.24	1.39	1.33	1.32	1.40	1.46	1.46
Picture completion	0.74	0.72	0.73	0.72	0.64	0.74	0.69	0.64	0.68	0.69	0.64	0.70
(SEm)	1.52	1.60	1.55	1.58	1.81	1.53	1.68	1.79	1.70	1.66	1.79	1.66
Coding	—	0.91	0.82	0.86	0.92	0.87	—	—	0.83	0.91	—	0.79
(SEm)	—	0.90	1.26	1.14	0.87	1.10	—	—	1.24	0.91	—	1.40
Picture arrangement	0.63	0.68	0.71	0.68	0.66	0.68	0.63	0.66	0.70	0.69	0.65	0.67
(SEm)	1.84	1.70	1.61	1.69	1.74	1.71	1.83	1.75	1.64	1.66	1.79	1.72
Block design	0.79	0.81	0.81	0.82	0.80	0.74	0.76	0.74	0.71	0.77	0.68	0.77
(SEm)	1.39	1.32	1.31	1.26	1.35	1.54	1.47	1.52	1.62	1.45	1.70	1.45
Object assembly	0.61	0.62	0.53	0.52	0.53	0.48	0.53	0.52	0.54	0.58	0.62	0.56
(SEm)	1.88	1.86	2.06	2.08	2.05	2.16	2.05	2.08	2.05	1.93	1.84	2.00

Symbol search	—	0.91	0.77	0.86	0.86	0.91	—	—	0.80	0.73	—	0.74
(SEm)	—	0.91	1.45	1.13	1.12	0.90	—	—	1.34	1.55	—	1.55
Mazes	0.65	0.72	0.59	0.58	0.63	0.58	0.52	0.52	0.53	0.54	0.48	0.58
(SEm)	1.78	1.60	1.91	1.95	1.82	1.94	2.07	2.07	2.06	2.02	2.16	1.95
Verbal IQ	0.86	0.89	0.91	0.92	0.93	0.94	0.94	0.94	0.93	0.93	0.90	0.92
(SEm)	5.66	4.89	4.43	4.13	4.05	3.67	3.68	3.63	3.93	3.94	4.77	4.30
Performance IQ	0.72	0.75	0.77	0.73	0.71	0.65	0.63	0.62	0.63	0.66	0.60	0.68
(SEm)	7.98	7.47	7.14	7.83	8.01	8.91	9.17	9.27	9.18	8.72	9.55	8.51
Full scale IQ	0.80	0.84	0.86	0.85	0.86	0.86	0.85	0.85	0.84	0.85	0.79	0.84
(SEm)	6.77	6.05	5.64	5.77	5.67	5.71	5.78	5.87	6.09	5.78	6.91	6.02
Verbal comp. index	0.84	0.88	0.90	0.92	0.92	0.93	0.93	0.94	0.92	0.92	0.89	0.91
(SEm)	5.93	5.15	4.65	4.34	4.28	3.91	3.84	3.81	4.12	4.18	4.96	4.51
Percept. organ. index	0.82	0.83	0.85	0.84	0.83	0.81	0.81	0.81	0.82	0.84	0.80	0.82
(SEm)	6.30	6.20	5.87	6.06	6.14	6.52	6.49	6.46	6.32	6.03	6.79	6.29
Freed. distract. index	0.75	0.77	0.75	0.79	0.83	0.86	0.83	0.85	0.84	0.85	0.78	0.81
(SEm)	7.48	7.27	7.44	6.85	6.17	5.55	6.22	5.75	6.09	5.90	7.10	6.57
Process. speed index	0.55	0.53	0.48	0.60	0.59	0.65	0.48	0.48	0.53	0.42	0.26	0.51
(SEm)	1.05	1.25	1.84	9.47	9.64	8.87	1.83	1.79	1.32	11.42	12.92	10.54

Data from Kwak, Choi, & Kim (Wechsler, 2001).

TABLE 15.6   Stability Coefficients of the Subtests, IQ Scales and Factor-Based Scales by Age

	6–9 (n = 63)	10–13 (n = 27)	14–16 (n = 31)
Information	0.81	0.90	0.76
Similarities	0.72	0.81	0.59
Arithmetic	0.74	0.66	0.70
Vocabulary	0.78	0.76	0.79
Comprehension	0.69	0.73	0.64
Digit span	0.73	0.73	0.81
Picture completion	0.70	0.90	0.79
Coding	0.75	0.87	0.81
Picture arrangement	0.53	0.49	0.54
Block design	0.83	0.76	0.71
Object assembly	0.66	0.77	0.55
Symbol search	0.71	0.84	0.55
Mazes	0.43	0.54	0.40
Verbal IQ	0.87	0.85	0.77
Performance IQ	0.84	0.86	0.83
Full scale IQ	0.86	0.88	0.84
Verbal comp. index	0.85	0.87	0.81
Percept. organ. index	0.81	0.86	0.80
Freedom distract. index	0.82	0.67	0.76
Processing speed index	0.78	0.87	0.75

Data from Kwak, Choi, & Kim (Wechsler, 2001).

VCI. The retest correlations for the subtests ranged from $r = 0.60$ for Mazes to $r = 0.90$ for Information.

Interscorer reliability was assessed for the Similarities, Vocabulary, Comprehension, and Mazes subtests. Sixty protocols were randomly selected from the sample (20 from each group: 6–8, 9–12, and 13–16 years). Two scorers independently scored all four subtests for all 60 cases. Interscorer reliabilities were $r = 0.92$ for Similarity, $r = 0.91$ for Vocabulary, $r = 0.93$ for Comprehension, and $r = 0.92$ for Mazes. These results indicated that those subtests that require scorer judgment were scored very reliably.

EVIDENCE OF VALIDITY

The intercorrelations of subtest scaled scores are presented in Table 15.7. The tables presented in other chapters compare the differences between the countries. The factor analysis of the subtests using the maximum-likelihood method of extraction with iterated communalities, followed by a Varimax rotation resulted in four factors (Table 15.8). The same factor structure was found as in the U.S.

The results of relationships of the K-WISC-III and other intelligence scales provide evidence of the convergence and discriminant validity of the K-WISC-III.

TABLE 15.7 Intercorrelation of Subtest Scaled Scores

Subtest/scale	Inf	Sim	Ari	Voc	Com	DS	PCom	Cd	PA	BD	OA	SS	Mz
Information													
Similarities	0.50												
Arithmetic	0.52	0.39											
Vocabulary	0.61	0.56	0.44										
Comprehension	0.48	0.50	0.38	0.59									
Digit span	0.35	0.30	0.39	0.37	0.29								
Picture completion	0.40	0.35	0.28	0.38	0.33	0.25							
Coding	0.20	0.23	0.23	0.23	0.24	0.24	0.17						
Picture arrangement	0.33	0.29	0.30	0.32	0.29	0.17	0.37	0.21					
Block design	0.33	0.29	0.39	0.32	0.26	0.27	0.36	0.20	0.31				
Object assembly	0.29	0.26	0.27	0.27	0.25	0.21	0.38	0.16	0.33	0.50			
Symbol search	0.22	0.20	0.23	0.23	0.21	0.19	0.22	0.44	0.26	0.24	0.20		
Mazes	0.17	0.12	0.22	0.14	0.10	0.16	0.20	0.13	0.19	0.28	0.21	0.18	

Data from Kwak, Choi, & Kim (Wechsler, 2001).

Evidence of convergent validity is demonstrated by high correlations between the K-WISC-III, KEDI-WISC, K-WPPSI, K-WAIS, and Kaufman Assesment Battery for Children (K-ABC). The correlations of VIQ and FSIQ scores between K-WISC-III and KEDI-WISC were 0.86 and 0.82, respectively.

The correlations of VIQ and FSIQ scores between K-WISC-III and K-WPPSI obtained from children ages 6 and 7 were 0.71 and 0.70, respectively, and the correlations of VIQ scores between K-WISC-III and K-WAIS obtained from children age 16 were 0.71. According to the result, it can be seen that correlations are higher between the scales in VIQ compared to PIQ.

The K-WISC-III was administered to special groups of children (gifted, learning disabled; LD, and attention deficit hyperactivity disorder; ADHD). In the case of 61 gifted children, the mean FSIQ was 130.6, with higher scores on VIQ (131.9) compared to PIQ (129.3). The mean FSIQ of 46 LD children was 91.7, with higher scores on PIQ (95.2) than on VIQ (90.5). They had a relatively low FDI score of 87.2. For the group of 31 children diagnosed in the child psychiatric hospital as ADHD, their FSIQ was found to be 86.3, with low PSI (84.3) and FDI scores (86.3).

Among the data obtained on K-WISC-III from clinical groups, the results of the comparison between the normal children and those with reading disabilities are the following. Results on the K-WISC-III Full Scale score and the result of reading ability test were the dependent variables. The VIQ score was lower than Performance in the reading disability group as compared to the normal group. Compared to the normal group, the reading disability group demonstrated significantly poorer performance on the subtests Information, Similarities, and Digit Span but did significantly better on Symbol Search. The reading disability group also demonstrated significantly worse performance on VCI and FDI, but did significantly better on PSI (Park, Lee, & Kwak, 2002).

TABLE 15.8 Maximum-Likelihood Factor Loadings (Varimax Rotation) for Four Factors

Subtest/scale	Factor 1: Verbal comprehension				Factor 2: Perceptual organization				Factor 3: Freedom from distractibility				Factor 4: Processing speed			
	Ages				Ages				Ages				Ages			
	6–7	8–10	11–13	14–16	6–7	8–10	11–13	14–16	6–7	8–10	11–13	14–16	6–7	8–10	11–13	14–16
Information	0.55	0.66	0.69	0.67	0.08	0.27	0.30	0.24	0.34	0.23	0.30	0.25	0.17	0.13	0.05	0.03
Similarities	0.54	0.61	0.72	0.64	0.23	0.17	0.15	0.23	0.17	0.14	0.12	0.08	0.12	0.08	0.16	0.15
Vocabulary	0.73	0.79	0.80	0.82	0.19	0.14	0.20	0.15	0.14	0.24	0.16	0.10	0.14	0.06	0.13	0.16
Comprehension	0.66	0.64	0.68	0.67	0.06	0.14	0.16	0.21	0.12	0.13	0.11	0.10	0.13	0.19	0.20	0.10
Picture completion	0.40	0.34	0.42	0.28	0.35	0.35	0.45	0.55	0.10	0.39	0.03	0.01	0.24	0.09	0.05	0.07
Picture arrangement	0.16	0.17	0.36	0.29	0.18	0.23	0.45	0.54	0.16	0.56	0.11	0.11	0.41	0.12	0.15	0.10
Block design	0.20	0.27	0.16	0.17	0.72	0.75	0.58	0.56	0.21	0.15	0.27	0.16	0.08	0.10	0.16	0.18
Object assembly	0.14	0.21	0.20	0.13	0.68	0.58	0.67	0.71	0.00	0.21	0.03	0.08	0.16	0.11	0.05	0.07
Mazes	0.07	0.11	0.02	0.05	0.42	0.30	0.29	0.24	0.12	0.17	0.24	0.13	0.20	0.12	0.03	0.17
Arithmetic	0.27	0.51	0.40	0.36	0.14	0.39	0.21	0.26	0.66	0.06	0.79	0.89	0.19	0.18	0.08	0.12
Digit span	0.26	0.42	0.37	0.34	0.18	0.26	0.13	0.16	0.36	0.01	0.30	0.23	0.20	0.15	0.15	0.26
Coding	0.08	0.21	0.17	0.12	0.14	0.12	0.00	0.04	0.08	0.07	0.03	0.07	0.66	0.97	0.90	0.73
Symbol search	0.20	0.17	0.15	0.10	0.12	0.28	0.22	0.18	0.12	0.23	0.09	0.02	0.52	0.43	0.53	0.46

Data from Kwak, Choi, & Kim (Wechsler, 2001).

The standardization study of K-WISC-III was conducted in December of 2001. Hence, while not many studies have been conducted using this test, many studies are expected to be conducted in the future on both normal and special children according to various diagnostic classifications.

CULTURAL ISSUES INFLUENCING WISC-III INTERPRETATIONS IN KOREA

Korea is a peninsula of about 10,000,000 km^2, located between Japan and China with a 5000-year history and a homogeneous population of 50 million people. The Gross National Product (GNP) in 1995 was $10,060, which was significantly less than that of Japan or U.S. However, since 1980 the GNP rate has been dramatically increased, and there is a high prospect of gaining first-nation status soon. According to the distribution of the level of education of the general population during the last 20 years, the ratio of the population with low-level education (i.e., below the completion of elementary education) has noticeably decreased, while population with higher educational background has been steadily increasing. The ratio in the population of below level elementary school education was 73.4% in 1970, but dropped to 27.6% by 1995. In contrast, the ratio of the population with higher education was 10.2% in 1970, but it has climbed to 37.5% by 1995 and above the level of completion of college education rose from 4.9% in 1970 to 19.1% by 1995. The ratio of population with higher education in 1995 was approximately 56.6%, which is about half of the adult population above the age of 25. This phenomenon reflects the development and movement of Korean society into a well-educated society. It is widely acknowledged that Korean parents are especially concerned about sending their children to universities with good reputations.

According to the recent national survey, parents' motivation to provide at least a college-level of education for their children varies greatly depending on the gender of the child and educational background of the head of the household. However, as a whole, "building character and becoming cultured" was most highly valued, followed by "getting a good job." In the case of males, "getting a good job" was valued, whereas "advantage in marriage selection, fostering of interests and skills" was the most important goal of achieving college education for females. Therefore, it could be explained that Korean parents still apparently have a biased attitude toward to the sex of their children.

Korean was officially recognized as the national language about 600 years ago, using its own identical language. Although English is taught from elementary school, they use Korean most of the time. The sentence structure of Korean is the reverse of English, and is seen as a unique language and clearly distinguished from the Japanese, Chinese, or any other Asian language. The nation, as a whole, is divided into several provinces (e.g., Kyunggi, Kyungsang, and Jeolla), and while local dialects do exist, the differences between them are not great. Moreover, since the standard Korean language is taught in schools, the Korean people as a whole do not have any difficulty or problem in communication in terms of misunderstanding from accent, intonation, slang, etc.

Therefore, if the IQ test has to be administered to a Korean child who is, recently immigrated to another country, he or she must be tested by a Korean tester with the Korean version of WISC-III in order to avoid the difficulty with language skill. On the other hand, using Korean WISC on these Korean children who were born and raised in a foreign country is highly discouraged. Especially in the Verbal test, the items in subtests, such as Vocabulary, Information, and Comprehension, which include proficiency in Korean, may measure Korean language skills of the child, rather than cognitive ability. As mentioned before, the Verbal subtests underwent more modification than Performance subtests in developing the Korean WISC-III, because they were more sensitive to cultural differences than Performance subtests.

For the Digit Span task, the names of numbers in Korean are one syllable. Therefore, it is questionable to expect a clear insightful investigation from the performance on this task as it varies from one country to another according to the length of the name of numbers.

The Korean education system is divided into 4 parts; elementary, middle, high school, and university, lasting 6, 3, 3, and 4 years, respectively. Presently, only elementary and middle schools are compulsory, funded by the government, while kindergarten is not yet compulsory. Since 1969, students are not required to take any test to be admitted into middle school; hence rate of admittance is reflective of the desire to pursue education. In 1970, the rate of entry into middle school was 63.2%, which gradually increased up to 98.7% in 1996. The entry into university from high school was 33.9% in 1970, 43.0% in 1980, 43.3% in 1990, and 78.9% in 1996, showing the greatest increase since 1995. In addition, there has been great interest in pursuing good college education because of the problems invading social issues for the last few decades.

There are about 5000 elementary schools, 2700 middle schools, and 2000 high schools in Korea. Although both public and private schools exist, there is no noticeable difference in curriculum. Nevertheless some variances may exist according to the policies of the Local Educational Authority (LEA). However, the differences do not have much influence on the curriculum and the contents of education between public and private school in terms of the level of schools. Most children are assigned to the school closest to their homes. There are a small number of schools with high academic achievement in the areas where families have a higher socioeconomic level. The tendency for people to move into areas where affluent families with higher educational aims are concentrated has become a significant social problem, along with the upsurge of expansive private lessons from private institutes around the area. There are criticisms that disparities exist between "privileged" students who have always had access to those private institutes versus those who have not, although there is not enough scientific evidence to support such criticisms. Therefore, these factors were considered in sampling for the standardization study, whereby some of the students from higher socioeconomic levels in the Seoul area were included in the standardized sample of the K-WISC-III.

The government plan to initiate the development of special education and special schools has not been realized yet, but many private organizations and institutes have been providing special education for gifted children. Unfortunately, however, due to the educational fever of the Korean parents, children are sent to these institutes at an extremely young age. Hence, the Wechsler IQ test is often administered in these kinds of institutes and in some rare cases, and parents have known how to train their child before taking the test.

In Korea, there is no psychologist assigned to each school, one must visit private institutes, such as consulting offices or clinics, in order to be given an intelligence test. Recently college-based research centers have attempted to administer these kinds of tests to children.

PROFESSIONAL ISSUES IN THE USE OF INTELLIGENCE TESTS IN KOREA

Compared to the Western countries, a relatively small number of tests have been standardized based on nationwide samples in South Korea. The Korean WISC-III has undergone rigorous adaptation and standardization with a representative sample. As the author of K-WPPSI standardized in 1996 and the present K-WISC-III, I have made the utmost effort in following the original construction process of the test material in order to develop the right instructions for the Korean version of the tests. The WISC has been used more often in clinical settings than in educational settings. However, not only clinical settings use it as a basic testing tool but also special schools use it with the same purpose. Therefore, all developmental, clinical, and counseling psychology majors must become familiar with the WISC test. However, since it is true that this test is also being administered by those not necessarily trained in psychology, guidelines for its use are necessary.

In Korea, it is difficult to follow the addressed law that only psychologists must administer psychological tests. While most psychological tests are indeed administered by psychologists, it is not the case for psychological tests for children. Since there are comparatively more education majors, including child welfare and special education, than psychology majors, they do in fact administer many child psychological tests. Therefore, education majors may not necessarily have sufficient background knowledge and training with psychological tests, and they may need to receive the appropriate training. This is especially true for tests that require professional training such as WISC.

For this purpose, the developers of this test, including myself, have held regular workshops for WISC, training people on the contents of the test material, administration and scoring, and interpretation of the results, as well as issuing a license. While such a licensing policy has no actual legal bearing, our workshop has provided much needed information and training to professionals, thereby earning a high reputation for its usefulness.

Recently, the Korean government attempted many new policies concerning the development of programs for gifted and talented children. Hence, the K-WISC-III is expected to be widely used for diagnosing such children. The Korean Psychological Association has 11 divisions and 7 committees and The Committee on Psychological Testing is one of the representative committees. Although its purpose is assisting with the development and use of psychological tests, it has been somewhat inactive. It has, however, published as a book titled *Standards for Psychological Testing in Korea* (1998), which outlines the various issues to be considered in test development and ethical guidelines in the sales and administration of psychological tests. Since the Committee on Psychological Testing has been established for only a few years, many efforts can be expected in the future. Meanwhile, although ethical guidelines concerning development and administration of psychological tests have been outlined, they have not been strictly enforced in Korea.

Among the 11 divisions under the Korean Psychological Association, the clinical, counseling, and developmental psychology sections issue licenses pertaining to psychological test administration and treatment. However, such licensing does not have any legal bearing, whereby even psychology-related majors can also administer tests merely after receiving some sort of training. Nonetheless, to the best of my knowledge, while the license issued by the Korean Psychological Association does not hold much legal significance, people are becoming aware of the need for licensed professionals with more specialized training.

In the case of the Korean WPPSI and WISC, the developers hold regular workshops on the test administration and interpretations and it is presently recognized as being the most effective training program. As a matter of fact, the developers are the members of The Committee on Psychological testing of Korean Psychological Association.

REFERENCES

Division of Clinical Psychology of KPA (1990). *Manual for Korean WAIS*. Seoul: Korean Guidance.

Korean Education Development Institute (1991). *Manual for KEDI-WISC*. Seoul: Special Education Publishers.

Korean Psychology Association (1998). *Standards for Psychological Testing*. Seoul: Jungangjuksung.

Kwak, K., Choi, P. H., & Kim, C. (2001). The standardization study for Korean–Wechsler Intelligence Scale for Children–III: Pilot Study. *The Korean Journal of Developmental Psychology, 14(3)*, 43–59.

Choi, P. H., Kwak, K., Park, K. (1996).*Manual for Korean–Wechsler Preschool and Primary Scale of Intelligence*. Seoul.

Park, S., Lee, C., & Kwak, K. (2002). Cognitive characteristic of 4th, 5th, 6th grade children with reading disability reflected in K-WISC-III. *The Korean Journal of Developmental Psychology, 14(4)*, 37–54.

Wechsler, D. (2001). *Korean–Wechsler Intelligence Scale for Children-III* (K. Kwak, P. H. Choi, & C. Kim, Trans.). Seoul, Korea: Special Education Publishers. (Original work published in 1991.)

16

TAIWAN

HSIN-YI CHEN

Department of Special Education
National Taiwan Normal University
Taipei Taiwan, ROC

YUNG-HWA CHEN

The Chinese Behavior Science
Corporation
Taipei, Taiwan

JIANJUN ZHU

The Psychological Corporation
San Antonio, Texas

After 3 years of translation and adaptation by Dr. Yung-Hua Chen and his staff at the Chinese Behavioral Science Corporation, the Taiwan Version of the Wechsler Intelligence Scale for Children—Third Edition (WISC-III) was published in 1997 (Wechsler, 1997). It is considered important to establish local norms of this well-recognized individualized intelligence test, and thus make the testing result meaningful for Taiwan users. Since publication of the Taiwan version of the WISC-III, psychologists and educators in Taiwan have been administering it in several critical decision-making areas such as determining IQs for exceptional children, and analyzing intra-individual differences in schools and clinical diagnoses.

ADAPTATION PROCESS

Considering the remarkable quality of the American WISC-III, the primary principle of the Taiwan research team was to maintain the original constructs and

Culture and Children's Intelligence:
Cross-Cultural Analysis of the WISC-III
241

TABLE 16.1 Number of Items Revised on the WISC-III Taiwan Version as Compared to U.S. Items

Subtests	U.S. test No. of items	No. of revised items	Revised items
Verbal subtests			
Information	30	3	No. 7, 22, 29
Similarities	19	0	
Arithmetic	24	6	No. 9, 15, 17, 18, 21, 23
Vocabulary	30	15	No. 15~30
Comprehension	18	1	No. 17
Digit span	15	0	—
Performance subtests			
Picture completion	30	0	—
Coding (A)	59	0	—
Coding (B)	119	0	—
Picture arrangement	14	1	No. 1
Block design	12	0	—
Object assembly	5	0	—
Symbol search (A)	45	0	—
Symbol search (B)	60	0	—
Mazes	10	0	—

to revise items only with significant cultural bias. In order to target culturally biased items, a panel of experienced examiners and professionals reviewed each of the U.S. items. They recommended that items in the subtests Digit Span, Similarities, and almost all Performance subtests could remain the same. However, revisions in various degrees were necessary for Verbal subtests such as Vocabulary, Information, Arithmetic and Comprehension. Subsequently, both new and adaptations of U.S. items were tested in a pilot study with a sample of 564 children, ages 6–16. Both item difficulty and item discrimination were examined through reviewing item p values, item-total correlations, and item-fit statistics, and the final item set was selected and order of difficulty was determined based on these data.

Table 16.1 summarizes the number of revised items for each subtest. As shown in the table, the majority of changes were made on the Verbal subtests. Some changes were made because of cultural bias, for example, item 29 of the U.S. Information subtest. Considering that Taiwan children are not as familiar with the distance between these cities as America children are, this item was changed to, "How far is it from Taipei to Singapore?" Another example, item 9 of the Arithmetic subtest was changed from "penny" to "dollars" to make this item more meaningful for Taiwan children.

TABLE 16.2 Demographic Characteristics of the Standardization Sample: Percentages by Parent Education Level, and Region

Age	n	Parent education level[a]					Region			
		E1	E2	E3	E4	E5	North	Central	South	East
6	100	14.0	20.0	40.0	15.0	11.0	35.0	35.0	24.0	6.0
7	100	12.1	21.2	41.4	11.1	14.1	43.0	24.0	27.0	6.0
8	100	22.4	20.4	36.7	10.2	10.2	40.0	26.0	28.0	6.0
9	100	22.0	16.0	37.0	14.0	11.0	43.0	25.0	26.0	6.0
10	100	21.0	22.0	34.0	13.0	10.0	45.0	22.0	27.0	6.0
11	100	19.2	26.3	38.4	9.1	7.1	40.0	26.0	28.0	6.0
12	100	20.0	23.0	38.0	8.0	11.0	43.0	22.0	29.0	6.0
13	100	18.0	26.0	33.0	11.0	12.0	41.0	24.0	30.0	5.0
14	100	19.0	25.0	36.0	9.0	11.0	42.0	23.0	29.0	6.0
15	100	12.4	24.7	39.2	11.3	12.4	41.0	30.0	28.0	1.0
16	100	17.5	21.6	39.2	12.4	9.3	42.0	28.0	30.0	0.0
Total	1100	18.0	22.4	37.5	11.3	10.8	41.4	25.9	27.8	4.9
Taiwan population		19.3	22.5	35.8	12.3	10.1	42.9	24.8	29.5	2.9

[a]Parent education level: E1: elementary school or below; E2: junior high school; E3: senior high school; E4: 2-year college; and E5: 4-year college or above.

SAMPLE CHARACTERISTICS

The Taiwan norms were based on a standardization sample of 1100 children representative of the Taiwan population. The sample included 100 children in each of 11 age groups ranging from 6 through 16 years with 50 males and 50 females in each age group. The data gathered in 1990 by the Taiwan Bureau of the Census provided the basis for stratification according to two variables: parent education and geographic region. Since the correlation between education and intelligence is high, parent education is an important variable in determining a representative sample. Because less than 2% of the population is indigenous people, ethnic composition is not as significant an issue in Taiwan as in the U.S. Most of these indigenous people live in eastern Taiwan. The number of indigenous children tested, all from Eastern Taiwan, was 2.9%. Table 16.2 shows the demographic characteristics of the Taiwan WISC-III Standardization Sample. The percentages of children in the standardization sample match very closely the Taiwan population in terms of parent education and geographic region.

RELIABILITY

Table 16.3 shows the average (across age) split-half reliability coefficients and standard errors of measurement of the subtests, IQ, and index scores by age and

TABLE 16.3 Reliability Coefficients and Standard Errors of Measurement of the Subtests Scaled Scores, IQ Scores, and Index Scores, by Age[a]

	Age in years											
Subtest/scale	6	7	8	9	10	11	12	13	14	15	16	Average[c]
Information	0.71	0.88	0.82	0.77	0.80	0.84	0.90	0.84	0.91	0.70	0.84	0.83
(SEm)	1.62	1.04	1.27	1.44	1.34	1.20	0.95	1.20	0.90	1.64	1.20	1.28
Similarities	0.89	0.90	0.88	0.86	0.88	0.86	0.82	0.80	0.88	0.82	0.86	0.86
(SEm)	0.99	0.95	1.04	1.12	1.04	1.12	1.27	1.34	1.04	1.27	1.12	1.12
Arithmetic	0.75	0.80	0.80	0.71	0.80	0.84	0.87	0.84	0.85	0.59	0.57	0.78
(SEm)	1.50	1.34	1.34	1.62	1.34	1.20	1.08	1.20	1.16	1.92	1.97	1.45
Vocabulary	0.83	0.86	0.86	0.90	0.89	0.92	0.92	0.94	0.93	0.92	0.92	0.90
(SEm)	1.24	1.12	1.12	0.95	0.99	0.92	0.92	0.73	0.79	0.85	0.85	0.95
Comprehension	0.76	0.82	0.87	0.79	0.91	0.84	0.82	0.88	0.87	0.80	0.79	0.84
(SEm)	1.47	1.27	1.08	1.37	0.90	1.20	1.27	1.04	1.08	1.34	1.37	1.23
Digit span	0.85	0.84	0.89	0.83	0.83	0.88	0.84	0.92	0.92	0.75	0.88	0.86
(SEm)	1.16	1.20	0.99	1.24	1.24	1.04	1.20	0.85	0.85	1.50	1.04	1.13
Picture completion	0.77	0.82	0.82	0.73	0.78	0.67	0.72	0.72	0.83	0.79	0.78	0.77
(SEm)	1.44	1.27	1.27	1.56	1.41	1.72	1.59	1.59	1.24	1.37	1.41	1.45
Coding	—[b]	—[b]	—[b]	0.83	—[b]	—[b]	—[b]	0.84	—[b]	—[b]	—[b]	0.83
(SEm)				1.24				1.20				1.22
Picture arrangement	0.77	0.61	0.80	0.71	0.81	0.81	0.87	0.80	0.77	0.63	0.69	0.76
(SEm)	1.44	1.87	1.34	1.62	1.31	1.31	1.08	1.34	1.44	1.82	1.67	1.49
Block design	0.86	0.86	0.88	0.83	0.84	0.84	0.86	0.85	0.87	0.68	0.89	0.85
(SEm)	1.12	1.12	1.04	1.24	0.20	1.20	1.12	1.16	1.08	1.70	0.99	1.19
Object assembly	0.74	0.61	0.60	0.65	0.64	0.63	0.68	0.72	0.79	0.71	0.60	0.68
(SEm)	1.53	1.87	1.90	1.77	1.80	1.82	1.70	1.59	1.37	1.62	1.90	1.72
Symbol search	—[b]	—[b]	—[b]	0.80	—[b]	—[b]	—[b]	0.72	—[b]	—[b]	—[b]	0.80
(SEm)				1.34				1.59				1.46
Mazes	0.80	0.77	0.74	0.73	0.73	0.73	0.76	0.63	0.62	0.61	0.68	0.72
(SEm)	1.34	1.44	1.53	1.56	1.56	1.56	1.47	1.82	1.85	1.87	1.70	1.62

Verbal IQ	0.93	0.96	0.96	0.94	0.96	0.96	0.96	0.96	0.97	0.94	0.94	0.95
(SEm)	3.97	3.00	3.00	3.67	3.00	3.00	3.00	3.00	2.60	3.67	3.67	2.91
Performance IQ	0.92	0.89	0.91	0.89	0.91	0.90	0.91	0.92	0.92	0.91	0.92	0.91
(SEm)	4.24	4.97	4.50	4.97	4.50	4.74	4.50	4.24	4.24	4.50	4.24	4.52
Full scale IQ	0.95	0.96	0.97	0.95	0.96	0.96	0.96	0.97	0.97	0.96	0.96	0.96
(SEm)	3.35	3.00	2.60	3.35	3.00	3.00	3.00	2.60	2.60	3.00	3.00	2.97
Verbal comp. index	0.93	0.95	0.95	0.94	0.96	0.96	0.96	0.96	0.97	0.94	0.96	0.95
(SEm)	3.97	3.35	3.35	3.67	3.00	3.00	3.00	3.00	2.60	3.67	3.00	2.91
Percept. organ. index	0.91	0.87	0.90	0.88	0.91	0.89	0.91	0.91	0.92	0.89	0.90	0.90
(SEm)	4.50	5.41	4.74	5.20	4.50	4.97	4.50	4.50	4.24	4.97	4.04	4.70
Freed. distract. index	0.88	0.88	0.90	0.86	0.88	0.90	0.89	0.92	0.93	0.79	0.81	0.88
(SEm)	5.20	5.20	4.74	5.61	5.20	4.74	4.97	4.24	3.97	6.87	6.54	5.27
Process. speed index	0.84	0.86	0.88	0.88	0.87	0.88	0.86	0.85	0.85	0.87	0.86	0.87
(SEm)	6.00	5.61	5.20	5.20	5.41	5.20	5.61	5.81	5.81	5.41	5.61	5.54

[a] $N = 100$ for each age group. The reliability coefficients for all subtests except Coding and Symbol Search are split-half correlations corrected by the Spearman-Brown formula. For Coding and Symbol Search, raw-score test-retest correlations are presented for six age groups, these coefficients, which are based on samples of about 60 children tested twice, were corrected for the variability of the appropriate standardization group (Guilford & Fruchter, 1978). The coefficients for the IQ and factor-based scales were calculated with the formula for the reliability of the composite (Nunnally, 1978);. The standard errors of measurement (SEM) are reported in scaled-score units for the subtests, in IQ units for the Verbal, Performance, and Full Scale scores, and in index units for the Verbal Comprehension, Perceptual Organization, Freedom from Distractibility, and Processing Speed scores.

[b] For Coding and Symbol Search, the best estimates of the reliability coefficient at an age level for which retesting was not done is the value obtained at the adjacent age level. The most reasonable estimate for age 6 through 11 is the value obtained at age 9, and the value obtained at age 13 is the estimate used for age 12 through 16. These "best estimates" for Coding and Symbol Search were used for computing the reliabilities of the composites to which these subtests contribute.

[c] The average r was computed with Fisher's z transformation. The average SEms were calculated by averaging the sum of the squared SEms for each age group and obtaining the square root of the results.

TABLE 16.4   Stability Coefficients of the Subtests, IQ Scales, and Factor-Based Scales by Age

	Age in years				
	9 ($n = 30$)		13 ($n = 30$)		All Ages
Subtest/scale	r_{12}	r_c^a	r_{12}	r_c^a	averages[b]
Information	0.78	0.86	0.89	0.88	0.87
Similarities	0.77	0.77	0.88	0.85	0.82
Arithmetic	0.42	0.72	0.81	0.68	0.70
Vocabulary	0.79	0.75	0.86	0.86	0.81
Comprehension	0.65	0.83	0.77	0.79	0.81
Digit span	0.79	0.87	0.95	0.93	0.90
Picture completion	0.73	0.84	0.79	0.73	0.79
Coding	0.83	0.82	0.84	0.84	0.83
Picture arrangement	0.73	0.71	0.68	0.70	0.71
Block design	0.76	0.79	0.91	0.84	0.82
Object assembly	0.40	0.65	0.80	0.70	0.68
Symbol search	0.80	0.85	0.72	0.60	0.75
Mazes	0.63	0.55	0.62	0.62	0.59
Verbal IQ	0.89	0.94	0.97	0.97	0.96
Performance IQ	0.80	0.88	0.93	0.91	0.90
Full scale IQ	0.88	0.94	0.97	0.96	0.95
Verbal comp. index	0.88	0.93	0.95	0.95	0.94
Percept. organ. index	0.77	0.87	0.93	0.90	0.89
Freed. distract. index	0.50	0.84	0.92	0.90	0.87
Process. speed index	0.86	0.88	0.83	0.83	0.86

[a] Correlations were corrected for the variability of WISC-III scores on the first testing (Guilford & Fruchter, 1978).

[b] Weighted average of corrected correlations for age 9 and age 13 were obtained with Fisher's z transformation ($N = 60$).

overall. The average reliability of the IQ scores ranged from $r = 0.91$ for Performance IQ (PIQ) to $r = 0.96$ for Full Scale IQ (FSIQ). The average reliability for the Index scores ranged from $r = 0.87$ for Processing Speed Index (PSI) to $r = 0.95$ for Verbal Comprehension Index (VCI). The subtest with the lowest average reliability was Object Assembly ($r = 0.68$), and the subtest with the highest average reliability was Vocabulary ($r = 0.90$). As expected, the standard error of measurement was high for subtests with low reliability.

Table 16.4 shows the average corrected retest correlations for the subtests, IQ, and index scores by age-band and overall. The retest correlation for the IQ scores ranged from $r = 0.90$ for PIQ to $r = 0.96$ for VIQ. The retest correlation for the index scores ranged from $r = 0.86$ for PSI to $r = 0.94$ for VCI. The subtest with the lowest retest correlation was Mazes ($r = 0.59$), and the subtest with the highest retest correlation was Digit Span ($r = 0.90$).

TABLE 16.5   Intercorrelation of Subtest Scaled Scores

Subtest/scale	Inf	Sim	Ari	Voc	Com	DS	PCom	Cd	PA	BD	OA	SS	Mz
Information													
Similarities	0.68												
Arithmetic	0.60	0.55											
Vocabulary	0.68	0.72	0.52										
Comprehension	0.64	0.67	0.50	0.70									
Digit span	0.43	0.40	0.47	0.38	0.39								
Picture completion	0.45	0.48	0.36	0.40	0.42	0.31							
Coding	0.31	0.29	0.34	0.29	0.30	0.25	0.21						
Picture arrangement	0.42	0.40	0.40	0.39	0.38	0.30	0.41	0.23					
Block design	0.46	0.45	0.50	0.43	0.43	0.40	0.47	0.32	0.44				
Object assembly	0.40	0.40	0.40	0.36	0.36	0.27	0.45	0.22	0.45	0.61			
Symbol search	0.38	0.40	0.44	0.36	0.37	0.34	0.32	0.50	0.35	0.42	0.37		
Mazes	0.22	0.20	0.27	0.23	0.21	0.29	0.22	0.17	0.27	0.36	0.27	0.20	

EVIDENCE OF VALIDITY

Regarding the validity evidence based on internal structure, the intercorrelations of the subtest scaled scores are reported in Table 16.5. The patterns of the intercorrelations are very similar to those reported in the U.S. WISC-III. In general, the subtests that make up each index score correlated with each other higher than with subtests that make up different index scores.

Table 16.6 presents results of the exploratory factor analysis. A principal axes factor analysis was applied, with iterated communalities (SMC inserted initially), followed by a Promax rotation. As shown in Table 16.6, the factor loadings are quite clean and the four proposed factors are easily identified. However, split loadings were found on Arithmetic and Mazes subtests. Roid, Prifitera, and Weiss (1993) reported similar split loadings of Arithmetic on both VCI and Freedom from Distractibility Index (FDI) while analyzing the factor structure with the U.S. standardization sample. This finding is considered reasonable since it takes both verbal comprehension and working memory abilities to solve arithmetic problems. The other finding, that the Mazes subtest showed a higher loading on FDI, was not as expected since Mazes has long been identified as an element in the performance domain. Actually, a similar finding was reported in the U.S. WISC-III Manual for children ages 6–7 only (Wechsler, 1991). This unstable result might be due to the fact that Mazes is the poorest measure of g compared to all the other 12 subtests, and it is the one with ample specificity (Sattler, 1992). Basically, both the exploratory and confirmatory factor analyses (Chen, Zhu, & Chen, 2000) provide evidence that the four-factor solution proposed in the U.S. WISC-III Manual is also the best solution found in Taiwan standardization data.

TABLE 16.6   Principal Axes Factor loadings (Promax Rotation) for Four Factors

	Verbal comprehension index	Perceptual organization index	Freedom from distractibility index	Processing speed index
Information	0.76	0.03	0.08	−0.03
Similarity	0.85	0.06	−0.07	0.02
Vocabulary	0.89	−0.04	0.00	−0.03
Comprehension	0.82	0.00	−0.06	0.02
Picture completion	0.27	0.51	−0.08	−0.04
Picture arrangement	0.14	0.44	0.09	0.01
Block design	−0.03	0.62	0.20	0.05
Object assembly	−0.02	0.76	−0.03	0.01
Mazes	−0.14	0.28	0.41	−0.10
Arithmetic	0.33	0.02	0.33	0.14
Digit span	0.17	−0.02	0.46	0.04
Coding	0.00	−0.07	−0.03	0.67
Symbol search	−0.01	0.11	−0.04	0.66

Note: Based on the standardization sample of $N = 1100$.

TABLE 16.7   Means and Standard Deviations of WISC-III IQ and Index Scores for Children with Mental Retardation, Autism, Learning Disabilities, and Attention Deficit Hyperactivity Disorder

Scale	Mental retardation ($n = 70$)		Autism ($n = 65$)		Learning disability ($n = 100$)		Attention deficit hyperactivity disorder ($n = 22$)	
	Mean	SD	Mean	SD	Mean	SD	Mean	SD
VIQ	61.69	8.54	85.42	17.65	84.37	13.54	91.86	15.11
PIQ	64.06	8.04	90.52	15.58	95.66	14.54	101.55	16.40
FSIQ	59.86	7.00	86.35	15.93	88.13	12.75	95.36	15.92
VCI	63.83	7.95	86.37	18.84	85.94	17.04	92.73	15.66
POI	65.51	9.45	95.17	16.44	99.18	16.81	104.32	18.33
FDI	65.28	10.50	86.51	18.35	81.20	11.79	90.05	13.24
PSI	69.44	10.07	79.97	15.68	83.92	13.28	91.36	17.09

Findings from comparison studies and clinical groups provide other validity evidence. Based on the Taiwan WISC-III standardization sample, Chen (1999b) found that the correlation between WISC-III FSIQ and teachers' ratings on children's school grades was $r = 0.44$, which is significant at the 0.01 level and consistent with findings of previous research on the relationship between ability and achievement.

In studies conducted by Chen and Yang (2000) and Chen, Yang, Zhu, and Chang (2001), WISC-III data were collected for various samples of exceptional children. Table 16.7 presents the means and standard deviations of WISC-III IQ and index scores for children with mental retardation (MR), autism, learning disability, and attention deficit hyperactivity disorder (ADHD). Similar to U.S. findings, PIQ scores for the MR group is a little higher than VIQ scores (Spruill, 1998). Also, this group obtained the highest mean scores on the PSI (Wechsler, 1991). For children with learning disabilities, their mean VIQ score was lower than the PIQ score, and their FDI and PSI scores were lower than VCI and Perceptual Organization Index (POI) scores (Prifitera & Dersh, 1993). For autistic children, VIQ is lower than PIQ (Rumsey, 1992; Yirmiya & Sigman, 1991). For the ADHD group, they scored lower on the PSI, FDI, and VCI, and achieved a significant higher POI score (Schwean, Saklofske, Yackulic, & Quinn, 1993).

CULTURAL ISSUES INFLUENCING WISC-III INTERPRETATIONS IN TAIWAN

There are several issues for psychologists to consider while testing a Taiwanese child in other countries. First of all, language could be a major problem. This could prevent the child from performing normally on the WISC-III. It is suggested not to test a child when his/her ability to listen and speak the local language is still immature. Among all 13 WISC-III subtests, Information, Vocabulary, and Comprehension would be influenced by examinee's language ability the most. Young immigrants from Taiwan could perform poorly on these subtests even though they are good at verbal comprehension. Secondly, "listen quietly and obey rules" has been informally encouraged within the Chinese society for a long time. Relatively speaking, educational programs in Taiwan do not pay attention to children's verbal expressive ability as much as they appreciate other abilities such as reading and memory. "Talkative" is a negative term in traditional Chinese culture, and children are not accustomed to talk about their own strengths because they are educated to be modest, humble, and polite. Recently, the Taiwan government became aware of this critical issue and has been trying to make some innovation in the way children are educated. Nonetheless, a current young Taiwan immigrant still could perform poorly on verbal subtests such as Vocabulary only because they are not used to talking more. Psychologists should consider this cultural difference, and always inquire further during testing with the WISC-III whenever it is appropriate. Some Taiwanese children may elaborate more on what he/she means and thus obtain higher scores when they are asked to explain further.

In Taiwan, less than 2% of the population are indigenous, and the majority live in the eastern part of Taiwan. The average IQ score for the indigenous population is less than the average IQ for non-aborigines. Their lower social economic level, which involves a combination of social, economic, and medical opportunities, could be one source for explaining this mean IQ difference. In a study of prediction bias (Chen, 1999a), the WISC-III FSIQ predicted teacher-rated school achievement equally well for children from different regions in Taiwan.

This result partially supports the fairness of using the WISC-III with the indigenous population of Taiwan.

In another study, which examined the base rate of Verbal-Performance differences across different IQ levels in Taiwan (Chen, 2001), results are quite consistent with U.S. findings (Kaufman, 1976; Matarazzo & Herman, 1985). It generally showed that the proportion of individuals with large differences between the Verbal and Performance abilities increases progressively with increase in FSIQ level. Interestingly, Ryan, Dai, and Paolo (1995) found the opposite pattern scores from a mainland China adult sample, where the proportion of individuals with large differences between the Verbal and Performance abilities decreased progressively with increase in FSIQ level. According to Ryan *et al.*, the Mainland China culture, which encourages extreme conformity, might be the reason for this observed Verbal-Performance pattern difference. This comparison provides evidence for the importance of cultural difference in cognitive development.

PROFESSIONAL ISSUES IN THE USE OF INTELLIGENCE TESTS IN TAIWAN

In Taiwan, test publishers restrict the sale of intelligence tests to qualified professionals who work in formal organizations (hospitals, schools, etc.) where administering IQ tests are necessary. Purchase requests of the WISC-III from non-psychologist professionals are typically rejected for confidential reasons. Intelligence tests are widely used in both psychological and educational settings. For example, test results are used to make diagnoses on patients' cognitive functions in hospitals, and to identify, place, and diagnose exceptional children (gifted, mentally retarded, and learning disabled children) in school.

Among all the individualized IQ tests available in Taiwan, the WISC-III is the most popular for multiple reasons. In addition to its worldwide name recognition, the quality of the adaptation process also plays an important role. That is, the items were revised carefully to minimize possible cultural bias, the standardization sample of 1100 cases was collected based on a stratified sampling plan, and the newly developed norms are both representative and appropriate. All these above characteristics make the WISC-III Taiwan edition a test with high quality for use by psychologists.

In practical settings, testing time is the major concern for some practitioners who do not have enough time to complete all subtests, and their goal is for a rough evaluation of examinees' overall cognitive functioning. In this case, appropriate short forms are needed. Chen (1999b) and Chen, Yang, Zhu, and Chang (2001) systematically examined the validity of several short forms across different samples. Results showed that the four subtest short forms using Vocabulary, Similarity, Block Design, and Picture Arrangement have the best predictive validity in the standardization sample and in highly heterogeneous samples where both normal and clinical children were combined together. Results also showed that when dealing with any specific exceptional children sample (such as Mental Retarded, Autism, or Learning Disabled group alone), different subtest combinations should be considered in order to obtain the best estimate of general intellectual ability.

Recently, theories such as "multiple intelligence" and "emotional IQ" get much attention in the field of IQ assessment. These concepts remind people to consider important factors other than IQ. However, it is worrisome that some people get the wrong impression and make distorted interpretations that the traditional IQ test is useless. We believe that professionals in every country have the responsibility to advocate a holistic view, to help people understand the role of IQ tests and how to interpret IQ test results correctly.

REFERENCES

Chen, H. (1999a). Comparison of WISC-III regression lines across gender and region for school achievement prediction in Taiwan. *Bulletin of Eastern Taiwan Special Education, 2*, 159–172.

Chen, H. (1999b). Four-subtest short forms of the Wechsler Intelligence Scale for Children (WISC-III) in Taiwan. *Psychological Testing, 46*, 13–32.

Chen, H. (2001). Base rates for verbal-performance discrepancies based on the Taiwan WISC-III standardization sample. *Journal of National Hualien Teachers College, 12*, 51–74.

Chen, H., & Yang, T. (2000). Base rates of WISC-III diagnostic subtest patterns in Taiwan: Standardization, learning disabled and ADHD sample applied. *Psychological Testing, 47*, 91–110.

Chen, H., Yang, T., Zhu, J., & Chang, B. (2001). *Validities of the WISC-III short forms based on multi-form/multi-sample/multi-method design.* Paper presented at the meeting of the 5th Symposium on Psychological and Educational Testing in Chinese Communities. Taipei, Taiwan.

Chen, H., Zhu, J., & Chen, Y. (2000). *The legitimacy and utility of the WISC-III factor-based indexes: Taiwan standardization sample applied.* Poster session presented at the annual meeting of the American Educational Research Association, New Orleans, LA.

Kaufman, A. S. (1976). Verbal-Performance IQ discrepancies on the WISC-R. *Journal of Consulting and Clinical Psychology, 44*, 739–744.

Guilford, J. P., & Fruchter, B. (1978). *Fundamental statistics in psychology and education* (6th ed.). New York, McGraw-Hill.

Matarazzo, J. D., & Herman, D. O. (1985). Clinical uses of the WAIS-R: Base rates of differences between VIQ-PIQ in the WAIS-R standardization sample. In B. B. Wolman (Ed.), *Handbook of intelligence: Theories, measurements, and applications* (pp. 899–932). New York: John Wiley.

Prifitera, A., & Dersh, J. (1993). Base rates of WISC-III diagnostic subtest patterns among normal, learning-disabled, and ADHD sample. *Journal of Psychoeducational Assessment Monograph Series. Advances in Psychological Assessment: Wechsler Intelligence Scale for Children—Third Edition*, 43–55.

Roid, G. H., Prifitera, A., & Weiss, L. G. (1993). Replication of the WISC-III factor structure in an independent sample. *Journal of Psychoeducational Assessment Monograph Series. Advances in Psychological Assessment: Wechsler Intelligence Scale for Children—Third Edition*, 6–21.

Ryan, J. J., Dai, X., & Paolo, A. M. (1995). Verbal-Performance IQ discrepancies on the Mainland Chinese version of the Wechsler adult intelligence scale (WAIS-RC). *Journal of Psychoeducational Assessment, 13*, 365–371.

Rumsey, J. M. (1992). Neuropsychological studies of high-level autism. In E. Schopler, & G. B. Mesibov (Eds.), *High-functioning individuals with autism* (pp. 41–64). New York: Plenum Press.

Sattler, J. M. (1992). *Assessment of children* (3rd ed.). San Diego, CA: Jerome Sattler.

Schwean, V. L., Saklofske, D. H., Yackulic, R. A., & Quinn, D. (1993). WISC-III performance of ADHD children. *Journal of Psychoeducational Assessment Monograph Series. Advances in Psychological Assessment: Wechsler Intelligence Scale for Children—Third Edition*, 56–70.

Spruill, J. (1998). Assessment of mental retardation with the WISC-III. In A. Prifitera & D. H. Saklofske (Eds.), *WISC-III clinical use and interpretation: Scientist-practitioner perspectives.* San Diego, CA: Academic Press.

Wechsler, D. (1991). *Wechsler Intelligence Scale for Children—Third Edition.* San Antonio, TX: The Psychological Corporation.

Wechsler, D. (1997). *Wechsler Intelligence Scale for Children—Third Edition, Taiwan Version* (Y. H. Chen, Trans.). Taipei, Taiwan: The Chinese Behavioral Science Corporation. (Original work published in 1991.)

Yirmiya, N., & Sigman, M. (1991). High functioning individuals with autism: Diagnosis, empirical findings, and theoretical issues. *Clinical Psychology Review, 11*, 669–683.

CROSS-CULTURAL ANALYSIS OF THE WISC-III

17

PRINCIPLES OF ADAPTATION OF INTELLIGENCE TESTS TO OTHER CULTURES

FONS J. R. VAN DE VIJVER

Department of Psychology
Tilburg University
Tilburg, The Netherlands

This chapter describes the conceptual background of the translations and adaptations of the international Wechsler Intelligence Scale for Children—Third Edition (WISC-III) project. An important development in cross-cultural research methodology of the last decades is the growing appreciation of the relationships between linguistic, cultural, and statistical issues of comparative studies (cf. Harkness, Van de Vijver, & Mohler, 2003). This chapter begins with a description of the types of translations that are employed in international studies; the second part is more specific and describes issues that had to be dealt with when translating the WISC-III. The third part embeds issues in translations in a broader framework and introduces the conceptual-methodological framework of the internal WISC-III project; the concept of equivalence is introduced and a taxonomy of equivalence is presented. The last part applies this framework to the WISC-III project and describes the main equivalence issues of the project.

TYPES OF TRANSLATIONS

Translating an intelligence test, such as the WISC-III, to a target language is more involved than rendering the test instructions and items in another language. An important question to consider is to what extent a close (literal) translation of the English version can be expected to yield an adequate test of the construct the

English-language version is supposed to cover. For some subtests, such as Digit Span, the answer is relatively straightforward. Within populations of schooled children who have gone through an arithmetic curriculum, digits are well known stimuli; a close translation of the original instrument will suffice to assess short-term memory skills in these schooled populations across the globe. Moreover, basic mechanisms observed in Western countries (e.g., item difficulty increases with the number of digits to be remembered; forward span is on average larger than backward span) can be expected to be universal. However, for other subtests a close translation would be more difficult to defend. Vocabulary items would often be easy to translate, but the question arises to what extent such a translation procedure will produce similar instruments in different languages. There is a fair chance that the familiarity and difficulty of at least some items vary across cultures. Clearly, translating an instrument requires both skills in designing adequate psychological measures and a thorough knowledge of the two languages and cultures involved.

Translators of the WISC-III set out to develop subtests that measure the target construct in the new version as adequately as possible. Three options are available to deal with the American version (Van de Vijver & Leung, 1997; cf. also Harkness, 2003). First, the English subtest can be closely translated (*application* of the original instrument). Applications have important advantages: they are easy to produce and they may allow for a straightforward comparison of scores (more is said about this comparability later in this chapter).

Experienced translators know that close translations are not always the preferred choice; they will often argue for good reasons that a close translation will not be appropriate and that a good representation of the target construct requires the *adaptation* of instructions or items. The Vocabulary subtest provides a good illustration. Close translations may be inappropriate for a variety of reasons: compared to the English originals, words in the target language may be relatively easy, difficult, uncommon, or (unlikely in the case of the WISC-III) even non-existent. So, adaptations attempt to generate more culture-appropriate instructions or stimuli while measuring the same underlying construct in all cultures (vocabulary knowledge is assumed to be a good indicator of intelligence in all cultures studied). There is an increasing appreciation in cross-cultural studies that close translations are often undesirable; maximizing the appropriateness of an instrument for a cultural context may make adaptation of at least some items necessary. In the cross-cultural literature the term "adaptation" seems to have replaced the term "translation" as the generic name (Harkness, Van de Vijver, & Mohler, 2002). The change of term is encouraging as it points to an increased cultural sensitivity of test designers and researchers.

On the other hand, test adaptations may be more difficult to work with in statistical analyses. A comparison of mean scores of different cultures is not straightforward if partly dissimilar items have been used in different cultures. The simplest solution would be to restrict the comparison to the common items. However, such a reduction would mean that information about the adapted items is not employed in the analysis, which is unattractive. Currently, two kinds of statistical techniques are available that can relatively easily deal with partly dissimilar item sets: item response theory (e.g., Hambleton & Swaminathan, 1985; Hambleton, Swaminathan, & Rogers, 1991) and structural equation modeling (e.g., Marcoulides & Schumacker, 1996; Tabachnik & Fidell, 2000). In both techniques it is important that adapted and closely translated items measure the same underlying construct. Within the context of the current international WISC-III project, the assumption means that all items of a subtest, both the closely translated as the adapted items, are indicators of the same underlying construct (e.g., vocabulary knowledge). If this assumption is met, both techniques allow for the comparison of the underlying construct in all cultural groups involved. Items that are common to sets or all cultures are used as anchors while items that are unique to cultures are used to add to the precision of the measure of the underlying construct.[1]

The third option is called *assembly.* A completely new instrument has to be assembled when the English items would be entirely inappropriate in the target culture. Such a drastic approach is needed when the underlying construct shows important cross-cultural differences. Indigenization (Sinha, 1997), which aims at maximizing the appropriateness of psychological theories and instruments to local cultures, will often amount to the assembly of new instruments. It has been argued that intelligence tests primarily assess school-related intelligence and do not adequately cover social aspects of intelligence. When Western respondents are asked which characteristics they associate with an intelligent person, skilled reasoning and extensive knowledge are frequently mentioned as well as social aspects of intelligence. These social aspects are even more prominent in everyday conceptions of intelligence in non-Western groups. Kokwet mothers (Kenya) expect that intelligent children know their place in the family and the fitting behaviors for children, such as proper forms of address. An intelligent child is obedient and does not create problems (Mundy-Castle, 1974; quoted in Segall, Dasen, Berry, & Poortinga, 1990). In this line of argument an intelligence test would need to contain a subtest of social aspects. Within the context of this book, the study of intelligence in schooled populations, the need to design a completely new instrument is unlikely (for examples, see Van de Vijver & Leung, 1997).

TRANSLATION OF THE WISC-III

The last type of translation, assembly, has almost never been applied to Western intelligence tests. In such an approach the suitability of an intelligence test for a cultural group is maximized by taking a local definition of intelligence as a

---

[1] It may be noted that the term "adapted" can have slightly a different meaning depending on the context. If an item is adapted, it means that the item content has been changed so as to increase its suitability in the new language and culture. However, when a test is adapted, it does not always mean that all items have been changed. Within the context of this book, an adapted subtest involves a subtest in which a smaller or larger part of the items was not closely translated.

starting point. An example of a test battery that was designed for a specific cultural context can be found in the work by Serpell (1993). He designed an intelligence test for children in Eastern Province (Zambia) after an extensive period of observation of children in their everyday environment and interviewing with local people in which he collected information these children had about everyday tasks and knowledge. The WISC-III translations described in this book never followed this anthropological, context-sensitive approach. At least two reasons can be envisaged for not adopting this anthropological approach. The first is pragmatic; there is much experience with previous WISC versions on which the translation of the WISC-III can build. In these projects, assemblies have never considered to be needed. The second is more theoretical; the cognitive structure of Western intelligence tests has shown remarkable stability across various cultural groups (e.g., Irvine, 1979; Jensen, 1980; Van de Vijver, 1997).

Translating WISC-III subtests did not involve the assembly of a completely new test in any of the countries, but depending on the suitability of the American original, on the application or adaptation of instructions and items (details about which items of which tests have been closely translated and which were adapted in which countries are given in Chapter 18 and the Appendix).

EQUIVALENCE

If closely translated or adapted instruments have been administered, the question arises to what extent the scores can be compared. Two simple examples illustrate the issue. If we have adequately measured height and weight of our subjects in different cultures, there is no doubt that the averages obtained in different cultures reflect real differences in the weight and height of the respective populations. By doing so, we assume that the scores are fully comparable across cultures. Let us now assume that using the format of the Digit Span, we read the names of American toys to children in the U.S. and some non-Western country in which American toys are not well known. We would be less inclined to believe that observed differences in the means observed in the different countries reflect genuine differences in short-term memory span of the children.

The previous example of differential stimulus familiarity (cultural knowledge) illustrates that cross-cultural comparisons may have to deal with sources of distortion that are uncommon to be important sources of variation in studies carried out within a single cultural group. So, cross-cultural comparisons have to deal with more sources of variation. Moreover, these sources of problems, often designated as bias sources, cannot be treated as non-systematic error. Rather, bias is a source of distortion that affects the scores of all individuals from a single cultural group. It can be defined as a source of differences in scores by individuals from different cultural groups that is not due to the construct measured by the instrument (e.g., Poortinga, 1989; Van de Vijver & Leung, 1997). In the case of the WISC-III this means that if bias would threaten score differences on, say, Arithmetic, one or more items of this subtest shows score differences that do not refer to arithmetic ability but to some other factor. Sources of bias in intelligence testing are, among other things, poor item translations, differential familiarity with item contents, or the testing situation in general, cultural inappropriateness of items or tests, differences in test administration conditions, and motivation of participants (Berk, 1982; Holland & Wainer, 1993; Van de Vijver & Tanzer, 1997).

An important aspect of analyses of cross-cultural data sets involves the question to what extent bias has challenged the comparability of scores. After all, only when there is no bias can scores can be directly compared across cultures. In the Anglo-Saxon literature on bias there is a focus on items as a source of distortion; these studies attempt to identify what is called "differential item functioning." A good example given by Hambleton (1994) is the test item "Where is a bird with webbed feet most likely to live?" which was part of a large international study of educational achievement. Compared to the overall pattern, the item turned out to be unexpectedly easy in Sweden. An inspection of the translation revealed why: the Swedish translation of the English was "bird with swimming feet" which gave examinees a strong clue about the solution, which was not present in the English original. In order to arrive at a valid cross-cultural comparison of scores the item has to be removed from the scale. Test scores of Swedes are overestimated because of the presence of this item. On the other hand, it is also clear that items that show bias are interesting from a cross-cultural perspective as they point to salient cross-cultural differences where researchers did not expect these to occur.

It is common to all sources of bias that they challenge the comparability of test scores. However, the impact of these sources is not always the same. For example, a poorly translated item has a specific influence that can be easily eliminated by removing the item from the comparison. However, differences with stimulus familiarity tend to have a more global impact on test scores that is more difficult to eliminate. The concept of equivalence is used to refer to the various levels of comparability of scores.

CONSTRUCT INEQUIVALENCE

The lowest level of comparability is called construct inequivalence. It will be observed when an instrument measures different constructs in two cultural groups (i.e., when "apples and oranges" are compared) or when the concepts of the construct overlap only partially across cultures. It may also result when constructs are associated with different behaviors or characteristics across cultural groups ("cultural specifics"). The assumption of construct inequivalence can be associated with an "emic" position which emphasizes the idiosyncrasies of each culture and, as a consequence, favors an indigenous approach to assessment.

CONSTRUCT EQUIVALENCE

A distinction can be made between three hierarchically linked types of equivalence (Van de Vijver and Leung, 1997; see also Poortinga, 1989). The first
is construct equivalence (also labeled structural equivalence and functional
equivalence). It means that the same construct is measured across all cultural
groups studied, regardless of whether or not the measurement of the construct
is based on identical instruments across all cultures. It implies the universal
(i.e., culture-independent) validity of the underlying psychological construct and,
in a terminology frequently used in cross-cultural psychology, can be associated
with an "etic" position (Berry, 1989).

As an example of construct equivalence, suppose that a researcher is interested
in traits and behaviors associated with loneliness in Austria and China. The study
could begin with a local survey in which randomly chosen adults are asked to generate such traits and behaviors. If the lists generated are essentially identical across
cultures, a loneliness questionnaire with identical questions in the two countries
could be composed. Data obtained with the instrument in the two countries can
be subjected to exploratory or confirmatory factor analyses in order to examine
construct equivalence (cf. Van de Vijver & Leung, 1997). If there are major differences in the traits and behaviors, one will need to tailor the measure to the cultural
context. This means that at least some items will be different in the two countries.
The construct equivalence of measures should then be addressed in a more indirect
way. A common procedure is to examine the nomological network of the measure
(Cronbach & Meehl, 1955): Does the measure show a pattern of high correlations
with related measures (convergent validity) and low correlations with measures of
other constructs (discriminant validity) as would be expected from an instrument
measuring loneliness?

MEASUREMENT UNIT EQUIVALENCE

The next level of equivalence is called measurement unit equivalence. This
level of equivalence can be obtained when two metric measures have the same
measurement unit but have different origins. In other words, the scale of one
measure is shifted with a constant offset as compared to the other measure.
An example can be found in the measurement of temperature using Kelvin and
Celsius scales. The two scales have the same unit of measurement, but their origins differ 273 degrees. Scores obtained with the two scales cannot be directly
compared but if the difference in origin (i.e., the offset) is known, their values
can be converted so as to make them comparable. In the case of cross-cultural
studies with measurement unit equivalence, no direct score comparisons can be
made across cultural groups unless the size of the offset is known (which is
rarely the case), but differences obtained within each group can still be compared across groups. For example, gender differences found in one culture can
be compared with gender differences in another culture for scores showing

measurement unit equivalence. Likewise, change scores in pretest-posttest designs can be compared across cultures for instruments with measurement unit equivalence.

SCALAR OR FULL-SCORE EQUIVALENCE

The highest level of equivalence is scalar equivalence or full-score equivalence. This level of equivalence can be obtained when two metric measures have the same measurement unit and the same origin. For instance, when temperature is measured using a Celsius scale (which is of interval level) in both groups, differences in temperature can be compared directly between the two groups.

EQUIVALENCE AND THE WISC-III

In a previous section it was stated that WISC-III subtests were never designed from scratch in any country (which was called the "assembly" option), but that items and instructions were either closely translated or adapted (called "application" and "adaptation," respectively). This choice has both advantages and disadvantages. An important advantage is the scope for psychometric comparisons (e.g., the comparison of internal consistencies, raw scores across countries, or patterns of scores, or the cognitive structure as identified in factor analysis). However, the preference for applications and adaptations also has disadvantages. A maximum suitability for a country may be more difficult to achieve if the American subtest is used as template for the translation. Using the American subtest as template may be more disadvantageous in cultures that share less with the American culture. Cross-national score differences could be a function of the cultural distance between a country and the U.S. This difference could be engendered by factors that are not supposed to create cross-national score differences, such as familiarity with the stimulus materials.

Bias sources, such as differential stimulus familiarity, tend to challenge and can lower the level of equivalence. If no direct score comparisons are intended across cultures, neither method nor item bias will be a threat to cross-cultural equivalence. However, method and item bias can seriously threaten scalar equivalence. An item systematically favoring a particular cultural group will obscure the underlying real cross-cultural differences in scores on the construct. Such a bias will reduce scalar equivalence to measurement unit equivalence.

The distinction between measurement unit and scalar equivalence is important in our cross-cultural data analysis. The latter assumes completely bias-free measurement. The debate about cross-cultural differences in cognitive test performance can be largely seen as a debate about the level of equivalence of cross-cultural score comparisons. For example, Jensen (1980) argues that when appropriate instruments are used (he mentions the Raven test as an example), cross-cultural differences in test performance reflect valid intergroup differences and show full score equivalence. Mercer (1984), on the other hand, states that common intelligence tests show problems such as differential familiarity and that this method bias will only allow measurement unit equivalence. The obvious implication is that group differences in the Raven scores reflect differences in intellectual abilities according to Jensen's reasoning while group differences mainly or exclusively reflect method bias in Mercer's reasoning.

The next chapter describes the procedures used for assessing which type of equivalence applies to the WISC-III subtests. It can be derived from the previous discussion that the distinction between measurement unit and full-score equivalence may be difficult to make. Therefore, our analysis first addresses structural equivalence (does the WISC measure the same construct in all countries involved?), followed by a combination of measurement unit and full-score equivalence.

REFERENCES

Berk, R. A. (1982). *Handbook of methods for detecting item bias.* Baltimore: Johns Hopkins University Press.

Berry, J. W. (1989). Imposed etics-emics-derived etics: The operationalization of a compelling idea. *International Journal of Psychology, 24,* 721–735.

Cronbach, L. J., & Meehl, P. E. (1955). Construct validity in psychological tests. *Psychological Bulletin, 52,* 281–302.

Hambleton, R. K. (1994). Guidelines for adapting educational and psychological tests: A progress report. *European Journal of Psychological Assessment, 10,* 229–244.

Hambleton, R. K., & Swaminathan H. (1985). *Item response theory: Principles and applications.* Dordrecht: Kluwer.

Hambleton, R. K., Swaminathan, H., & Rogers, H. J. (1991). *Fundamentals of item response theory.* Newbury Park, CA: Sage.

Harkness, J. A. (2003). Questionnaire translation. In J. A. Harkness, F. J. R. van de Vijver, & P. Ph. Mohler (Eds.), *Cross-cultural survey method* (pp. 35–56). New York: Wiley.

Harkness, J. A., Van de Vijver, F. J. R., & Mohler, P. Ph. (2003). *Cross-cultural survey method.* New York: Wiley.

Holland, P. W., & Wainer, H. (1993). *Differential item functioning.* Hillsdale, NJ: Erlbaum.

Irvine, S. H. (1979). The place of factor analysis in cross-cultural methodology and its contribution to cognitive theory. In L. Eckensberger, W. Lonner, & Y. H. Poortinga (Eds.), *Cross-cultural contributions to psychology* (pp. 300–343). Lisse, The Netherlands: Swets and Zeitlinger.

Jensen, A. R. (1980). *Bias in mental testing.* New York: Free Press.

Marcoulides, G. A., & Schumacker, R. E. (1996). *Advanced structural equation modelling: Issues and techniques.* Mahwah, NJ: Erlbaum.

Mercer, J. R. (1984). What is a racially and culturally nondiscriminatory test? A sociological and pluralistic perspective. In C. R. Reynolds & R. T. Brown (Eds.), *Perspectives on bias in mental testing* (pp. 293–356). New York: Plenum Press.

Poortinga, Y. H. (1989). Equivalence of cross-cultural data: An overview of basic issues. *International Journal of Psychology, 24,* 737–756.

Segall, M. H., Dasen, P. R., Berry, J. W., & Poortinga, Y. H. (1990). *Human behavior in global perspective. An introduction to cross-cultural psychology.* New York: Pergamon Press.

Serpell, R. (1993). *The significance of schooling. Life journeys in an African society.* Cambridge: Cambridge University Press.

Sinha, D. (1997). Indigenizing psychology. In J. W. Berry, Y. H. Poortinga, & J. Pandey (Eds.), *Handbook of cross-cultural psychology* (2nd ed., Vol. 1, pp. 129–169). Boston: Allyn and Bacon.

Tabachnick, B. G., & Fidell, L. S. (2000). *Using multivariate statistics* (4th ed.). New York: Allyn and Bacon.

Van de Vijver, F. J. R. (1997). Meta-analysis of cross-cultural comparisons of cognitive test performance. *Journal of Cross-Cultural Psychology, 28,* 678–709.

Van de Vijver, F. J. R., & Leung, K. (1997). *Methods and data analysis for cross-cultural research.* Newbury Park, CA: Sage.

Van de Vijver, F. J. R., & Tanzer, N. K. (1997). Bias and equivalence in cross-cultural assessment: An overview. *European Review of Applied Psychology, 41,* 263–279.

18

METHODOLOGY OF COMBINING THE WISC-III DATA SETS

FONS J. R. VAN DE VIJVER

Department of Psychology
Tilburg University
Tilburg, The Netherlands

KOSTAS MYLONAS

Department of Psychology
The University of Athens
Athens, Greece

VASSILIS PAVLOPOULOS

Department of Psychology
The University of Athens
Athens, Greece

JAMES GEORGAS

Department of Psychology
The University of Athens
Athens, Greece

This chapter consists of three parts. In the first part an overview is given of which items were adapted and which items were closely translated per subtest in each of the countries. This presentation provides the background for the statistical analyses reported in Chapter 19; however, the overview is also interesting in its own right. It provides insight in the judgmental bias of the subtest, which refers to nonstatistical procedures to identify bias, based on a content analysis of the items. All local test development teams had to address two questions: (1) which American items were expected to be transferable to a new linguistic and cultural context without major alterations and (2) which items were assumed to require adaptations. As a consequence, country comparisons of the number of adapted items of the 11 subtests provide information about the judgmental bias in these subtests. The second part of this chapter describes (in a largely nontechnical way) the statistical analyses that are reported in Chapter 19. Conclusions are drawn in the third part.

OVERVIEW OF TEST ADAPTATIONS
PER COUNTRY

In Chapter 17, a distinction was made between three ways of translating Wechsler Intelligence Scale for Children—Third Edition (WISC-III) subtests: applications (i.e., close translations of items), adaptations (i.e., change of item contents in order to enhance the suitability of an item for a particular cultural context), and assemblies (i.e., the development of a completely new instrument, needed when the original instrument would be entirely inappropriate in the new culture). Aggregated across countries, the vast majority of the items in the WISC-III adaptations described in this book, about 90%, has been closely translated or simply copied (in the case of pictorial stimuli), while a small minority of the items, about 10%, has been adapted. Assemblies were not used.

A detailed overview of the similarity of each subtest in each country to the U.S. subtest is presented in the Appendix. The tables indicate for each subtest whether the item was closely translated or adapted. In the case of a close translation, an item may appear in a different place in the item order. The order of the items is always determined by the empirically observed difficulty order. As a consequence, the order in a specific country may differ somewhat from the order in the U.S. subtest. The tables in the Appendix contain information about both the nature of the translation (application or adaptation) and the rank order of the closely translated items. So, the tables have three types of items: closely translated items with the same position in the item order in the U.S. as in a target country, closely translated items that have moved to a different place in the item rank order, and adapted items.

From a bias perspective, an interesting feature of the Appendix involves the proportion of adapted items across subtests and countries. An overview of these proportions is given in Table 18.1. The rows of the table present the country names in ascending order of proportions of adapted items. Analogously, the columns present the subtests in increasing order of their proportion of adapted items. A comparison of countries shows that, as could be expected, the smallest number of adaptations were found in the three English-speaking countries (Australia, Canada, and the UK). The largest proportions are found in Japan, The Netherlands and Flanders, and France. The rank order of the countries has some face validity in that culturally and geographically proximate countries tend to be close to one another. However, there was one notable exception. Whereas Korea and Taiwan are close to each other (with relatively low numbers of adapted items), Japan had the highest proportion of all countries. The reason behind the deviant position of Japan is not clear.

A column-wise comparison of Table 18.1 shows that the items of Object Assembly and Digit Span are identical in all countries. Block Design, Mazes, Picture Arrangement, and Picture Completion are identical in all countries except Japan; the test constructors in each country apparently judged that the performance subtests were culturally appropriate in their cultures. Thus, the Performance

TABLE 18.1   The Proportion of Adapted Items per Subtest and Country (in Order of Increasing Row and Column Means)

Country[a]	Object assembly	Digit span	Block design	Mazes	Picture arrangement	Picture completion	Arithmetic	Similarities	Comprehension	Information	Vocabulary	Mean
AUS	0.00	0.00	0.00	0.00	0.00	0.00	0.00	0.00	0.00	0.00	0.00	0.00
CAN	0.00	0.00	0.00	0.00	0.00	0.00	0.00	0.00	0.00	0.00	0.00	0.00
UK	0.00	0.00	0.00	0.00	0.00	0.00	0.00	0.00	0.06	0.07	0.00	0.01
LITH	0.00	0.00	0.00	0.00	0.00	0.00	0.00	0.00	0.00	0.13	0.23	0.03
SLO	0.00	0.00	0.00	0.00	0.00	0.00	0.00	0.05	0.00	0.17	0.23	0.04
TAI	0.00	0.00	0.00	0.00	0.00	0.00	0.00	0.00	0.06	0.10	0.30	0.04
KOR	0.00	0.00	0.00	0.00	0.00	0.00	0.17	0.05	0.17	0.20	0.23	0.07
GRE	0.00	0.00	0.00	0.00	0.00	0.00	0.00	0.11	0.11	0.37	0.33	0.08
SWE	0.00	0.00	0.00	0.00	0.00	0.00	0.08	0.00	0.00	0.43	0.43	0.09
GER	0.00	0.00	0.00	0.00	0.00	0.00	0.42	0.11	0.17	0.17	0.37	0.11
FRA	0.00	0.00	0.00	0.00	0.00	0.00	0.08	0.16	0.56	0.33	0.77	0.17
DUT	0.00	0.00	0.00	0.00	0.00	0.00	0.27	0.29	0.53	0.32	0.77	0.20
JAP	0.00	0.00	0.08	0.10	0.21	0.40	0.08	0.37	0.28	0.57	0.93	0.28
Mean	0.00	0.00	0.01	0.01	0.02	0.03	0.08	0.09	0.15	0.22	0.35	0.09

Note: The country of reference is the U.S.; cell means represent the proportion of subtest items that were adapted from the U.S. subtest version.

[a]Country codes: AUS: Australia; CAN: Canada; DUT: The Netherlands and Flanders (Dutch language area); FRA: France and Francophone Belgium; GER: Germany, Austria, and Switzerland (German language area); GRE: Greece; JAP: Japan; KOR: South Korea; LITH: Lithuania; SLO: Slovenia; SWE: Sweden; TAI: Taiwan; UK: United Kingdom; U.S.: United States of America.

subtests showed fewer adaptations than the Verbal subtests. The largest score was obtained by Vocabulary (with 35% of adapted items).

A possibly less apparent, though salient feature of Table 18.1 is the overall patterning of the proportions; going from left to right and from the top to the bottom, numbers tend to increase. Although there are various distortions of the consistency, there appeared to be quite some agreement among the local teams about which U.S. subtests needed more and which subtests required less adaptation. An intraclass coefficient, measuring consistency across countries (with subtests as replications) showed a highly significant value of 0.92 ($p < 0.001$). An intraclass correlation estimating the consistency across subtests (with countries as replications) obtained a significant value of 0.83 ($p < 0.001$). Both values indicate that there is a remarkable consistency across the various teams who developed the local versions of the WISC-III about which subtests travel better.

In sum, the judgmental bias analysis shows a clear result: there is considerable agreement across countries about the question which subtests are more susceptible to bias. However, as indicated by the large country differences in an average number of adapted items, the local teams did not agree on the absolute proportions that required adaptation.

CROSS-CULTURAL DATA ANALYSES

The cross-cultural data analysis consists of three parts. The first part addresses the structural equivalence of the subtests. To what extent is the cognitive structure identical across cultures that presumably underlies test behavior? It was stated in Chapter 17 that much cross-cultural work, dealing with the different versions of the WISC (usually the WISC-R) as well as other intelligence tests, has shown the stability of the cognitive structure underlying intelligence tests (e.g., Kush *et al.*, 2001; Naglieri & Jensen, 1987; Reschly, 1978; Sandoval, 1982; Taylor & Ziegler, 1987; Valencia, Rankin, & Oakland, 1997). However, as usual, the proof of the pudding is in the eating: We need to demonstrate that this also holds for the WISC-III subtests in the twelve data sets of our study. The WISC-III was adapted to 16 countries: the U.S., Canada, UK, Austria, Germany, and Switzerland, France and French-speaking Belgium, The Netherlands and Dutch-speaking Belgium, Greece, Sweden, Slovenia, Lithuania, Japan, South Korea, and Taiwan. However, there are 12 data sets: the U.S., Canada, The Netherlands and Flanders (Dutch language area), France and French-speaking Belgium, Germany, Austria, and Switzerland (German language area), Greece, Japan, South Korea, Lithuania, Slovenia, Sweden, and Taiwan. Data are not available from the UK. In the unlikely event that we would not find evidence to support the structural equivalence of the subtests, a further analysis of the nature of the differences would be needed.

If we find evidence to support the structural equivalence of the subtests, we can proceed with the next step. The second type of statistical analysis addresses the metric equivalence of the data (measurement-unit and full-score equivalence).

As argued before, we treat these together in order to avoid the theoretically complex and ideology-laden discussion whether country differences in raw scores on WISC-III subtests are due to valid differences or to method bias (e.g., differential stimulus and test familiarity).

The third stage of the analysis further addresses the nature of the cross-cultural differences in scores in more detail. The importance of the distinction between measurement-unit and full-score equivalence is seen here as less important than often suggested in the literature. We do not claim that the present data set can settle an issue that has been around for so long: the nature of the cross-cultural differences in scores on intelligence tests (e.g., Bruner, 1914; Burks, 1928; Herrnstein & Murray, 1994; Jensen, 1980; Leahy, 1935; Vernon, 1969, 1979). We argue in favor of a more pragmatic perspective, in which we examine the nature of the cross-cultural score differences by relating these to various country-level indicators, such as educational expenditure (per capita). Thus, Van de Vijver (1997) found that educational expenditure could partly explain cross-cultural differences in cognitive test scores. Correlations between these country-level indicators and observed cross-cultural score differences on raw test scores on the WISC-III subtests can provide important information about the nature of these differences.

In the following section each of the statistical analyses are described in more detail.

ANALYSIS OF STRUCTURAL EQUIVALENCE

Various statistical techniques can be employed to examine structural equivalence, such as factor analysis (exploratory or confirmatory), multidimensional scaling, and cluster analysis (Van de Vijver & Leung, 1997). In the context of intelligence tests exploratory factor analysis has been used most frequently. This technique is also used here for different reasons. First and foremost, factor analysis is a tried and tested procedure for examining the similarity of the cognitive structure underlying intelligence tests. Second, in the initial stage of the analysis the interest is not in the measurement unit of the subtests (in which confirmatory factor analysis would be the preferred choice) but in the factors underlying the battery. As a consequence, an analysis is needed that is based on correlations (rather than covariances). Finally, the usage of exploratory factor analysis allows us to relate our findings to common findings in the literature (notably the discussion on the dimensionality of the WISC-III; cf. Allen & Thorndike, 1995; Blaha & Wallbrown, 1996; Bracken & McCallum, 1993; Kush *et al.*, 2001; Prifitera & Saklofske, 1998; Reynolds & Ford, 1994).

An examination of the structural equivalence of an intelligence battery could start with an analysis of the similarity of the structure of the subtests, followed by an analysis of the subtest scores. The first step scrutinizes item scores and the second subtest scores (raw or standard scores). Unfortunately, the opportunity to analyze the subtests separately and to examine the structural equivalence of the subtests is very limited. For the speeded tests item responses are typically not recorded and if they would be recorded, they would not yield meaningful inter-correlations because of the small number of errors per item. Furthermore, for the adapted tests (i.e., subtests containing items that were not closely translated but substituted) only the items that are common can be examined for structural equivalence. As will become clearer in the second part of this chapter, this number varies across the subtests and countries involved; yet, for some subtests the number of items shared with the American subtests (from which the other language versions were developed) is very small, thereby precluding a meaningful analysis. Another problem in the item-level factor analyses is the variable number of respondents across items. More difficult items are answered by fewer children. The factor analysis would have to accommodate this difference in number of respondents. Finally, we share the preference in the literature to focus on subtest scores in the study of structural equivalence. If we are interested in comparing cognitive structures across cultures, subtest scores provide a more comprehensive picture than item-level scores. In sum, without belittling the value of item-level studies when addressing structural equivalence, we focus here on the analysis of subtest scores.

The procedure to use exploratory analysis in the study of structural equivalence has two stages. In the first stage the factor analyses are carried out (suppose that we want to compare the American and British data). The American and British data are analyzed separately. The factor loadings (suppose that four factors were extracted) are then compared to each other. Rotations are an important part of factor analysis, aimed at increasing the interpretability of the solution. However, rotation methods have some arbitrariness. This arbitrariness needs to be resolved before the similarity of the factors can be evaluated. One of the countries is designated as target, (e.g., the American factor loadings. Usually the choice is immaterial; however, in this study, because the WISC tests were originally developed in the U.S., this country is the obvious target. Thus, the Greek factor loadings are rotated so as to maximize their similarity with the American factor loadings. It should be noted that this is not done to artificially boost the similarity, but the need for target rotations is a consequence of the arbitrariness of the rotations in the two country solutions.

The most frequently employed agreement (or congruence) coefficient is Tucker's phi (originally due to Burt). The coefficient is insensitive for positive constants with which loadings are multiplied (Tucker's phi between the loadings the vectors $\{0.1, 0.2, 0.3\}$ and $\{0.2, 0.4, 0.6\}$ is perfect as the values of the second vector are exactly twice as large as the value of the first vector). However, the coefficient is sensitive to differences in means (Tucker's phi between the loadings of vectors $\{0.1, 0.2, 0.3\}$ and $\{0.2, 0.3, 0.4\}$ is not perfect). The insensitivity to differences in (positive) multiplicative constants is deliberately chosen; it makes the coefficient invariant for differences in eigenvalues of the factors. The underlying idea is that differences in the reliability of factors across cultures do not challenge the structural equivalence of the factors. Values of Tucker's phi larger than 0.90 are often taken to indicate equivalent factors. More recently, this value has been challenged by Van de Vijver and Poortinga (1994), who showed in a simulation study that values substantially higher than 0.90 can be obtained even when one or two items show markedly different loadings on factors with high eigenvalues (factors with many items with high loadings). The major problem with congruence coefficients is that statistical tests cannot be performed on these coefficients as their sampling distribution is unknown. To address this problem, Chan, Ho, Leung, Chan, and Yung (1999) propose using a bootstrap procedure to estimate the standard error of Tucker's phi. A visual inspection of differences in loadings of the target matrix and rotated source matrix may also help to identify anomalous items.

In our description of the factor analytic procedure we conveniently simplified the analysis to two groups. However, we employ 12 data sets, which means that we have 66 ($= (12 \times 11)/2$) comparisons per factor. The obvious question to address is how it is possible to deal with such a multitude of comparisons. Two types of different approaches can be envisaged to deal with comparisons involving a larger number of countries (see Welkenhuijsen-Gybels & Van de Vijver, 2002, for a more elaborate description). The first is a "one-to-all" approach. It amounts to pooling all data in a single data matrix (controlling for confounding differences in mean country-levels on the variables studied). Statistical details have been described by Van de Vijver and Poortinga (2002; see also Muthén, 1994). The factor analysis of the pooled data yields the target solution with which the factor solutions of each country are compared. The agreement is evaluated by means of Tucker's phi. If all countries show values larger than some critical value, evidence for structural equivalence is obtained. If some values show lower values, structural equivalence is not supported and reasons for the lower values need to be identified.

The second is a "one-to-one" procedure, in which all country comparisons are computed. The advantage of this procedure is its level of detail; however, from a computational perspective the procedure is cumbersome. The output of the procedure is a country-by-country matrix with values of Tucker's phi in the cells (there is one matrix per factor). Each cell indicates the level of similarity between two factors obtained in the two countries. Cluster analysis or multidimensional scaling can be employed to identify homogenous groups of countries with a high internal factorial for each cluster.

In principle, both approaches could be applied here. An attractive feature of the first approach is that it starts from the overall pooled solution that is based on data from 12 data sets. If the factor solutions in all countries show a good agreement with this overall structure, the latter is the global structure which has a wide applicability and is based on an impressive sample size. However, when there are country differences in structure, a comparison to a pooled solution may mask the patterning of the differences. In the latter case a one-to-one comparison would be more informative.

In conclusion, the analysis of structural equivalence consists of three parts. The first is a factor analysis per country of the subtest scores; four factors are extracted. In order to control for age effects standard scores are used. In the second stage the factorial agreement for all pairs of countries is computed. Four matrices, indicating the factorial agreement for each pair of countries, form the output of this stage. Finally, per factor a cluster analysis is employed to identify sets of countries with a high factorial agreement.

METRIC EQUIVALENCE

Assuming an affirmative answer to the question of the structural equivalence of the WISC-III, possibly amended for the fourth factor, we can continue with an analysis of metric equivalence. The adapted items may seem to preclude a direct comparison of raw scores across countries. The first and easiest solution would be to disregard the adapted items and to restrict the comparison to the items, used in all countries. A quick scan of the tables in the Appendix quickly reveals the unattractiveness of this option. If we would be forced to restrict the comparison to the common items, the comparisons would be based on very small item numbers, which would challenge the validity and replicability of the comparison. So, if we were to restrict the comparison to common items, some subtest comparisons not involving the U.S. may be based on small item sets.

The problem can be tackled using Item Response Theory (for introductions, see Fischer & Molenaar, 1995; Hambleton & Swaminathan, 1985; Hambleton, Swaminathan, & Rogers, 1991). Item Response Theory assumes that a person has a certain ability, which is statistically estimated on the basis of his or her responses on the subtest items; analogously, each item has a certain difficulty level, which is estimated on the basis on the number of correct responses to the item. The theory assumes that all items of a subtest measure the same underlying trait in all countries involved; in the case of cross-cultural data we also need to assume that items have the same item parameters in all countries involved (items should not be biased in favor of or against any country). Furthermore, Item Response Theory assumes local independence, which formally means that within groups of equal ability responses are statistically independent. In more informal terms, the assumption means that each subject answers each item independently and that there are no carry-over effects across items (e.g., effects due to memory or fatigue). If these assumptions are met, Item Response Theory allows for the estimation of a person's ability even if not all items are identical in all groups. As long as there are "anchors" (a set of items that are common to the countries to be compared), Item Response Theory can estimate the ability level of each person (and, by implication, the mean ability level of the country).

What does the application of Item Response Theory amount to in the present case? Let us take Vocabulary as an example. Suppose that two countries have 10 common and 20 country-specific items. We need to assume that in the two countries each of the 30 items measures the same underlying trait, say vocabulary knowledge (and nothing else than this trait). We also assume that the difficulty level of the common items is identical. The occurrence of an item that is much more difficult in one country, compared to the difficulty of the other items, would invalidate the applicability of Item Response Theory for that item; an item that appears very early in the list of words in one country should not appear at the end of the subtest in another country. Finally, we assume the absence of carry-over effects. If this set of (restrictive) assumptions is met, we can use both the 10 common items (as anchor) and the 20 country-specific items (as helping to improve the estimate of the ability of each person). The average of these person's abilities gives us a country mean for that subtest, in which all responses of all children have been used.

NATURE OF THE CROSS-CULTURAL
SCORE DIFFERENCES

The distinction between measurement unit and full score equivalence is difficult to make in the present data set. Full score equivalence requires the absence of any form of bias; when dealing with a large number of cultures it is difficult to demonstrate the absence of bias. Therefore, a more modest approach is chosen here in which the nature of the cross-cultural score differences observed is examined by correlating these differences with country indicators. In other words, we validate the cross-cultural score differences by examining their nomological network (Cronbach & Meehl, 1955). In this analysis we shift the focus from the individual to the country level. Each country is represented by its average score on each subtest.

The study of psychological indicators at country level is gaining popularity in cross-cultural psychology (Georgas & Berry, 1995; Georgas, Van de Vijver, & Berry, 2003; Lynn & Martin, 1995; McCrae & Allik, 2002; Poortinga, Van de Vijver, & Van Hemert, 2002; Van de Vijver, 1997; Van Hemert, Van de Vijver, Poortinga, & Georgas, 2002). Building on Berry's Ecocultural Framework, Georgas *et al.* (2002) examined the patterning of cross-cultural differences in attitudes and values (Hofstede, 2001; Schwarz, 1992) and subjective well-being (Inglehart, 1997). Two sets of country indicators were found to be relevant: religion and affluence. Some religions, such as Islam and traditional beliefs, and countries with low levels of affluence were found to place more emphasis on interpersonal aspects, such as power, loyalty, and hierarchy. Protestant countries and more affluent countries placed more emphasis on intrapersonal values, such as individualism and well-being. Van de Vijver (1997) examined cross-cultural differences in scores on cognitive tests. He found affluence to be related to these differences. More specifically, educational expenditure (per capita) was a good predictor of cross-national score differences.

From a statistical perspective the country-level studies mentioned are usually simple and straightforward. Correlational and multiple regression analyses are employed to examine relationships between psychological variables and country indicators. In the present study correlations will be used. Correlations are computed between country indicators and subtest scores (either the mean raw scores for the subtests that are identical across the countries or the means of the ability distributions based on Item Response Theory in the case of subtests with adapted items).

CONCLUSION

The quality of large cross-cultural projects such as described in this book is based on a combination of substantive and methodological factors. The current chapter focused on the latter. The approach adopted in this chapter starts with a careful analysis of the question to what extent the various subtests of the WISC-III measure the same underlying construct(s). A comparison of the factor structures obtained in each country to the structure of all countries combined is expected to yield valuable information about the similarity of the structure of intelligence underlying the WISC-III in the countries examined. Based on the literature and on the judgmental bias analysis, which showed a remarkable consistency across countries about which subtests needed more and which needed fewer adaptations, we expect to find a good cross-cultural agreement of the factor structure. In the next step mean scores are computed per subtest and country. Item Response Theory is used to deal with the problem that several subtests do not have exactly the same number of items. Finally, these mean scores are related to country-level variables (such as educational expenditure) in order to understand the nature of the differences in scores.

REFERENCES

Allen, S. R., & Thorndike, R. M. (1995). Stability of the WAIS-R and WISC-III factor structure using cross-validation of covariance structures. *Journal of Clinical Psychology, 51,* 648–657.

Blaha, J., & Wallbrown, F. H. (1996). Hierarchical factor structure of the Wechsler Intelligence Scale for Children-III. *Psychological Assessment, 8,* 214–218.

Bracken, B. A., & McCallum, R. S. (1993). *Wechsler Intelligence Scale for Children—Third Edition.* Brandon, VT: Clinical Psychology Publishing Company.

Bruner, F. G. (1914). Racial differences. *Psychological Bulletin, 11,* 384–386.

Burks, B. S. (1928). The relative influence of nature and nurture upon mental development: A comparative study of parent-foster child resemblance. *Twenty-Seventh Yearbook of the National Society for the Study of Education, 27,* 219–316.

Chan W., Ho, R. M., Leung, K., Chan, D. K.-S., & Yung, Y.-F. (1999). An alternative method for evaluating congruence coefficients with Procrustes rotation: A bootstrap procedure. *Psychological Methods, 4,* 378–402.

Cronbach, L. J., & Meehl, P. E. (1955). Construct validity in psychological tests. *Psychological Bulletin, 52,* 281–302.

Fischer, G. H., & Molenaar I. W. (1995). *Rasch models. Foundations, recent developments, and applications.* New York: Springer-Verlag.

Georgas, J., & Berry, J. W. (1995). An ecocultural taxonomy for cross-cultural psychology. *Cross-Cultural Research, 29,* 121–157.

Georgas, J., Van de Vijver, F. J. R., & Berry, J. W. (2003). The ecocultural framework, ecoso-cial indices and psychological variables in cross-cultural research. *Journal of Cross-Cultural Psychology.* In press.

Hambleton, R. K., & Swaminathan, H. (1985). *Item response theory: Principles and applications.* Dordrecht: Kluwer.

Hambleton, R. K., Swaminathan, H., & Rogers, H. J. (1991). *Fundamentals of item response theory.* Newbury Park, CA: Sage.

Herrnstein, R. J., & Murray, C. (1994). *The bell curve. Intelligence and class structure in American life.* New York: Free Press.

Hofstede, G. (2001). *Culture's consequences* (2nd ed.). Thousand Oaks, CA: Sage.

Inglehart, R. (1997). *Modernization and postmodernization: Changing values and political styles in advanced industrial society.* Princeton, NJ: Princeton University Press.

Jensen, A. R. (1980). *Bias in mental testing.* New York: Free Press.

Kush, J. C., Watkins, M. W., Ward, T. J., Ward, S. B., Canivez, G. L., & Worrell, F. C. (2001). Construct validity of the WISC-III for White and Black students from the WISC-III standardization sample and for Black students referred for psychological evaluation. *School Psychology Review, 30,* 70–88.

Leahy, A. M. (1935). Nature-nurture and intelligence. *Genetic Psychological Monographs, 17,* 237–308.

Lynn, R., & Martin, T. (1995). National differences for thirty-seven nations in extraversion, neuro-ticism, psychoticism and economic, demographic and other correlates. *Personality and Individual Differences, 19,* 403–406.

McCrae, R. R., & Allik, J. (2002). *The five-factor model across cultures.* New York: Kluwer Academic/Plenum Publishers.

Muthén, B. O. (1994). Multilevel covariance structure analysis. *Sociological Methods and Research, 22,* 376–398.

Naglieri, J. A., & Jensen, A. R. (1987). Comparison of Black-White differences on the WISC-R and the K-ABC: Spearman's hypothesis. *Intelligence, 11,* 21–43.

Poortinga, Y. H., Van de Vijver, F. J. R., & Van Hemert, D. A. (2002). Cross-cultural equiva-lence of the big five: A tentative interpretation of the evidence. In A. J. Marsella (Series Ed.), R. R. McCrae & J. Allik (Eds.), *The five-factor model across cultures* (pp. 271–292). New York: Kluwer Academic/Plenum Publishers.

Prifitera, A., & Saklofske, D. H. (1998). *WISC-III clinical use and interpretation: Scientist-practitioner perspectives.* San Diego, CA: Academic Press.

Reschly, D. (1978). WISC-R factor structures among Anglos, Blacks, Chicanos, and Native-American Papagos. *Journal of Consulting and Clinical Psychology, 46,* 417–422.

Reynolds, C. R., & Ford, L. (1994). Comparative three-factor solutions of the WISC-III and WISC-R at 11 age levels between 6-1/2 and 16-1/2 years. *Archives of Clinical Neuropsychology, 9,* 553–570.

Sandoval, J. (1982). The WISC-R factorial validity for minority groups and Spearman's hypothesis. *Journal of School Psychology, 20,* 198–204.

Schwartz, S. H. (1992). Universals in the content and structure of values: Theoretical advances and empirical tests in 20 countries. In M. Zanna (Ed.), *Advances in experimental social psychology* (Vol. 25, pp. 1–65). Orlando, FL: Academic Press.

Taylor, R. L., & Ziegler, E. W. (1987). Comparison of the first principal factor on the WISC-R across ethnic groups. *Educational and Psychological Measurement, 47,* 691–694.

Valencia, R. R., Rankin, R. J., & Oakland, T. (1997). WISC-R factor structures among White, Mexican American, and African American children: A research note. *Psychology in the Schools, 34,* 11–16.

Van de Vijver, F. J. R. (1997). Meta-analysis of cross-cultural comparisons of cognitive test performance. *Journal of Cross-Cultural Psychology, 28,* 678–709.

Van de Vijver, F. J. R., & Leung, K. (1997). *Methods and data analysis for cross-cultural research.* Newbury Park, CA: Sage.

Van de Vijver, F. J. R., & Poortinga, Y. H. (1994). Methodological issues in cross-cultural studies on parental rearing behavior and psychopathology. In C. Perris, W. A. Arrindell, & M. Eisemann (Eds.), *Parental rearing and psychopathology* (pp. 173–197). Chicester: Wiley.

Van de Vijver, F. J. R., & Poortinga, Y. H. (2002). Structural equivalence in multilevel research. *Journal of Cross-Cultural Psychology, 33,* 141–156.

Van Hemert, D. D. A., Van de Vijver, F. J. R., Poortinga, Y. H., & Georgas, J. (2002). Structure and Score Levels of the Eysenck Personality Questionnaire across individuals and countries. *Personality and Individual Differences.*

Vernon, P. E. (1969). *Intelligence and cultural environment.* London: Methuen.

Vernon, P. E. (1979). *Intelligence: Heredity and environment.* San Francisco: Freeman.

Welkenhuysen-Gybels, J., & Van de Vijver, F. J. R. (2002). *Methods for the evaluation of construct equivalence in studies involving many groups.* In review.

19

A CROSS-CULTURAL
ANALYSIS OF THE WISC-III

JAMES GEORGAS

Department of Psychology
The University of Athens
Athens, Greece

FONS J. R. VAN DE VIJVER

Department of Psychology
Tilburg University
Tilburg, The Netherlands

LAWRENCE G. WEISS

The Psychological Corporation
San Antonio, Texas

DONALD H. SAKLOFSKE

Department of Educational Psychology
and Special Education
University of Saskatchewan
Saskatoon, Saskatchewan, Canada

This chapter describes the cross-cultural analysis of the Wechsler Intelligence Scale for Children—Third Edition (WISC-III) data presented in the country chapters of Part II. The reader is also referred to Chapters 17 and 18 for a description of the theoretical and methodological background of this chapter. Three different types of analyses are reported. The first section addresses the structural equivalence of the subtests. The question examined here is the extent that the factor structure of the WISC-III is similar across countries. The analysis is based on the idea that similarity of factor structure across groups (i.e., structural equivalence; Van de Vijver & Leung, 1997) is indicative of the similarity of psychological structures involved in the different cultural groups to solve the WISC-III test items. The second section employs Item Response Theory (IRT; Fischer & Molenaar, 1995; Hambleton & Swaminathan, 1985; Hambleton, Swaminathan, & Rogers, 1991) to manage the subtest data that were not identical in all countries. About 10% of the items are adapted, which precludes a direct score comparison across cultures. The use of IRT enables us to estimate mean ability level of each cultural group,

Culture and Children's Intelligence:
Cross-Cultural Analysis of the WISC-III
277

even when not all stimuli are identical. The third section explores the relationships between these average scores at the country level and the ecocultural indices of Affluence and Education.

STRUCTURAL EQUIVALENCE OF THE
WISC-III ACROSS CULTURES

The purpose of the analysis of structural equivalence is to determine to what extent the construct of intelligence as measured by the WISC-III is similar across the cultures. In cross-cultural cognitive psychology the analysis is related to the issue of universals in cognitive processes and variations in manifestations of cognitive processes, as discussed in Chapter 2. The 12 country data sets are from the standardization studies of the WISC-III in Canada ($n = 1100$); Germany, Austria, and German-speaking Switzerland ($n = 1570$); France and French-speaking Belgium ($n = 1120$); Greece ($n = 956$); Japan ($n = 1125$); Lithuania ($n = 452$); The Netherlands and Dutch-speaking Belgium ($n = 1229$); Slovenia ($n = 1080$); South Korea ($n = 2231$); Sweden ($n = 1036$); Taiwan ($n = 1100$); and the U.S. ($n = 2200$). The total number of subjects in the data set is 15,999.

The first step was to conduct an exploratory factor analysis of the standard scores for the 13 subtests of the entire data set extracting from one to four factors. While it might be expected from a test with a second-order general mental ability factor that first-order factors would therefore be correlated, it was still necessary in this study to decide whether the method of rotation of the factors should be Varimax or oblique. Thus, solutions employing both methods were explored. The presence of a strong first factor (accounting for 41.77% of the variance, the scree plot is presented in Fig. 19.1) and the positive correlations between the factors supported the usage of oblique rotations.

The four-factor solution (including the Mazes subtest in the data set) resulted in factors that could clearly be labeled Verbal Comprehension, Processing Speed, Perceptual Organization, and Freedom from Distractibility. However, Freedom from Distractibility contained Mazes and Digit Span, while Arithmetic was found to load on Verbal Comprehension. In the one-factor solution, Mazes had the lowest factor loading (0.39). As well, Mazes was not listed under any factor in the WISC-III Manual (Wechsler, 1991). Kaufman (1994) has expressed reservations about Mazes because of its low loading on g and poor reliability. For these reasons, the decision was made to exclude Mazes from the analyses and to proceed with the remainder of the analyses based on 12 subtests. The exploratory factor analysis and the oblimin-rotations were repeated, but without Mazes. The four-factor solution was clear and stable as presented in Table 19.1.

The exploratory factor analysis solution described above, based on pooling all the data in a single data matrix, may yield a less clear picture and would overrate the cross-cultural similarity if there are differences in factor structure in some countries. This would appear to be the case here in that the literature vis-à-vis the

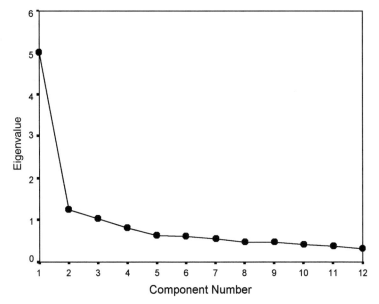

FIGURE 19.1   Scree plot of the combined data set.

fourth factor of the WISC-III, Freedom from Distractibility, composed of Arith-metic and Digit Span, suggests some inconsistent findings (Blaha & Wallbrown, 1996; Konold, Kush, & Canivez, 1997; Kush, Watkins, Ward, Ward, Canivez, & Worrell, 2001; Logerquist-Hansen & Barona, 1994; Prifitera, Weiss, & Saklofske, 1998; Reynolds & Ford, 1994; Roid, Prifitera, & Weiss, 1993; Roid & Worrall, 1996; Sattler, 1992; Sattler & Saklofske, 2001; Wechsler, 1991). Thus, in order to investigate the Freedom from Distractibility factor more carefully, we decided to proceed with a next step that involves a "one-to-one" procedure in which factor solutions of all countries are compared in a pairwise manner.

The one-to-one procedure consisted of determining the factorial agreement of all pairs of countries. Exploratory factor analyses of the standard scores of the 12 subtests were again computed, this time one for each of the 12 data sets, and four factors were extracted. One country was arbitrarily designated as the target and the factor loadings of the second country were rotated so as to maximize their similarity with the target country. Similarity of factor structure was determined by comparisons of the factor loadings of all pairs of countries for each of the four factors with Tucker's phi as the factorial coefficient of agreement. This resulted in a country-by-country matrix of 66 ($12 \times 11/2$) Tucker's phi coefficients (see Table 19.2). A value of at least 0.90 is taken to be sufficient that the two factors are identical. As can be seen in Table 19.2, all the coefficients are larger than 0.90 for Factors 1, 2, and 3, indicating factorial stability in the factor equivalence across all the 12 data sets on these factors. Indeed many of the phi coefficients are at the

TABLE 19.1 Factor Loadings of Combined Data: One-Factorial, Two-Factorial, Three-Factorial, Four-Factorial Solutions

Subtest	One factor	Two factors[a]		Three factors[a]			Four factors[a]			
	Factor 1	Factor 1	Factor 2	Factor 1	Factor 2	Factor 3	Verbal comprehension	Processing speed	Perceptual organization	Freedom from distractibility
Picture completion	0.61	0.46	0.25	0.16	-0.14	0.69	0.22	-0.09	0.67	-0.10
Information	0.76	0.84	-0.04	0.79	-0.05	0.09	0.74	-0.03	0.08	0.14
Coding	0.46	-0.14	0.80	-0.01	0.86	0.01	0.00	0.91	-0.09	0.00
Similarities	0.75	0.84	-0.06	0.79	-0.06	0.08	0.78	-0.01	0.05	0.05
Picture arrangement	0.60	0.32	0.41	0.10	0.09	0.59	0.20	0.19	0.52	-0.19
Arithmetic	0.69	0.59	0.19	0.58	0.18	0.10	0.38	0.07	0.14	0.45
Block design	0.69	0.31	0.54	0.05	0.15	0.71	-0.03	0.09	0.73	0.20
Vocabulary	0.76	0.88	-0.09	0.87	-0.05	0.01	0.87	0.02	-0.03	0.04
Object assembly	0.60	0.23	0.51	-0.11	0.03	0.86	-0.13	-0.01	0.87	0.07
Comprehension	0.68	0.79	-0.08	0.77	-0.05	0.01	0.83	0.05	-0.05	-0.08
Symbol search	0.56	-0.05	0.81	-0.01	0.76	0.19	-0.01	0.80	0.11	0.03
Digit span	0.52	0.37	0.23	0.47	0.34	-0.11	0.07	0.05	0.01	0.87
Eigenvalue	5.01	5.01	1.25	5.01	1.25	1.04	5.01	1.25	1.04	0.81
Percentage explained	41.77	41.77	10.40	41.77	10.40	8.62	41.77	10.40	8.62	6.78
Correlations of factors		1.00	0.47	1.00	0.33	0.51	1.00	0.33	0.50	0.29
		0.47	1.00	0.33	1.00	0.30	0.33	1.00	0.35	0.22
				0.51	0.30	1.00	0.50	0.35	1.00	0.23
							0.29	0.22	0.23	1.00

[a]Oblimin-rotated loadings (pattern matrix).

TABLE 19.2   Coefficients of Factorial Agreement: Four-Factor Solution

	Neth/Flan	Canada	France/Belgium	Ger/Aus/Swit	Greece	Japan	South Korea	Lithuania	Slovenia	Sweden	Taiwan
First factor: verbal comprehension											
Neth/Flan											
Canada	0.987										
France/Belg	0.993	0.996									
Ger/Aus/Swit	0.988	0.987	0.982								
Greece	0.992	0.992	0.997	0.985							
Japan	0.996	0.997	0.994	0.995	0.990						
South Korea	0.989	0.993	0.990	0.991	0.989	0.996					
Lithuania	0.989	0.984	0.980	0.988	0.970	0.993	0.982				
Slovenia	0.975	0.987	0.972	0.987	0.961	0.992	0.989	0.986			
Sweden	0.990	0.995	0.994	0.993	0.988	0.996	0.989	0.989	0.982		
Taiwan	0.994	0.993	0.987	0.994	0.981	0.997	0.987	0.997	0.993	0.993	
U.S.	0.995	0.995	0.999	0.989	0.996	0.995	0.989	0.990	0.980	0.996	0.989
Second factor: processing speed											
Neth/Flan											
Canada	0.979										
France/Belg	0.997	0.986									
Ger/Aus/Swit	0.972	0.985	0.983								
Greece	0.992	0.985	0.997	0.993							
Japan	0.987	0.987	0.987	0.971	0.990						
South Korea	0.988	0.989	0.990	0.987	0.989	0.983					
Lithuania	0.980	0.984	0.985	0.993	0.982	0.972	0.983				
Slovenia	0.971	0.983	0.977	0.987	0.975	0.983	0.987	0.984			
Sweden	0.977	0.976	0.987	0.973	0.985	0.978	0.968	0.966	0.953		
Taiwan	0.997	0.984	0.991	0.998	0.989	0.974	0.993	0.990	0.993	0.993	
U.S.	0.970	0.987	0.979	0.984	0.977	0.986	0.982	0.972	0.978	0.984	0.980

(*Continues*)

TABLE 19.2 (Continued)

	Neth/Flan	Canada	France/Belgium	Ger/Aus/Swit	Greece	Japan	South Korea	Lithuania	Slovenia	Sweden	Taiwan
Third factor: perceptual organization											
Neth/Flan											
Canada	0.986										
France/Belg	0.996	0.993									
Ger/Aus/Swit	0.995	0.990	0.995								
Greece	0.997	0.987	0.998	0.980							
Japan	0.993	0.984	0.995	0.992	0.994						
South Korea	0.987	0.987	0.988	0.992	0.989	0.986					
Lithuania	0.986	0.971	0.985	0.991	0.989	0.991	0.980				
Slovenia	0.991	0.990	0.990	0.994	0.986	0.983	0.991	0.981			
Sweden	0.993	0.988	0.993	0.993	0.991	0.994	0.981	0.990	0.983		
Taiwan	0.990	0.973	0.990	0.969	0.990	0.989	0.970	0.978	0.949	0.987	
U.S.	0.976	0.992	0.986	0.981	0.983	0.985	0.979	0.973	0.973	0.991	0.963
Fourth factor: freedom from distractibility											
Neth/Flan											
Canada	0.937										
France/Belg	0.963	0.964									
Ger/Aus/Swit	0.937	0.978	0.944								
Greece	0.977	0.939	0.988	0.915							
Japan	0.949	0.979	0.971	0.952	0.965						
South Korea	0.902	0.950	0.945	0.918	0.935	0.980					
Lithuania	0.879	0.918	0.882	0.958	0.875	0.838	0.791				
Slovenia	0.925	0.981	0.937	0.985	0.934	0.956	0.949	0.949			
Sweden	0.946	0.994	0.972	0.981	0.957	0.975	0.936	0.936	0.968		
Taiwan	0.941	0.971	0.953	0.951	0.921	0.939	0.891	0.923	0.931	0.974	
U.S.	0.906	0.978	0.968	0.922	0.941	0.972	0.949	0.821	0.922	0.970	0.938

Note: Neth/Flan: The Netherlands and Flanders (Dutch-speaking area of Belgium); France/Belgium: France and French-speaking area of Belgium. Ger/Aus/Swit: Germany, Austria, German-speaking area of Switzerland (German-speaking countries).

level of 0.99. This was not the case with Factor 4. Inspection of the coefficients of Table 19.2 reveals that some are below 0.90.

Frequency distributions of Tucker's phi coefficients are presented in Fig. 19.2. As can be seen, for Factor 1, almost all the coefficients are at the level of 0.98 or above (the lowest coefficient is 0.96). For Factor 2, again, almost all coefficients are at the level of 0.98 or above, and the lowest coefficient is 0.95. Factor 3 shows a similar distribution, with the lowest coefficient 0.95. However, the distribution of the frequencies of the coefficients in Factor 4 is spread out, with the lowest coefficient of 0.79. This suggests that although the coefficients of factorial agreements are in general above 0.90, the overall agreement is lower than was found for the other three factors.

The dispersion of the coefficients for the fourth factor may be due to the existence of clusters of countries with different factor structure patterns. A closer inspection of the factor structures suggested that the Arithmetic subtest was the

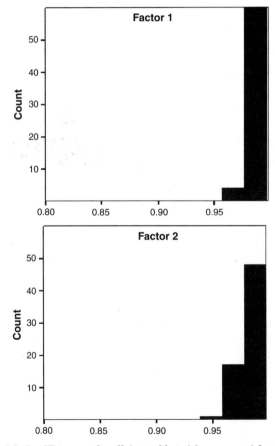

FIGURE 19.2   Histogram of coefficients of factorial agreement: 4-factorial solution.

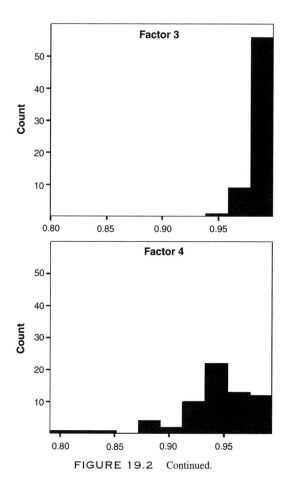

FIGURE 19.2   Continued.

main source of distortion (see Table 19.3). In contrast, Digit Span was not further considered as this subtest had a high loading on the fourth factor in all countries. In order to further examine the nature of the cross-cultural differences on the fourth factor, a hierarchical cluster analysis of the loadings of Arithmetic on the Verbal Comprehension and Freedom from Distractibility factors of each of the 12 country data sets was carried out. The results (Fig. 19.3) suggest three clusters of countries. These three clusters of countries can be identified in terms of on which factor the Arithmetic subtest loads in each country (the exploratory factor analyses), on Factor 1 (Verbal Comprehension) or Factor 2 (Freedom from Distractibility). This can be illustrated by the loadings in Table 19.3. Canada, Sweden, Japan, South Korea, and Taiwan constituted the first cluster. These countries all have moderate loadings of Arithmetic on Verbal Comprehension (median loading: 0.34) and a slightly higher loading on Freedom of Distractibility (median: 0.45). The second cluster contained the following countries: Greece, The Netherlands and

TABLE 19.3 Loadings of Arithmetic Subtest on the First and Fourth Factor in Each Country (before Target Rotation)

	Verbal comprehension	Freedom from distractibility
Cluster 1		
Canada	0.30	0.51
Sweden	0.31	0.50
Japan	0.38	0.44
Korea	0.40	0.45
Taiwan	0.34	0.42
Cluster 2		
Greece	0.52	0.28
Neth/Flan	0.52	0.26
USA	0.48	0.37
France/Belgium	0.46	0.33
Cluster 3		
Lithuania	0.28	0.66
Ger/Aus/Swit	0.23	0.66
Slovenia	0.13	0.64

Note: Neth/Flan: The Netherlands and Flanders (Dutch-speaking area of Belgium); France/Belgium: France and French-speaking area of Belgium; Ger/Aus/Swit: Germany, Austria, German-speaking area of Switzerland (German-speaking countries).

Dutch-speaking Flanders, U.S., and France and French-speaking Belgium. In these countries the loadings of Arithmetic were somewhat higher for Verbal Comprehension (median = 0.50) than for Freedom from Distractibility (median = 0.31). Lithuania, Germany/Austria/German-speaking Switzerland and Slovenia were in the third cluster. These countries showed relatively low loadings of Arithmetic on Verbal Comprehension (median = 0.23) and relatively high loadings on Freedom from Distractibility (median = 0.66). In comparing Table 19.3 with Table 19.1, in which all countries are combined, the loadings of the first cluster were closest to the pooled solution, which is not surprising because this cluster contained the largest number of countries. Compared to Verbal Comprehension, Freedom from Distractibility plays a somewhat more important role in Arithmetic in the second cluster and less important role in the third cluster.

From a cross-cultural perspective it is interesting to address the imperfect consistency of Arithmetic across the countries. One might speculate that the cognitive processes necessary for solution of the Arithmetic tasks might be the basis of this problem. The Arithmetic subtest is a multifactorial task involving elements of auditory comprehension of word problems, numerical skill, and verbal working memory. Purer measures of working memory may be more useful in clarifying the factor structure for the next edition of the WISC. That is, although the cognitive task is purported to measure arithmetic skills, the questions are framed in terms of a comprehension of the context. For example an arithmetic task might be: "John

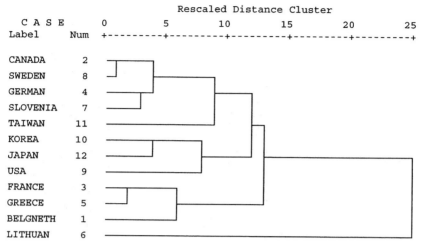

FIGURE 19.3 Hierarchical cluster analysis of the loadings of the 12 countries on the Verbal Comprehension and Freedom from Distractibility Factors (dendrogram). *Note*: BELGNETH: The Netherlands and Flanders (Dutch-speaking area of Belgium). FRANCE: France and French-speaking area of Belgium. GERMAN: Germany, Austria, and German-speaking area of Switzerland (German-speaking countries).

and Mary set out on a ride with their bikes. They cycled for 1 hour, stopped 1 hour for a picnic lunch, and then continued for another 2 hours. Their average speed was 15 kilometers per hour. How many kilometers did they travel?" One aspect of the task is the ability to make the computations. However, the second aspect requires them to comprehend the context, that is: "It is John and Mary," "They are riding bikes," "They stop for a picnic, thus do not take into account this 1 hour," "They continue for another 2 hours." It may be that in some countries, success in solving the problem is correlated more with verbal comprehension processes, while success in other countries is dependent on skills in decontextualizing the computations. This explanation may be intuitively appealing as a first and global explanation of the overall patterning of the loadings of Arithmetic. However, it does not yet specify the distribution of loadings across countries; for example, it is unclear why Arithmetic showed a higher loading on the fourth factor in, say, the U.S. than Slovenia. In addition to this theoretical issue, there may be a more methodological reason for the inconsistent loadings of Arithmetic. In almost all countries that report a fourth factor, Freedom from Distractibility had the lowest eigenvalue. In other words, of the four factors it had the weakest and least robust statistical underpinning. If the countries were completely identical and the samples would constitute mere random drawings from a single parent population, the fourth factor would be the first one that would not be adequately retrieved. Possibly compounding this issue is that the Digit Span subtest score is based on a composite of both digits forward and backward. Repeating digits backward involves much more working memory than digits forward, which taps short-term auditory memory for numbers. Again, this points to the need to further refine this factor on new versions of the Wechsler scales for children (e.g., a letter-number span task was included on the WAIS-III).

In sum, the one-factorial solution is very stable, indicating construct equivalence of the WISC-III across the 12 country data sets. The two-factorial solution is also very stable, except for low values in some comparisons on the second factor, but overall the results again indicate construct equivalence. The three-factorial equivalence also indicates construct equivalence. The four-factorial solution is very stable for the first three factors and fairly stable for the fourth factor. The median value of the coefficient of factorial agreement for the fourth factor is 0.95, which is well above the minimum threshold value of 0.90. Yet, some comparisons yielded lower values than the threshold level. If one looks at the factor analyses reported in the country chapters, some countries extracted three-factor solutions while most extracted four-factor solutions. Also, the factor analyses of each country as presented in the country chapters were often done with Varimax rotations, while oblique rotations were employed in the above factor analyses which are also more in line with current hierarchical theories of intelligence (e.g., Carroll, 1993). However, we recognize that the difference in rotation method might have led to some differences in the outcomes. Such differences are more likely when a factor does not have a clearly defined set of indicators, such as the fourth factor in this study. For example, Chapter 3 reported a higher loading of Arithmetic on Freedom from Distractibility than on the verbal factor, while the analyses of this chapter showed the opposite pattern; the discrepancy may be due to the method of rotation (which was oblique here and orthogonal in Chapter 3).

FACTOR STRUCTURE OF THE WISC-III

Having established with the one-to-one comparison of factors across countries that the Freedom from Distractibility factor is less stable across the 12 country data sets, we can now return to the overall exploratory factor analysis of the pooled data set (Table 19.1). This exploratory factor analysis method presents an "average" of the pooled data of 12 data sets, and based on evidence from the one-to-one analyses, we can conclude that there is factor equivalence on the first three factors of the four-factor solution. We can now examine more closely the subtests loaded on the factors in the one-, two-, three-, and four-factor solutions.

The one-factor solution (see Table 19.1) extracted 41.77% of the variance. Vocabulary and Information had the highest loadings (0.76), closely followed by Similarities (0.75). Arithmetic and Block Design (0.69) and Comprehension (0.68) are next. Lower loadings were observed for Picture Completion (0.61), Object Assembly (0.60), Symbol Search (0.56), Digit Span (0.52), and Coding (0.46). Thus, the Verbal subtests, with the exception of Digit Span and with the addition of Block Design, loaded the highest in the one-factor solution.

In the two-factor solution with oblimin-rotations, the second factor extracted 10.40% of the variance. The first factor was composed primarily of the Verbal subtests, with their loadings in approximately the same order as the one-factor solution. However, Picture Completion (0.46) also loaded on this factor. The correlation between the two factors was relatively high ($r = 0.47$).

The three-factor solution extracted 8.63% of the variance on the third factor. The eigenvalues for the three factors are respectively, 5.01, 1.25, and 1.04. The correlation between Factor 1 and Factor 2 is $r = 0.33$, between Factor 1 and Factor 3 is $r = 0.51$, and between Factor 2 and Factor 3 is $r = 0.30$, indicating a relatively high statistical relationship between the three factors. Factor 1 is composed of Vocabulary (0.87), Information and Similarities (0.79), Comprehension (0.77), Arithmetic (0.58), and Digit Span (0.47) and is primarily composed of Verbal Comprehension subtests. Factor 2 is defined by Coding (0.86) and Symbol Search (0.76) and reflects Processing Speed. Factor 3 contained Object Assembly (0.86), Block Design (0.71), Picture Completion (0.69), and Picture Arrangement (0.59), and clearly describes Perceptual Organization.

The four-factor solution extracted an additional 6.78% of the variance; its eigenvalue was 0.81. Factor 1, Verbal Comprehension, is composed of Vocabulary (0.87), Comprehension (0.83), Similarities (0.78), Information (0.74), but also Arithmetic (0.38). Factor 2 is Processing Speed with Coding (0.91) and Symbol Search (0.80). Factor 3 is Perceptual Organization with Object Assembly (0.87), Block Design (0.73), Picture Completion (0.67), and Picture Arrangement (0.52). Factor 4, Freedom from Distractibility, was composed of Digit Span (0.87) and Arithmetic (0.45).

There has been some debate in the literature about the number of factors underlying the WISC-III with both three- and four-factor solutions having been reported. The variability in factor structure was also illustrated in the various chapters in which the validation studies of the various countries were discussed. France and the French-speaking area of Belgium (Chapter 6), Greece (Chapter 13), The Netherlands and Flanders (the Dutch-speaking area of Belgium) (Chapter 7) all reported three-factorial solutions, while all other countries reported four factors. Most factor analytic studies of the WISC-III have supported the four-factor structure (Blaha & Wallbrown, 1996; Konold, Kush, & Canivez, 1997; Kush, Watkins, Ward, Ward, Canivez, & Worrell, 2001; Roid, Prifitera, & Weiss, 1993; Roid & Worrall, 1996; Sattler & Saklofske, 2001; Wechsler, 1991), although others have supported a three-factor structure (Logerquist-Hansen & Barona, 1994; Reynolds & Ford, 1994; Sattler, 1992). Thus, the current results are consistent with previous research in that two-thirds of the countries studied supported four factors while one-third supported three factors. In spite of mixed empirical support for the fourth factor, Prifitera, Weiss, and Saklofske (1998) point out that factor analysis should not be the sole criterion for determining how to summarize test performance, but that this decision should be informed by clinically meaningful patterns in the performance of diagnostic groups as well. Clearly, there is a wealth of research supporting the clinical utility of the concept of working memory (Baddeley, 1977).

Do our data provide an unambiguous support for either the extraction of three or four factors? If we base our conclusion on the pooled solution (i.e., all countries are considered jointly), both the three- and four-factorial solutions are clearly interpretable and in full agreement with the factor structures reported in the literature. We could certainly identify the fourth factor with a loading for Arithmetic and a much higher loading for Digit Span. There are no firm statistical grounds for favoring either solution in the pooled data. The choice has to be derived from other considerations, such as theoretical preference or clinical significance of either solution. In addition, it may be pointed out that in all our multifactorial solutions the factors showed strong, positive correlations, which clearly demonstrates the presence of a single second-order factor reflecting general mental ability. In hierarchical models the distinction between three- and four-factor solutions is less salient than in orthogonal solutions.

Three reasons can be envisaged as to why the factor structure could not be retrieved in all countries: real differences between countries in the composition of the fourth factor, differences in factor extraction methods, and sampling fluctuations because of the relative weakness of the fourth factor. Whichever factor or combination of factors could be held responsible, the differences that are reported could be erroneously seen as inconsistencies. The lack of uniformity in the number of factors that were reported in the previous chapters could be easily misconstrued. Seen from the perspective of a psychologist working in a single country, there is no inconsistency. Researchers in the countries that report three factors have considered both three- and four-factor solutions. In these countries the researchers felt that the fourth factor was insufficiently clear and too ambiguous to be used. It should be emphasized that this represents a best practices perspective. After all, factor-based indices are often used in practice and it is recommendable to use only those indices that can be adequately retrieved in a country. Statements about individual clients must be based on sound psychometric and clinical practice. In everyday practice, applications of the WISC-III are almost always aimed at statements about individuals and not about different cultural groups. These statements should be as valid, both psychometrically and clinically, as possible. The question of whether an index is unique for a country or is shared with other countries does not have much relevance for the psychologist who works with a single client in a single country.

The overall conclusion is that the WISC-III shows a remarkable similarity in factor structure across these countries. The factor equivalence suggests cognitive universality in the WISC-III across these cultures, as discussed in Chapter 2.

CROSS-CULTURAL COMPARISONS
OF WISC-III SCORES

In this section, the WISC-III scores of the Subtests, the Verbal and Performance IQs, and three- and four-factor solutions of the index scores are compared across

TABLE 19.4   Number of Items Changed on Subtests per Country

Subtest	CN	FR	GE	GR	JA	KO	LI	NE	SL	SW	TA	UK	Total
							Country						
Inf		10	5	11	17	6	4	9	5	13	3	2	85
Sim		3	2	2	7	1		4	1				20
Ari		2	10		2	4		6		2			26
Voc		23	11	10	28	7	7	22	7	13	9		137
Com		10	3	2	5	3		9			1	1	34
DS													0
PC					12								12
Cd													0
PA					3								3
BD					1								1
OA													0
SS													0
Total		48	31	25	75	21	11	50	13	28	13	3	318

Countries: CN: Canada; FR: France and French-speaking Belgium; GE: Germany, Austria and German-speaking Switzerland; GR: Greece; JA: Japan; KO: South Korea; LI: Lithuania; NE: The Netherlands and Dutch-speaking Belgium; SL: Slovenia; SW: Sweden; TA: Taiwan; UK: United Kingdom.

Subtests: Inf: Information; Sim: Similarities; Ari: Arithmetic; Voc: Vocabulary; Com: Comprehension; DS: Digit Span; PC: Picture Completion; Cd: Coding; PA: Picture Arrangement; BD: Block Design; OA: Object Assembly; SS: Symbol Search.

countries. The comparisons will be at the level of raw scores, since employing scaled scores would obviously result in equal means in all comparisons.

As discussed in Chapter 17, adapted items create the problem of comparison since they are not identical to the U.S. items. Table 19.4 shows the number of items changed for each subtest and for each country. The largest number of items changed across countries was on Vocabulary, with highest country changes noted for Japan with 28 items out of 30, followed by France with 23, and The Netherlands with 22. The second largest number of items changed was on Information, with Japan first (17 out of 30), followed by Sweden (13), Greece (11), and France (10). No items were changed for Digit Span and the Performance subtests Coding, Object Assembly, and Symbol Search. Overall, Japan changed the largest number of items (75), followed by The Netherlands (50) and France (48).

Item Response Theory (IRT) (Fischer & Molenaar, 1995; Hambleton & Swaminathan, 1985) enables the estimation of the ability level of each person and the mean ability level of each cultural group, when not all stimuli are identical. The ability level of each person and country means on all the subtests were estimated using conditional maximum likelihood estimation; the OPLM program (One-Parameter Logistic Model) was used for the computations (Verhelst, Glas, & Verstralen, 1995). This procedure has the advantage that no assumptions have to be made about the form of the ability distribution in the various countries. The OPLM

TABLE 19.5   Mean Scores of the Countries with many Adapted Items on the Vocabulary Subtest

	Netherlands/ Flanders	France/ Belgium	Sweden	Japan	Total
Item 1			0.99		0.98
Item 2	0.99	0.99	0.99	0.99	0.98
Item 3	0.99		0.97		0.99
Item 4		0.96	0.99	0.98	0.97
Item 5			0.96		0.98
Item 6		0.91	0.95		0.93
Item 7					0.92
Item 8	1.00		0.99		0.95
Item 9					0.86
Item 10			0.93		0.80
Item 11	0.85	0.76	0.92		0.74
Item 12			0.44		0.59
Item 13			0.50		0.61
Item 14	0.34	0.63			0.52
Item 15			0.55		0.45
Item 16		0.39	0.64		0.49
Item 17	0.42				0.42
Item 18			0.97		0.49
Item 19	0.20		0.17		0.38
Item 20					0.35
Item 21					0.42
Item 22					0.31
Item 23			0.57		0.27
Item 24	0.15	0.10	0.37		0.32
Item 25					0.23
Item 26					0.33
Item 27					0.34
Item 28					0.20
Item 29					0.12
Item 30					0.12

model used for the analysis is a slight variation of the Rasch model, in that the item discrimination parameter is allowed to vary across items; however, unlike a real two-parameter model, the current model requires the researcher to specify the values of the item discrimination parameter prior to the analyses. The computer program has an option to suggest values of these parameters to the user in an initial run. This option was used here. In order to increase the fit of the data to the underlying model, item discrimination parameters varied across items.

The IRT procedure implemented in the OPLM program to estimate children's abilities was used for all adapted tests in all countries, with one exception: the Vocabulary subtest. As can be seen in Table 19.4 (see also Table 18.1), some countries introduced many different items; the most items were changed in Japan, where only two of the original items were retained. The two items were very easy items, as shown in Table 19.5. The very small overlap of items and extreme scores on these items made the Japanese Vocabulary unsuitable for the cross-cultural analysis. France and French-speaking Belgium and The Netherlands and Dutch-speaking Flanders changed 77% of the items, and Sweden changed 43% of the items. In each of these countries one finds items that are much easier or more difficult than in the overall data set (see Table 19.5). This observation points to an important problem in the translations of Vocabulary items whereas the same problem was not found in any other subtest. In a few cases a close translation of the American Vocabulary yielded items that were adequate from a psychometric point of view, but were so different in difficulty level (measured by the proportion of correct responses) from the global data set that the assumption of equal item difficulty indices vis. psychometric theory was seriously challenged. Therefore, the Japanese, French, Dutch, and Swedish Vocabulary scores were not included in the cross-cultural analyses.

MEANS OF COUNTRY SCORES

How Were the Mean Scores Computed?

The observed means of the closely translated subtests and the OPLM estimates of the adapted tests are expressed on different scales. In order to increase the comprehensibility for the reader, all raw scores were transformed into the widely employed Scaled Scores of the Wechsler tests. For each subtest the scores of all countries were given an average of 10 and a standard deviation of 3. In line with common practice, we have transformed the Full-Scale, Verbal, and Performance IQ to a scale with a mean of 100 and a standard deviation of 15. The factor-based indices (of both the three- and the four-factor model) were also rescaled to have a mean of 100) and standard deviation of 15.

The IQ and factor-based indices could not be computed for the full data set because of the exclusion of the Vocabulary subtests country means from the four countries. Because of this large proportion of missing data on a single variable, it was decided not to impute missing values using some advanced statistical modeling procedure. Therefore, the computed IQ scores and factor-based indices were based on the available data so that the scores presented are not always based on the same sets of countries for each subtest.

In addition to the widely employed Scaled Scores and IQ scales, which are presented in graphical form (Figs. 19.5–19.8), the country scores are also presented in tabular form. The numbers represented here are deviation scores of the country on a subtest or aggregate score, such as IQ, from the global mean. The standard deviations of the distributions are always equal to one so that the scores can be interpreted as z scores. Because of the large sample size ($n = 15,999$) even small differences are statistically significant. Thus, these differences are reported in terms of effect size. Cohen (1988) has defined effect sizes of 0.20 as small, 0.50 as medium, and 0.80 as high.

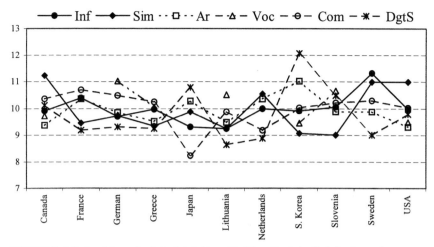

FIGURE 19.4 Means (scaled: global $M = 10$, SD $= 3$) of the Verbal subtests, by country. *Note*: Inf = Information. Sim = Similarities. Ar = Arithmetic. Voc = Vocabulary. Com = Comprehension. DgtS = Digit Span.

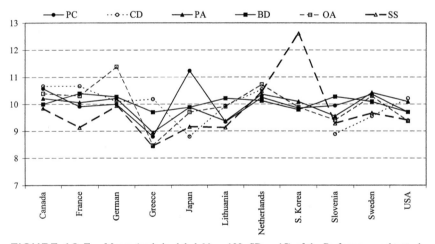

FIGURE 19.5 Means (scaled: global $M = 100$, SD $= 15$) of the Performance subtests, by country. *Note*: PC = Picture Completion. CD = Coding. PA = Picture Arrangement. BD = Block Design. OA = Object Assembly. SS = Symbol Search.

COMPARISON OF MEAN SCORES

An inspection of the means for the Verbal subtests (Fig. 19.4) and Performance subtests (Fig. 19.5) shows that there is much cross-cultural score variation, but that there is no obvious patterning of high- and low-scoring countries. Another

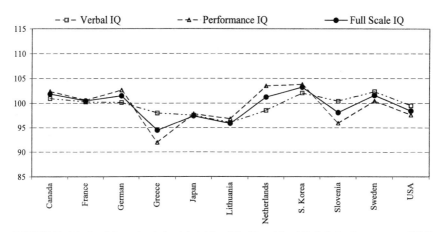

FIGURE 19.6   Means (scaled: global $M = 100$, SD $= 15$) of Verbal, Performance, and Full Scale IQ, by country.

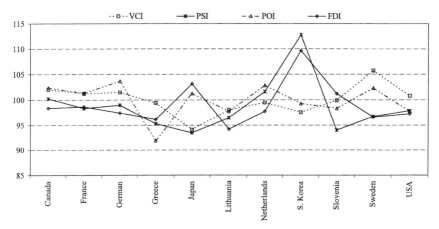

FIGURE 19.7   Means (scaled: global $M = 100$, SD $= 15$) of the index scores based on the four-factor solution per country. *Note*: VCI = Verbal Comprehension Index. PSI = Perceptual Speed Index. POI = Perceptual Organization Index. FDI = Freedom from Distractibility Index.

remarkable feature of both figures is the dominance of small differences from the global mean (as can also be confirmed in the upper part of Table 19.6). Of the 128 effect sizes for the subtests that were computed, only five had an absolute value of at least 0.50 and only one was higher than 0.80. The average absolute effect size of the upper part of Table 19.6 is 0.17. This means that on average countries showed a difference of 0.17 standard deviation units from the global mean. In Cohen's terminology this means that the average effect size observed here is small. Similarly, of the 100 effect sizes computed for the aggregate scores (IQs and index

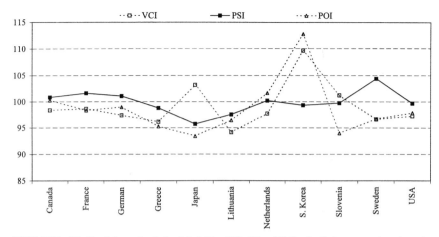

FIGURE 19.8 Means (scaled: global $M = 100$, SD $= 15$) for the Index scores based on the three-factor solution per country. *Note*: VCI = Verbal Comprehension Index. PSI = Perceptual Speed Index. POI = Perceptual Organization Index.

scores), 6 had an absolute value higher than 0.50 and 2 an absolute value higher than 0.80. The average value is 0.19. So, a first visual impression strongly points to the presence of small cross-cultural differences. As an aside, it may be noted that the global mean was computed on the basis of all countries; this means that when the effect size of, e.g., Slovenia on Digit Span was computed, Slovenia itself was part of the data employed to compute the global mean. Including a country in the computation of the effect sizes leads to an underestimation of the real difference of the country from the global mean. However, as the total number of countries for these analyses was 12, the total effect of a single country on the global mean was small; consequently, the underestimation of the effect size was limited.

In addition, the cross-cultural differences in mean scores were also tested in analyses of variance of the Subtest scores, the factor-based index scores, and the Full-Scale, Verbal, and Performance IQ with Country as the independent variable. It should be emphasized that the analyses of variance were not primarily meant to test the significance of the independent variable. It is obvious that with the large sample size, differences that are negligibly small from a psychological perspective can be statistically highly significant. Rather, our main interest was in evaluating the size of the cross-cultural differences observed (in line with our visual impression of small cross-cultural differences based on effect size). The size of these differences was evaluated by means of η^2 values, which estimate the proportion of variance accounted for by country in the explanation of the dependent variable. As can be verified in Table 19.7, all country differences were highly significant ($p < 0.001$). However, the η^2 values were low; the mean value was 0.033 (range: 0.003–0.103). Applying Cohen's criteria, this effect size is small. In sum, the main conclusion to be derived from our analyses is that cross-cultural differences in

TABLE 19.6 Effect Sizes for the 12 Subtest Scores

						Subtests						
	Inf	Sim	Ari	Voc	Com	DS	PC	CD	PA	BD	OA	SS
Canada	-0.03	0.41	-0.21	-0.09	0.12	0.04	0.19	0.22	0.07	0.00	0.13	-0.05
France	0.13	-0.18	0.12		0.23	-0.27	-0.03	0.22	0.02	0.13	0.10	-0.29
German	-0.10	-0.09	-0.05	0.34	0.16	-0.23	0.00	0.03	0.07	0.09	0.46	-0.02
Greece	-0.01	-0.22	-0.16	0.02	0.08	-0.25	-0.40	0.06	-0.35	-0.10	-0.51	-0.52
Japan	-0.23	-0.04	0.09		-0.59	0.26	0.41	-0.40	-0.04	-0.04	-0.10	-0.28
Lithuania	-0.25	-0.25	-0.17	0.17	-0.04	-0.45	-0.22	-0.02	-0.21	0.07	-0.03	-0.29
The Netherlands	0.00	0.18	0.12		-0.27	-0.37	0.08	0.18	0.12	0.04	0.24	0.16
South Korea	-0.03	-0.31	0.34	-0.18	0.01	0.69	-0.05		0.03	-0.07	-0.04	0.87
Slovenia	0.02	-0.33	-0.04	0.22	0.07	0.16	-0.02	-0.37	-0.15	0.09	-0.20	-0.24
Sweden	0.44	0.33	-0.04		0.10	-0.33	0.12	-0.15	0.14	0.03	0.10	-0.11
U.S.	-0.01	0.33	-0.23	-0.17	0.01	-0.07	-0.10	0.07	0.03	-0.10	-0.21	-0.20

Aggregate Scores

	IQ scores			4-Factor indices				3-Factor indices		
	Verbal	Perf.	Total	VCI	PSI	POI	FDI	VCI	PSI	POI
Canada	0.06	0.16	0.12	0.14	0.02	0.16	-0.11	0.06	0.02	0.16
German	0.01	0.04	0.03	0.08	-0.11	0.09	-0.09	0.11	-0.11	0.09
Greece	0.01	0.18	0.10	0.10	-0.07	0.25	-0.17	0.07	-0.07	0.25
Japan	-0.13	-0.53	-0.37	-0.04	-0.31	-0.54	-0.26	-0.08	-0.31	-0.54
Lithuania	-0.16	-0.14	-0.17	-0.39	-0.44	0.09	0.21	-0.29	-0.44	0.09
The Netherlands	-0.26	-0.21	-0.27	-0.13	-0.24	-0.15	-0.39	-0.16	-0.24	-0.15
South Korea	-0.10	0.23	0.08	-0.04	0.11	0.19	-0.15	0.01	0.11	0.19
Slovenia	0.14	0.25	0.21	-0.16	0.85	-0.05	0.64	-0.05	0.85	-0.05
Sweden	0.03	-0.27	-0.13	-0.01	-0.40	-0.11	0.08	-0.02	-0.40	-0.11
U.S.	0.16	0.03	0.11	0.38	-0.22	0.15	-0.23	0.29	-0.22	0.15

Note: Effect size is defined here as the difference of the country mean and the global mean, divided by the average standard deviation (of the individual scores per country). German refers to Germany, Austria, and Switzerland. France refers to the French-speaking area of Belgium. The Netherlands refers to The Netherlands and Dutch-speaking part of Belgium. Aggregate indices are based on available test scores (in order to avoid missing values).

Subtests: Inf: Information; Sim: Similarities; Ari: Arithmetic; Voc: Vocabulary; Com: Comprehension; DS: Digit Span; PC: Picture Completion; CD: Coding; PA: Picture Arrangement; BD: Block Design; OA: Object Assembly; SS: Symbol Search.

Factor Indices: VCI = Verbal Comprehension Index; PSI = Perceptual Speed Index; POI = Perceptual Organization Index; FDI = Freedom from Distractibility Index.

TABLE 19.7 Analysis of Variance Results for the Subtests, IQ, and Index Scores (Country as Independent Variable)

Dependent variable	F	df	η^2
Subtest			
Picture completion	20.18	10, 13970	0.014
Information	8.69	10, 13970	0.006
Coding	27.84	9, 11719	0.021
Similarities	48.52	10, 13871	0.034
Picture arrangement	15.10	10, 13962	0.011
Arithmetic	24.52	10, 13964	0.017
Block design	13.26	10, 13963	0.009
Vocabulary	35.07	6, 9557	0.022
Object assembly	49.64	10, 13960	0.034
Comprehension	34.57	10, 13838	0.024
Symbol search	159.82	10, 13947	0.103
Digit span	139.17	10, 13968	0.091
IQ scores			
Verbal IQ	14.49	6, 9361	0.009
Performance IQ	65.39	9, 11670	0.048
Full Scale IQ	36.70	5, 7153	0.025
Factor-based indices: 4 factors			
Verbal comprehension (VCI)	17.79	6, 9369	0.011
Processing speed (PSI)	42.27	9, 11699	0.034
Perceptual organization (POI)	60.37	10, 13942	0.042
Freedom from distractibility (FDI)	146.54	10, 13960	0.095
Factor-based indices: 3 factors			
Verbal comprehension (VCI)	4.98	6, 9361	0.003
Processing speed (PSI)	42.27	9, 11699	0.034
Perceptual organization (POI)	60.37	10, 13942	0.042

Notes: All *F* ratios are significant at 0.001 level. The last column represents the proportion of the total variance accounted for by country. The four- and three-factor Perceptual Organization and Processing Speed indices are exactly the same.

both subtests and aggregate scores (IQ scores and factor-based index scores) of the 12 countries in the study were small.

In the first section of this chapter we found strong evidence for the structural equivalence of the WISC-III across the countries of our study. Combined with the present results, a picture of considerable similarity in describing cognitive structure and level emerges. We found cross-cultural differences in test scores for all subtests; however, these differences are small and appear against a background of similar cognitive structures underlying the WISC-III.

A first impression of Figs. 19.5 and 19.6 could easily convey the impression that the cross-cultural differences observed are random fluctuations. The seemingly random nature of the score variation may be partly due to small effect sizes observed and the relatively large error component associated with such small effects. Random fluctuations due to sampling, small inaccuracies in item translations, estimation errors of ability estimates, and other sources of unsystematic error may add to this picture. However, any conclusions regarding explanation of the variability in subtests across countries cannot be made on the basis only of these results. Moreover, some effect sizes turned out to be large. As can be seen in Table 19.7, Symbol Search and Digit Span showed effect sizes that were much larger than those of other subtests. An inspection of the effect sizes of Table 19.6 shows that South Korean data had a major impact. The score of South Korea on Symbol Search is 0.87 standard deviation above the mean and 0.69 standard deviation on Digit Span; no other country showed this large a difference. It could be speculated that South Korea's high score on Symbol Search reflects a strong motivational component and it is known from other studies and international comparisons of educational achievement that South Koreans often show a high motivation in education-related matters (Hong, Milgram, & Perkins, 1995; Kim & Chun, 1994; Song & Ginsburg, 1987). It is unfortunate that no South Korean data for Coding were available as this could have shown to what extent this subtest might also show the same difference, in support of the above interpretation.

The background of the high score of South Korea on Freedom from Distractibility may be less speculative. Freedom from Distractibility is based on scores on Digit Span and Arithmetic. As can be seen in Fig. 19.4 and Table 19.6, the average Digit Span score of South Korea was high (effect size = 0.69). Various East Asian languages have short words for numbers (short refers here to the time it takes to say a number). Relevant theoretical work pertaining to this difference has been initiated by Baddeley and colleagues in their work on the so-called phonological loop hypothesis. There is some evidence that persons speaking languages with relatively short words for numbers tend to have a longer short-term memory span for numbers than persons speaking languages with long words for numbers (Baddeley, 1997; Ellis & Hennelly, 1980; Naveh-Benjamin & Ayres, 1986). The high South Korean scores and the above-average Japanese scores on Digit Span are in line with the phonological loop hypothesis. However, further work would be needed to examine to what extent the phonological loop hypothesis could explain the whole patterning of country differences in Digit Span scores.

RELATIONSHIPS BETWEEN COUNTRY MEANS AND SOCIAL INDICATORS

The first section of this chapter showed the universality of the factor equivalence of the WISC-III across these countries. The second section compared the average scores on the subtests, the Verbal, Performance, and Full Scale scores, as well as the index scores across these countries. A further question, to be explored in this section, is the relationship of the scores on these WISC-III variables with cultural variables. To what extent can observed differences in these scores be attributed to cultural variables? The 12 WISC-III data sets come from 15 countries.

But, as indicated in Chapter 2, 15 nations do not necessarily constitute 15 cultural groups. From the perspective of cross-cultural psychology, country (like culture) is an umbrella concept. If we are interested in exploring the nature of cross-cultural differences, it is often more interesting and revealing to examine the role of underlying dimensions that can be used to order countries than to treat country as a nominal variable that covers a myriad of underlying differences.

A major issue in cross-cultural methodology is the identification of cultural variables which might explain differences or similarities in psychological factors across nations. As discussed in Chapter 2, culture is a broad concept which includes all aspects of human activity. However, recent methodological advances have proposed employing ecocultural indices at the country level as potential measures of cultural variables (Georgas & Berry, 1995; Georgas, Van de Vijver, & Berry; 2002; Lynn & Martin, 1995; McCrae & Allik, 2002; Poortinga, Van de Vijver, & Van Hemert, 2002; Van de Vijver, 1997; Van Hemert, Van de Vijver, Poortinga, & Georgas, 2002). The goal would be to explore the relationship between ecocultural indices and psychological variables.

Georgas and Berry (1995) examined the ecocultural indices from 174 nations selected from a pool of over 500 indices from various statistical yearbooks. Cluster analysis based on five *a priori* ecocultural dimensions, *ecology, education, economic, mass communications,* and *population,* resulted in 23 ecological and social indicators. Two types of ecocultural indices at a country-level were chosen for this analysis: Affluence, composed of measures of economic activity, and education. The analyses in the previous two sections of this chapter were at the individual level; scores were based on data from each of the children in the 11 data sets (Taiwan is excluded). The following analysis is at the country level; average scores are examined for each of the 11 countries on the WISC-III subtests, Verbal, Performance, and Full Scale averages, and the index scores determined by the three- and four-factor solutions. Correlations are computed between the various WISC-III-derived scores and ecocultural indices.

THE SOCIAL INDICATORS: AFFLUENCE AND EDUCATION

The social indices for the 11 countries were collected from archival data from the year 2002, from the World Bank Organization, UNESCO Institute for Statistics, and other sources. Taiwan was not included in the analyses because of missing Affluence and Educational indices. The indices were gathered separately for France, Belgium and Holland, and Germany, Austria, and Switzerland. However, determining a composite index of Affluence for these countries would necessitate taking into account population size of these countries, standardization sample sizes, together with data on the economic indices for the German-speaking region of Switzerland, the French-speaking region of Belgium, and the Dutch-speaking region of Belgium; regional breakdowns of these areas were not available. Thus, the indices employed were France, for France and French-speaking Belgium,

Germany for Austria and German-speaking Switzerland, and The Netherlands for Dutch-speaking Flanders.

The economic indices, labeled Affluence, initially chosen were: Gross Domestic Product (per capita in USD), energy use per capita (in kg of oil equivalent), electricity consumption (per capita in kWh), percent of labor force in industry, percent of labor force in agriculture, national electricity consumption (in kWh per capita), unemployment rate, imports (in USD), exports (in USD), inflation rate, and industrial production growth rate.

A factor analysis of the indices was carried out in order to see whether the country differences in the various variables showed any patterning. The analysis showed a strong first factor; Inflation Rate and Industrial Production Growth Rate indices were the only indices that did not load highly on the overall factor. Thus, a second model, without these two indices resulted in a one-factor solution explaining 58.5% of the total variance and yielding factor scores for the countries; loadings are presented in Table 19.8 and factor scores of the countries in Table 19.9.

TABLE 19.8 Factor Loadings for Economic Indices

Economic index	Loading
Energy use per capita (in kg of oil equivalent)	0.95
Percent of labor force in agriculture	−0.88
Electricity consumption per capita (in kWh)	0.86
National electricity consumption (in kWh) (weighted for population variations)	0.85
Gross domestic product per capita (in USD)	0.83
Exports (in USD)	0.73
Imports (in USD)	0.68
Unemployment rate (%)	−0.58
Percent of labor force in industry	−0.31

TABLE 19.9 Factor Scores for Affluence (in Ascending Order)

Country	Score
Lithuania	−1.60
Greece	−1.21
Slovenia	−0.92
South Korea	−0.45
France/Belgium	0.01
Germany/Austria/Switzerland	0.10
The Netherlands/Belgium	0.19
Japan	0.30
Sweden	0.74
Canada	1.10
U.S.	1.75

The Educational indices were: percent of tertiary education level students enrolled in Education, Humanities, Social Sciences, Natural Sciences, and Medicine; pupil-teacher ratio for pre-primary, primary, and secondary education (secondary education level data from Japan were not provided); age of pre-primary, primary, and secondary enrollment; duration of each education level; male and female tertiary education enrollment percentages.

The indices were factor analyzed and a unifactorial structure was obtained, explaining 52.1% of the variance. The indices employed could be labeled *access to education*. More males and females were enrolled in tertiary education in countries with higher factor scores. Fewer tertiary students focus on a specific field; thus, they are more pluralistic in their educational choices. Pupil-teacher ratio is higher, meaning that the demand for pre-primary, primary, and secondary education is also high. Duration of educational level in each country is negatively correlated with countries with higher overall factor scores (loadings are given in Table 19.10 and factor scores in Table 19.11). That is, countries with a longer duration of pre-primary, primary, and secondary education have fewer number of pupils per teacher, while countries with shorter duration have higher numbers of pupils per teacher.

The correlation between the factor scores of Affluence and Education was positive and significant, $r = 0.61$, $p < 0.05$. In Table 19.12 the correlations are presented between Affluence and Access to Education and the scores of the WISC-III (subtests, the Verbal, Performance, Full Scale IQs, and the four- and three-factor index scores). It should be noted that, as explained above, the correlations in the upper part, labeled "Subtests," are based on 11 countries for all subtests except for Vocabulary (7 countries) and Coding (10 countries). In order to avoid the problem that because of missing scores for Vocabulary and Coding, almost no aggregate scores could be computed, all correlations involving IQ and index scores are based on incomplete data. The procedure to deal with missing data to compute effect sizes in Table 19.6 was also employed here. Significance tests of the correlations reported in Table 19.12 are one-tailed, because it is known from the research literature that

TABLE 19.10   Factor Loadings for the Educational Indices

Index	Loading
Pupil-teacher ratio (pre-primary education)	0.85
Pupil-teacher ratio (primary education)	0.61
Pupil-teacher ratio (secondary education)	0.86
Duration of educational level	−0.66
Male % enrolling in tertiary education	0.96
Female % enrolling in tertiary education	0.65
% of students in natural sciences	−0.54
% of students in humanities	0.51

both Affluence and Education tend to be positively correlated with cognitive test performance (e.g., Van de Vijver, 1997).

At the subtest level, Affluence showed significant correlations with Similarities ($r = 0.86$, $p < 0.001$), Picture Completion ($r = 0.54$, $p < 0.05$), and Picture Arrangement ($r = 0.75$, $p < 0.001$). Education was significantly correlated with Digit Span ($r = 0.64$, $p < 0.05$), Picture Arrangement ($r = 0.57$, $p < 0.05$), and Symbol Search ($r = 0.68$, $p < 0.05$). None of the three IQ measures correlated significantly with Affluence (although the correlations were in the expected direction and the probability levels of 0.06 and 0.09 were close to significance). The correlations of the IQ scores with Education were somewhat higher and reached significance (Verbal IQ: $r = 0.55$, $p < 0.05$; Performance IQ: $r = 0.63$, $p < 0.05$; Full-Scale IQ: $r = 0.68$, $p < 0.05$). The index scores showed a similar pattern in that only Education showed significant correlations. Education was positively associated with Processing Speed ($r = 0.72$, $p < 0.05$) and Freedom from Distractibility ($r = 0.59$, $p < 0.05$).

What can be concluded from these analyses? At the subtest level the patterning of the correlations is difficult to interpret. Caution is needed here because the number of countries is small and a single country with a very high or low score can have a large impact on the correlations. For example, if the South Korean data are not considered, the correlations of Education with Digit Span and Symbol are no longer significant. Similarly, the removal of the South Korean data has the same effect on the significance of the correlations of the index scores with Education. However, we feel more confident in interpreting the correlations of the three IQ scores and the overall patterning of the subtest correlations. The median correlation of subtest scores with Affluence is 0.18 and 0.28 with Education. After aggregation of subtest scores into IQ scores (which can be expected to increase the correlation), we found a correlation of 0.49 for Affluence and 0.68 for Education.

TABLE 19.11   Factor Scores for Education (in Ascending Order)

Country	Score
Lithuania	−1.513
Greece	−0.918
Slovenia	−0.829
Sweden	−0.572
Germany/Austria/Switzerland	−0.132
Japan	−0.069
France/Belgium	−0.065
The Netherlands/Belgium	0.077
U.S.	0.827
Canada	1.477
South Korea	1.719

TABLE 19.12 Correlation Coefficients with the WISC-III Subscales, the Verbal, Performance, Full Scale IQs, and the Four-Factor and Factor-Based Index Scores for 11 Countries[a]

	Affluence	Education
Subtests		
Information	0.33	0.02
Similarities	0.86[e]	0.38
Arithmetic	−0.15	0.31
Vocabulary[a]	—	—
Comprehension	−0.04	0.03
Digit span	0.06	0.64[c]
Picture completion	0.54[c]	0.35
Coding	0.25	0.24
Picture arrangement	0.75[d]	0.57[c]
Block design	−0.23	−0.39
Object assembly	0.30	0.21
Symbol search	0.10	0.68[c]
Mazes	0.10	0.00
IQ scores		
Verbal IQ[b]	0.43	0.55[c]
Performance IQ[b]	0.43	0.63[c]
Full Scale IQ[b]	0.49	0.68[c]
Index Scores: four-factor solution		
Verbal comprehension[b]	0.38	−0.00
Processing speed[b]	0.07	0.72[c]
Perceptual organization[b]	0.50	0.32
Freedom from distractibility[b]	−0.01	0.59[c]
Index scores: three-factor solution		
Verbal comprehension[b]	0.38	0.11
Processing speed[b]	0.07	0.72[c]
Perceptual organization[b]	0.50	0.32

[a] Due to large number of missing values for the Vocabulary subtest (for Japan, The Netherlands/Flanders, France/Belgium, and Sweden) no correlation is computed.
[b] Correlations based on available tests (not all tests scores available for computing the aggregate score).
[c] $p < 0.05$.
[d] $p < 0.01$.
[e] $p < 0.001$ (one-tailed).

Our analyses suggest that the country differences in scores on intelligence tests are small but patterned. Almost half of the country variation in IQ scores can be statistically accounted for by educational factors.

In order to adequately interpret the size of this number some aspects should be taken into consideration. The first is the impact of random error on the correlations. The psychological test scores were based on carefully chosen samples, which are supposed to adequately represent their respective populations. However, various sources of incomparability across countries still remain; for example, there is no standard way to deal with multicultural populations in the samples. Second, the data sets that were based on more than one country (French and Walloon; Dutch and Flemish; German, Austrian, and Swiss) were treated here as coming from a single country; their country scores were the scores of the largest country/region involved (i.e., France, The Netherlands, and Germany). Obviously, this simplification introduces some error. Third, samples are drawn from school-going populations, which means that country differences in who is attending regular schools will affect the outcomes (e.g., country differences in proportion of children in special education). The country-level indicators have their own sources of incomparability. It is common to find that indicators, such as enrollment ratios, are not defined in exactly the same way in all countries. These factors can be expected to reduce the size of the correlation between IQ and education. It is more difficult to think of factors that boost the correlation. So, it is probably fair to say that the estimate that almost half of the country variation in IQ scores can be accounted for by educational differences is conservative.

Another important factor to consider in the interpretation of the correlations is the ambiguous nature of the Education factor. From a statistical perspective the factor was clearly defined and supported the unidimensional nature of educational indicators, reported by Georgas and Berry (1995). However, from a psychological perspective the meaning of the factor is less clear. Various factors may explain the country differences observed. For example, the education factor could be a proxy for school quality. A higher quality will provide more intellectual stimulation and foster cognitive growth in children. Alternatively, it may well be that children from better schools have been more exposed to evaluation practices including psychological and educational tests, are more used to being individually tested, and know better how to find a balance between speed and accuracy in speed tests. In general, education may foster cognitive growth and it may make children more test-wise.

A final caveat in the interpretation of the correlations with education involves the role of Affluence. We found that Education showed slightly smaller correlations with IQ scores than Affluence did. However, the difference was small and nonsignificant in our small sample, and the correlation between Education and Affluence was positive and significant. As a consequence, it may well be that more general, affluence-related factors (e.g., physical quality of the child's living environment) also play a role in explaining cross-cultural score differences in IQ.

Future researchers might also consider the role of educational access and affluence in explaining IQ score differences between cultural subpopulations within countries.

In sum, the current analysis cannot pinpoint the factors and processes which underlie cross-cultural differences in IQ scores. However, our analysis demonstrates that there are important education-related factors in explaining cross-cultural score differences and that these factors explain possibly more than half of the country score variation in IQ scores.

THE WISC-III IN CULTURAL CONTEXT:
A SYNTHESIS OF FINDINGS

The goal of this book was to analyze the WISC-III in terms of cultural context from two perspectives: culture-specific (or indigenous) and cross-cultural.

From the culture-specific or indigenous psychology perspective, authors from each of the countries described in detail the standardization of the WISC-III in their country according to a standard format. These chapters described the standardization sample, the closely translated items and the adapted items, data on reliability and validity, the factor analyses of the index scores, cultural issues related to test performance in the country, as well as information about the use of intelligence tests and other psychological tests in the country. The test standardization, the care taken to adapt new items when the U.S. items were judged culturally biased, efforts taken to obtain representative samples of children, and the analysis of the data are all at very high levels. Only data sets that met these standards were included in this book. The result was a very reliable and carefully gathered data set, which, in turn, was manifested in the clarity of the statistical analyses.

In addition to information on the psychometric analysis of the WISC-III, these chapters provide valuable information on the clinical use of the WISC-III in each country. These descriptions will be of use to psychologists in today's multicultural world, when evaluating the cognitive functioning of a child who has recently immigrated to the host country and does not yet have the linguistic competence nor adequate knowledge of the cultural and educational "new world" to which it is adapting. The most common theme running through these country chapters, to which a psychologist should pay attention, is the important role of language in the intelligence test performance of the children, as well the psychologist's adequate knowledge of the child's first or native language. A recently immigrated child with a low level of language skills might well be tested with one of the WISC-III versions described above, or WISC-III adaptations in progress in different countries at the present time. In some cases, a child might be tested with a combination of the American WISC-III and the "home" country WISC-III. The child's performance could then be scored and evaluated in terms of both the "home" and "host" country norms.

A related theme is the relationship of language to certain cognitive tasks. For, example, that Korean words for numbers are very short, which may very much contribute to Korean children doing better on Digit Span items, as was found in the cross-cultural analysis. The opposite is the case for, e.g., Lithuanian children, whose language contains similarly sounding three-syllable names of digits, so that the structure of the task, i.e., short-term memory of the digits, is inherently more difficult.

Another common theme across the country chapters is that certain subtests did not require much revision. This was the case mostly with the Performance subtests, but also with some of the Verbal subtests. One of these was Comprehension and another was Similarities. These two tests contain items about ethical and practical behavior, knowledge of societal institutions, as well as finding similarities among items at an abstract level. The processes of adapting these two subtests in the countries as well as the results from the cross-cultural analysis indicated that these two tasks are well-constructed, with items that require little adaptation across cultures, at least across the countries of North America, Northern and Southern Europe, and East Asia of our sample. Similarly, the Performance tests were very comprehensible to all the children. In other words, these test items appear to travel well across country, cultural, and language "borders."

The overall conclusion regarding the subtests of the WISC-III is that the item content is comprised of relatively familiar stimuli across these countries. The word "universal" can be employed here in relation to the task stimuli as well as cognitive demands. Up to now it has been employed in relation to cognitive processes. That is, the WISC-III affords itself to adaptation to different cultures, *if* the test constructor abides by the proper psychometric procedures for selecting test items and test construction, and if the standardization is based on a representative sample of children in the culture, as has been described in these country chapters.

The cross-cultural analysis of the WISC-III was the second major goal of this book. Several major findings resulted from this study. The first major finding is the remarkable cross-cultural similarity of the structure underlying the WISC-III. The one-, two-, and three-factor solutions as well as the first three of the four-factor solution were very stable across cultures; it is only in some countries that the fourth factor showed somewhat lower values. This finding provides evidence of universal cognitive processes across cultures, as measured by the WISC-III, and as discussed by other researchers (e.g., Berry, Poortinga, Segall, & Dasen, 2002; Irvine, 1979; Van de Vijver, 1997). Certainly the finding of a robust second-order factor of general intelligence and group factors in both the separate country data as well as the cross-cultural analyses of the WISC-III supports Carroll's model (1993) of a second level of group factors and a general factor that are also common to the subsets of the WISC-III. The finding of a universal construct with the WISC-III represents a derived emic (Berry, 1969) in that the indigenous researcher in each country constructed a similar intelligence test, changing some items, and comparison of the etic and emic tests resulted in a derived emic.

That most of the countries have a four-factor structure, such as the U.S., and some have a three-factor structure, such as France and French-speaking Belgium, is consistent with the theoretical framework discussed by Berry *et al.* (2002), which proposes the same cognitive processes can be manifested in different ways in different cultures. This, however, has not been unequivocally demonstrated in this study. A more simple explanation may be, as discussed in this chapter, that these differences are more likely attributed to error variance due to variables such as differences in sampling fluctuations, item differences, or other variables. The statistical method of determining structural equivalence is essentially an "average" across cultures. Thus, each clinician who administers the WISC-III to a child and interprets the results does so with the items of its culture and the structure manifested in the culture. The issue of structural equivalence or cognitive universals is of theoretical and psychometric interest, while the clinician is more interested in how appropriate an intelligence test is in his/her culture in the evaluation of cognitive functioning of a specific child.

The second major finding is that there are no major mean score differences on the WISC-III across the countries; neither the subtests, the Full Scale, Verbal, Performance IQ, or the index scores showed large cross-cultural score differences. The few differences found did not manifest a particular pattern and might be explained by sampling error, or by phenomena such as the phonological loop hypothesis on Digit Span (Baddeley, 1997). That the different countries did not show large differences in mean scores is an important finding, not only in relation to the WISC-III, but also in relation to comparisons of average IQs across ethnic groups or across countries. Studies have reported mean differences between ethnic or cultural groups, some at the beginning of the 20th century, others more recently.

Our study differs from most of these studies in that the participants were carefully sampled (i.e., representative sampling based on relevant demographic factors), while past studies often used convenience sampling. Our sampling procedure reduced the effects of sample particulars and presumably made it easier to find significant correlations of subtest and IQ scores with country-level variables. Furthermore, the careful sampling procedure added to the adequacy of the statistical tests of the country differences. In psychology we often ignore the fact that sampling procedures have an impact on the statistical tests that are carried out. The not uncommon approach in some studies where a convenience sample is treated as a simple random sample (in which it is assumed that all eligible units have an equal and known probability of being included) may lead to entirely wrong conclusions about significance (e.g., Häder & Gabler, 2003; Kish, 1965). It is remarkable that the extensive literature in survey research on which sampling procedures are adequate and on the implications of sampling for statistical testing has not had a greater impact on psychology. Another important difference between our study and many previous studies is the bias analysis that was carried out here. Comparisons of means between ethnic groups and cultures lead to questionable results without a careful examination of potential sources of bias. Only when the various forms of bias in tests can be eliminated in different cultures can scores be directly compared across cultures. As described in Chapter 17, sources of bias are inequivalence at the item level, score level, and construct level. Although item bias is an important source of systematic error in comparisons between groups, it is only one source of bias. Equivalence at the score level and construct level are also important sources of bias. In addition, other variables such as population distributions of a culture in terms of socioeconomic measures, education, etc., can also be potential sources of bias.

A further issue is comparisons of ethnic groups within a polyethnic country as compared to cross-cultural comparisons of countries. Comparisons of ethnic groups within a country must take into account socioeconomic and educational measures of the ethnic groups, but must also control for other acculturation measures such as duration of immigration, language facility, occupational and educational opportunities, and degree of acculturation to the societal institutions. The assessment of acculturation is a neglected issue in multicultural societies (Arends-Tóth & Van de Vijver, 2002; Van de Vijver & Phalet, 2003).

The present study has carefully examined the potential sources of cultural bias, and made adjustments to eliminate or minimize these sources of bias. This process began at the country level with the processes of selection of items, closely translated and adapted, based on pilot studies, selecting the standardization sample on the basis of demographic measures, and administering the test in a standardized manner. The process continued with the analysis of the data. Construct equivalence was established at the cross-cultural level. Item Response Theory was employed to estimate the ability level of each person on the adapted items. Thus, the conclusion of no differences in means between countries on the WISC-III appears to have a sound basis in psychometric practice.

An incidental finding is of interest to cross-cultural studies of item bias. As discussed in Chapter 17, item equivalence is of utmost importance in cross-cultural research. Care must be taken that the items in different countries are not culturally biased. Importance is stressed on the necessity of adapting items to attain item equivalence. However, there is evidence from the results of this study of the phenomenon of "quasi-adaptation" of an instrument, which can result in reducing construct equivalence. The example of the Vocabulary subtest is pertinent to this phenomenon. The number of adapted items in some countries was so high that the number of common items needed, according to IRT, to compute item level difficulties became too small, thereby reducing the scope for cross-cultural comparisons. The problem was further aggravated by the finding that the difficulty level of some of the closely translated items differed significantly from the global data set. Thus, it was not possible to employ IRT to estimate the ability level of persons on the adapted items, leading to the questioning of the construct equivalence of the Vocabulary subtest in these countries. This does not necessarily invalidate the use of the Vocabulary subtest for intracultural use by clinicians, but it did not permit its use in the cross-cultural analyses. Researchers should be aware of this problem of "quasi-adaptations" of items in cross-cultural studies. The choice to adapt or not to adapt should be made with specific criteria in mind. The test constructor should attempt to keep the number of adapted items as small as possible, or risk the possibility of changing the construct, or of not being able to demonstrate its equivalence with IRT.

We have attempted to be very careful in the degree of generalization of the results of this cross-cultural study and in use of the term "construct equivalence." We have stated that there is cross-cultural equivalence in the factor-structure of the WISC-III and that there are no major cross-cultural differences in score means *in the countries of the sample*. As discussed in Chapter 2, cross-cultural methodology is not merely about comparing a large number of countries on a psychological variable. There should be independent measures of the social structural and other cultural dimensions so as to ensure the countries represent different positions across these dimensions. These countries represent different geographical and cultural zones around the world: North America, North and Central Europe, the Balkans, and East Asia. We can intuitively assume there are cultural similarities within the countries of these cultural regions, e.g., "European culture," as well as differences between others, e.g., "Asian and European culture," but this is not enough. In order to place each country in its position, we employed secondary county-level data from the two social indices, Affluence and Education.

The affluence and educational indices we employed indicated differences between these countries, and the correlations between the WISC-III scores and these two indices were statistically significant. However, the indices of affluence and education of the countries in our sample do not represent the wide range of economic level, and educational systems of countries throughout the world. Our sample does not include the poor countries of Africa, South America, and East and West Asia. Thus, although this is a cross-cultural analysis, the range of country samples in this study is restricted in terms of economic and educational measures. Thus, the generalization of the results regarding cross-cultural universality of construct equivalence and mean differences has been carefully stated so as to reflect the sample cultures. These countries represent the upper extreme positions on the social indices of affluence and education. They share similar social structural features. They are among the most affluent countries in the world. In Georgas and Berry (1995) most of these countries emerge in the same cultural cluster on economic and educational social indices. Lithuania and Slovenia are exceptions here, although among the former socialist countries of Eastern Europe, they are among those whose economic level is increasing more rapidly than some of their neighbors. All have highly developed educational systems. Their governments and their people place high value on the role of education in achievement of occupational success, leading to a better life. These countries all have invested highly in information technology.

The correlations between the WISC-III scores and access to education and affluence are few and difficult to interpret in terms of cognitive processes. However, one might predict that if countries with a greater range of educational and economic indices were included, more significant relationships with cognitive processes would emerge. It could be argued that the proportion of variance accounted for by affluence and education will depend on the countries involved in a study. In a comparison of countries with comparable levels of affluence and expenditure on education per capita, these variables may hardly be relevant. However, in a cross-cultural study in which the majority of the world is better represented than in our data set, affluence and educational expenditure will most likely play an even more dominant role. It seems fair to conclude from our finding that about half of the variance in country means on the aggregated IQ measures was due to these social indices and this would be a conservative estimate if countries of all levels of affluence were to be included.

Although we have been careful to restrict the generalization of the results to the countries of the sample, the findings of universality of the factor structure

and of no mean score differences across countries on the subtests, the Full Scale
IQ, Verbal IQ, Performance IQ, or the Index scores are noteworthy. They beg the
question of whether these findings could be generalized to Africa, South America,
and East and West Asia and are indications of universal cognitive processes across
cultures. Studies in which the structure of intelligence has been compared across
cultures usually point to strong similarities of basic cognitive functions across cultures (e.g., Van de Vijver, 1997). Compared to various other cross-cultural studies
of intellectual performance, we found remarkably small differences in mean scores
obtained in the countries involved. The relationship we found between affluence
and WISC-III subtest and aggregated total scores suggests that by enlarging the
cultural variation in our data set, the variation in these scores would also increase.
Although our findings cannot shed light on purported genetic factors in intelligence, they suggest, both directly and indirectly, that environmental factors,
notably economic development (possibly as a proxy for educational expenditure
and quality), play an important role in cross-cultural differences in intelligence
scores. The direct evidence comes from the relationship between WISC-III scores
and affluence. The indirect evidence is also related to the changes in affluence of
some of the countries participating. Although some of the countries in the sample
are the most affluent countries of the world at the present time, Lithuania and
Slovenia are not at this high level. Indeed, Taiwan, South Korea, Greece were
not among the affluent countries 30 or 40 years ago. Although the mechanisms
behind the presumed relationship of gains in affluence and intelligence scores are
unclear (and could range from improved nutrition and health to education to test-
wiseness), the powerful role of economic factors in producing cognitive change
is undisputed. Countries throughout the world are rapidly acculturating to the
demands of modern society. Globalization and economic changes have resulted in
improvements in educational systems in almost all countries, e.g., Nigeria, South
Africa, Saudi Arabia, Pakistan, India, Brazil, Chile, Mongolia, and Indonesia.
Performance on the WISC-III is correlated with educational achievement. Thus,
one could speculate that with increasing levels of affluence, globalization, and
expenditures on schooling, the cross-cultural differences in scores on intelligence
tests will become smaller. This hypothesis requires systematic cross-cultural studies as has been described in this book, but the authors believe that the results of
this study may be a harbinger of such a finding.

What are the implications of these findings for the WISC-III? The cross-cultural
analysis of the data strongly indicates that the WISC-III is a remarkably robust
measure of intelligence with cross-cultural relevance. The IQ and index scores
measure the same constructs in each of the countries, and further, these constructs appear to indicate that the WISC-III measures cognitive processes that are
universal across these cultures. It would appear that over fifty years of experience with the Wechsler tests and the periodic revisions during this period have
resulted in a refined and valid measure of cognitive processes that has considerable power for assessing children's intelligence, even in different cultural
contexts.

REFERENCES

Arends-Tóth, J. V., & Van de Vijver, F. J. R. (2002). *Assessment of acculturation: Conceptual and methodological issues.* Under review.

Baddeley, A. (1997). *Human memory: Theory and practice.* Mahwah, NJ: Erlbaum.

Berry, J. W. (1969). On cross-cultural comparability. *International Journal of Psychology, 4,* 119–128.

Berry, J. W., Poortinga, Y. H., Segall, M. H., & Dasen, P. R. (2002). *Cross-cultural psychology: Research and applications.* New York: Cambridge University Press.

Blaha, J., & Wallbrown, F. H. (1996). Hierarchical factor structure of the Wechsler Intelligence Scale for Children—III. *Psychological Assessment, 8,* 214–218.

Carroll, J. B. (1993). *Human cognitive abilities. A survey of factor-analytic studies.* Cambridge: Cambridge University Press.

Cohen J. (1988). *Statistical power analysis for the behavioral sciences* (2nd ed.). Hillsdale, NJ: Erlbaum.

Ellis, N. C., & Hennelly, R. A. (1980). Bilingual word length effect: Implication for intelligence testing and the relative ease of mental calculation in Welsh and English. *British Journal of Psychology, 71,* 43–51.

Fischer, G. H., & Molenaar, I. W. (Eds.) (1995). *Rasch models: Foundations, recent developments and applications.* New York: Springer.

Georgas, J., & Berry, J. W. (1995). An ecocultural taxonomy for cross-cultural psychology. *Cross-Cultural Research, 29,* 121–157.

Georgas, J., Van de Vijver, F. J. R., & Berry, J. W. (2003). *The ecocultural framework, ecosocial indices and psychological variables in cross-cultural research. Journal of Cross-Cultural Psychology.* (In press).

Häder, S., & Gabler, S. (2003). Sampling and estimation. In J. A. Harkness, F. J. R. van de Vijver, & P. Ph. Mohler (Eds.), *Cross-cultural survey research.* New York: Wiley.

Hambleton, R. K., & Swaminathan H. (1985). *Item response theory: Principles and applications.* Dordrecht, The Netherlands: Kluwer.

Hambleton, R. K., Swaminathan, H., & Rogers, H. J. (1991). *Fundamentals of item response theory.* Newbury Park, CA: Sage.

Hong, E., Milgram, R. M., & Perkins, P. G. (1995). Homework style and homework behavior of Korean and American children. *Journal of Research and Development in Education, 28,* 197–207.

Irvine, S. H. (1979). The place of factor analysis in cross-cultural methodology and its contribution to cognitive theory. In L. H. Eckensberger, W. J. Lonner, & Y. H. Poortinga (Eds.), *Cross-cultural contributions to psychology* (pp. 300–341). Lisse, The Netherlands: Swets and Zeitlinger.

Kaufman, A. S. (1994). *Intelligent testing with the WISC-III.* New York: Wiley.

Kim, U., & Chun, M. B. J. (1994). Educational "success" of Asian Americans: An indigenous perspective. *Journal of Applied Developmental Psychology, 15,* 329–339.

Kish, L. (1965). *Survey sampling.* New York: Wiley.

Konold, T., Kush, J., & Canivez, G. L. (1997). Factor replication of the WISC-III in three independent samples of children receiving special education. *Journal of Psychoeducational Assessment, 15,* 123–137.

Kush, J. C., Watkins, M. W., Ward, T. J., Ward, S. B., Canivez, G. L., & Worrell F. C. (2001). Construct validity of the WISC-III for white and black students from the WISC-III standardization sample and for black students referred for psychological evaluation. *School Psychology Review, 30,* 70–88.

Logerquist-Hansen, S., & Barona, A. (1994, August). *Factor structure of the Wechsler Intelligence Scale for Children-III for Hispanic and Non-Hispanic white children with learning diabilities.* Paper presented at the meeting of the American Psychological Association, Los Angeles.

Lynn, R., & Martin, T. (1995). National differences for thirty-seven nations in extraversion, neuroticism, psychoticism and economic, demographic and other correlates. *Personality and Individual Differences, 19,* 403–406.

McCrae, R. R., & Allik, J. (2002). *The five-factor model across cultures.* New York: Kluwer Academic/Plenum Publishers.

Naveh-Benjamin, M., & Ayres T. J. (1986). Digit span, reading rate, and linguistic relativity. *Quarterly Journal of Experimental Psychology, 38A,* 739–751.

Poortinga, Y. H., Van de Vijver, F. J. R., & Van Hemert, D. A. (2002). Cross-cultural equivalence of the big five. A tentative interpretation of the evidence. In A. J. Marsella (Series Ed.), R. R. McCrae & J. Allik (Eds.), *The five-factor model across cultures* (pp. 271–292). New York: Kluwer Academic/Plenum Publishers.

Prifitera, A., Weiss, L. G., & Saklofske, D. H. (1998). The WISC-III in context. In A. Prifitera & D. H. Saklofske (Eds.), *WISC-III clinical use and interpretation: Scientist-practitioner perspectives* (pp. 1–38). San Diego, CA: Academic Press.

Reynolds, C. R., & Ford, L. (1994). Comparative three-factor solutions of the WISC-III and WISC-R at 11 age levels between $6\frac{1}{2}$ and $16\frac{1}{2}$ years. *Archives of Clinical Neuropsychology, 9,* 553–570.

Roid, G. H., Prifitera, A., & Wiess, L. G. (1993). Replication of the WISC-III factor structure in an independent sample. *Journal of Psychoeducational Assessment WISC-III Monograph,* 6–21.

Roid, G. H., & Worrall, W. (1996, August). *Equivalence of factor structure in the U.S. and Canada editions of the WISC-III.* Paper presented at the annual meeting of the American Psychological Association, Toronto.

Sattler, J. M. (1992). *Assessment of children* (revised and updated, 3rd ed.). San Diego, CA: Author.

Sattler, J. M., & Saklofske, D. H. (2001). Wechsler Intelligence Scale for Children—III (WISC-III): Description. In J. M. Sattler (Ed.), *Assessment of children: Cognitive applications* (4th ed.) (pp. 220–297). San Diego, CA: Author.

Song, M.-J., & Ginsburg, H. P. (1987). The development of informal and formal mathematical thinking in Korean and U.S. children. *Child Development, 58,* 1286–1296.

Van de Vijver, F. J. R. (1997). Meta-analysis of cross-cultural comparisons of cognitive test performance. *Journal of Cross-Cultural Psychology, 28,* 678–709.

Van de Vijver, F. J. R., & Leung, K. (1997). *Methods and data analysis for cross-cultural research.* Newbury Park, CA: Sage.

Van de Vijver, F. J. R., & Phalet, K. (2003). Assessment in multicultural groups: The role of acculturation. *Applied Psychology: An International Review* (special issue).

Van Hemert, D. D. A., Van de Vijver, F. J. R., Poortinga, Y. H., & Georgas, J. (2002). Structure and Score Levels of the Eysenck Personality Questionnaire across individuals and countries. Personality and Individual Differences.

Verhelst, N. D., Glas, C. A. W., & Verstralen, H. H. F. M. (1995). *One-parameter logistic model: OPLM* [Computer program]. Arnhem, The Netherlands: CITO Groep.

Wechsler, D. (1991). *Wechsler Intelligence Scale for Children—Third Edition.* San Antonio, TX: The Psychological Corporation.

APPENDIX

OVERVIEW OF CLOSELY TRANSLATED AND ADAPTED TEST ITEMS PER SUBTEST

The Appendix described which items were closely translated and which items were adapted. The American version was the reference version in all countries. The first column gives the U.S. item numbers. The following columns describe the item numbers in the other countries; the numbers in the cell represent item numbers. Three types of entries are found in the tables. In the first one a cell is set in regular typeface and a row has the same number for a cell in the U.S. and in a specific country, say Slovenia. This means that the American item has been closely translated and that the item appears at the same place in the Slovenian subtest; for example in Picture Completion, the American and Slovenian items are identical. The second type of cell is also set in regular typeface, but the number of the U.S. item and the country item are not identical. This means that the original U.S. item is retained but appears at a different position. For example, the ninth item in the Slovenian Picture Completion is the seventeenth item of the U.S. subtest. The third type of cell uses bold and italic typeface. These cells refer to adapted items. For example, the first five items of the Japanese version of Picture Completion have a country-specific content, not found in any other country.

The following country codes are used in the tables (note that DUT refers to a standardization sample composed of data from the Dutch language area of The Netherlands and Flanders, FRA to French language areas of France and Belgium, and GER to German language areas of Germany, Austria, and Switzerland)::

USA   United States of America
AUS   Australia
CAN   Canada
DUT   The Netherlands and Flanders (Dutch language area)
FRA   France and Belgium (French language area)

GER   Germany, Austria, and Switzerland (German language area)
GRE   Greece
JAP   Japan
KOR   South Korea
LITH   Lithuania
SLO   Slovenia
SWE   Sweden
TAI   Taiwan
UK   United Kingdom

TABLE A.1   Picture Completion

USA	AUS	CAN	DUT	FRA	GER	GRE	JAP	KOR	LITH	SLO	SWE	TAI	UK
1	1	1	1	1	1	1	*1*	1	1	1	1	1	1
2	2	2	2	2	2	2	*2*	5	2	2	2	2	2
3	3	3	3	3	3	3	*3*	3	3	3	3	3	3
4	4	4	4	4	4	4	*4*	2	4	4	4	4	4
5	5	5	5	5	5	5	*6*	4	5	5	5	5	5
6	6	6	6	6	6	6	5	6	8	6	8	6	6
7	7	7	7	7	7	7	13	9	6	7	6	7	7
8	8	8	8	8	8	8	8	8	7	8	7	8	8
9	9	9	9	9	9	9	15	17	13	17	13	9	9
10	10	10	10	10	10	10	11	14	16	10	9	10	10
11	11	11	11	11	11	11	10	12	10	11	11	11	11
12	12	12	12	12	12	12	*9*	10	14	12	14	12	12
13	13	13	13	13	13	13	16	18	18	13	15	13	13
14	14	14	14	14	14	14	7	11	12	14	10	14	14
15	15	15	15	15	15	15	*21*	7	11	15	12	15	15
16	16	16	16	16	16	16	*19*	16	9	16	17	16	16
17	17	17	17	17	17	17	14	13	17	9	19	17	17
18	18	18	18	18	18	18	17	15	15	18	20	18	18
19	19	19	19	19	19	19	20	19	20	19	18	19	19
20	20	20	20	20	20	20	*12*	27	19	20	16	20	20
21	21	21	21	21	21	21	24	21	22	21	22	21	21
22	22	22	22	22	22	22	*18*	20	21	22	21	22	22
23	23	23	23	23	23	23	*23*	23	25	23	27	23	23
24	24	24	24	24	24	24	*27*	22	26	24	25	24	24
25	25	25	25	25	25	25	25	25	24	25	23	25	25
26	26	26	26	26	26	26	22	24	23	26	24	26	26
27	27	27	27	27	—	27	—	26	30	27	26	27	27
28	28	28	28	28	27	28	26	28	28	28	29	28	28
29	29	29	29	29	28	29	28	29	27	29	28	29	29
30	30	30	30	30	29	30	29	30	29	30	30	30	30

TABLE A.2 Information

USA	AUS	CAN	DUT	FRA	GER	GRE	JAP	KOR	LITH	SLO	SWE	TAI	UK
1	1	1	1	1	1	1	*1*	*11*	1	1	1	1	1
2	2	2	*4*	2	*22*	2	2	*13*	2	2	2	2	2
3	3	3	2	3	2	3	3	1	3	3	3	3	3
4	4	4	3	8	4	4	*5*	2	4	4	4	4	4
5	5	5	5	4	3	5	*4*	3	5	8	*7*	6	8
6	6	6	9	5	5	9	*8*	*17*	8	*10*	5	10	5
7	7	7	8	9	7	7	*9*	*18*	7	6	*6*	*12*	6
8	8	8	7	7	6	6	7	5	6	7	26	5	7
9	9	9	11	*6*	8	8	6	4	10	9	8	7	9
10	10	10	*6*	13	14	*10*	*10*	7	24	11	*11*	11	11
11	11	11	10	14	9	11	*13*	6	9	5	*9*	8	10
12	12	12	14	12	10	14	12	10	11	13	10	14	12
13	13	13	15	15	11	*12*	20	21	14	15	28	21	14
14	14	14	*12*	*10*	23	17	*18*	23	15	20	18	17	15
15	15	15	13	*11*	12	18	14	14	13	14	12	15	13
16	16	16	27	25	*27*	*13*	11	8	12	*17*	15	9	19
17	17	17	*16*	*16*	13	*15*	*15*	27	19	16	13	19	16
18	18	18	22	*17*	16	*16*	19	25	18	21	14	23	17
19	19	19	29	21	24	20	*17*	22	26	23	*30*	22	23
20	20	20	*17*	*18*	*15*	*19*	16	9	*21*	12	*24*	13	*18*
21	21	21	25	27	20	22	*21*	12	22	24	17	16	21
22	22	22	18	22	19	*21*	26	*29*	29	*18*	19	*24*	24
23	23	23	21	*20*	17	23	22	20	17	26	25	20	20
24	24	24	*19*	*23*	28	*24*	*24*	26	20	29	23	25	25
25	25	25	20	19	18	*25*	27	24	23	19	*27*	27	22
26	26	26	*23*	24	21	26	23	19	27	27	*16*	18	27
27	27	27	*24*	26	25	28	*25*	16	28	22	21	29	26
28	28	28	31	*29*	30	29	28	28	30	*25*	*22*	28	29
29	29	29	30	*30*	26	*27*	*29*	30	*25*	*28*	*20*	*30*	28
30	30	30	*26*	28	*29*	30	*30*	15	*16*	30	29	26	*30*
—	—	—	*28*	—	—	—	—	—	—	—	—	—	—

TABLE A.3 Similarities

USA	AUS	CAN	DUT	FRA	GER	GRE	JAP	KOR	LITH	SLO	SWE	TAI	UK
1	1	1	1	5	3	4	*3*	1	3	3	5	5	5
2	2	2	2	1	2	5	*4*	4	2	1	1	1	2
3	3	3	*7*	4	4	2	*7*	3	5	*2*	4	4	3

(Continues)

TABLE A.3   (*Continued*)

USA	AUS	CAN	DUT	FRA	GER	GRE	JAP	KOR	LITH	SLO	SWE	TAI	UK
4	4	4	4	2	1	3	6	2	1	4	3	3	1
5	5	5	3	3	*5*	7	1	*19*	4	5	2	2	4
6	6	6	5	6	7	1	*5*	5	6	6	6	6	6
7	7	7	6	7	6	6	2	6	7	7	7	7	7
8	8	8	9	*8*	8	8	9	8	8	8	8	8	8
9	9	9	12	*9*	10	9	8	7	9	10	9	9	10
10	10	10	10	12	11	11	10	14	11	9	10	10	9
11	11	11	*11*	11	13	13	—	9	12	12	12	14	12
12	12	12	8	10	12	10	*14*	13	10	11	11	11	11
13	13	13	15	*15*	15	12	13	10	13	13	13	12	13
14	14	14	17	13	14	14	12	11	15	15	16	13	15
15	15	15	*13*	16	16	*15*	*11*	15	14	14	17	15	14
16	16	16	19	17	17	16	17	18	16	17	15	16	17
17	17	17	16	14	*9*	*17*	15	16	18	16	14	17	16
18	18	18	20	18	19	18	*16*	17	17	18	18	18	18
19	19	19	*14*	19	18	19	18	12	19	19	19	19	19
—	—	—	*18*	—	—	—	—	—	—	—	—	—	—
—	—	—	*21*	—	—	—	—	—	—	—	—	—	—

TABLE A.4   Picture Arrangement

USA	AUS	CAN	DUT	FRA	GER	GRE	JAP	KOR	LITH	SLO	SWE	TAI	UK
1	1	1	1	1	1	1	*1*	1	1	1	1	1	1
2	2	2	2	2	2	2	2	2	2	2	2	2	2
3	3	3	3	3	3	3	5	3	3	3	3	3	3
4	4	4	4	4	4	4	8	5	4	4	4	4	4
5	5	5	5	5	5	5	6	6	5	5	5	5	5
6	6	6	6	6	6	6	*3*	7	6	6	6	6	6
7	7	7	7	7	7	7	10	9	7	7	7	7	7
8	8	8	8	8	8	8	*4*	4	8	8	8	8	8
9	9	9	9	9	9	9	9	8	9	9	9	9	9
10	10	10	10	10	10	10	7	10	10	10	10	10	10
11	11	11	11	11	11	11	11	11	11	11	11	11	11
12	12	12	12	12	12	12	12	12	12	12	12	12	12
13	13	13	13	13	13	13	13	13	13	13	13	13	13
14	14	14	14	14	14	14	14	14	14	14	14	14	14

TABLE A.5   Arithmetic

USA	AUS	CAN	DUT	FRA	GER	GRE	JAP	KOR	LITH	SLO	SWE	TAI	UK
1	1	1	1	1	1	1	1	1	1	1	1	1	1
2	2	2	2	2	2	2	2	2	2	2	2	2	2
3	3	3	7	3	3	3	3	17	3	3	3	3	3
4	4	4	4	4	4	4	4	3	4	4	4	4	4
5	5	5	3	5	5	5	5	4	5	5	5	5	5
6	6	6	5	6	19	6	23	7	6	6	6	6	6
7	7	7	10	7	20	9	7	21	8	9	8	7	9
8	8	8	11	8	10	12	6	5	10	12	10	8	12
9	9	9	6	9	6	7	9	24	7	7	7	9	7
10	10	10	12	10	8	8	8	8	9	11	9	10	8
11	11	11	8	12	7	10	11	9	12	10	12	11	10
12	12	12	9	11	9	11	10	6	11	8	11	12	11
13	13	13	13	13	11	13	12	10	13	13	13	13	13
14	14	14	14	15	12	14	13	11	14	14	14	14	14
15	15	15	15	14	13	15	15	13	15	15	15	15	15
16	16	16	16	16	14	16	14	12	16	16	16	16	16
17	17	17	18	17	15	17	16	15	17	17	17	17	17
18	18	18	17	18	16	18	24	14	18	18	18	18	18
19	19	19	19	20	18	20	18	16	20	20	20	19	20
20	20	20	20	19	17	19	17	18	19	19	19	20	19
21	21	21	24	22	22	23	20	19	22	23	23	21	23
22	22	22	22	23	23	22	22	20	23	22	22	22	22
23	23	23	21	21	21	21	19	23	21	21	21	23	21
24	24	24	26	24	24	24	21	22	24	24	24	24	24
—	—	—	23	—	—	—	—	—	—	—	—	—	—
—	—	—	25	—	—	—	—	—	—	—	—	—	—

TABLE A.6   Vocabulary

USA	AUS	CAN	DUT	FRA	GER	GRE	JAP	KOR	LITH	SLO	SWE	TAI	UK
1	1	1	1	2	1	1	1	2	1	3	6	4	1
2	2	2	4	5	4	3	2	1	3	19	2	2	3
3	3	3	5	3	2	4	3	5	2	1	3	1	2
4	4	4	3	1	13	7	4	4	6	2	5	3	6
5	5	5	6	4	8	2	5	9	5	25	7	7	5
6	6	6	7	7	6	5	6	10	7	8	10	11	8
7	7	7	8	6	3	12	7	11	9	4	1	8	7
8	8	8	2	8	5	6	8	3	4	5	4	5	4
9	9	9	9	9	20	8	9	7	10	7	12	10	10
10	10	10	10	10	7	10	10	6	8	6	9	9	11
11	11	11	11	11	9	11	11	8	14	11	11	14	12
12	12	12	12	12	15	9	12	13	13	17	14	6	9
13	13	13	13	13	10	13	13	15	23	20	19	16	14
14	14	14	24	14	25	14	14	23	15	23	16	22	13

(*Continues*)

TABLE A.6 (*Continued*)

USA	AUS	CAN	DUT	FRA	GER	GRE	JAP	KOR	LITH	SLO	SWE	TAI	UK
15	15	15	*14*	*15*	17	*18*	*15*	21	*16*	*13*	17	13	19
16	16	16	*15*	21	19	*21*	*16*	*18*	20	14	13	12	15
17	17	17	22	*16*	11	20	*17*	17	27	*18*	*22*	15	18
18	18	18	*16*	*17*	27	15	*18*	25	12	*24*	8	18	21
19	19	19	27	*18*	16	*24*	*19*	28	11	27	29	*17*	16
20	20	20	*17*	*19*	14	*25*	*20*	29	*17*	15	*20*	*29*	20
21	21	21	*18*	*20*	12	17	*21*	20	22	12	*15*	*27*	17
22	22	22	*19*	*22*	*28*	22	*22*	14	28	22	*21*	19	24
23	23	23	*20*	*23*	26	19	*23*	30	25	26	18	26	23
24	24	24	30	28	21	16	*24*	12	24	29	25	*24*	22
25	25	25	*35*	*24*	24	29	*25*	24	*19*	21	*23*	*21*	25
26	26	26	*21*	*25*	23	*26*	*26*	22	*21*	10	*24*	*30*	26
27	27	27	*23*	*26*	18	23	*27*	19	*29*	16	*26*	*20*	28
28	28	28	*25*	*27*	22	30	*28*	16	18	*9*	*27*	*25*	27
29	29	29	*26*	*29*	*30*	27	*29*	27	*30*	28	*28*	23	30
30	30	30	*28*	*30*	29	*28*	*30*	26	26	30	*30*	28	29
—	—	—	*29*	—	—	—	—	—	—	—	—	—	—
—	—	—	*31*	—	—	—	—	—	—	—	—	—	—
—	—	—	*32*	—	—	—	—	—	—	—	—	—	—
—	—	—	*33*	—	—	—	—	—	—	—	—	—	—
—	—	—	*34*	—	—	—	—	—	—	—	—	—	—

TABLE A.7 Comprehension

USA	AUS	CAN	DUT	FRA	GER	GRE	JAP	KOR	LITH	SLO	SWE	TAI	UK
1	1	1	1	4	*2*	1	3	4	1	1	1	1	1
2	2	2	2	2	5	2	5	3	2	4	4	4	4
3	3	3	*3*	*1*	1	3	6	1	4	3	3	5	3
4	4	4	*4*	*3*	18	5	4	5	5	2	2	2	2
5	5	5	*6*	7	3	4	2	2	3	5	5	3	5
6	6	6	9	*5*	6	6	8	6	7	8	8	6	8
7	7	7	8	9	11	8	13	10	10	9	7	10	9
8	8	8	*7*	*6*	8	10	7	*7*	11	7	6	7	7
9	9	9	5	*8*	4	9	*1*	11	9	6	9	11	6
10	10	10	13	*10*	7	7	*10*	8	6	10	10	8	10
11	11	11	11	13	9	11	9	9	8	11	12	9	11
12	12	12	*10*	16	15	16	*12*	12	15	14	14	12	14
13	13	13	17	14	14	14	17	17	13	15	15	14	15
14	14	14	*12*	*11*	10	18	11	15	14	12	11	15	12
15	15	15	*14*	18	12	*12*	*14*	*13*	17	16	16	16	16
16	16	16	*15*	*12*	13	13	16	14	12	13	13	13	13
17	17	17	*16*	*15*	*17*	17	15	*18*	16	17	17	*17*	*17*
18	18	18	19	*17*	16	15	—	16	18	18	18	18	18
—	—	—	*18*	—	—	—	—	—	—	—	—	—	—

TABLE A.8   Block Design

USA	AUS	CAN	DUT	FRA	GER	GRE	JAP	KOR	LITH	SLO	SWE	TAI	UK
1	1	1	1	1	1	1	1	1	1	1	1	1	1
2	2	2	2	2	2	2	2	2	2	2	2	2	2
3	3	3	3	3	3	3	3	3	3	3	3	3	3
4	4	4	4	4	4	4	4	4	4	4	4	4	4
5	5	5	5	5	5	5	5	5	5	5	5	5	5
6	6	6	6	6	6	6	6	6	6	6	6	6	6
7	7	7	7	7	7	7	7	7	7	7	7	7	7
8	8	8	8	8	8	8	8	8	8	8	8	8	8
9	9	9	9	9	9	9	9	9	9	9	9	9	9
10	10	10	10	10	10	10	10	10	10	10	10	10	10
11	11	11	11	11	11	11	11	11	11	11	11	11	11
12	12	12	12	12	12	12	*12*	12	12	12	12	12	12

TABLE A.9   Mazes

USA	AUS	CAN	DUT	FRA	GER	GRE	JAP	KOR	LITH	SLO	SWE	TAI	UK
1	1	1	1	1	1	1	1	1	1	1	1	1	1
2	2	2	2	2	2	2	2	2	2	2	2	2	2
3	3	3	3	3	3	3	3	3	3	3	3	3	3
4	4	4	4	4	4	4	4	4	4	4	4	4	4
5	5	5	5	5	5	5	5	5	5	5	5	5	5
6	6	6	6	6	6	6	6	6	6	6	6	6	6
7	7	7	7	7	7	7	*7*	7	7	7	7	7	7
8	8	8	8	8	8	8	8	8	8	8	8	8	8
9	9	9	9	9	9	9	9	9	9	9	9	9	9
10	10	10	10	10	10	10	10	10	10	10	10	10	10

AUTHOR INDEX

SUBJECT INDEX

ADHD, *see* Attention deficit hyperactivity
    disorder
Arithmetic test
    adaptation and translation by country, 333
    Hamburg Wechsler Intelligence Test for
        Children adaptation, 139
    loadings of Arithmetic subtest on first and
        fourth factor in each country, 283–286
Attention deficit hyperactivity disorder (ADHD)
    German assessment, 127, 132
    Taiwan assessment, 248–249
Austria
    cultural and language diversity issues in
        intelligence testing, 137–138
    Hamburg Wechsler Intelligence Test for
        Children adaptation
        adaptation process, 138–139
        arithmetic subtest, 139
        cultural issues influencing interpretation,
            145–146
        reliability coefficients of subtests and IQ
            scales by country and two age bands,
            140–142
        sample characteristics, 140–141
        scoring comparison with Germany and
            Austria, 126–127, 130, 143–144
        validity evidence, 143–145
    historical perspective of Hamburg Wechsler
        Intelligence Test for Children
        development, 121–122, 137

professional issues in intelligence test use,
    146–147
Autism, Taiwan assessment, 248–249

Belgium, *see* Dutch adaptation, Wechsler
            Intelligence Scale for Children: Third
            Edition; French-speaking adaptation,
            Wechsler Intelligence Scale for
            Children: Third Edition
Binet-Simon tests
    development, 5
    history of use, 5–6
Block design test, adaptation and translation by
        country, 335

Canada
    demographics, 63–65, 72
    educational opportunity, 63
    immigration, 72
    Wechsler Intelligence Scale for Children:
        Third Edition adaptation and use
        adaptation process, 62, 71
        cultural issues influencing interpretation,
            69–71
        exploratory factor analysis, 64
        intercorrelations of subtest scaled scores,
            IQs, and indexes, 68
        need for modification, 61–62
        professional issues in use, 71–74

However, the decision to take measures regarding learning and other disabilities in the public educational system started in 1990. In addition, the visiting consultation project in 1995 and the learning disabilities educational measures project in 2000 were initiated as model projects nationwide. These projects are still in a trial stage in each prefecture and their eventual adoption is still several years away.

For this model project, each prefecture's educational committee has a team of experts that includes not only members from the education sector but also psychologists and physicians. The nationwide application of the project has demonstrated the need for the utilization of intelligence tests for making decisions about the educational measures for children with first-degree intellectual disabilities and learning disabilities.

Currently, there is no official or legally qualified status or positions for school psychologists, but only a "collaboratively authorized qualification" certified by academic societies exists.

The qualifications for school psychologists were established in 1997 in collaboration with five academic societies: The Japanese Association of Educational Psychology, the Japanese Association of Special Education, the Japanese Academy of Learning Disabilities, the Japan Society of Developmental Psychology, and the Japanese Association for the Study of Developmental Disabilities. As discussed above, with the rapid increase of concern for the training of children with first-degree developmental disabilities including learning disabilities, the environment for the full-scale utilization of psychological tests in the educational field has been facilitated. This trend can be seen as a resurgence of the value of intelligence tests, and indicates progressive use of psychological tests "from the clinic to the classroom." We predict that we are beginning a totally new era concerning the utilization of the WISC-III and related tests in the field of education in Japan.

In the future, with expansion of educational measures for lightly disabled children, we can expect the legal provision and maintenance for those qualifications to be improved.

REFERENCES

Guilford, J. P. (1954). *Psychometric methods.* (2nd ed.) New York: McGraw-Hill.
Guilford, J. P., & Fruchter, B. (1978). *Fundamental statistics in psychology and education.* (6th ed.) New York: McGraw-Hill.
Hayashi, S. (1971). *Vocabulary research and basic vocabulary.* Report of the National Institute for Japanese Language 39.
Japan Educational Research Institute (1985). *Studies on the basic vocabulary in school learning I.* Tokyo, Japan: Kyoiku-shuppan.
Ministry of Education (1995). *School basic survey.* Tokyo, Japan: Printing Bureau, Ministry of Finance.
National Institute for Japanese Language (1980). *Vocabulary of infants.* Tokyo, Japan: Tokyo-shoseki.
Okubo, A., & Kawamata, R. (1982). *Vocabulary for under school age.* Report of the National Institute for Japanese Language 71.